Lines of Thinking:
Reflections on the Psychology
of Thought

Lines of Thinking: Reflections on the Psychology of Thought

Volume 2: Skills, Emotion, Creative Processes, Individual Differences and Teaching Thinking

Edited by

K.J. GILHOOLY
University of Aberdeen

M.T.G. KEANE
Open University

R.H. LOGIE
University of Aberdeen

G. ERDOS
University of Newcastle

JOHN WILEY & SONS
Chichester · New York · Brisbane · Toronto · Singapore

Copyright © 1990 by John Wiley & Sons Ltd,
Baffins Lane, Chichester,
West Sussex PO19 1UD, England

Other Wiley Editorial Offices

John Wiley & Sons, Inc., 605 Third Avenue,
New York, NY 10158–0012, USA

Jacaranda Wiley Ltd, G.P.O. Box 859, Brisbane,
Queensland 4001, Australia

John Wiley & Sons (Canada) Ltd, 22 Worcester Road,
Rexdale, Ontario M9W 1L1, Canada

John Wiley & Sons (SEA) Pte Ltd, 37 Jalan Pemimpin 05–04,
Block B, Union Industrial Building, Singapore 2057

Library of Congress Cataloging-in-Publication Data:

Skills, emotion, creative processes, individual differences, and
  teaching thinking/edited by K. J. Gilhooly ... [et al.].
    p. cm. — (Lines of thinking: reflections on the psychology
  of thought ; v. 2)
    Includes bibliographical references.
    ISBN 0-471-92477-6
    1. Thought and thinking. I. Gilhooly, K. J. II. Series: Lines
  of thinking ; v. 2.
  BF441.S58 1990
  153—dc20   89–37262
                                                       CIP

British Library Cataloguing in Publication Data:

Lines of thinking: reflections on the psychology of
  thought.
  Vol. 2 : Skills, emotion, creative processes, individual
  differences and teaching thinking.
  1. Thought processes
  I. Gilhooly, K. J.
  153.4'2

ISBN 0-471-92477-6

Typeset by Mathematical Composition Setters, Salisbury, England.
Printed and bound in Great Britain by Courier International Ltd, Tiptree, Essex.

Contents

Part II: Emotion and Thinking

Part III: Creative Processes

Part IV: Individual Differences

Part V: Teaching Thinking

Preface

This two-volume work arises from the International Conference on Thinking which was held at the University of Aberdeen in August 1988, under the auspices of the British Psychological Society's Cognitive Psychology Section. However, the resulting book is not simply raw conference proceedings but rather selected and expanded papers based on the talks given at Aberdeen. The chapters making up the two volumes together provide a broad, cross-sectional snap-shot of current empirical and theoretical research on human thinking.

In common with other complex psychological concepts, 'thinking' is very difficult to define neatly. In broad-brush terms, we take 'thinking' to refer to those mental processes that enable intelligent systems to go beyond the information given by perception or memory and so make available new inferred representations. Particular theoretical approaches provide more specific definitions within their own perspectives and areas; examples will be found throughout the book.

Despite the evident importance of thought processes in everyday life and in art, science and technology, the general topic of thinking was relatively neglected in scientific psychology for many years during which the behaviourist approach predominated. Complex internal processes such as thinking did not lend themselves to analysis in terms of S–R chains or even in terms of mediational s–r chains. Happily, research on thinking has been growing steadily since the beginnings of the information-processing revolution (c. 1956 onwards). The persuasive correspondence between computer programs for solving symbolic problems and strategies in human problem solving opened the way for the development of the computer metaphor for mental processes. Since the mid-1950s an ever-wider range of thinking tasks have been studied with an ever-growing battery of techniques. As a result the field has taken on a fragmented appearance and the many sub-areas seldom connect with one another. And yet, the same cognitive system solves syllogisms, uses analogies, makes decisions, acquires specialized thinking skills, is subject to emotional influences, is creative and can benefit from instruction in thinking skills. Joint consideration of results from these disparate areas should help indicate the shape of the underlying cognitive architecture. A major aim of the conference was to bring together researchers from diverse sub-areas in the hope that common concerns would be recognized and linking concepts be developed. The material in this book will, it is hoped, assist readers in 'thought exercises' aimed at integrating currently distinct sub-areas. In the Introductions to different parts of the book certain interconnections are pointed out: no doubt there are others waiting, implicit, to be discovered by interested readers. In addition to 'internal' integrations, we believe there are many signs in the chapters of outward connections from thinking research to education, computing science, and to developmental, motivational and clinical psychology.

Certain key issues arise repeatedly across sub-areas. One such issue, for example, is the role of limited-capacity working memory in thinking. Working memory limitations are frequently invoked in explanations of thinking task difficulty without being tested. Detailed examination of working memory limitations in a range of thinking tasks would seem to be a promising area for future research. Also, longstanding issues of representation naturally arise throughout the book. Are the internal representations manipulated in thought best considered to be symbolic or subsymbolic, propositional or analogue, mental models or schemata, locally or globally defined?

Even in these two volumes not all aspects of thinking are discussed. Thinking is an exceedingly broad subject and the present book largely focuses on normal individual adult human thought directed toward problem solving and reasoning. Thus we have little or no treatment of thinking in children, in group situations or in non-human organisms. Thought disorders and undirected thinking are discussed, and while thinking in artificially intelligent systems is considered this is in comparison to human processes rather than in its own right.

The sequential organization of the book is into topics that, roughly speaking, increase in their time-scale and complexity. The four parts of Volume 1 focus on representational issues; a wide range of approaches to reasoning; analogy; and decision making.

In Volume 2, more extended and still more complex processes are considered. These are: skilled thinking (Part I); emotion and thought (Part II); creative processes (Part III); individual differences (Part IV); and teaching thinking (Part V).

In conclusion, we believe that the chapters in this book represent the main lines of current thinking about thinking and we hope that the many studies and arguments contained here will assist readers to reflect fruitfully on the psychology of thought.

K.J. GILHOOLY
M.T.G. KEANE
R.H. LOGIE
G. ERDOS

Acknowledgements

We should like to thank our colleagues on the committee of the British Psychological Society's Cognitive Psychology Section for their support of our proposal for the International Conference on Thinking (which is the basis of the present book); the British Psychological Society's Conference Office staff, particularly Jackie Millington and Amanda Biggs, for assistance in organizing the conference; and our Local Committee Members, Paul Kinnear and Caroline Green, who helped greatly in making the conference a pleasant and memorable event.

We should also like to thank Mike Coombs, Wendy Hudlass and Lewis Derrick of John Wiley very much for their many problem-solving efforts in transforming this book from a thought into a concrete product. Valuable assistance in the production of the book was also given by Caroline Green and Valerie Wynn at Aberdeen.

Acknowledgen...

Contributors

R. K. E. BELLAMY: *MRC Applied Psychology Unit, 15 Chaucer Rd, Cambridge CB2 2EF, UK.*

D. BERRY: *Department of Experimental Psychology, University of Oxford, South Parks Road, Oxford OX1 3UD, UK.*

M. BRABECK: *Department of Psychology, Boston College, Chestnut Hill, MA 02167, USA.*

P. G. CARYL: *Department of Psychology, University of Edinburgh, 7 George Square, Edinburgh EH8 9JZ, UK.*

M. BETH CASEY: *Department of Psychology, Boston College, Chestnut Hill, MA 02167, USA.*

A. J. CLARKE: *Unit for Cognitive Development of Vista University, Private Bag X634, Pretoria, 0001, RSA.*

M. CONWAY: *Psychology Department, Lancaster University, Lancaster LA1 4YF, UK.*

I. DEARY: *Department of Psychology, University of Edinburgh, 7 George Square, Edinburgh EH8 9JZ, UK.*

R. L. DOMINOWSKI: *Department of Psychology, University of Illinois at Chicago, Box 4348, Chicago, Illinois 60680, USA.*

J. J. DOWNES: *Department of Experimental Psychology, University of Cambridge, Downing Street, Cambridge CB2 2EB, UK.*

G. ERDOS: *Department of Social Studies, The University, Newcastle-upon-Tyne NE1 7RU, UK.*

K. A. ERICSSON: *Department of Psychology, University of Colorado at Boulder, Muenzinger Psychology Building, Campus Box 345, Boulder, Colorado 80309–0345, USA.*

J. GEAR: *Psychology Department, University of Hull, Hull HU16 4DJ, UK.*

K. J. GILHOOLY: *Department of Psychology, University of Aberdeen, King's College, Aberdeen AB9 2UB, UK.*

D. GILMORE: *Department of Psychology, University of Nottingham, University Park, Nottingham NGT 2RD, UK.*

A. GREEN: *MRC Applied Psychology Unit, 15 Chaucer Road, Cambridge CB2 2EF, UK.*

D. GREGORY: *Humberside College of Higher Education, Inglemire Avenue, Hull HU6 7LU, UK.*

J. HAWORTH: *Department of Psychology, University of Manchester, Manchester M13 9PL, UK.*

H. KREITLER: *Department of Psychology, Tel Aviv University, Ramat Aviv, Tel Aviv 69928, Israel.*

S. KREITLER: *Department of Psychology, Tel Aviv University, Ramat Aviv, Tel Aviv 69928, Israel.*

R. H. LOGIE: *Department of Psychology, University of Aberdeen, King's College, Aberdeen AB9 2UB, UK.*

C. MCGUINNESS: *Department of Psychology, Queen's University, Belfast, Northern Ireland BT7 1NN, UK.*

R. MORRIS: *Department of Clinical Psychology, Institute of Psychiatry, De Crespigny Park, Denmark Hill, London SE5 8AF, UK.*

K. OATLEY: *Department of Psychology, Adam Smith Building, University of Glasgow, Glasgow G12 8RT, UK.*

H. PALM: *Unit for Cognitive Development of Vista University, Private Bag X634, Pretoria, 0001, RSA.*

M. J. POWER: *MRC Social Psychiatry Unit, Institute of Psychiatry, De Crespigny Park, London SE5 8AF, UK.*

T. W. ROBBINS: *Department of Experimental Psychology, University of Cambridge, Downing Street, Cambridge CB2 2EB, UK.*

P. SAARILUOMA: *Department of Psychology, University of Helsinki, Division of Applied Psychology, Fabianinkatu 28, 00100 Helsinki 10, Finland.*

A. F. S. SALWAY: *Department of Psychology, University of Aberdeen, King's College, Aberdeen AB9 2UB, UK.*

B. SEAGULL: *NCAS, Rutgers University, New Jersey, USA.*

D. SLEEMAN: *Department of Computing Science, University of Aberdeen, King's College, Aberdeen AB9 2UB, UK.*

K. SULLIVAN: *Department of Psychology, Boston College, Chestnut Hill, MA 02167, USA.*

F.N. WATTS: *MRC Applied Psychology Unit, 15 Chaucer Rd, Cambridge CB2 2EF, UK.*

J. WILLIAMSON: *Department of Psychology, Liverpool Institute of Higher Education, Stand Park Rd, Liverpool L16 8ND, UK.*

E. WINNER: *Department of Psychology, Boston College, Chestnut Hill, MA 02167, USA.*

Part I

Skilled Thinking

Thinking Skills

K.J. GILHOOLY
King's College, Aberdeen University

The papers in this part deal with the nature, acquisition and performance of skilled thinking. Paradigm cases of skilled thinking are exemplified by experts who, for example, rapidly identify winning moves in chess (Saariluoma), accurately interpret contour maps (Williamson and McGuiness), or show exceptional immediate memory performance (Ericsson).

A basic factor in skilled thinking in many domains seems to be the acquisition of an extensive repertoire of familiar patterns or schemata that enable new information to be rapidly encoded in a way appropriate for further action. Ericsson shows how use of pre-existing knowledge can effectively increase as apparently basic a capacity as immediate memory. Extended practice is clearly a necessary condition for the acquisition of sufficient familiar patterns to reach expert levels in any domain. Indeed, over a wide range of domains, a 'ten-year-rule' operates. At least ten years intensive practice is necessary for world-class performance in any complex area. Ericsson's analysis brings to the foreground issues of motivation and long-term processes of cognitive change that will require new out-of-laboratory methods of study.

The role of familiar patterns and of extensive background knowledge clearly emerges in Williamson and McGuiness' study of skilled map-reading. Saariluoma also supports the role of familiar patterns, in the case of chess problem perception and solving. Familiar patterns help cut down chess problem spaces to manageable sizes. Interestingly, this work also reveals a negative aspect of using familiar patterns—'set' effects that can lead players to overlook optimal but unfamiliar lines of play. Within chess problem spaces, differences in search processes become important and a model combining pattern-recognition and evaluation-based search is proposed.

Bellamy and Gilmore present evidence that, in the domain of programming, familiar patterns in the form of stored 'programming plans' appear to play little actual role in writing programs. Previous evidence for the utility of such plans was based on studies of memory for programs rather than program writing.

While practice is a necessary condition for skill acquisition, it is also surely true that different approaches to practice will differ in effectiveness. Green and Gilhooly examine the role of learning strategies in the complex domain of statistical computing. The strategies typical of faster learners are contrasted with those more characteristic of slower learners in the domain of study. More effective learners showed more-frequent executive-level processing. They monitored their performance better and made more strategic decisions as against local, tactical decisions.

Another factor affecting acquisition of cognitive skills is the appropriateness of the coding used during the study period. Berry's chapter concerns the effects of concurrent verbalization on cognitive skill acquisition: her work indicates that concurrent verbalization can help by bringing relevant pieces of information together in working memory at critical points in learning. Logie and Salway examine in more detail the relative roles of working-memory components in the performance of a spatial thinking task (mental rotation). Their work indicates the utility of dual task methodology for specifying, more closely than is common, the nature of working memory involvement in skilled thinking.

In conclusion, the chapters in this part indicate that the study of real-life complex thinking skills is a lively area of research showing good signs of progress and with considerable potential for development.

1

Theoretical Issues in the Study of Exceptional Performance*

K. ANDERS ERICSSON
University of Colorado at Boulder

INTRODUCTION

In all human activities and endeavours there are always some people who do better and are considered more successful than the majority. When these people perform at a very high level, they are called talented and gifted or specialists and experts. The label used to characterize them, whether intended to do so or not, reflects attribution of their successful behaviour to some major factor. Similar conceptions and attributions have guided scientific efforts to understand the source of such 'successful behaviour'.

All theoretical positions recognize that extensive preparation and practice are necessary to attain exceptional levels of performance. The point of disagreement is the extent to which unmodifiable genetic factors limit the ultimate level of performance. Let me briefly present the two main approaches.

Researchers who have de-emphasized the role of innate factors have studied exceptional performers to discover how to improve training for normal subjects as well as to determine the potentials of human development. A nice quote from Maslow (1971, p. 7) illustrates this position:

> 'If we want to answer the question of how tall the human species can grow, then obviously it is well to pick out the ones who already are tallest and study them. If we want to know how fast a human being can run, then it is no use to average out the speed of a "good sample" of the population; it is far better to collect Olympic gold medal winners and see how well they can do. ...The highest possibilities of human nature have practically always been underrated. Even when "good specimens", the saints and sages and great leaders in history, have been available for

---

* Thoughtful comments and suggestions on earlier drafts of this chapter from Janet Grassia, Laura Thompson and Susan Silverberg are gratefully acknowledged.

Lines of Thinking, Volume 2   Edited by K.J. Gilhooly, M.T.G. Keane, R.H. Logie and G. Erdos
© 1990 John Wiley & Sons Ltd

study, the temptation too often has been to consider them not human but supernaturally endowed.'

Even the most optimistic humanist has to concede that not all human attributes can be improved by environmental interventions. For example, the evidence for strong genetic determination of height is very compelling (Wilson, 1986). Given the solid evidence for genetic determination of many physical attributes, it seems reasonable to think that mental capacities and other cognitive factors that appear critical for attaining exceptional levels of performance may also be genetically determined.

Those who emphasize the role of genetic factors cannot, of course, argue that it is possible to design instructional training programmes that will enable individuals to attain exceptional levels of performance. Because genetic factors are immutable, the best one can hope for is to identify those that are critical to exceptional performance. Society then benefits because individuals with the critical attributes can be identified early and provided with whatever limited educational resources are of value.

The first step towards identifying critical attributes is analysis of the attributes displayed by exceptional performers during childhood and assessed retrospectively through interviews and biographical records. Constraining the search to genetically determined attributes has led investigators to focus on basic capacities for which a neural and physiological mechanism is plausible. One area of performance that has produced clear support for differences in talent or genetically determined ability is sports. There is overwhelming evidence that the bodies of élite athletes differ from those of normal subjects and less successful athletes with respect to the composition of the muscles, the blood supply to the muscles, the size of the heart, and other characteristics. It has been proposed that such differences could be the result of long-term training; but in a recent chapter of the *Annual Review of Psychology*, Browne and Mahoney (1984, p. 609) wrote:

'There is good evidence that the limits of this psychological capacity to become more efficient with training is determined by genetics. Muscle fiber type (fast-twitch versus slow-twitch percentage) and the maximal amount of oxygen consumed per minute per body weight (called max VO_2) are prime examples. Both are more than 90% determined by heredity for both males and females (Fox & Mathews, 1981).'

One might conclude that élite performance in sports is almost completely determined by genetic differences. However, I will re-examine the evidence in this quotation and consider more recent evidence on this issue later in the chapter.

Similar evidence is available in the arts. The area I am most familiar with is the performance of musicians. One of the best-known attributes of excellent musicians is absolute pitch—that is, the ability to recognize musical notes when they are played in isolation. Individuals apparently discover their ability to make judgements of absolute pitch at a young age. Another characteristic of many exceptional musicians is their ability to play a musical piece after a single hearing. For example, Mozart is alleged to have had such a tape-recorder-like memory for music.

Superior memory is often claimed to characterize eminent authors and scientists. Rather than attempt an exhaustive review of the evidence, I will provide a specific example from the childhood of Marie Curie, who shared a Nobel prize with her husband for the discovery of radium. Madame Curie grew up in Poland, which at the time was under Russian occupation. The official language in the schools was Russian instead of the familiar Polish. Memorization of text in a foreign language is difficult, but the young Marie did not find it so:

> 'Her memory was such that her comrades, hearing her faultless recitation of a poem they had seen her read no more than twice, thought at once of a trick, and accused her of learning verses secretly.' (Curie, 1938, p. 26)

The idea that individual differences in ability to memorize are genetically determined has various sources of support and evidence. The most striking individual differences are observed for memorization of unfamiliar and meaningless information. Normal subjects claim to use rote methods to grind and stamp the information on to memory. Subjects with exceptional memory report that they are able to store the information in sensory form—for example, as visual images (Luria, 1968) or auditory images (Binet, 1894). If superior memory draws on direct storage of sensory impressions, a genetic account of individual differences is theoretically plausible. Further evidence for the genetic account comes from *idiot savants*: that is, individuals with a very low level of general intelligence but with a single superior ability—for example, to memorize numbers.

In this chapter I scrutinize the evidence for the claim that differences in memory ability, in perceptual abilities like absolute pitch, and in athletic ability as reflected by physiological differences in élite athletes, are immutable and genetic in origin. These differences have been identified and studied primarily in individuals who already display exceptional performance. To examine the alternative possibility that these differences are acquired, I shall first briefly review some recent evidence on the amount and timing of preparation and training required to attain exceptional levels of performance.

A recent review (Ericsson and Crutcher, in press) of exceptional performance in chess, sports, the arts and the sciences shows that exceptional performance appears to be impossible without extensive practice. The review finds remarkably consistent support for Chase and Simon's (1973) claim that world-class performance requires a minimum of about ten years of committed practice.

The finding that exceptional levels of performance require a decade of intense preparation strengthens the hypothesis that differences in memory, perception and physiological capacity are acquired through and result from practice. I want to focus here on an empirical issue; namely, is it possible to dramatically improve one's basic physiological, perceptual and memory capacity through training and practice? I deliberately use the phrase *basic capacity* and appreciate the underlying logical inconsistency of being able to improve something that is basic.

Hence an important part of my enterprise is to demonstrate that the processes underlying high and exceptional performance on many tests alleged to measure basic capacities are in fact not basic.

The claim that one is studying a basic capacity in psychology is nearly always a theoretical inference. Psychological studies are thus quite different from the studies of exceptional performance in sports, in which actual physiological differences have been observed. Our knowledge about the physiology of the sensory system is a plausible basis for the inference that exceptional perceptual abilities like absolute pitch reflect a basic capacity. In the case of memory ability, the precise localization of the relevant neurological processes is still largely unknown, and the inference about basic processes or capacities is theoretically derived. Let me illustrate the line of argument for the measurement of basic memory processes.

MEMORY ABILITY

Research on the processes and capacity of basic memory dates back to the origin of experimental psychology. Ebbinghaus (1964/1885) quickly realized that his search for general laws of human memory would not be successful if he studied memory for familiar material because of individuals' experience with such material differs markedly. Instead, he determined to study memory for unfamiliar material such as nonsense syllables, for which no one would have formed basic or simple associations between the elements he presented and prior experience. Furthermore, he used a rapid rate of presentation to eliminate any mediating cognitive processes. This claim that experimental control over material and presentation rate can constrain subjects to rely on basic processes is very important. Even to this day many investigators hold this belief.

If unfamiliar material and fast presentation rates force subjects to rely on basic memory processes, then subjects with exceptional performance on memory tasks with these conditions have to have exceptional basic memory processes or even memory processes that are different from those of average subjects. This argument for a different memory system in some individuals was apparently accepted in the field of psychometrics (Wechsler, 1952).

One testable implication of this hypothesis is that memory performance for unfamiliar, rapidly presented material should be stable and not markedly influenced by practice. Bill Chase and I decided to replicate some earlier studies showing that memory span could be improved. By studying verbal reports on subjects' cognitive processes during the memory trials, we wanted to understand how the fixed capacity of short-term memory could allow, through practice, systematic increases in the amount of material remembered.

Chase and Ericsson (1981, 1982) provided subjects with several hundred hours of practice on the digit-span task. In this task, a sequence of random digits is read to a subject at the rate of one digit per second, and the subject is asked to recall the sequence of digits. If the sequence is reported correctly, the length of the next sequence is increased by one digit; otherwise, the length is decreased by one digit.

Figure 1.1 shows average digit span as a function of practice for several

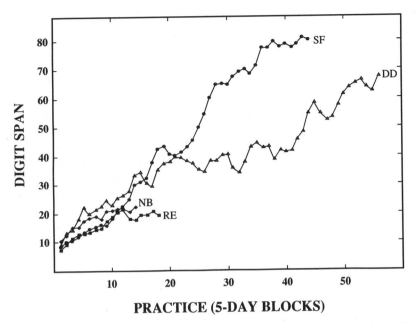

FIGURE 1.1   Average digit span for form trained subjects as a function of practice. The data for S.F. and D.D. are obtained from Chase and Ericsson (1982), for R.E. from Chase and Ericsson (1981), for N.B. from Ericsson, Fendrich and Faivre (in preparation).

subjects. These subjects were selected as representative college students, and their initial digit spans were in the normal range; that is, seven plus or minus two (Miller, 1956). However, after 50–100 hours of practice, all subjects attained digit spans of over 20 digits with a presentation rate of one digit per second. These digit spans are higher than those reported for allegedly exceptional subjects (Ericsson, 1985).

The improvements with practice and training shown in Figure 1.1 clearly refute the claim that digit-span performance reflects basic, unmodifiable memory capacity. From the retrospective verbal reports given after the memory trials and from series of experiments testing hypotheses derived from these reports, a fairly clear picture emerges of the nature of improvements in digit span. Because the results of these studies have been reported in detail elsewhere (Chase and Ericsson, 1981, 1982; Ericsson, 1985, 1988; Ericsson and Chase, 1982; Ericsson, Chase and Faloon, 1980), I shall simply give examples of and summarize the findings here.

From the performance data alone one might argue that practice with the digit-span task simply makes the rehearsal strategy used by normal subjects more rapid and efficient. This explanation becomes more and more unreasonable when it has to account for digit spans of over 80 digits, which two of the subjects attained. Several other pieces of evidence refute this explanation. According to the rehearsal method, subjects would retain the information only temporarily and store essentially no information about earlier memory trials. However, when our subjects were tested after the session, they were able to recall around

90% of all the 200–300 digits presented during different trials. The improvement in digit-span performance appeared to be limited to the type of stimulus material used in practice (i.e. digits) and no improvements were observed in memory span for consonants. Hence, with practice subjects do not extend the general capacity of their short-term memory, but rather acquire skill in rapidly storing a particular type of information in long-term memory.

Verbal reports on cognitive processes during digit-span trials give a detailed picture of acquired skill for memory. I shall focus on S.F., the first subject Chase and I studied. S.F.'s retrospective reports indicated that his cognitive processes were initially the same as those of other college students in the digit-span task. In the first practice session S.F. rehearsed the presented digit sequences. In subsequent sessions he would group the first three digits of a series, concentrate on the group for a moment, and then rehearse the remaining digits in the sequence. At recall he would retrieve and report the three-digit group and then the digits in the rehearsal group.

During session 5, S.F. reported realizing that a three-digit sequence could be interpreted as a running time for a mile. For example, 418 could be a 4-minute, 18-second mile time. S.F.'s average digit span for this session jumped four standard deviations from the average of the previous session. S.F. was a long-distance runner with extensive knowledge of both specific and general categories of running times for many different races. In subsequent sessions, S.F. retrieved a set of races ($\frac{1}{4}$-mile, $\frac{1}{2}$-mile, $\frac{3}{4}$-mile, mile, 2-mile) that covered the range of most three-digit numbers from 100 to 959. Chase and I argued that S.F.'s use of pre-existing knowledge and patterns to encode the information rapidly in long-term memory was a necessary characteristic of exceptional memory, and we called this characteristic the *principle of meaningful encoding*.

With further practice, S.F. was able to encode several three-digit or four-digit groups and store them in long-term memory. To retrieve these digit groups in order during the recall test, S.F. reported associating spatial labels with each digit group: 'first', 'middle', and 'last'. Further increases in S.F.'s digit span occurred when he began to group digit groups into several supergroups, an example of which appears in Figure 1.2.

S.F. reported that prior to the presentation of a digit sequence, he would plan how to group and organize the sequence. During the presentation he would associate a unique location within the hierarchy with each digit group. We (Chase and Ericsson, 1982) called these locational cues within the hierarchy *retrieval cues*. At the time of recall S.F. could activate these retrieval cues and recall the associated digit groups in the presented order. The general principle of associating presented information with a well-known, organized set of retrieval cues we called *the retrieval structure principle*.

During some of the test sessions, we presented S.F. with a self-paced version of the digit-span task in which he could control the presentation of digits on a CRT by pressing a response key. With practice he could memorize digit sequences below his current digit span at a rate much faster than his usual rate of one digit per second. This observation, along with other evidence, led us to propose a third general principle for acquired exceptional memory, or as we call it *skilled memory*. According to this principle, the speed of encoding and retrieval

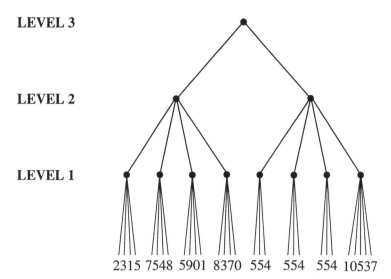

FIGURE 1.2 Proposed hierarchical organization of S.F.'s memory encoding of 30 presented digits. The first level contains mnemonic encodings of digit groups, and the second level consists of supergroups in which the relative location of several digit groups are encoded.

operations can be dramatically increased by practice, so that they can be performed within seconds and thus exhibit the storage and access characteristics of short-term memory.

In a recent review (Ericsson, 1985) I showed that results from other studies that assessed the detailed cognitive processes of subjects with exceptional memory performance are remarkably consistent with the three principles of skilled memory. For example, consistent with the principle of meaningful encoding, all of these studies produced evidence that subjects segmented the digit sequences into groups and verbally reported encoding these digit groups by drawing on pre-existing knowledge and patterns. Some of these exceptional subjects were skilled in mental calculation and had extensive experience in mathematics. They reported using their knowledge of mathematics to encode the digit groups (Bryan, Lindley and Harter, 1941; Mueller, 1911, 1913). Professor Rueckle, for example, reported encoding six-digit groups by identifying relations between prime factors of the two three-digit numbers (Mueller, 1911), as shown in Figure 1.3. Mathematicians, as well as people who are not mathematicians, also used knowledge of dates and patterns (Hunt and Love, 1972). The remaining subjects (Gordon, Valentine and Wilding, 1984; Susukita, 1933, 1934) reported using the mnemonic technique of phonemic recoding, by which two to four numbers can be recorded as concrete nouns.

There is also considerable evidence for the retrieval structure principle. In the extensive experimental analyses of Professor Rueckle, Mueller (1911, 1917) was able to provide evidence for Rueckle's use of a hierarchical retrieval structure for the digit groups that is very similar to those structures identified for the digit-span experts studied by Chase and Ericsson (1981, 1982; Ericsson, 1985, 1988).

Encodings of a professor in mathematics (Rueckle)

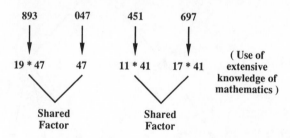

Encodings of a subject (TE) trained in mnemonics

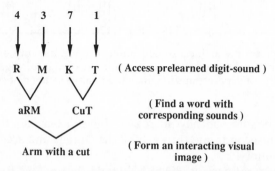

FIGURE 1.3 Examples of types of encodings used by a mathematics professor, Rueckle (Mueller, 1911) and by a subject, T.E. (Gordon, Valentine and Wilding, 1984), who had extensive training in mnemonics.

Susukita (1933, 1934) described the retrieval structure used by a professional mnemonist, Isahara. This retrieval structure consisted of a fixed sequence of about 400 physical locations, such as a brook near Isahara's house. Using the 'method of loci' to memorize a series of digits, Isahara would recode the first group of digits as a concrete word and then form a visual image of the word and the first physical location. He would then recode the next group of digits and imagine the second location, and so on. At the time of recall, Isahara would use his knowledge of the fixed series of locations to cue his retrieval of the stored images and would then decode the words to obtain the presented digits. The mnemonically trained subject studied by Gordon, Valentine and Wilding (1984) used a similar method but relied on a prelearned sequence of concrete objects instead of locations.

In sum, several independent investigations of subjects displaying exceptional memory performance have shown that exceptional memory performance involves mediating knowledge and cognitive processes. The exceptional subjects differed in the type of knowledge used and in the details of their retrieval structures, but the structure of their memory skills is completely consistent with the principles of skilled memory.

Only a few studies have explicitly rejected cognitive mediation of exceptional memory. Chase and I carefully reviewed them (Ericsson and Chase, 1982), and showed that the performance of our own trained digit-span experts could match and even surpass the memory performance of the allegedly exceptional subjects. A critical piece of evidence supporting the use of sensory images in allegedly exceptional memory (Binet, 1894; Luria, 1968) involved memorization of visually presented matrices like the one shown in Figure 1.4. The allegedly exceptional subjects were able to efficiently recall the digits in the matrix in any of the orders of recall shown in this figure. We found that, without special training, our digit-span experts could match or surpass the performance of exceptional subjects on this task. Our subjects' recall times for different orders of recall were highly correlated with those obtained for the allegedly exceptional subjects. This finding is important because it shows that allegedly exceptional subjects most likely rely on the same mediating processes that normal subjects do. Furthermore, this finding demonstrates that, with a retrieval structure, subjects can recall presented information in a much more efficient and flexible manner than previously believed possible.

When Irene Faivre and I (Ericsson and Faivre, 1988) reviewed the empirical evidence on *idiot savants* and mentally retarded subjects exhibiting exceptional memory, we found that their performance was exceptional only in contrast to

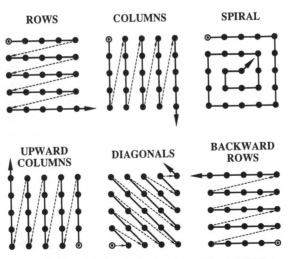

FIGURE 1.4 A 25-digit matrix of the type used by Binet (1894) to test his memory experts. He asked subjects to repeat the whole matrix in the various orders shown or to repeat individual rows as five-digit numbers.

their low level of general abilities. We also found evidence that several of the mentally retarded subjects encoded information with mediating knowledge.

In conclusion, exceptionally good memory performance has been shown to reflect not superior basic memory capacity but rather acquired memory skills with encoding processes and retrieval structures. Exceptional memory performance by a small number of subjects has invariably been demonstrated for meaningless materials like digits, nonsense syllables, and foreign languages, for which normal subjects show very poor memory. Normal subjects show much better memory for the text of stories and other meaningful materials, and their rates of memorization for such materials are comparable to exceptional subjects' rates for memorizing digits after extensive practice (Ericsson, 1985).

Chase and Ericsson (1982; Ericsson, 1985) argued that the superior memory of experts for information within their field of expertise, as demonstrated in chess, music, computer programming, and so forth, can be accounted for by these experts' superior acquired knowledge in those domains. Ericsson and Staszewski (1989) have gone one step further and described how experts in many fields develop memory skills with the structure of skilled memory to cope with great demands on working memory. In support of the memory-skill hypothesis, Chi (1978) has shown that 10-year-old chess players participating in chess tournaments show superior memory for chess positions but not for other materials such as digits. It is a reasonable conjecture that the superior memory displayed by many exceptional performers during their childhood reflects the knowledge and expertise they have already acquired at that point in their lives and is not a talent prerequisite for attaining future eminence.

PERCEPTUAL ABILITY

Experience and familiarity are critically important to the ability to perceive and recognize objects and their attributes. As with memory ability, the most intriguing evidence of superior perceptual abilities is found for stimuli that normal people find lacking in apparent meaning and meaningful organization. Tasks in which some people demonstrate clearly superior perceptual abilities are determining the sex of chickens, identifying heart murmurs, diagnosing X-rays, and wine and food tasting (Gibson, 1969). The traditional explanation for these superior abilities is that, after considerable experience with particular complex stimuli, individuals learn to selectively attend to the critical aspects. A recent study by Biederman and Shiffrar (1987) demonstrated the importance of such attentional factors in chicken sexing. This study showed that naive subjects' performance after short-term instruction was dramatically changed in the direction of performance by experts with years of practice.

Researchers in the field of perception have tended to avoid complex stimuli in favour of simple stimuli whereby the basic processes of sensory perception can be studied. The use of simple stimuli eliminates any problems with selective attention because each stimulus differs from the others in only a single physical dimension, such as pitch and loudness for sounds. The sensory nature of the attributes of simple stimuli should rule out the mediation of cognitive and experimental factors.

Many experimental paradigms have been used in studies of sensory perception and I shall focus here on one of them, absolute judgement. In an absolute judgement task, a subject tries to identify which of several possible simple stimuli was presented. The absolute judgement paradigm is interesting for several reasons. In a classic paper, Miller (1956) showed that the number of identifiable stimuli remain constant (4–10) over a wide range of stimulus dimensions and modalities (taste, hearing, vision, etc.). One well-known exception to this overwhelming constancy is that a small proportion of musicians have absolute pitch and can identify quickly and correctly 88 different pitches.

In the traditional view, absolute pitch is not just a feat of performance but an automatic perception revealed in childhood. Individuals who report using mediating processes to achieve very high levels of pitch recognition are not said to have absolute pitch. (Examples of mediating processes are attempts to reproduce the note by humming and singing, to identify the note with the same note in well-known pieces of music, and to identify the note by estimating musical intervals.) Several attempts have been made to identify unique performance criteria for individuals with 'true' absolute pitch, but evaluations of a large number of subjects on many tests and measures have produced no clear evidence for any such criteria. As the tests of ability to recognize pitch get harder, as they do when artificially generated sine tones are used, for example, fewer and fewer subjects pass the tests (Oakes, 1955). This finding suggests that the best subjects are merely the extreme end of a normal distribution of ability.

The widespread belief among musicians that absolute pitch is inherited is in itself important. Most musicians have very good relative pitch; that is, they identify notes in relation to other available notes. However, relative pitch must be a very different ability from absolute pitch because although many musicians desire absolute pitch, few are able to attain it. Differences in these two abilities were confirmed by Brady (1970), a musician who was able to attain absolute pitch performance through training. His training involved learning to identify a single tone. Once he had established that tone as an internal referent, he was able to identify other tones quickly and easily by drawing on his previously developed relative pitch. Brady reported that once developed, the identification task required little effort and that no conscious practice was necessary to maintain the skill. No decrement in performance was reported after six months, and only a slight decrement was reported after 13 years (Costall, 1985).

It thus appears that once absolute pitch is acquired, no deliberate efforts to maintain the skill are necessary—at least for active musicians. This raises the possibility that subjects with absolute pitch in the traditional sense acquired the necessary skill as children and then simply maintained it effortlessly for the rest of their lives. In their literature review Ericsson and Faivre (1988) found several pieces of evidence supporting this hypothesis. Children with absolute pitch tend to start their music training early, and memorization of individual tones appears to be easier before children start perceiving notes as part of larger musical structures.

If absolute pitch is an acquired skill, it is not simply a uniform improvement of the judgement processes used by untrained subjects in determining pitch. The

pattern of errors in pitch identification produced by subjects with absolute pitch
is quite different from that produced by untrained subjects. Those with absolute
pitch tend to confuse tones with the same location in different subscales rather
than tones having the smallest difference in fundamental frequencies. For
example, an untrained subject might confuse C with B, whereas a subject with
absolute pitch would confuse C in one octave with C in a different octave (Ward
and Burns, 1982). The ability to perceive the similarity of the same tone in
different octaves is also an attribute of relative pitch. In her doctoral dissertation
Faivre (1986) made a detailed analysis of the mediating cognitive processes in
two untrained subjects in a task involving identification of musical notes. One
subject showed a three- to four-fold increase in ability during the practice
period. Faivre's analysis showed that this subject acquired the ability to identify
the same note in different octaves. This result is consistent with current
proposals in neurology that in addition to information about the height of the
tone, information about the chroma or the quality of the same note across
octaves is encoded by the receptors of the ear.

There have been several other demonstrations of improvements in judgement
of simple stimuli with practice. However, surprisingly little is known about the
mechanism mediating this acquired improvement or skill. Ericsson and Faivre
(1982, 1988) studied one subject (I.F.) learning to identify colours differing only
slightly in hue. At first, I.F. could correctly identify on the average five of the 21
colour stimuli, the same level of performance observed for control subjects in
this task. After 80 sessions of practice I.F. could reliably identify 18 out of the 21
stimuli, a result that is comparable to the control subjects' performance when,
with all stimuli simultaneously available, they rank-ordered the stimuli with
respect to hue.

Several efforts were made to make certain that I.F. did not base her performance on technical imperfections, scratches, and other additional cues making the
stimuli unique in an artifactual manner. For example, I.F. showed perfect
transfer to a parallel set of the same colour stimuli never seen before. From an
analysis of verbal reports and errors over the duration of practice, Ericsson and
Faivre (1982, 1988) were able to show that, although I.F.'s overall performance
increased gradually, discrete improvements were due to the sudden emergence
of perfect identification of particular stimuli, which were reported to have
distinct colour attributes like 'bright', 'gold' and 'orange'. Although perfect
recognition of these stimuli was initially restricted to these stimuli alone, with
practice these stimuli functioned as anchors and enabled I.F. to correctly identify
other stimuli with nearly the same hue. In several tests of transfer throughout
the period of training I.F. also tried to identify 21 stimuli from a different part of
the colour spectrum, and no transfer was observed. The specificity of the
observed improvement is quite consistent with the learning of labels for specific
attributes, which are distinct in the set of training stimuli (Ericsson and Faivre,
1982, 1988). Many other studies (Gibson, 1969) have found similar specificity of
improvement of performance: for example, training of absolute auditory threshold in one frequency range shows no transfer when the threshold is tested in a
different frequency range.

In sum there is considerable evidence that perceptual judgements even of simple stimuli can be dramatically improved through practice. The improvements are often remarkably specific, and the mediating mechanisms are not dissimilar to those identified for other skills such as skilled memory.

The evidence for acquired skill is clearer for perceptual judgements of complex stimuli. The highest levels of performance in diagnosis of X-rays (Lesgold, 1984) and evaluation of livestock (Phelps and Shanteau, 1978) are achieved by individuals with 10–30 years of experience in making such judgements. Through analysis of the judgement processes of individuals at different levels of expertise, the research on diagnosis of X-rays (Lesgold, 1984) has demonstrated the emergence of rules and constructive analysis with increased levels of expertise. Furthermore, some interesting research has been done relating experts' perception of dogs to characteristics of normal, meaningful perception of faces (Diamond and Carey, 1986). If further research confirms that the cognitive structure and level of performance exhibited by experts in unfamiliar and 'meaningless' perceptual domains is similar to those of normal subjects' engaged in everyday perception, our understanding of both everyday perception, and expertise will be greatly enhanced.

SPORTS PERFORMANCE AND PHYSIOLOGICAL CHARACTERISTICS

Performance in sports did not attract the attention of psychologists until relatively recently. The simplicity of the tasks, the high degree of automatism in mediating cognitive processes, and the critical importance of motor processes did not appear to leave much room for interesting psychological phenomena. This is particularly true for events such as running and swimming. For the same reasons these sports activities have been intensively studied by sports physiologists.

The most successful efforts to identify physiological correlates of performance have been made with long-distance running. This sport is attractive to study because it involves maintaining a comparatively simple motor activity for extended periods of time. It is also relatively easy to set up a laboratory situation for steady-state running on a treadmill. During steady-state running or cycling on an exercise bicycle, the body converts energy into work through the metabolism of oxygen. In the laboratory, it is possible to measure both the maximal ability to take up oxygen (aerobic power) and the efficiency with which oxygen is converted into work at submaximal levels of running. The aerobic power of runners is highly predictive of their long-distance running performance. Correlations between running times and maximal oxygen uptake (aerobic power) range between -0.82 and -0.91 for several studies of well-trained and experienced runners (Conley and Krahenbuhl, 1980).

Aerobic power is a measure of the overall ability of the body to metabolize oxygen and produce muscular energy. Through examination of the physiological components mediating the circulation of oxygen and its metabolism in the muscles, it might be possible to identify those components that account for the superior aerobic power of élite long-distance runners. Most of the studies have essentially used a cross-sectional approach and compared the physiological characteristics of élite athletes with those of normal subjects. One of the first findings was that athletes have hearts that are larger than normal (see Morganroth and Maron, 1977). A larger heart provides the capacity to circulate more oxygen-rich blood, which is critical to high aerobic power. The oxygen-rich blood eventually needs to reach the muscles, and studies have shown that subjects' aerobic power is closely related to the number of capillaries supplying each muscle fibre with blood (Saltin *et al.*, 1977). Muscles are composed of muscle fibres with different characteristics. Some muscle fibres, such as slow-twitch muscle fibres, are particularly suited to the sustained activity involved in long-distance running. A high proportion of slow-twitch muscle fibres is highly predictive of good long-distance running performance (see Bouchard, 1986, for a review). The superior aerobic power of athletes can, at least in part, be accounted for by their larger hearts and the larger number of capillaries for each muscle fibre. In a similar manner, it is possible to account for the greater running efficiency of long-distance runners by their higher percentage of slow-twitch muscle fibre.

The empirical evidence that these physiological differences are stable genetic characteristics of élite runners is remarkably weak. We know only that the élite long-distance runners exhibit these differences after many years of practice. The nature of these physiological differences has led investigators to believe that they reflect stable individual genetic differences and that élite runners lie at the extreme end of normal variation. Some of the early studies tended to confirm this view by showing extremely high (over 90%) genetic determination (i.e. heritability) for these differences (see Fox and Mathews, 1981, for a review). However, more recent genetic studies have been unable to replicate the previous high heritability estimates and indicate a much lower degree of genetic determination (Bouchard, 1986). The role of genetic factors in determining sports performance appears to be considerably less important than originally believed. Recent research summarized in a symposium on genetic factors in sports performance clearly shows that many factors, including maximal aerobic power and capacity and proportion of muscle fibre types, 'are characterized by only a moderate heritability component' (Bouchard and Malina, 1986, p. 184). Hence there appears to be considerable room for improvement and influence by environmental factors. Let me therefore turn to empirical evidence demonstrating the effects of practice on these physiological characteristics.

Recent research has shown that the human physiological system is far more adaptable than was once believed possible. Changes in the number of capillaries supplying blood to muscle fibres are found to take place as a result of practice (Salmons and Henriksson, 1981). Salmons and Henriksson (1981) also reviewed evidence showing that in animals fast-twitch muscle fibres can be completely converted into slow-twitch muscle fibres through sustained electric stimulation of muscles.

A subsequent review of Howald (1982) showed that these results can be generalized to human skeletal muscles. The evidence presented included case studies of top athletes who were forced to stop or reduce training because of injuries. Drastic decrements in the percentage of their slow-twitch fibres occurred within six months to one year. Howald also showed that training studies and studies using electrical stimulation produced a very consistent pattern of results. The transformation from fast-twitch to slow-twitch muscle fibres appears to be gradual and involves a number of intermediate muscle types. Although studies of limited training rarely demonstrate a complete conversion of fast-twitch to slow-twitch fibres, clear changes to intermediate muscle types are regularly seen. In addition, Howald (1982) reviewed developmental data on the percentage of slow-twitch fibres in children of different ages and found that changes in activity pattern could readily account for these differences.

If extensive training does affect any of these physiological characteristics those that are affected must closely correspond to specific functions central to the training activities. Hence, characteristics acquired or improved through training should be adaptations to the demands of training. As noted earlier, aerobic power is closely related to long-distance running performance, except in élite long-distance runners, for whom a ceiling effect may be present. Elite long-distance runners differ from other élite runners in their running efficiency at rates lower than maximum. At rates similar to their regular running speeds during races, élite long-distance athletes are able to run more efficiently; that is, they can maintain speed with a minimal consumption of oxygen (Conley and Krahenbuhl, 1980; Daniels *et al.*, 1986).

One of the most striking examples of adaptation with training is the anatomical differences in the hearts of different types of athletes. Morganroth and Maron (1977) reviewed research showing that the mass of the heart was larger in both endurance athletes, such as runners and swimmers, and athletes focusing on strength, such as wrestlers and shot-putters. However, the increase was due to different factors in the two types of athletes. In athletes focusing on sudden exhibitions of strength, the thickness of the left ventricular wall was increased and facilitated rapid transport of oxygen-rich blood to the muscles. Endurance athletes benefit from a larger volume of circulated, oxygen-rich blood, and their hearts showed an increased left ventricular diastolic volume, a measure that was essentially normal in wrestlers. Except for the critical characteristics, the athletes' hearts were found to be within the normal range.

Tesch and Karlsson (1985) examined the size and frequency of fast- and slow-twitch fibres in the muscles of different types of élite athletes as well as of students serving as control subjects. They found, as would be expected, that middle- and long-distance runners had a significantly higher percentage of slow-twitch fibres in the legs than did the control subjects, but the runners' back muscles were no different from those of the control subjects. For élite kayakers the pattern was reversed. There was no difference in the proportions of fibres in kayakers' leg muscles compared with those of the control subjects, but large differences were found for the back muscles. From these and other findings Tesch and Karlsson (1985) argued that differences in the muscles of élite athletes occur only for muscles specifically trained for a sport (legs in running and back muscles in kayaking), with no differences for untrained muscles.

It is only quite recently that sports physiologists have started to make longitudinal studies of these adaptation processes. Part of the problem is that it appears necessary for athletes to train intensively for years before these physiological adaptations occur. The available data clearly support this claim.

Long-distance runners participate for about 10 years in active competition before attaining their peak performance (Wallingford, 1975). Highly trained and experienced long-distance runners were found to have trained for ten years on the average (Conley and Krahenbuhl, 1980). Élite long-distance athletes usually run twice a day and cover distances from 110 to 240 km essentially every week of the year (Hagan, Smith and Gettman, 1981; Wallingford, 1975).

The best evidence linking intensive training directly to observed physiological adaptations comes from a longitudinal study of élite long-distance runners, who acquired larger maximal aerobic power and larger relative heart volumes during a five-year period of training but who showed no suggestion of initial superiority at age 14 (Elovainio and Sundberg, 1983). A much larger body of evidence links the maintenance of superior physiological characteristics to sustained intensive training and shows a remarkably rapid deterioration to normal characteristics with the termination of practice (Ericsson, in press). The nature of the adaptation processes is perhaps better revealed by a number of negative effects associated with sustained high levels of training. Intensive running occasionally leads to 'runner's knee', 'runner's heel bumps', shin splints, Achilles' tendonitis, and bone deformities of the foot such as bunions and hammer-toes (Subotnick, 1977).

I want to close this section with a quotation on the high degree to which élite athletes adapt to the physical conditions of their sport. The quotation is taken from a biography of Roger Bannister (1955) who was the first person to break the magical four-minute limit for the English mile. Bannister (1955, p. 112) is reflecting on the fact that, through training, athletes acquire a low resting pulse, which occasionally gives them trouble:

> 'Sometimes an athlete's pulse at rest may have minor irregularities. A case is known of a world record holder who fainted in the course of an ordinary medical examination. The key to this paradox is found when the athlete begins to exercise. Far from being a sick man he quickly passes to a state of extreme efficiency. His integration of heart and lungs may be more efficient when he is running at ten miles an hour than when he is sitting in an arm chair. This is perhaps as striking a tribute to the body's philosophy, which seems to prefer movement, as to its physiology, which makes this movement possible. The waddling gait and breathlessness of a muscle-bound weight-lifter are salutary warnings of the dangers of over-specialization, and of what occurs when muscular development has been carried to excess.' (p. 112)

CONCLUDING REMARKS

My review has shown that in three different domains of ability performance assumed to reflect stable basic capacities can be dramatically improved by training and practice. The improvements observed are consistent in several respects with the traditional view of stable capacities, in that short-term practice is insufficient for attaining improvements, and in that the improvements are not simple extrapolations from the processes observed in untrained subjects. The memory tasks most clearly show the qualitative change in the mediating cognitive processes from untrained subjects to the trained memory experts. Mere exposure to the stimulus material or even practice in memorization is not in itself sufficient for acquiring very high levels of memory performance. Ericsson and Polson (1988) found that waiters and waitresses who regularly memorized their customers' dinner orders, did not acquire the elaborate memory skill of an expert waiter, who exhibited far superior performance. Ericsson and Crutcher (in press) reviewed additional evidence and pointed out the critical problem-solving processes leading one subject to the discovery and design of a superior memory skill with an effective retrieval structure. A similar argument for active learning and discovery of critical sensory attributes can be made for the improvement of perceptual abilities, although the evidence currently available is less complete. Finally, in the domain of sports, evidence on the mediation of cognitive processes in training is essentially lacking. However, it is clear that extreme intensity and extended duration of training are critical for improvements in élite long-distance running (Ericsson, in press).

On the basis of these findings it is reasonable to question the traditional account that attributes exceptional performance to inherited talents. The conception of exceptional performance as a skill acquired during a decade provides a better account of the evidence I have presented. However, it is also necessary to account in terms of acquired skill for the original evidence cited in support of the talent hypothesis. This evidence includes the early emergence of signs of giftedness, the high degree of specialization, and the scarcity of exceptional performers.

The skill-acquisition hypothesis can account for these three phenomena. First, I will review evidence on the emergence of signs of giftedness at an early age and then discuss the specialization and scarcity of exceptional performance. Recent research on the developmental history of international-level performers in games, sports, and the arts and sciences has shown that these individuals begin to pursue their chosen activity at a very early age (see Table 1.1).

From interviews with parents and coaches Bloom (1985b) found that future exceptional performers showed promise as children in activity only compared with other children in the same residential area. Such early involvement leads to early acquisition of skill, which in turn is responsible for superior memory in the target domain (Chi, 1978). Some research reviewed earlier indicated that young children more easily acquire absolute pitch than adults do. Together with the early starting age of exceptional pianists, this observation could account for early demonstrations of absolute pitch and for the observation that many exceptional musicians exhibit absolute pitch.

Table 1.1 also displays the evidence for the conclusion that around ten years of preparation appear necessary to reach an international level of performance. The ages at which individuals make outstanding artistic and scientific contributions or break the world record in sports are not uniform across the adult life-span; the highest frequencies of peak sports performance are normally observed for ages between 18 and 25, and for the other activities, below the age of 40. Hence in the framework of skill acquisition an early start appears to be beneficial and in some domains perhaps even necessary to attain truly exceptional levels of performance.

The early intense involvement in the target domain by exceptional performers is important for two reasons. The exceptional performers would have good

Table 1.1 Some statistics on the time when exceptional performers in various domains started, reached international level of performance, and reached their peak level of performance

Domain	Starting age	Time until international level of performance was attained after start	Age of peak performance
Sports			
Tennis players	6.5^a	$>10^b$	
Swimmers	4.5^c	10^d	$18–20^e$
Long-distance running		$\sim 10^f$	$25–30^{e,g}$
Arts			
Pianists	6^h	17^i	
Musical composers	$6–9^j$	$\sim 20^j$	$30–40^k$
Science			
Mathematicians		$\sim 10^l$	
Scientists			$30–40^k$
Games			
Chess	9.75^m	14.25^n	$30–40^o$

[a] Monsaas (1985); average age.
[b] Derived from Monsaas (1985) by Ericcsson and Crutcher (1989).
[c] Kalinowski (1985); average.
[d] Kalinowski (1985); average duration of competitive swimming.
[e] Scholtz and Curnow (1988); estimates based on Olympic gold medal winners.
[f] Wallingford (1975); estimated duration of competitive running.
[g] Ericsson (1990); estimates based on age at which world record was broken.
[h] Sosniak (1985); average age.
[i] Sosniak (1985); average duration from start to win major competition.
[j] Hayes (1981). [k] Lehmann (1953). [l] Gustin (1985).
[m] Krogius (1976); average age. [n] Krogius (1976); average duration since start.
[o] Elo (1965); Lehmann (1953); Krogius (1976).

opportunities to acquire characteristics and skills, which have been attributed to endowed talent. Secondly, exceptional athletes, artists and scientists are fully committed to their specific vocation and for years spend essentially all of their time attaining excellence in the particular field of their choice. The exceptional performers studied by Bloom (1985a) subordinated for extended periods all other aspects of their lives to optimizing their development and chances for success. For example, they minimized social and leisure time, spent money and time to travel substantial distances for training and competition, and moved far from family and friends to receive the best training and coaching. It is important to recognize that motivation and commitment must endure in the face of sickness, disease, injuries, lack of progress, and even successive failures. These strict requirements for enduring motivation provide a major selection factor and account for the scarcity of people attaining exceptional levels of performance to a high degree.

The attainment of exceptional levels of performance is severely constrained by both cognitive and motivational factors. In the earlier sections of this chapter I described examples of the cognitive analysis leading subjects to the discovery of methods and strategies necessary for the cognitive structure of the skill. In most task domains this cognitive analysis is facilitated by the instruction and feedback given by coaches and teachers. Beyond these cognitive factors subjects need to supply time and energy to maintain regular and intensive practice. There is a fair consensus that some activities involved in the acquisition of exceptional performance are inherently enjoyable and rewarding. Examples of such activities are the play of children and the flow state, which is defined by Csikszentmihalyi (1975) as the optimal match between the individual's skill level and the demands of the chosen field, leading the individual to be fully consumed by the activity. But play and flow experiences are very different from the reflective analysis of one's performance and the deliberate fine-tuning and massive repetition that are the critical activities in learning and in improving performance. Both of these learning-related activities require concentration and effort, and most people seem to view them with aversion, especially when they extend over long periods of time. Furthermore, to reach the highest levels of performance it appears necessary for individuals to fully dedicate themselves to an activity, give complete priority to that activity, and thereby give up and postpone other desirable social and cognitive activities which would require a share of the limited resources of time and 'mental energy'.

The transition to full-time commitment in exceptional performers in a domain does not appear to be sudden but develops gradually over many years and overlaps with development during childhood and adolescence. The motivational factors engaging the individual appear to change during this long period. In the work by Bloom and his associates (Bloom, 1985b), three phases can be distinguished in the ten-year or longer process of attaining exceptional performances. During the early childhood years (first phase), the individual is introduced to the domain, and play and enjoyment are emphasized. In general the parents are interested in this particular domain and give all kinds of encouragement and support. The parents stress the importance of doing one's best and working hard, and they exemplify this ethic themselves. During the middle years of training (second phase), competition and work receive more emphasis. During the late years, a definite commitment is required, and the individual decides to pursue training and activity full time. Figure 1.5 shows these three phases and a fourth phase, which is associated with disengagement from the activity. In many activities such as science and music it may never be necessary for the individuals to disengage, but athletes need almost invariably to terminate their full-time practice with increasing age.

Associated with the description of each phase in Figure 1.5 are three types of activities. Analysis of current performance to set up useful goals for immediate training and preparation is called 'cognitive analysis' and can be done by the individual or by a coach or teacher. During the second and especially the third phase, it seems essential that the individual works with a teacher or coach who has also performed at an exceptional level or coached other exceptional performers (Bloom, 1985b). To maximize training gains it is essential for individuals to so organize their lives that sufficient time and energy—maximal during the third phase—can be allocated to training and preparation. This

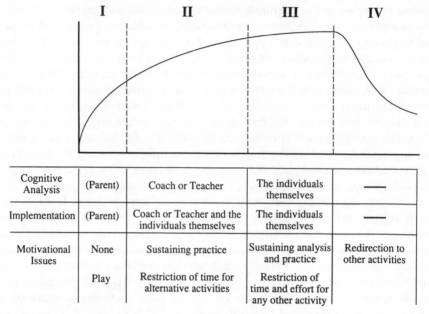

FIGURE 1.5 Phases of the acquisition of exceptional performance with their motivational and instructional characteristics.

organization is implemented through both cognitive and motivational effort, as shown in Figure 1.5. Motivation involving the delay or even exclusion of many social activities and, during the third phase, when full commitment to the chosen field is required, is particularly interesting.

I have been searching for empirical evidence on these motivational issues, and have been continually impressed by the devotion and even obsession documented in scholarly biographies of exceptional performers. As an illustration I will simply give a brief quotation about the third phase from the biography of one of the all-time great performers—Isaac Newton:

> 'Near the end of his life he was asked how he had discovered the law of universal gravitation. "By thinking on it continually," was the answer. I do not know of any story that better describes Newton, both in its suggestion of a life whose central adventure lay in the world of thought and in its indication of his mode of work. Newton had a rare capacity for esctacy, for stepping outside of himself and becoming wholly absorbed in the problems on which he worked. In a state of ecstacy he would forget to sleep and to eat. Innumerable stories about neglected meals have survived, to the extent that I sometimes wonder if the age's primary measure of Newton's genius did not lie in the fact that he could become so interested in a problem as not to eat. (Westfall, 1980, p. 110)

Westfall goes on to list the 'innumerable' independent documents verifying Newton's behaviour.

On this note I will make some concluding remarks. For three different domains of ability (memory, perception and sports) evidence has shown that with long-term practice remarkable improvements can be achieved on tasks originally believed to measure basic capacities and processes. Furthermore, striking physiological changes have been found to occur as the body adapts to extensive training. Hence, through intensive extended practice physiological limits can be changed and information processing limits can be circumvented by acquired skill. New evidence has shown that exceptional performance in a wide range of domains is attained only after ten or more years of intensive preparation. In light of these findings, I have argued that many so-called indicators of talent are not inherited prerequisites for exceptional performance but rather capabilities acquired as a result of intensive practice.

It would be a mistake to conclude that the skill-acquisition hypothesis for exceptional performance eliminates all constraints on the attainment of exceptional levels of performance. Instead, it entails new constraints involving the necessity of long-term motivation to sustain optimal learning and improvement for a decade or more. This presentation has shown that the results of extended practice cannot be extrapolated from short-term practice. Similarly, evidence indicates that long-term motivation cannot be understood or extrapolated from short-term studies of motivation. This evidence also demonstrates that human adaptability and the potential for human performance is far greater than normally believed.

At the same time, these results present a number of empirical and methodological challenges to theories of general psychology. It is no longer possible to dismiss exceptional levels of performance as special cases or genetic exceptions. Theories should be able to account for the full range of human performance. The fact that the acquired characteristics are attained over years and decades presents a real challenge to the current state of experimental methodology and forces us to search for ways of incorporating a longitudinal perspective in our work. I think that the empirical study of exceptional performance and its acquisition is a fascinating area of research with the potential for becoming a major field of research in the cognitive science.

REFERENCES

Bannister, R. (1955). *First four minutes*. London: Putnam.

Biederman, I., & Shiffrar, M. M. (1987). Sexing day-old chicks: a case study and expert systems analysis of a difficult perceptual-learning task. *Journal of Experimental Psychology: Learning, Memory and Cognition, 13*, 640–645.

Binet, A. (1894). *Psychologie des grands calculateurs et joueurs d'echecs* [Psychology of exceptional mental calculators and chess players]. Paris: Librarie Hachette.

Bloom, B. S. (ed.) (1985a). *Developing talent in young people*. New York: Ballantine Books.

Bloom, B. S. (1985b). Generalizations about talent development. In B. S. Bloom (ed.), *Developing talent in young people* (pp. 507–549). New York: Ballantine Books.

Bouchard, C. (1986). Genetics of aerobic power and capacity. In R. M. Malina & C. Bouchard (eds.), *Sport and human genetics* (pp. 59–88). Champaign, IL: Human Kinetics.

Bouchard, C., & Malina, R. M. (1986). Concluding remarks. In R. M. Malina & C. Bouchard (eds.), *Sport and human genetics* (pp. 183–184). Champaign, IL: Human Kinetics.

Brady, P. T. (1970). The genesis of absolute pitch. *Journal of the Acoustical Society of America, 48*, 883–887.

Brown, M. A., & Mahoney, M. J. (1984). Sport psychology. *Annual Review of Psychology, 35*, 605–625.

Bryan, W. L., Lindley, E. H., & Harter, N. (1941). *On the psychology of learning a life occupation*. Bloomington, IN: Indiana University Publications.

Chase, W. G., & Ericsson, K. A. (1981). Skilled memory. In J. R. Anderson (ed.), *Cognitive skills and their acquisition* (pp. 141–189). Hillsdale, NJ: Lawrence Erlbaum.

Chase, W. G., & Ericsson, K. A. (1982). Skill and working memory. In G. H. Bower (ed.), *The psychology of learning and motivation*, Vol. 16 (pp. 1–58). New York: Academic Press.

Chase, W. G., & Simon, H. A. (1973). The mind's eye in chess. In W. G. Chase (ed.), *Visual information processing* (pp. 215–281). New York: Academic Press.

Chi, M. T. H. (1978). Knowledge structures and memory development. In R. S. Siegler (ed.), *Children's thinking: What develops?* (pp. 73–96). Hillsdale, NJ: Erlbaum.

Conley, D. L., & Krahenbuhl, G. S. (1980). Running economy and distance running performance of highly trained athletes. *Medicine and Science in Sports and Exercise*, **12**, 357–360.

Costall, A. (1985). The relativity of absolute pitch. In P. Howell, I. Cross & R. West (eds.), *Musical structure and cognition* (pp. 189–208). London: Academic Press.

Csikszentmihalyi, M. (1975). *Beyond boredom and anxiety*. San Francisco: Jossey-Bass.

Curie, E. (1938). *Madame Curie: A biography*. Garden City, NY: Doubleday, Doran & Company.

Daniels, J., Scardina, N., Hayes, J., & Foley, P. (1986). Elite and subelite female middle- and long-distance runners. In D. M. Landers (ed.), *Sport and élite performers* (pp. 57–72). Champaign, IL: Human Kinetics.

Diamond, R., & Carey, S. (1986). Why faces are and are not special: an effect of expertise. *Journal of Experimental Psychology: General*, **115**, 107–117.

Ebbinghaus, H. (1964). *Memory: A contribution to experimental psychology* (translated by H. A. Ruger & C. E. Bussenius). New York: Dover. (Original work published 1885.)

Elo, A. E. (1965). Age changes in master chess performance. *Journal of Gerontology*, **20**, 289–299.

Elovainio, R., & Sundberg, S. (1983). A five-year follow-up study on cardiorespiratory function in adolescent élite endurance runners. *Acta Paediatrica Scandinavica*, **72**, 351–356.

Ericsson, K. A. (1985). Memory skill. *Canadian Journal of Psychology*, **39**, 188–231.

Ericsson, K. A. (1988). Analysis of memory performance in terms of memory skill. In R. J. Sternberg (ed.), *Advances in the psychology of human intelligence*, Vol. 5 (pp. 137–179). Hillsdale, NJ: Erlbaum.

Ericsson, K. A. (in press). Peak performance and age: an examination of peak performance in sports. In P. B. Baltes & M. M. Baltes (eds.), *Successful aging: Perspectives from the behavioral sciences*. New York: Cambridge University Press.

Ericsson, K. A., & Chase, W. G. (1982). Exceptional memory. *American Scientist*, **70**, 607–615.

Ericsson, K. A., Chase, W. G., & Faloon, S. (1980). Acquisition of a memory skill. *Science*, **208**, 1181–1182.

Ericsson, K. A., & Crutcher, R. J. (in press). The nature of exceptional performance. In P. B. Baltes, D. L. Featherman & R. M. Lerner (eds.), *Life-span development and behavior*, Vol. 10. Hillsdale, NJ: Erlbaum.

Ericsson, K. A., & Faivre, I. A. (1982). Acquiring 'absolute pitch' for colours. Paper presented at the meeting of the Psychonomic Society, Minneapolis, MN.

Ericsson, K. A., & Faivre, I. (1988). What's exceptional about exceptional abilities?. In L. K. Obler & D. Fein (eds.), *The exceptional brain: Neuropsychology of talent and special abilities* (pp. 436–473). New York: Guilford.

Ericsson, K. A., Fendrich, D., & Faivre, I. (in preparation). A chronometric analysis of the acquisition of exceptional digit-span performance.

Ericsson, K. A., & Polson, P. G. (1988). An experimental analysis of the mechanisms of a memory skill. *Journal of Experimental Psychology: Learning, Memory and Cognition*, **14**, 305–316.

Ericsson, K. A., & Staszewski, J. (1989). Skilled memory and expertise: mechanisms of exceptional performance. In D. Klahr & K. Kotovsky (eds.), *Complex information processing: The impact of Herbert A. Simon*. Hillsdale: NJ: Erlbaum.

Faivre, I. A. (1986). *A theory of skill development in the absolute judgment of tones*. Unpublished doctoral dissertation, University of Colorado at Boulder.

Fox, E. L., & Mathews, D. K. (1981). *The physiological basis of physical education and athletics* (3rd edn.). Philadelphia, PA: Saunders.

Gibson, E. J. (1969). *Principles of perceptual learning and development*. Englewood Cliffs, NJ: Prentice-Hall.

Gordon, P., Valentine, E., & Wilding, J. (1984). One man's memory: a study of a mnemonist. *British Journal of Psychology*, **75**, 1–14.

Gustin, W. C. (1985). The development of exceptional research mathematicians. In B. S. Bloom (ed.), *Developing talent in young people* (pp. 270–331). New York: Ballantine Books.

Hagan, R. D., Smith, M. G., & Gettman, L. R. (1981). Marathon performance in relation to maximal aerobic power and training indices. *Medicine and Science in Sport and Exercise*, **13**, 185–189.

Hayes, J. R. (1981). *The complete problem solver*. Philadelphia, PA: The Franklin Institute Press.

Howald, H. (1982). Training-induced morphological and functional changes in skeletal muscle. *International Journal of Sports Medicine*, **3**, 1–12.

Hunt, E., & Love, T. (1972). How good can memory be. In A. W. Melton and E. Martin (eds.), *Coding processes in human memory*. New York: Holt.

Kalinowski, A. G. (1985). The development of Olympic swimmers. In B. S. Bloom (ed.), *Developing talent in young people* (pp. 139–192). New York: Ballantine Books.

Krogius, N. (1976). *Psychology in chess*. New York: RHM Press.

Lehman, H. C. (1953). *Age and achievement*. Princeton, NJ: Princeton University Press.

Lesgold, A. M. (1984). Acquiring expertise. In J. R. Anderson & S. M. Kosslyn (eds.), *Tutorials in learning and memory: Essays in honor of Gordon Bower* (pp. 31–60). San Francisco: Freeman.

Luria, A. R. (1968). *The mind of a mnemonist*. New York: Avon.

Maslow, A. H. (1971). *The farther reaches of human nature*. New York: Viking Press.

Miller, G. A. (1956). The magical number seven, plus or minus two. *Psychological Review*, **63**, 81–97.

Monsaas, J. A. (1985). Learning to be a world-class tennis player. In B. S. Bloom (ed.), *Developing talent in young people* (pp. 211–269). New York: Ballantine Books.

Morganroth, J., & Maron, B. J. (1977). The athlete's heart syndrome: a new perspective. *Annals of the New York Academy of Sciences*, **301**, 931–941.

Mueller, G. E. (1911). Zur Analyse der Gedächtnistätigkeit und des Vorstellungsverlaufes: Teil I [Towards analyses of memory and imagery: Part I], *Zeitschrift für Psychologie*, Supplement 5.

Mueller, G. E. (1913). Neue Versuche mit Rueckle [New experiments with Rueckle], *Zeitschrift für Psychologie und Physiologie der Sinnesorgane*, **67**, 193–213.

Mueller, G. E. (1917). Zur Analyse der Gedächtnistätigkeit und des Vorstellungsverlaufes: Teil II [Toward analyses of memory and imagery: Part II]. *Zeitschrift für Psychologie*, Supplement 9.

Oakes, W. F. (1955). An experimental study of pitch naming and pitch discrimination reaction. *Journal of Genetic Psychology*, **86**, 237–259.

Phelps, R. M., & Shanteau, J. (1978). Livestock judges: how much information can an expert use?. *Organizational Behavior and Human Performance*, **21**, 209–219.

Salmons, S., & Henriksson, J. (1981). The adaptive response of skeletal muscle to increased use. *Muscle and Nerve*, **4**, 94–105.

Saltin, B., Henriksson, J., Nygaard, E., Andersen, P., & Jansson, E. (1977). Fiber types and metabolic potentials of skeletal muscles in sedentary man and endurance in runners. *Annals of the New York Academy of Sciences*, **301**, 3–29.

Schultz, R., & Curnow, C. (1988). Peak performance and age among superathletes: track and field, swimming, baseball, tennis, and golf. *Journal of Gerontology: Psychological Sciences*, **43**, 113–120.

Sosniak, L. A. (1985). Learning to be a concert pianist. In B. S. Bloom (ed.), *Developing talent in young people* (pp. 19–67). New York: Ballantine Books.

Subotnick, S. I. (1977). A biomechanical approach to running injuries. *Annals of the New York Academy of Sciences*, **301**, 888–899.

Susukita, T. (1933). Untersuchung eines ausserordentlichen Gedächtnisses in Japan (I) [An investigation of a subject with exceptional memory in Japan (I)], *Tohoku Psychologica Folia*, **1**, 111–154.

Susukita, T. (1934). Untersuchung eines ausserordentlichen Gedächtnisses in Japan (II) [An investigation of a subject with exceptional memory in Japan (II)], *Tohoku Psychologica Folia*, **2**, 14–43.

Tesch, P. A., & Karlsson, J. (1985). Muscle fiber types and size in trained and untrained muscles of élite athletes. *Journal of Applied Physiology*, **59**, 1716–1720.

Wallingford, R. (1975). Long distance running. In A. W. Tayler & F. Landry (eds.), *The scientific aspects of sports training* (pp. 118–130). Springfield, IL: Thomas.

Ward, W. D., & Burns, E. M. (1982). Absolute pitch. In D. Deutsch (ed.), *The psychology of music* (pp. 431–451). New York: Academic Press.

Wechsler, D. (1952). *The range of human capacities*. Baltimore, MD: Williams & Wilkins.

Westfall, R. S. (1980). Newton's marvelous years of discovery and their aftermath: myth versus manuscript. *Isis*, **71**, 109–121.

Wilson, R. S. (1986). Twins: genetic influence on growth. In R. M. Malina & C. Bouchard (eds.), *Sports and human genetics* (pp. 1–21). Champaign, IL: Human Kinetics.

2

The Role of Schemata in the Comprehension of Maps

JANIS WILLIAMSON
Liverpool Institute of Higher Education

CAROL MCGUINNESS
Queen's University, Belfast

INTRODUCTION

Maps are intrinsically interesting and often visually attractive representations of aspects of the world. They can be used to depict the Earth's physical surface, or to represent some abstract variable which has a distribution across the Earth's surface; for example, prevailing wind directions. Maps are used for innumerable purposes, from general use such as finding a location, to specialist uses by military personnel, surveyors or geologists.

In spite of the widespread use and importance of maps, Keates (1982) has suggested that map skills among the general population are low. People often cannot fully interpret the significance of what is depicted on a map. Even among specialist users map interpretation often presents difficulties (Cross, Rugge and Thorndyke, 1982). One might think that observations such as these might have stimulated much fruitful research, but strangely perhaps, compared with the amount of research conducted on processes involved in prose reading and comprehension, little work has been reported on map-reading skills. That which does exist is fragmented, and is to be found in three major areas—cartography, education, and more recently psychology. Researchers in these areas have different reasons for studying maps and map-reading; they use different traditions and methods, and may ultimately be working towards different goals.

The psychological approach is naturally that of most interest here, but a brief introduction to the cartographic and educational perspectives will help to place the psychological research on maps into context.

Lines of Thinking, Volume 2   Edited by K.J. Gilhooly, M.T.G. Keane, R.H. Logie and G. Erdos
© 1990 John Wiley & Sons Ltd

Cartographic research is mainly concerned to develop more legible maps: that is, with finding the optimal method for communicating extremely complex information in the most comprehensible way. Typical areas of research would include evaluating the best symbols to use (see, for example, Clarke, 1959; Flannery, 1971); the most effective colour coding (for example, Christner and Ray, 1961); and the best methods of relief portrayal (for example, Phillips, De Lucia and Skelton, 1975; Potash, Farrell and Jeffrey, 1978). For a long time the map-reader was regarded as a relatively unimportant participant in the map-reading process, as compared with the importance of the map itself. Recently, however, cartographers have begun to recognize the importance of the map-reader's cognitive processes and abilities in the communication of map information, and have called for greater cooperation with psychologists (Olson, 1979: Gilmartin, 1981; Griffin, 1983; Eastman, 1985). It must be said that on the whole psychologists have been slow to take up the challenge of map-reading as a potential research area, from both theoretical and applied perspectives.

Educational research into map-reading tends to be much more concerned with the teaching and instruction of map-reading skills. Within this broad field many areas of research coexist. One major focus is the identification of difficult concepts within map-reading, and of developing ways to overcome the difficulties. Examples of difficult concepts would include scale, distance and relief portrayal (Salt, 1971; Charlton, 1975; Boardman, 1982, 1983). Another major area of interest in this field is to identify abilities which may correlate with successful map-reading; visuo-spatial skills are one obvious candidate (see, for example, Underwood, 1981; Riding and Boardman, 1983). Although many studies of this type have been reported, no clear-cut conclusions are able to be drawn about the role of such mental abilities in map-reading.

In summary, the cartographic and educational approaches to maps and map-reading are directly concerned with making maps easier to read, and with training people to become more competent map-readers. In contrast, the cognitive psychological literature on maps and map knowledge concentrates on more abstract issues. Many studies have used maps as a context for testing theories about mental representation. Studies exist which examine ideas on dual coding, analogical versus propositional representation, mental rotation, imagery strategies, and effective learning strategies (Thorndyke and Stasz, 1980; Eley, 1981; Kulhavy, Schwartz and Shaha, 1982, 1983; Steinke and Lloyd, 1983; Lloyd and Steinke, 1984; Kulhavy, Lee and Caterino, 1985). The focus in these studies tends to be the application of principles of representation to an analysis of maps and mapping, rather than an investigation of the cognitive process involved in mapping *per se*. In addition, very few researchers have attempted to use conventional or realistic topographic or atlas maps, or to use tasks related to actual map-reading activities (with the exception of some recent studies on map-reading with military applications see, for example, Cross, Rugge and Thorndyke, 1982; Simutis and Barsam, 1983). Generally the maps used are simple outlines drawn specifically for the purposes of the experiment, and bear no relation to a 'real' map of a 'real' landscape (as opposed to, for example, an Ordnance Survey map).

The authors were interested in peoples' reaction to maps showing real and complex landscapes. What conceptions does a person have when looking at such a map? What does he or she notice and think about? Are there different levels at which people are able to extract and understand information from maps? Most interesting of all, from the cognitive psychologists' viewpoint, what kind of knowledge representation might underlie such understanding?

Research was carried out on such questions using a variant of the expert/novice paradigm. Subjects with varying levels of map-reading experience were observed across a range of tasks. Several experiments were carried out, using large numbers of subjects, and involving lengthy analyses. Consequently, this chapter concentrates on describing only one aspect of the findings. The most experienced map-readers tested (the 'expert' group) consisted of a group of 36 A-level geography students, who had seven years' experience of reading and using maps, both for their own sake, and in conjunction with other geographical projects. This paper reviews their performance as a group across three quite different tasks, and places the findings within a schema-theoretic framework. (Note that the reports of performance will be purely descriptive. Detailed accounts of the experiments containing statistical comparisons with other groups are in preparation.) The current research is then placed in the context of contemporary cognitive research on maps, and recommendations made for future research possibilities.

A brief introduction to the types of materials and tasks used in the research will be helpful at this point. Ordnance Survey map sections depicting aspects of the British landscape in detail were used as stimuli for the first two tasks to be described (the third required no map stimuli). The tasks used were not conventional map-reading tasks. It was thought that little insight into cognitive processes would be gained by simply asking subjects to locate particular grid references, or find highest points, etc. Instead, much more open-ended tasks were employed, with loosely defined objectives; this followed recommendations encountered in some of the literature on expertise (Chi, Feltovich and Glaser, 1981; Chi, Glaser and Rees, 1982). It was hoped that such techniques would permit more insight into the nature of subjects' conceptual and schematic frameworks.

TASK 1: MAP DESCRIPTIONS

Subjects were presented with a series of three Ordnance Survey map sections, depicting very different terrains. These were reproduced as colour slides, and projected on a screen. Subjects were asked to provide a written description of what the maps represented. Five minutes were allowed for the description of each map. No further instructions were given.

The analysis of these descriptions was lengthy and complex, and covered aspects of the data such as simple length of description in words, the actual features mentioned, and an analysis of the structure of the description. This final analysis of structure and content provided the most consistent and reliable differences between the groups tested, in that the 'expert' group demonstrated significantly more sophisticated strategies in their descriptive style. Looking globally, the type of description most often produced by the expert group was a connected and structured piece of writing, where map elements were identified, described and placed into context with one another. An example of one of these descriptions is included later, for illustrative purposes. By way of contrast, other descriptive styles involved simply copying a list of place names from the map, or listing items with no additional structure or context. Following these overall assessments of the descriptions, more detailed categories of descriptive style were derived and these are summarized below.

Technical terms. Descriptions were assessed for the use of specific geographical terminology to describe map elements (e.g. 'truncated spurs', 'oxbow lakes').

Evaluation of elements. Descriptions were assessed for the manner in which elements were described. Map elements were judged to have been evaluated if they were accompanied by an adjective or other qualifying term (e.g. '*minor* roads', *many small* islands', '*widespread* settlement').

Locational information. Descriptions were assessed to examine whether subjects imposed any frame of reference on map elements (e.g. 'in the top left corner of the map', 'in the south-west region of the map').

Relational statements. Descriptions were assessed for the presence of statements which linked map items together (e.g 'The *road* follows the path of the *river* along the *valley* floor').

Explanation/implication. Descriptions were assessed to examine whether reasons were given for the presence or absence of particular elements (e.g. a particular valley shape was because of glaciation). The other focus of interest was on implications, where mention was made of concepts or ideas not actually present on the map (e.g. relation of map elements to farming, tourism or potential for power sources).

The expert group, being looked at in detail here, used these categories of descriptive style significantly more than the other groups tested. The pattern of their performance can be summarized thus. The very large majority of group members (80%) described the maps in terms of connected discourse, using an elaborated mode of description. They used many specific geographic terms to characterize map contents. Evaluation of map elements was a strong feature in their descriptions. Map elements they referred to were located in particular areas of the map ('in the north-east corner is an area of forested ground'). Many of the group used cardinal directions, which can be interpreted as demonstrating more sophisticated thinking than simple top/bottom, right/left directions. The descriptions provided by the group related map information together in integrated ways ('the map shows a nucleated settlement, with some linear development out along the main roads'). In addition, subjects in this group often explained why things happened as they did on the map ('the population is very sparse *because* of the barren rocky land'); or they drew inferences about concepts not physically represented ('this area would be suitable for hydroelectric power'). Part of an actual description containing examples of all five categories described above is included below, for illustrative purposes:

The map illustrated a glaciated region, demonstrating many of the main features of glaciation. There were 2^2 U-shaped valleys[1], one from the west to the east[3] of the map, and the other in the north-east[3] of the map, both containing rivers. Major[2] roads followed the path of these rivers along the valley floors[4]. In the U valleys were also misfit rivers[1] and ribbon lakes[1]. There were many[2] corries on the map, with tarns. The surrounding land was very high, and there were very many[2] hanging valleys[1]. There was little evidence of settlement, because of the rocky, barren[2] landscape[5].

Key:
[1] technical geographical terms
[2] evaluation
[3] locational information
[4] relational information
[5] explanation.

Extensive use of such descriptive categories combines to give an impression of a person who has a concept of the map as a complete entity; as a whole and meaningful information array, and not simply as a collection of isolated and random elements. Perhaps the most striking and important qualitative difference in thinking between this group, and others examined, is this degree of integration and relationship seen among the map elements; this is a quality of thinking referred to in much of the literature on expertise (see, for example, Egan and Schwartz, 1979; Jeffries *et al.*, 1981; Lesgold, 1984).

As a result of time and experience, this group has accumulated large amounts of map information which has been assimilated into their existing knowledge base in such a way that items no longer exist in isolation but are meaningfully integrated into the system; this naturally influences perception and thinking about maps they subsequently encounter. In many studies on expertise, skilled subjects' performance is attributed to their having knowledge organized in the form of schemata, which are said to be indexed by pattern-recognition abilities (Chase and Simon, 1973; Larkin *et al.*, 1980). These can quickly guide the expert to the correct or most likely interpretation of a stimulus or problem. Schemata probably exist at various stages of development, which are reflected in the amount of knowledge contained, and in its organization, integration and flexibility. Performance differences observed between experts and novices can be attributed to the effectiveness of the appropriate schemata in retrieving and structuring knowledge for output. The claim made here is that the experienced group under discussion have developed flexible and pattern-indexed map schemata which greatly facilitated their task performance. An illustration of this was provided by the tendency of subjects to see the maps as identifiable types. Often they characterized the whole map in the first sentence of their description, before going on to detailed analysis ('This is a busy market town, in a low-lying area, served by efficient communication networks.') The appearance of the map may have triggered a pattern-recognition device which allowed subjects to rapidly identify the map type. Once this has happened, and the appropriate schema is activated, expectations are aroused for what one would expect to see on that particular map type, and the description follows naturally.

TASK 2: MAP SORTING

Subjects were presented with an assortment of 24 Ordnance Survey map sections, reproduced as large colour prints, and were asked to sort them into groups on the basis of their subjective criteria. The number of groups was left open, and no time limit was imposed.

As in the previous task, many aspects of performance were assessed, including time taken to do the task, the number of groups produced, length of protocol, and the number of dimensions of information considered by the subjects in assigning maps to particular groups. As before, the pattern of performance which emerged for the 'expert' group will be described, without involving statistical comparisons with other groups. The expert group took on average 10 minutes to sort the maps, though a few subjects took up to 20 minutes; in any case, a fair amount of consideration was devoted to the task. The subjects typically formed the maps into five or six groupings, and were able to give full and clear explanations with regard to what the map groups signified, and how and why one differed from another. Although there were naturally individual differences among the subjects in terms of sorting, there was strong consistency on major map groupings. The basis of subjects' sortings was strongly linked to the dimensions of information they were considering. For most of the maps, there were about six potential types of information to be considered, and these are listed below for illustration:

a) shape of land—hill, mountainous, low-lying
b) settlement and population patterns
c) communication patterns
d) water features and drainage
e) glaciation features
f) vegetation patterns.

While subjects in less-experienced groups would tend to categorize maps on the basis of one of these dimensions (e.g. 'They all have mountains', 'They all have big towns'), the expert group would typically consider three or four of the above dimensions for each of the maps, and weigh up the relative importance of each before assigning a map to a particular group. A sorting profile emerged for the expert group which suggested that they considered more information as the basis for their map groupings; this consideration took quite some time, and resulted in the production of a larger number of map groupings than those observed in less-experienced subjects.

Evidence from the protocols of the experienced group indicated that they were responding to the underlying structure of the map, and not simply the surface representation. These subjects considered information which could be inferred but was not explicitly represented. Examples of what could be referred to as 'deep' processing included: the type of farming prevalent in an area; the potential for tourism and recreation; the glaciated features of mountainous areas; types of rock underlying depicted terrain; ratio of artificial to natural drainage, and the reasons for it; type of settlement on the map, and why it was that type, and so on. Fully 80% of subjects in the expert group used this type of analysis and description in their protocols. How does this pattern of results fit into a schema-theoretic framework? Again it was shown that the experienced subjects have more information at their disposal, and that as experience has increased, this has developed into structured and integrated knowledge. A sophisticated level of processing is required to consider three or four dimensions of information for each map, while constructing relatively homogeneous classifications. Integration of information is of particular importance here, because once various aspects of map information have become integrated, it may become easier to deal with more than one aspect simultaneously. Different dimensions of map information may be perceived in conjunction with one another; for example, settlement patterns and communication networks do not exist randomly side by side, but have a necessary and logical relationship (one which is not necessarily obvious to the novice). It may be that two or three dimensions of information such as these are perceived as constituting a pattern or 'chunk' of information (Chase and Simon, 1973), consequently easing the load on memory and information processing. The realization of such relationships, and the creation of such 'chunks', probably comes about in the later and more sophisticated stages of schema development; a stage which only the experienced group in these studies have actually achieved.

TASK 3: MAP CONCEPTS

Subjects were presented with a list (shown below) of 15 map-related geographical concepts, and asked to produce as many relevant associations to each as they could, in an interval of 30 seconds per concept. This word-association paradigm has commonly been used to explore cognitive structure (Deese, 1962; Shavelson, 1974). Concepts used were as follows: cliffs, communications, contours, drainage, glaciation, human activity, mountains, population, railway, relief, river, roads, settlement, valley, vegetation.

The rationale for this task was based on conclusions drawn from the findings relating to the preceding tasks. It was becoming increasingly obvious as the research progressed that levels of map understanding *per se* were closely linked to geographical understanding in general. The experienced group had developed, and indeed were still developing, a complex network of map schemata, in which map concepts and features became interdependent and logically interconnected. A high-level organization of knowledge such as this also implies a deep understanding of the physical world. Experienced geographers have knowledge of the geographical regularities which occur in the world. For example, they know that rivers and valleys tend to co-occur in the real world, that settlements grow around rivers, that underlying geology produces certain kinds of physical landscapes. These relationships can be deduced by the novice, or the man in the street, but they are probably explicitly represented in the experienced geographer's schemata network, and need no deduction. Map understanding goes far beyond seeing what is represented on the map's surface. An understanding of the landscape and how it functions is also necessary. It is reasonable to suggest that the ability to comprehend the underlying regularities of the physical world is intimately related to the well-developed map schemata of the experienced geographer. Thus, this task was designed to explore subjects' understanding of geographical, map-related concepts. The previous tasks had probed map understanding by presenting subjects with actual map stimuli. This task assessed the idea that map schemata were stable mental representations which could be accessed without the presence of actual map stimuli, and that good map understanding is to a large extent conceptually driven rather than data driven.

As in previous tasks much complex analysis was undertaken on the lists of associations produced, including simple numbers of associations, the most frequently occurring associations and their rank orders, and the integration and cohesion among concepts, as evidenced by subjects' lists. Analysis of the most frequently occurring associations to particular concepts did not distinguish in important ways between the expert group and other subjects. For a few of the concepts there was some indication of a more superordinate or abstract mode of thinking in the expert group. Two examples are described. For the concept 'drainage' the expert group's associations concerned types and patterns of drainage (artificial/trellis/radial), whereas less-experienced subjects' associations concerned water, pipes and drains. For the concept 'river', the expert group's associations concerned ideas on velocity, erosion and stages of the river. Less-experienced subjects concentrated on streams, tributaries and banks. However, cluster analysis performed on subjects' association lists provided far more interesting and important results in terms of implications for knowledge representation and schematic networks.

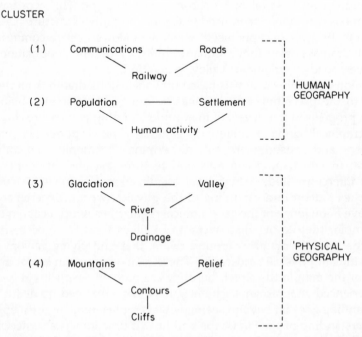

FIGURE 2.1 The content and arrangement of map concept clusters demonstrated by the 'expert' group.

One would by now predict that the expert group should have demonstrated high cohesion and integration among concepts, and this hypothesis was indeed strongly supported. Figure 2.1 shows a graphic representation of the results of cluster analysis for this particular group of subjects. Analysis was based on calculations of amount of similarity and overlap in subjects' responses to particular concepts. The concepts clustered clearly into four groups (with the exception of 'vegetation' which was very much an outlier in that it did not cluster into the groups of any of the subjects tested). These clusters appear to be sensible and meaningful within the geographical context. In addition, the clusters can be further subsumed under two major headings. The first two clusters relate clearly and strongly to human geography (population/communications), and the latter two clusters to physical geography (valley/river/mountains).

The main point to be emphasized from these subjects' results is that they demonstrated structured and stable representations of map knowledge, without the prompting of concrete map stimuli, a factor which indicates that their map knowledge is indeed conceptually rather than data driven. Because these subjects already conceive of interconnections and relationships between valleys, glaciation, rivers and drainage, for example, that prior knowledge can be drawn on in the interpretation of maps they encounter. The observation that prior knowledge and experience drive and direct the comprehension of new information is, of course, one of the main tenets of schema theory.

DISCUSSION

Experienced subjects, in their performance on these tasks, demonstrated many aspects of knowledge representation and use previously attributed to experts in many diverse areas. Factors such as the ability to quickly recognize types of stimuli, the ability to see below the surface to the important underlying structure of information, the ability to chunk information into meaningful units, and task performance being conceptually rather than data driven, are all aspects of skilled performance reported in the expertise literature. These experienced geographers had their map and geographical knowledge highly structured and integrated, as demonstrated by their performance across all tasks reported here. These qualitative changes in the structure of knowledge are also typical of the developmental changes in conceptual structure as described by Rhys (1972) with specific reference to geography, and more generally by Biggs and Collis (1982). In terms of schema development, it is suggested that all subjects tested in this series of experiments had some kind of schema framework for dealing with the tasks, but that those of the expert group were qualitatively very different from those of less-experienced subjects, being immensely more complex and sophisticated.

Even within the limited range of stimuli and concepts used in these tasks it is evident that the experienced geographer has an impressive understanding of the regularities and relationships which exist within the physical geographical environment, and the way in which those physical aspects relate to human activities. This knowledge may be learned partly from maps, but it is also likely to be gained from direct instruction, interaction with different landscapes and so on. The resulting knowledge is a stable mental representation, and independent from specific maps in the sense that it can be elicited without the presence of map stimuli. Geographical knowledge from whatever source, and map understanding, are inextricably linked. Although the initial goal of the studies was to explore map understanding, the important role of general geographical knowledge in the process became more and more obvious. Maps are representations of objects in space. Understanding the representation cannot be separated from understanding that which is represented.

CONCLUSIONS AND RECOMMENDATIONS

These studies need now to be placed in the context of the current state of research on maps and map skills within cognitive psychology. It is acknowledged that the studies undertaken have been exploratory, and were not designed to test specific hypotheses; nevertheless they have established a basis from which to develop more stringent and sophisticated paradigms and experiments. The studies have demonstrated that using 'real' maps as experimental stimuli is a possibility, and can lead to theoretical advancement in map understanding. Several possible avenues of research have been extended, not only in the cognitive field, but also in cartography and education. Real maps could be used for map-reading studies and evaluations in paradigms similar to those reported by Boardman (1982) on visualization and interpretation of contours. Real maps could be used in paradigms such as Kulhavy et al.'s (1982–85) recall experiments, Eley's (1981) contour-identification study, or Thorndyke and Stasz's (1980) learning task. The way has also been opened for further examination of the relationship between levels of competence, defined in terms of schema development, and many more conventional map-reading tasks. The research here could range from studying patterns of visual search involved in finding the highest point on a map, to processes involved in reasoning about particular settlement patterns. This latter is a complex task which has certainly not been tackled from a cognitive perspective. In-depth evaluation studies of cognitive structure and associated schema networks could be developed over a wider range of expertise, and the relationship between geographical knowledge and map understanding needs to be further explored.

REFERENCES

Biggs, J., & Collis, K. (1982). *Evaluating the quality of learning*. New York: Academic Press.
Boardman, D. (1982). Graphicacy through landscape models. *Studies in Design, Education Craft and Technology*, **14**, 95–108.
Boardman, D. (1983). *Graphicacy and geography teaching*. Beckenham, Kent: Croom Helm.
Charlton, K. (1975). *A study of pupil understanding of map symbolism, scale, direction and location in the age range 8–13 years*. M.Phil. thesis, University of Leeds.
Chase, W., & Simon, H. (1973). Perception in chess. *Cognitive Psychology*, **4**, 55–81.
Chi, M., Feltovich, P. & Glaser, R. (1981). Categorisation and representation of physics problems by experts and novices. *Cognitive Science*, **5**, 121–152.

Chi, M., Glaser, R., & Rees, E. (1982). Expertise in problem solving. In R. Sternberg (ed.), *Advances in the psychology of human intelligence*. Hillsdale, NJ: Erlbaum.

Christner, C., & Ray, H. (1961). An evaluation of the effect of selected combinations of targets and background coding on map reading performance. *Human Factors*, **3**, 131–146.

Clarke, J. (1959). Statistical map reading. *Geography*, **44**, 96–104.

Cross, K., Rugge, S., & Thorndyke, P. (1982). Cognitive processes in interpreting the contour line portrayed of terrain relief. Technical report NR157-454, Anacapa Sciences Inc., California.

Deese, J. (1962). On the structure of associative meaning. *Psychological Review*, **69**, 161–175.

Eastman, R. (1985). Cognitive models and cartographic design research. *Cartographic Journal*, **22**, 95–101.

Egan, D., & Schwartz, B. (1979). Chunking in recall of symbolic drawings. *Memory and Cognition*, **7**, 149–158.

Eley, M. (1981). Imagery processing in the verification of topographical cross-sections. *Educational Psychology*, **1**, 39–48.

Flannery, J. (1971). The relative effectiveness of some common graduated point symbols in the presentation of quantitative data. *Canadian Cartographer*, **8**, 96–109.

Gilmartin, P. (1981). The interface of cognitive and psychophysical research in cartography. *Cartographica*, **18**, 9–20.

Griffin, T. (1983). Problem solving on maps—the importance of user strategies. *Cartographic Journal*, **20**, 101–109.

Jeffries, R., Turner, A., Polson, P., & Atwood, M. (1981). The processes involved in designing software. In J. Anderson (ed.), *Cognitive skills and their acquisition*. Hillsdale, NJ: Erlbaum.

Keates, J. S. (1982). *Understanding maps*. Harlow, Essex: Longman.

Kulhavy, R., Lee, J., & Caterino, L. (1985). Conjoint retention of maps and related discourse. *Contemporary Educational Psychology*, **10**, 28–37.

Kulhavy, R., Schwartz, N., & Shaha, S. (1982). Interpretative framework and memory for map features. *American Cartographer*, **9**, 141–147.

Kulhavy, R., Schwartz, N., & Shaha, S. (1983). Spatial representation of maps. *American Journal of Psychology*, **96**, 337–351.

Larkin, J., McDermott, J., Simon, D., & Simon, H. (1980). Expert and novice performance in solving physics problems. *Science*, **208**, 1335–1342.

Lesgold, A. (1984). Acquiring expertise. In J. Anderson & S. Kosslyn (eds.), *Tutorials in learning and memory*. San Francisco: Freeman.

Lloyd, R., & Steinke, R. (1984). Recognition of disoriented maps; the cognitive process. *Cartographic Journal*, **21**, 55–59.

Olson, J. (1979). Cognitive cartographic experimentation, *Canadian Cartographer*, **16**, 34–44.

Phillips, R., Delucia, A., & Skelton, N. (1975). Some objective tests of the legibility of relief maps. *Cartographic Journal*, **13**, 39–46.

Potash, L., Farrell, J., & Jeffrey, T. (1978). A technique for assessing map relief legibility. *Cartographic Journal*, **15**, 28–35.

Rhys, W. (1972). Geography and the adolescent. *Educational Review*, **24**, 183–196.

Riding, R., & Boardman, D. (1983). The relationship between sex and learning style and graphicacy in 14-year-old children. *Educational Review*, **35**, 69–79.

Salt, C. (1971). *An investigation into the ability of 11–12 year old pupils to read and understand maps*. M.A. thesis, University of Sheffield.

Shavelson, R. (1974). Methods for examining representations of a subject matter structure in a student's memory. *Journal of Research in Science Teaching*, **11**, 231–249.

Simutis, Z., & Barsam, H. (1983). Terrain visualisation and map reading. In H. Pick & L. Acredolo (eds.), *Spatial orientation: Theory, research and applications*. New York: Plenum Press.

Steinke, T., & Lloyd, R. (1983). Images of maps—a rotation experiment. *Professional Geographer*, **25**, 455–461.

Thorndyke, P., & Stasz, C. (1980). Individual differences in procedures for knowledge acquisition from maps. *Cognitive Psychology*, **12**, 137–175.

Underwood, J. (1981). Skilled map interpretation and visual spatial ability. *Journal of Geography*, **80**, 55–58.

3

Apperception and Restructuring in Chess Players' Problem Solving

PERTTI SAARILUOMA
University of Helsinki

INTRODUCTION

A characteristic of skilled thinking is its high selectivity. In mathematics, physics, medicine and computer science, skilled persons are able to segregate the essential from unessential far more effectively than the less skilled (Chi, Feltovich and Glaser, 1979; Larkin *et al.*, 1980; Lesgold, 1984). Skilled chess players are able to achieve a very high performance level by considering fewer than ten continuations in problem spaces where there are potentially millions of alternative paths, yet they do not search any deeper or wider than novices (de Groot, 1965). Skilled players just see the good moves while the less skilled miss them. The performance of skilled persons is possible only if they use some highly efficient information selection mechanisms.

The problem of selectivity has been actively considered in research into skilled chess from the very beginning (de Groot, 1965, 1966; Newell and Simon, 1963, 1972). Two competing theoretical approaches have been suggested. The first of them is evaluation controlled search, in which selectivity is achieved by using probabilistic evaluation rules to decide which of the many possible paths is the most promising. A good goal is found by a maze search, in which the evaluation rules suggest which path one should select at decision nodes. The heuristic search model suggested by Newell and Simon (1963, 1972) and the SEEK-model outlined by Holding (1985) are typical examples of evaluation-based search models.

The second type of explanation has been called 'recognition–association' by Holding (1985) (Chase and Simon, 1973; Newell and Simon, 1972; Hartstone and Wason, 1983). In recognition–association models some characteristic pattern of pieces activates in the mind of a player a series of associated moves. The associated series leads from the current position to a good goal position (Chase and Simon, 1973; Hartstone and Wason, 1983).

Discussion of the advantages and disadvantages of these explanations has, for want of empirical data, proceeded relatively slowly. In the early sixties the heuristic search model had a strong position but it was replaced by the recognition–association models in the early seventies (Chase and Simon, 1973; Newell and Simon, 1963, 1972). In the eighties, Holding (1985) managed to prove that the empirical evidence supporting recognition–association models was not yet sufficient and he decided to revise evaluation-based explanations (Holding and Reynolds, 1982). In this chapter a new type of empirical evidence will be presented for recognition-based search, but it will also be shown that the two approaches can be united.

APPERCEPTION

The key argument in favour of the recognition–association theory by Chase and Simon (1973) was indirect. It was known that good players are better than the less skilled at recalling chess positions after short presentations. So it was very natural to assume that they are better at finding good moves, because they have a larger 'vocabulary' of chess specific patterns (Chase and Simon, 1973). The association of chess specific patterns used in chunking with the ones used in the activation of sterotypical moves was the critical assumption in this argumentation.

Holding and Reynolds (1982) constructed pseudorandom positions in which skilled players found better moves than less skilled but in which they were not able to recall the positions essentially better than novices. So it was not correct to assume that chess masters use the same chunks in recalling as they do in solving problems. A similar incompatibility had also been found for the game Go (Reitman, 1976). Holding (1985) completed his empirical argument by reanalysing a small part of the data presented by Chase and Simon (1973) and concluded that the recognition–association theory is wrong.

Holding and Reynolds' (1982) experiment does not yet prove, however, that skilled players do not base their search on familiar combinational themes such as standard queen mates, piece-supporting schemes or blockades. Recognition can be based on a few suitably located pieces, while recall presupposes coding of all pieces. The argumentation supporting recognition–association models was not valid, but Holding and Reynolds' (1982, Holding, 1985) argument does not yet reject the possibility of recognition-based search. It is necessary to make further experiments which test directly the relevance of recognition.

Recognition–association models assume that the associated sequence of moves is automatically activated when a familiar pattern of pieces is recognized and this activated schema or production controls information intake. This would suggest that chess players may, in ambiguous positions (positions with two very effective lines), miss one important line as their attention is concentrated on a familiar continuation. It would suggest that people are apt to select familiar but suboptimal playing lines rather than unfamiliar but optimal. In problem-solving literature these kinds of phenomena are common. Point-of-no-return, set,

Einstellung and fixation effects are good examples (Bartlett, 1958; Duncker, 1945; Luchins, 1942).

First Experiment

In the first experiment an ambiguous position with two main lines (a series of good moves) was presented to the subjects. The familiar main line was a very well-known combinational theme called 'smothered mate'. The alternative was a shorter line embedded into the smothered-mate line. If problem solving is recognition-based, subjects should be likely to choose the familiar but longer line. If subjects selected the longer line they would be asked to look for a better solution to see if they were aware of the shorter line at the moment of selection.

Method

Subjects. Twelve subjects participated in the experiment. They were all members of the Pittsburgh chess club. They were divided into four skill groups on the basis of their ratings: (1) 1300–1700, (2) 1701–2000, (3) 2001–2100, and (4) over 2100. The USCF-rating system is basically an ELO-rating system, details of which have been presented in Elo (1978).

Stimuli. In this experiment one position was presented to the subjects. This position was 'ambiguous'; that is, there were two main lines in it. One of them was a very familiar five-moves or ten-plies long line (A) called 'smothered mate' or 'de Legacy's mate' (see Figure 3.1). A ply is a 'half move', a move made by white or black. Usually a chess move refers to a pair of moves, one by white and one by black. So the smothered-mate line is actually nine plies long. The other main line (C) was one move or two plies shorter, but is not so familiar. In addition to the two main lines, subjects generated usually one line more (B).

Method and design. Standard protocol analysis was used. The position was presented to the subjects and their verbal protocols were collected by means of a tape recorder. Subjects were told that they had white pieces and they should find the best solution in the given position. The position was presented with a standard chessboard and standard pieces.

Subjects had ten minutes to solve the problem on their own, and after that the experimenter began to give them cues. Also, if a subject was satisfied with a solution, but this was not the best, the experimenter began to give them cues. All the cues were given in the form of a question. The questions were relatively general at first.(e.g. 'Can you find a better line?') If it was necessary the questions were made more specific, such as 'Is there any other move which would be better than knight h6'? Finally, all the subjects were led to the shortest solution.

Results

The main results are presented in Figure 3.1. It shows the position, four selected playing lines, and the order in which each line appeared in each subjects' protocol.

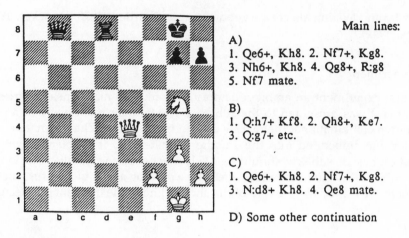

Main lines:

A)
1. Qe6+, Kh8. 2. Nf7+, Kg8.
3. Nh6+, Kh8. 4. Qg8+, R:g8
5. Nf7 mate.

B)
1. Q:h7+ Kf8. 2. Qh8+, Ke7.
3. Q:g7+ etc.

C)
1. Qe6+, Kh8. 2. Nf7+, Kg8.
3. N:d8+ Kh8. 4. Qe8 mate.

D) Some other continuation

The order of main lines in the protocols:

Subject

1.	A	B	C
2.	A	B	C
3.	A	B	C
4.	A	B	C
5.	A	B	C
6.	A	B	C
7.	A	B	C
8.	A	B	C
9.	A	B	C
10.	B	D	C
11.	B	D	C
12.	B	D	C

FIGURE 3.1 Summary of the results of the first experiment.

All the skilled players selected the familiar line (A) first. They obviously recognized this line as they were able to name it. The three beginners, who were not familiar with the line, selected the second alternative (B). When the skilled players were asked to look for a better line, they consistently selected the second line, which is *not* based on smothered mate. Only after prolonged cuing were they able to find the shortest solution (C). This shows how totally unaware subjects were about the optimal alternative, since it was unfamiliar to them.

Second Experiment

The behaviour of the subjects in the first experiment had a clear resemblance to a fixation phenomenon, which was due to familiarity with the longer main line. The second experiment aimed at studying whether it was possible to produce task-induced fixation. First subjects were shown four very easy smothered-mate combinations, then a critical position with three mating lines (A, B, C). The first of them (A) was a five-moves (nine-plies) long smothered mate, and the two others were shorter. After the critical position, subjects were shown two new introductory positions, either with line B or C. Finally, they were shown the critical position anew. If recognition is an essential part of chess players' problem solving, it might be possible to fixate some subjects twice with the same position.

Method

Subjects. Twelve subjects participated in the experiment. They were chess players whose Finnish SELO grading varied from 1600 to 2450. In the SELO grading system the mean is 1700 and standard deviation is 200 points, so none of the subjects were absolute beginners.

Stimuli. Four simple positions with smothered mate were constructed. The fifth position was critical and contained three different mates. Two series of two positions, with one of the alternative mates in the critical position, were constructed. All the positions were made using transfers and they were presented to the subjects by means of 10×10 cm pictures, not with a normal chess board and pieces.

Design and procedure. Subjects were told that they were to be given a series of chess positions. They were to assume that they had white pieces in each position. Their task was to find the mates as fast as possible. The experimenter presented a new position to a subject immediately he found a correct solution.

Subjects were first given four introductory positions, which entailed very easy smothered mates. After that they were presented with the critical position with three different mates (A, B, C). The smothered mate was the longest of the three.

Immediately after solving the critical position they were given two new introductory positions with either theme B or theme C. Finally, the subjects were presented with the critical position again. The solutions of the subjects in the two presentations of the critical position were collected (see the positions in the Appendix).

Results

All subjects but one proposed the suboptimal smothered-mate line when they saw the critical position for the first time. In the second stage, five subjects in the group given the introductory B solution suggested theme B as the second alternative, and five subjects from the other group suggested the theme C solution. So 10 out of the 12 subjects were fixated twice. The exceptions were the one master who was not fixated the first time, and the grandmaster, who saw both of the two alternatives. The result supports the fixation hypothesis and is statistically significant ($p < 0.05$, sign test).

Third Experiment

The first two experiments showed that it is possible to fixate subjects along familiar or activated lines in ambiguous positions. In the third experiment these results were put into a more general context. Six ambiguous positions with one intuitively easy but suboptimal line (A) and one more difficult but optimal line (B) were presented to the first group of subjects. The second group of subjects were presented with six positions in which—with small transformations, such as transposing one piece or putting one extra piece on the board—one line (A) was eliminated but the other line (B) remained.

If there was a large difference in the number of B lines between the two groups, then the familiar and suboptimal A line had blocked the activation of the B-line in the first group. This would indicate that the activation of one line was the reason for the fixation effects in the first two experiments, and that these kinds of effects are not absolutely rare in chess players' problem solving.

Method

Subjects. Two matched groups of six subjects participated in the experiment. The strength of the players in the groups varied from 1600 to 2400.

Materials. Two series of six positions were made. In the first series there were two alternative main lines. The first of them was easy to recognize but suboptimal, the second was more difficult. The positions and lines were shown to 15 chess players whose ratings varied from 1400 to 2200 and 71% of them chose the first lines as more stereotypical and familiar. In the second series of six positions the first line was eliminated either by replacing pieces or adding new pieces for black (see the Appendix).

Design and procedure. A between-subjects design was used. The first series of positions was presented to the first group of subjects and the second series to the second group. The thinking-aloud method was used. The maximum time the subjects had per position was five minutes.

Results

The key variable in this experiment is the number of B-type solutions or the selections of the unfamiliar lines in the two groups. The results are presented in Table 3.1. The difference between the two groups in the number of B-type solutions is almost 60% and is statistically significant ($t(10) = 5.76$, $p < 0.001$).

Table 3.1 The percentage of subjects who selected line B in the experimental (A) and control groups (B)

Group A		
Familiar	Non-familiar	Other
67%	11%	22%
Group B		
Familiar	Non-familiar	Other
—	69%	31%

The results suggest that it was not the difficulty of B-type solutions which prevented subjects in the first group from finding them, but it was rather the activity of A-type solutions that blocked the activation of the B-type solutions in the first group.

Discussion

In all three experiments it was shown that subjects are very likely to select familiar but suboptimal lines instead of non-familiar but optimal ones. The natural explanation for this phenomenon is recognition-based search. Subjects recognize typical piece configurations and generate the associated moves. Recognition theory may also be supported by the fact that subjects are able to name the most familiar themes of combination such as smothered mate in the first experiment.

The results of the three experiments suggest that the recognition of a familiar theme or a prototypical problem space (that is, a familiar piece pattern with associated stereotypical move series) has a very important role in selective thinking. The activation of a prototypical problem space makes it possible to neglect millions of possible alternatives and concentrate on the most relevant one or ones. Recognition controlled search is a very strongly top-down process. It has an obvious resemblance with fixation and *Einstellung* effects, which was demonstrated in the first two experiments. Subjects literally do not see the alternatives, though the stimulus is one and the same.

This is not seeing in the same sense of the word that it is normally used in the psychology of visual perception. It is important to distinguish between the indirect seeing which is typical of thinking and simple perception, as has been recently suggested by Neisser (1987). Anyone can see all the pieces on a chessboard. Only skilled subjects are able to see the right prototypical problem spaces, as was shown in the first experiment. This kind of 'second-order seeing' or conceptual perception could best be described with an old but recently almost forgotten term *apperception* (James, 1890; Leibniz, 1704/1979).

Apperception is one of the few important terms from the late nineteenth century which have not been rehabilitated during the last three decades. Presumably one of the main reasons has been its vagueness. After it was introduced by Leibniz it was used in many different contexts by different authors, and James (1890) justly took it as a very vague concept. Only very recently has it been used incidentally in some texts outside the testing literature, and it may be that it still has a position to fill in the psychology of human thinking, in describing how theoretical problem spaces are transformed into small searchable problem spaces.

RESTRUCTURING

Strong recognition–association models do not presuppose genuine search. A recognition–association scheme entails both the base-move and the goal, so the previous experiments fit very well with this scheme. The instant activation of a familiar line led easily to a very good position and it was not necessary to search in the ordinary sense. No node-evaluation was presupposed. This is not, however, the general case. Very often it is not possible to find a solution directly, but the finding of a solution takes much pain and effort (de Groot, 1965; Saariluoma, 1984). These may be called restructuring tasks, to be studied in the second series of experiments.

In these kinds of tasks subjects' protocols are usually episodic. This means that subjects relate a few moves and after that they return to the base-move or shift to another episode (de Groot, 1965; Newell and Simon, 1972; Saariluoma, 1984). This kind of episodic shifting is a sign of restructuring. A new episode focuses the attention of a player to a new aspect of the stimulus position.

Earlier research has shown that the organization of episodes is highly selective. Chess players do not usually generate more than five to seven different base-moves and still they are able to find good solutions. In addition they do not usually search deeper than five to six moves (Charness, 1981; de Groot, 1965, 1966; Newell and Simon, 1972, Saariluoma, 1984). In this part of the chapter the main attention is paid to the mechanisms of episodic selectivity.

Fourth Experiment

A simple test for the strong forms of recognition–association models is the analysis of failed and biased episodes. Recognition–association models predict that the main reason for failure is the inability to 'find the idea' (the correct goal). If somebody is able to recognize the right prototypical problem space, he or she should be able to find the solution as well, because the goal is embedded into the associated sequence of moves. If subjects are able to find the right goal but not the solution, and they have a great number of episodes with the right goal but not the solution, it is a clear sign of the inadequacy of strong recognition–association models.

If a recognition–association scheme is not sufficient to explain the problem-solving process, it is necessary to do close reading of the protocols and try to understand the inner structure of episodes to find some other explanation for the episodic selectivity. This presupposes studying of the protocols and the analysis of the distribution of valuative sentences in the protocols.

Method

Subjects. Ten subjects participated in the experiment. They were all experienced amateur players having SELO ratings the mean of which was about 2150 points. The best subjects were masters having over 2200 SELO points, and the weakest were second-class players with over 1800 points.

Materials and procedure. One relatively difficult position was presented to the individually tested subjects (see the Appendix). It was selected because it began with a knight sacrifice, which was difficult to find directly. The think-aloud protocols of all subjects were collected.

Results

Only three of the ten subjects found the solution, but all of them found the right goal and tried to achieve it. They generated 77 episodes in all, of which the bulk were failed attempts to make the back-row mate with the rooks, which was also the goal of the right solution. The percentage of episodes with a right goal and wrong goal are presented in Table 3.2. The episodes with a right goal are divided into two groups: successful and unsuccessful.

In the major parts of the episodes in the protocols there is a right goal, but fewer than 20% of them contain the right solution. So over 50% of the episodes with the correctly recognized goal do not lead to anything. This means that subjects are not able to find the solution immediately but they must make a search.

The necessity of a search can be better seen in the protocols than in the above figures. All the subjects were aware of the basic goal (a back-row mate) but only three of them could avoid errors and find the solution. The course of the problem-solving process is here essentially different from the previous experiments, since it presupposes genuine search. The search is, however, hardly of the kind heuristic search models would predict, since there is practically no intermediate node evaluation in the protocols, but all evaluative sentences are associated to terminal nodes.

The selectivity of search is also higher than heuristic search models would predict. Subjects tried seven different base-moves out of 42 possibilities in all. The mean number of the episodes and sub-episodes with a different content per person was 7.5. If it is assumed that both sides have 40 legal moves in each position after two moves (four plies), there will be 2.56×10^6 paths, and after four moves (eight plies) there will be 6.5536×10^{12} paths, etc. So the set of possible continuations is far larger than the set of considered ones. In heuristic search subjects should generate on each depth level a number of alternatives and compare them with each other to select the best. This means that subjects should generate around 40 moves and select the best of them, but nothing comparable to this procedure can be found in the protocols. There is neither intermediate node evaluation nor parallel move generation: subjects just generate direct paths.

The suggested moves in the episodes appear to be very coherent. People do not generate random moves but they all seem to have some common core (de Groot, 1965). Close reading of protocols shows that the moves of the opponent

Table 3.2 Correct and incorrect goal in the episodes

Correct goal	
Successful	18%
Unsuccessful	57%
Incorrect goal	25%

Table 3.3 An example of a protocol

Black threatens to take a pawn, but it is possible to threaten a mate in the h-line.

E1: (1) f6, R : g5; (2) Rd.h4, N : f6 and black loses a rook. Is there anything else for black?

E2: If first f6, then the king cannot go to f8.

E3: It is not possible to take (1) −, R : g5, because Rd.h4.

E4: If bishop c6, does that change anything? The rook steps a few squares up to avoid the exchange of rooks (1) f6, Bc6; (2) Rh2 R : g5; (3) Rd.h4. Oh, no. The knight is able to make an intermediate move and the rook check is not effective. If (3) −, N : f6; (4) Rh8+, and black loses a rook.

E5: Something else ... if ... there should be something else for black. This is too simple... The same idea all the time. (1) f6 R : g5; (2) Rd. h4, and threatens mate... WOW!! (2) −, Kf8, and the rook is able to blockade the threat. Good grief...

E6: Well, it is necessary to start from the beginning. So if (1) Nd5, e : d5, and then (2) f6, and next Rd.h4. Does he have intermediate moves? Bf5 does not help.

E7: If (1) Nd5, e : f5; (2) Nf6. It looks very bad for black. Knight cannot take f6. Move (3) f4 might help a little. R : f4 and the rook is able to intervene.

E8: Well, if (1) Nd5, e : f5; (2) Rd.h4...

E9: (1) Nd5, e : f5; (2) Nf6+, N : f6; (3) g : f6, so Rd.h4 threatens. (3) −, f4; (4) R : f4, Rg5, and then Rh7 and Be6.

E10: So, (1) Nd5, e : f5, (2) Nb6, Rb8, and (3) R : d6... No, its parried. It does not work.

E11: Aha! (1) Nd5, e : f5; (2) Nf6, N : f6; (3) g : f6, f4; (4) Rg1+, Kf8; (5) R : f4 ... Rh5; (6) Rg7, Be6; (7) N : e6, R : d6.

E12: (1) Nd5, R : d5; (2) B : d5, e : d5; (3) f6 ... Directly f6 threatens Rd.h4.

I shall play (1) Nd5 ...

(here black) fall into a small number of categories (Table 3.3). All the opponents' moves in the main episodes in which the intention was basically correct (back-row mate with rooks) fall into four categories. These categories are the exchange of one of the attacker's active pieces (i.e. the pieces which participate in the attack), blockade of the attacker's path to the goal (i.e. placing one of one's own pieces so as to prevent the attacker from moving to the goal), escape of the target, counter-attack. In this particular position around 45% of all the defenders' moves were exchange moves, 40% escape moves, 10% blockade moves and 5% counter-attacks.

Only a very small fraction of all the possible moves and the combinations of moves may fulfil the four criteria. Four out of the ten black pieces can never play any role in preventing the attack, and only a very small fraction of the possible moves these pieces have may be used for this purpose. Moreover, each move by white eliminates some further sequences of possible moves. So, if white plays f6 in his first move, black has precisely one move which may help. After Nd5 he has three choices, and after Rd.h4 two effective choices. In addition, the set of possible moves is limited by the fact that only a small number of the attacker's pieces participate actively in the attack. In this position the number is from four to six pieces depending on the chosen line.

These overall considerations can be expressed more precisely to formulate some principles chess players use in the construction of the representation. The active side has some goal, which he tries to achieve by making a definite series of moves. The other side tries to prevent this. The series of moves of the active side defines a path from the initial position to some goal position. The path runs though a set of squares and it is thus spatially limited. Now, only those defender's moves are rational, which are directly related to his actions on the path to a possible goal. Turning off from the path would lead the opponent into an even worse position.

The last question is: Why do people abandon an active path and shift their representation? A close reading of the protocols shows that the main reason is failure to find a closed path from the initial position to a goal position. In Table 3.3, changes are not made in the main episodes, but all the time white works for back-row mate with his rooks. However, he abandons his first plan, immediate f6, because he finds in E5 that he is not able to mate. Rook c5 comes via g5 to g8 and blocks white's attack. So that path cannot be closed.

A closed path is a forced series of moves from an initial position to a goal position. 'Forced' means that the goal position is the best achievable position for the opponent. Many of the shifts from one episode to another were caused by abandoning paths, which cannot be closed. In Table 3.3 another motive for shifts was the necessity to check if the opponent could play better by making some other moves and thus prevent the closing of a path. In Table 3.3 the episodes E4, E5, E7, E9, E10, E11 and E12 are motivated by attempts to find a better move for the defender. All the moves are directly attached to the goal.

To summarize, chess players' problem solving is a search for a closed path from an initial position to a goal position. The path spans a small subspace of the basic problem space and the search takes place in it. In restructuring one path is shifted to another as a consequence of a failure to close the path.

Fifth Experiment

In the fifth experiment the tentative findings of the fourth experiment are tested with six randomly chosen positions. The main attention is given to the number of generated moves and episodes, their length, their relation to the level of skill, and the location of the evaluative sentences in them. Important parameters are also the number of episodes with the right goal and the number of solved problems.

Method

Subjects. Eleven subjects participated in the experiment. Two of them were international level players: one grandmaster and one international master. Three were national master-class players with ratings above 2200 SELO points. Another three were first-class players having ratings between 1900 and 2050 SELO points. Three of the subjects were beginners with no rating.

Stimuli and procedure.   Six randomly chosen tactical positions were presented to
the subjects in the same way as in the previous experiment (see the Appendix).
There was a time limit of ten minutes per position. In two of the six positions
subjects had black pieces.

Results

The main quantitative parameters of the protocols are presented in Table 3.4.
The most skilled players were the best but they did not make the widest search,
which can be seen in both the number of generated moves and episodes. This
supports the earlier findings by de Groot (1965, 1966; for contrary results see
Charness, 1981). Really skilled players do not necessarily need to search wider
than less skilled ones to achieve a higher level of performance. Presumably,
strongly automatized and chunked prototypical problem spaces help them
in this.

The number of episodes with the correct base-move and goal is again
somewhat larger than the number of solutions, which indicates that chess
players must do some search in spite of finding the right idea. This time the
number of positions in which subjects did not find the idea at all was quite high,
especially in the lowest skill groups. This suggests that they do not know the
prototypical problem spaces.

The shifts of episodes were again motivated by the inability to close a path
from the initial position to a goal position. When subjects detect a move the
effects of which they are not able to parry, they are apt to restructure and shift to
another episode. There was no exception to this rule, but regularly in the third
and sometimes in the fifth position the subjects accepted a continuation which
they could not analyse to the end. In chess these kinds of moves are called
'intuitive sacrifices' and in such moves evaluation of a position is very
important.

Evaluation is a very central part of restructuring, since it is the way in which

Table 3.4 Main quantitative parameters for the fifth experiment

	International	Master	Second-class	Beginner
Correct solutions	75%	66%	39%	0%
Number of moves	23	52	21	3.6
Length of episodes	3.6	5.1	4.6	1.6
Mean number of correct episodes per player				
Successful	8	10	4	0
Non-successful	6	11	4	4
Average number of incorrect episodes per player	15	19	9	16

one is able to define if goals have been really worth something and if the defender's moves are real obstacles to the search process. There was no sign, however, of the node evaluation typical of the heuristic search model. The evaluative sentences concentrated on the terminal nodes.

Discussion

It is not justifiable to think that no search or evaluation would take place in chess players' problem solving. Recognition of the prototypical problem spaces is not a sufficient explanation. It is necessary to assume limited search, which seems to be controlled by an activated path through which the active side tries to achieve a good goal position. All the moves of a defender are directed towards the elimination of the path actions, and this abstracts a subspace of the basic problem space, in which the search takes place. The abstraction is based on four relatively simple and well-formulated principles.

On the other hand, it is also wrong to think that search would be a pure heuristic search. There is a very strong evaluative component in it, but it appears only in the terminal nodes. In heuristic search one would expect to see assessments about the value of the intermediate nodes. The restricted nature of search and its strong association with the generated path and absence of intermediate node evaluations all suggest that the path controls the information selection during the search process, as was suggested after the fourth position.

GENERAL DISCUSSION

The series of experiments reported here shows that strong recognition–association models as well as evaluation-based models are not in themselves sufficient to explain chess players' problem solving. Evaluation-based models can hardly provide a satisfactory explanation of the fixation and *Einstellung* phenomena of the experiments in the first part. On the other hand the experiments in the second part have shown that chess players do, in fact, search, but it is restricted by the path of action. All the generated defence moves are directed to eliminate the realization of the path.

One link in this chain is open: What is the origin of the path? How does a player select the path he is going to work with during a particular episode? The experiments in the first part suggest as the natural solution that the origin of the paths is in the prototypical problem spaces. Activation of a prototypical problem space in the mind of a player defines some global idea about a goal and a stereotypical series of moves which could be used to achieve it. The series of moves forms the active path, and so the stereotypical series of moves may be used in filtering an abstract problem space. The actual search takes place in this space.

In the fourth experiment all the subjects instantly found the goal but only a few of them fully solved the problem. Since the goal and attack are very stereotypical in these kinds of situations, and some subjects also say this explicitly, there is no reason to doubt that this would not be a recognition process. A close reading of the protocols of the fifth experiment points to the same conclusion. Evaluation is not focused on the individual moves but on the episodes as a whole.

The above scheme also explains why subjects have such great difficulties in the first three experiments in finding the optimal lines. After having found one way to a good path they simply give up further search and the alternative prototypical problem spaces do not activate at all. This can be seen very well in the third experiment, in which abandoning one alternative brings the other alternative into focus.

On a more general psychological level this all means that chess players' problem solving takes place in abstracted problem spaces, which are small subspaces of the basic problem space. The abstraction is based on the recognition of familiar prototypical problem spaces. The process of abstraction is called apperception, since it provides a set of task-necessary cues, which define strongly the perceptual world of a subject. The activation is also a process of analogical problem solving, since the player has not usually previously seen the prototypical problem spaces in precisely the same conditions.

The activated prototypical problem space defines a hypothetical path to a goal position and all the actions of the defender are directed to this path, which essentially limits the size of the problem space. A path is open as long as there is no forced way from the initial position to the goal. The basic task of a problem solver in chess is to show that the path can be closed. The process of closing is a path-controlled search process in which evaluation has an important role. If it is not possible to close a problem space, subjects abandon it and they restructure their problem representation. The whole process of chess players' problem solving can be interpreted as an apperception and restructuring cycle, which makes it possible to find effective solutions with very small search spaces. Apperception is necessary for restricting a searchable problem space, and restructuring for modifying or abandoning it when it does not lead to a solution.

APPENDIX
THE POSITIONS USED IN THE FIVE EXPERIMENTS

First Experiment

White: Kg1, Qe4, Ng5, f2, g3, h2
Black: Kg8, Qb8, Rd8, g7, h7

Second Experiment

A-line:
White: Ka1, Qd2, Ng5, a3, b2
Black: Kg8, Qb8, Re8, g7, h7

White: Kb1, Da4, Ng5, a2, b2
Black: Kg8, Qb8, Re8, g7, h7

White: Ka1, Qb1, Ng5, a3, b2
Black: Kg8, Qa7, Re8, c7, g7, h7

White: Ka2, Qe2, Ng5, Bb3, a3, b2
Black: Kg8, Qb8, Rc8, Rf8, a6, b5, e6, g7, h7

Critical position:
White: Ka2, De2, Rb1, Bb2, Ng5, a3, b3, f3, g3, g2
Black: Kg8, Qb8, Rc8, Rd8, Bc6, a6, b5, d5, g7, h7

B-line:
White: Ka1, Rb1, Rg1, Bb2, Bb3, Ng5, f4, g3
Black: Kh8, Qb8, Rc8, Rd8, a6, b7, g7, h7

White: Ka2, Qd4, Rg1, Bb2, Ng5, a3, b3, c2, f4, g3
Black: Kh8, Qb8, Re8, Rf8, a6, b5, c7, g7, h7

C-line:
White: Ka2, Qe6, Bb2, Bf5, a3, b3
Black: Ka8, Qb8, Re8, Rg8, Nh6, a6, b5, g7, h7

White: Ka2, Qe2, Ng5, Bb2, a3, b3, f3, g2
Black: Kg8, Qb8, Rc8, Rf8, a6, b5, c5, g7, h7

Third Experiment

First series:

White Kg1, Qe4, Ra1, Re1, Nc5, Bd2, b2, b4, f2, g2, h3
Black: Kh8, Qd6, Ra8, Rb5, Nd3, Nf4, a6, b7, d4, g7, h7

White: Kg2, Qd6, Ra3, Rh1, Ne3, Nf5, a4, c6, f2, g3
Black: Kg8, Qb3, Rb6, Re8, Bc7, Be6, b5, f7, g7

White: Kh2, Qd3, Rf1, Bb1, Bd6, b4, c3, g2, h3
Black: Kg8, Qa3, Rb7, Bc6, Nf6, a4, d7, e6, f7, g7, h7

White Kb2, Qd2, Rd4, Ne6, Be2, b3, c2, g4
Black: Kh7, Qb7, Rd7, Nd5, Bg8, a7, g6, h6

White:Kh2, Qe3, Re5, Bc5, Ng3, d5, f2, g2, h3
Black: Kg8, Qb7, Rf6, Nb4, Bd7, f7, g6, h7

White: Kc1, Qd2, Rh1, Bb1, Bf6, Ne4, b2, c3, e3
Black: Kg8, Qa6, Rb8, Rf8, Be8, Na4, a7, e6, f7, g6, h7

Second series:

White: Kg1, Qe4, Ra1, Re1, Nc5, Bd2, b2, b4, f2, g2, h3
Black: Kh8, Qd6, Ra8, Rb5, Bg5, Nd3, Nf4, a6, b7, d4, g7, h7

White: Kg2, Qd6, Ra3, Rh1, Ne3, Nf5, a4, c6, f2, g3
Black: Kg8, Qb3, Qb8, Rb6, Re8, Bc7, Be6, b5, f7, g7

White: Kh2, Qd3, Rf1, Bb1, Bd6, b4, c3, g2, h3
Black: Kg8, Qa3, Rb7, Bg6, Nf6, a4, d7, e6, f7, g7, h7

White: Kb2, Qd2, Rd4, Ne6, Be2, b3, c2, g4
Black: Kh7, Qb7, Rd7, Ra8, Nd5, Bg8, a7, g6, h6

White: Kh2, Qe3, Re5, Bc5, Ng3, d5, f2, g2, h3
Black: Kg8, Qb7, Rf6, Nb4, Bd7, e6, f7, g6, h7

White: Kc1, Qd2, Rh1, Bb1, Bf6, Ne4, b2, c3, e3
Black: Kg8, Qc8, Rb8, Rf8, Be8, Na4, a7, e6, f7, g6, h7

Fourth Experiment

White: Kc1, Rd4, Rh1, Bb3, Nc3, a2, b2, c2, f5, g5
Black: Kg8, Rc5, Ra8, Ne8, Bd7, a6, b7, d6, e6, f7

Fifth Experiment

White: Kg1, Qe2, Rd1, Rf1, Ba3, a2, f2, g2, h2 ... black to move
Black: Kg8, Qd5, Rd8, Rc8, Bc5, a7, e6, f7, g6, h7

White: Kg2, Qf6, Ra1, b4, b2, e5, f2, g3
Black: Kg8, Qe2, Rh8, Nh6, a7, e4, e6, f7, g6, h7

White: Kg1, Qd2, Rd1, Re1, Ng3, Ne5, a3, b2, c2, f2, g2, h4
Black: Kg7, Qc8, Ra8, Rd8, Bb7, Rd7, a7, b6, d4, e6, f7, g6, h5

White: Kd1, Qd3, Ra1, Re1, Nc3, Ng7, Bc1, a3, b4, c2, f3, g2
Black: Kf7, Qh2, Ra8, Rh8, Nd7, Ne7, Bb6, a7, b7, d5, f6

White: Kh2, Qg3, Ra1, Rg2, Nh4, Bg6, Bc5, b2, c2, d4, e5, f4, h3
Black: Kh8, Qd8, Rf8, Rb5, Nc6, Ne7, a5, c4, d5, e6, f5, h6

White: Kf2, Qe4, Rc2, Be2, a2, b2, e3, f3, h4 ... black to move
Black: Kh8, Qe6, Rg1, Be5, a7, b5, d6, e7, f7, h6

REFERENCES

Bartlett, F. (1958). *Thinking*. London: Allen & Unwin.

Charness, N. (1981). Search in chess: age and skill differences. *Journal of Experimental Psychology: Human Perception and Performance*, 7, 467–476.

Chase, W. G., & Simon, H. A. (1973). The mind's eye in chess. In W. G. Chase (ed.), *Visual information processing* (pp. 215–281). New York: Academic Press.

Chi, M., Feltovich, P., & Glaser, R. (1981). Categorization and representation of physic problems by experts and novices. *Cognitive Science*, 5, 121–152.

Chi, M., Glaser, R., & Rees, E (1982). Expertise in problem solving. In R. J. Sternberg (ed.), *Advances in the psychology of human intelligence*, Vol 1. Hillsdale, NJ: Erlbaum.

de Groot, A. D. (1965). *Thought and choice in chess*. The Hague: Mouton.

de Groot, A. D. (1966). Perception and memory versus thought: some old ideas and recent findings. In B. Kleinmuntz (ed.), *Problem solving*. New York: John Wiley.

Duncker, K. (1945). *On problem solving* (Psychological Monographs 270). Washington: APA.

Elo, A. (1978). *The ratings of chess players, past and present*. London: Batsford.

Hartstone, W. C. & Wason, P. C. (1983). *The psychology of chess*. London: Batsford.

Holding, D. (1985). *The psychology of chess skill*. Hillsdale, NJ: Erlbaum.

Holding, D. H. & Reynolds, R. I. (1982). Recall or evaluation of chess positions as determinant of chess skill. *Memory and Cognition*, 10, 237–242.

James, W. (1890). *The principles of psychology*. New York: Dover.

Larkin, J., McDermott, J., Simon, D. P., & Simon, H. A. (1980). Expert and novice performance in solving physics problems. *Science*, **208**, 1335–1342.

Leibniz, G. (1704). *New essays on human understanding*. Cambridge: Cambridge University Press.

Lesgold, A.M. (1984). Aquiring expertise. In J. R. Anderson & S. M. Kosslyn (eds), *Tutorials in learning and memory: Essays in honor of Gordon Bower*. San Francisco: Freeman.

Luchins, A. (1942). *The mechanization in problem solving: The effect of Einstellung* (Psychological Monographs 54; Whole no. 248).

Neisser, U. (1987). From direct perception to conceptual structure. In U. Neisser (ed.), *Concepts and conceptual development: Ecological and intellectual factors in categorization* (pp. 11–24). Cambridge: Cambridge University Press.

Newell, A., & Simon, H. A. (1963). GPS: A program that simulates human thought. In E. A. Feigenbaum & J. Feldman (eds.), *Computers and thought* (pp. 279–309). New York: McGraw-Hill.

Newell, A., & Simon, H. A. (1972). *Human problem solving*. Engelwood Cliffs, NJ: Prentice-Hall.

Reitman, J. (1976). Skilled perception in Go: deducing memory structures from inter-response times. *Cognitive Psychology*, **8**, 336–356.

Saariluoma, P. (1984). Coding problem spaces in chess. *Commentationes Scientiarum Socialium*, **23** (Societas Scientiarum Fennica, Turku).

4

Programming Plans: Internal or External Structures

R. K. E. BELLAMY
MRC Applied Psychology Unit, Cambridge

D. J. GILMORE
University of Nottingham

INTRODUCTION

'Studies on the cognitive strategies of experts have shown that performance in complex problem solving domains, at least for human practitioners, is not based on elaborate algorithms but on mental storage and use of large incremental catalogues of pattern-based rules (Michie, 1980). Therefore, considerable effort has been expended by psychologists and AI researchers in understanding the nature and organisation of human memory for problem solving and knowledge acquisition (Bobrow and Collins, 1976; Anderson, 1983; and Wilensky, 1983). ' (Barfield, 1986, p. 16)

The literature on the psychology of programming has also been strongly oriented towards obtaining a description of the structure of expert knowledge. To this end, a large number of comparisons of expert–novice performance have been made (Shneiderman, 1976; Adelson, 1981; Atwood and Ramsey, 1978; Greeno, 1980; Soloway *et al.*, 1982; Barfield, 1986). The results here show that the 'programming plan'—described below—is an effective description of expert knowledge in certain limited circumstances.

In this chapter we shall argue that the static organization of knowledge is not a coherent object to pursue. Recent studies in cognition (Suchman, 1987; Winograd and Flores, 1987; Gammack, 1988) have moved steadily towards the viewpoint that knowledge is fluid and its characteristics, as revealed by experimental data, are determined more by the characteristics of the experiment than by the conceptual organization.

Lines of Thinking, Volume 2   Edited by K.J. Gilhooly, M.T.G. Keane, R.H. Logie and G. Erdos
© 1990 John Wiley & Sons Ltd

In the first part of this chapter we discuss the role of the programming plan and the evidence for it, concluding that it is called into being by the task of structured programming. In the second part, we propose that a more coherent object of study is the process of programming and identify ways in which the process may be related to characteristics of the device, task and notation, showing that certain combinations give rise to what are currently called programming plans. Finally, we discuss an alternative paradigm for the study of complex skills.

THE PROGRAMMING PLAN

Many studies have found evidence suggesting that programming plans represent the fundamental structure of programming knowledge (Soloway and Ehrlich, 1983; Rist, 1987; Gilmore and Green, 1987). Programming plans derive from the theory of goals and plans proposed by Schank and Abelson (1977). This theory suggests that a plan once formed is then internalized, so that in the future it can be accessed directly. Access to the internalized plans is through pattern matching.

Soloway *et al*. (1983) propose a three-level, hierarchical classification of Pascal programming plans: strategic plans, describing the algorithmic level; tactical plans, showing how smaller problem elements are solved; and implementation plans, describing the mapping between the problem and the code. Thus, programming plans are hierarchical in nature; programming, as described in this theory, is a process of top-down goal-decomposition. It should be noted that such a structure does not fit neatly into the linear structure of a Pascal program. Thus, programmers are often required to interleave plans, at lower levels in the goal hierarchy. Figure 4.1 shows two interleaved plans.

The evidence for programming plans from studies of Pascal programmers is not clear cut. Tasks involving the inference of plan structure show marked

```
10
    Restore
20 Dim data%(9)
   : Dim Reversed%(9)
30 For I% = 0 to 9: Read data%(I%):
   Reversed
   %
   (9-I%) = data%(I%):
   Print; data%(I%)" ": Next
40
   Print: For I% = 0 TO 9:
       Print; Reversed%(I%);" ": Next
50   Data   1,2,3,4,5,6,7,8,9,0
```

FIGURE 4.1   A Basic program to print an array, reverse it and then print the reversed array. There are three interleaved plans: a 'print array' plan (*italic* font), a 'reverse array' plan (roman font), and a second 'print array' plan (**bold** font).

novice–expert differences, but tasks involving the utilization of information about plan structure do not show reliable effects (see, for example, Rist, 1985). Gilmore (1986) suggests that some of the novice–expert differences reported by Soloway and Ehrlich (1983) may not be statistically significant (according to the available published data).

Evidence from studies on languages other than Pascal suggest that plans are only used by programmers doing structured programming. Gilmore (1986) compared debugging performance in Pascal and Basic. He found that the highlighting of plan structures aided Pascal programmers, but only for tasks in which plan-related information was important. Basic programmers showed no evidence of using plans. In this experiment it is unclear whether the real cause of the difference between Pascal and Basic experts was due to language differences, or whether it was a difference in their programming experience and culture. The results of Davis (1988) suggest that it is the programming culture that is the real cause of the difference found in Gilmore's study. Plans are only found in programming cultures where structured programming methods predominate.

The majority of this evidence is limited both in the tasks and the languages investigated. Studies have addressed only the tasks of comprehension and debugging, which may be fundamentally different tasks from that of program generation. Surprisingly, given the number of languages in current use, only the languages Pascal and Basic have received attention. Below we describe a cross-language investigation of Pascal, Basic and PROLOG, using a generative task.

EXPERIMENTAL EVIDENCE FOR PROGRAMMING PLANS IN CODE GENERATION

Our analysis was based on the parsing–gnisrap model of coding (Green, Bellamy and Parker, 1986). Coding starts when the programmer has already solved the main problems of how to write the program, and wishes to translate this into the programming language. The parsing–gnisrap model borrows directly from that of Rist (1986) in that it proposes expert coding to be a process of forward chaining, matching elements in a skeletal plan to programming plans expressing these plan elements in terms of the program notation. These programming plans describe purely syntactic knowledge. Semantic knowledge is required for solving a problem but not for coding the solution in a specified language.

In the model proposed by Rist, generation will always occur in plan order. He states: '... once created ... it (*the plan*) will be retrieved and implemented ... in the order in which plan pieces occur in the final program.' (The italics have been added for clarification.) Figure 4.2 shows the predicted order of generation using Rist's model.

The parsing–gnisrap model makes different predictions for the order of generation (illustrated in Figure 4.3). This difference is due to two extensions to Rist's model, incorporated into the parsing–gnisrap model. Firstly, it describes the process by which a skeletal plan element gets instantiated in the programming notation. Programming knowledge is represented in schemata which state

```
1       Program  =   find(input, output);
2       Var
5           x: boolean;
6           i: integer;
7           a: array(1..10) of integer;
3       Begin
8           x := false;
10          for i = 1 to 10 do
11              begin
9                   if a(i) = 10 then x := true
12              end
4       End.
```

FIGURE 4.2   The left-hand numbers indicate the order in which the lines of code would be generated. There are two plans here. The first is a 'found' plan (lines 5, 6, 7, 8 and 9), the second a 'loop' plan (lines 10, 11 and 12).

```
1       Program  find(input,  output);
2       Var
5           x: boolean;
9           i: integer;
6           a: array(1..10) of integer;
3       Begin
8           x := false;
10          for i = 1 to 10 do
11              begin
7                   if a(i) = 10 then x := true
12              end
4       End.
```

FIGURE 4.3   The plans are the same as in Figure 4.2. Working-memory limitations cause the focal line (line 7) to be generated before the preconditions (lines 8 and 9).

the code, its purpose, the role of components within the code, the preconditions for using the schema and the conditions after using it. Plans are built around 'focal lines', lines of code encoding the main goal of the plan. Once the focal line has been invoked, additional preconditions are found by matching preconditions to the conditions after other schemata. The 'ideal' programmer, blessed with an infinite working memory, could build up the whole code like this. However, the second addition to Rist's model is that the parsing–gnisrap model has a severely limited internal working memory, forcing it to use an external medium (e.g. the VDU screen) as a temporary store or as a dump when overload threatens it. Rather than build up the whole program internally and then output it to the editor from start to finish, it outputs fragments as they are completed, or incomplete fragments if working memory becomes overloaded. Code fragments that have been output to the external system are simply deleted from internal memory—a simplifying assumption. When subsequently the programmer needs to refer to the fragment, it will need to be parsed. Parsing aims to recreate the original plan structure, in which the roles of each component were marked. The parser is based on that of Bever (1970).

For instance, in Figure 4.3 the model generates lines 1 to 7 in working memory. This is then output to the screen. Line 7 is the focal line of the found plan and therefore according to the model is accessed from long-term memory before lines 8 and 9 which are preconditions of the found plan. If the model forgets a subgoal or a precondition, it must reparse from the screen to see what to do next. Lines 8 and 9 are added after the model has parsed the contents of the screen and noticed that the preconditions of the found plan are missing.

The model is not a serially staged model. Instead, processes can be driven by need, by availability, or by agenda-list: the programmer outputs code to external memory when a fragment is ready or when the limitations of memory make it necessary. Similarly, material that has been output to external memory is parsed when the construction of a plan demands information no longer in internal memory, or when an agenda-list contains a note that unfilled gaps remain in the external memory.

The experiment described in the next section compares the order of programme generation in Pascal, Basic and PROLOG. A suitable metric for the order of program generation is a count based on the number of deviations from pure linear generation. Pure linear generation would start at the top left-hand corner and write until reaching the bottom right-hand corner. A deviation occurs when a programmer goes back to insert code at a point in the existing structure. In this experiment, such deviations from pure linear generation were called *nonlinearities*: further details are given below.

Rist's model predicts that nonlinearities will only occur when a programmer starts to interleave a new plan into the existing structure. The parsing–gnisrap model allows for far more flexibility in the type of nonlinearities that can occur. For instance it suggests that minor parts often get missed out of plans. Therefore, programmers may go back to fill in these code fragments after generating later (in terms of the linear structure of the program) parts of the plan.

To enable comparison of the Rist and parsing–gnisrap models, the nonlinearities were divided into those occurring between plans and those occurring within plans. A between-plan nonlinearity can only be to insert another plan or plan fragment after completion of the current plan. A within-plan nonlinearity is one that occurs during generation of the current plan, to insert a code fragment into either the current or a previous plan.

The Rist model predicts that there will be more between-plan than within-plan nonlinearities. The parsing–gnisrap suggests that generation will be in plan order, but within-plan nonlinearities will occur because of working-memory limitations. Further, these within-plan nonlinearities will be to insert the preconditions of plans.

The Method

Fourteen expert programmers were subjects in this study, using the language of their expertise, which were Basic ($N = 5$), Pascal ($N = 4$) and PROLOG ($N = 5$).

These three languages were chosen to exemplify some important differences in language design. Pascal and Basic are imperative, assignment-based languages, while PROLOG is nearer to logic programming. PROLOG and Basic have lower degrees of right-to-left constraint than Pascal; this means that Pascal programmers are forced to make decisions about fragments of code at the beginning of a program, when these decisions are based on code occurring further on in the program (for example, variable declarations). Pascal contains more cues about the purpose of fragments of code than Basic or PROLOG; that is, it is more role-expressive. Plan structures in Pascal and Basic are easily identified, but are more conjectural in PROLOG.

Subjects solved three simple problems. The first was to reverse an array in place (Basic and Pascal) or reverse a list (PROLOG). The second was based on the 'traffic counting' problem (Ratcliff and Siddiqi, 1986); the problem here is to analyse a data file from a survey in which each passing vehicle generated one signal and each elapsed time interval a different signal. Our programmers had to write a program to count the vehicles, the length of the survey period, and the longest time without a vehicle. The third problem was to consult a timetable of Cambridge–London trains and find the last train to arrive at or before a stated time. These problems were all easy by professional standards—indeed, we assumed they would be trivial. In retrospect, it was clear that they demanded more problem solving than we expected, so that the results were not purely coding behaviour, as we had hoped.

The programmers used the screen editor Microsoft Word on a Macintosh, and their actions were recorded using the Journal desk accessory. They were not allowed to use paper for drafting but could make notes on-screen if so desired.

Results

Owing to the lack of any formal definition of a programming plan, independent raters (experts in the field) were then asked to indicate the programming plans in each of the programs written by the subjects. The nonlinearities were then compared with the plan analyses, to produce a score of within-plan and between-plan nonlinearities for each rater.

There are several ways to score nonlinearities, but of the metrics we examined the most conservative (the one that minimized between-group differences) was to count only those nonlinearities which went backwards from the end of the program to some earlier point. No further jumps were scored, whatever the programmer did, until new material had been added at the end of the program. In this way a sequence of jumps through the program to change related items would be scored as a single jump. Note that moving the cursor to inspect code elsewhere, without altering the code, was not counted. Finally, nonlinearities to refer to or to alter on-screen notes, which were often placed at the head of the text, were not counted.

The plan analyses produced by the individual raters were fundamentally different and were therefore dealt with independently. The major difference in the plan analysis was that the inclusion of variable declarations and **begin...end** statements were only included in the definition of a programming plan by one of the raters. Apart from these code fragments the plans varied very little between the two raters. *Post hoc* discussion revealed that both raters had used the same method, a goal hierarchy, to produce the plan analysis.

These differences in the plan analysis are interesting in their own right, and are discussed below. However, they make it difficult to combine the scores of our two raters. Therefore, a statistical analysis was performed independently on each plan analysis. For each plan analysis, the counts of backward nonlinearities were subjected to a two-way analysis of variance, language and jump-type (between-plan nonlinearities versus within-plan nonlinearities) taken as factors.

For each of the raters, there was a significant difference between the languages. There is a possibility that this difference may be due to differences in the length of the programs giving some programmers a greater opportunity to make nonlinearities (the average length of a program for each language was: Pascal = 123.73 words, PROLOG = 167.92 words, Basic = 76.5 words). To ensure that the difference between the languages was not due to program length, scores were corrected for the word length of programs. Possible measures could have been lines, words, characters or syntactic structures. The question of what the correct size of unit to take as indicative of program length would need a separate paper, so we made the arbitrary choice of number of words. Languages were still found to differ significantly in the number of nonlinearities even when a correction was made for program length (see Figure 4.4). This suggests that for Pascal programmers the absolute number of nonlinearities per unit length is significantly greater than for Basic or PROLOG programmers.

Unfortunately the other effects were not robust across raters. The first analysis

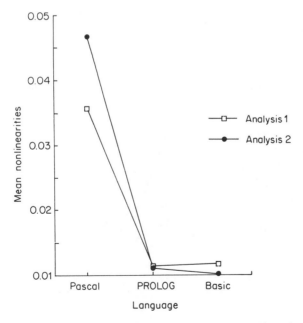

FIGURE 4.4   In both analyses, Pascal programmers make a significantly greater number of nonlinearities than Basic or PROLOG programmers.

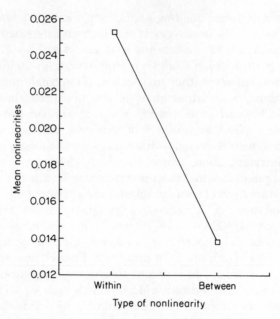

FIGURE 4.5 Analysis 1 shows significantly more within-plan nonlinearities than between-plan.

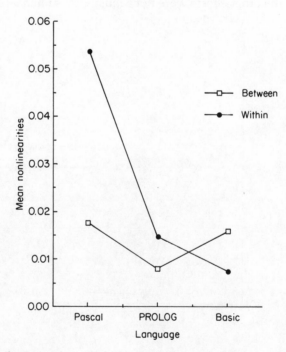

FIGURE 4.6 Analysis 1 shows that Pascal programmers make a significantly greater number of nonlinearities than PROLOG or Basic programmers.

(analysis 1) found significant differences for all the effects: language ($f = 25.505$, $p < 0.001$), jump-type ($f = 11.772$, $p < 0.006$; see Figure 4.5), and the interaction ($f = 20.168$, $p < 0.001$; see Figure 4.6). These effects were still significant when program length was taken into account. The other rater's analysis (analysis 2) showed only the language effect ($f = 4.421$, $p < 0.05$); jump-type and the interaction of language by jump-type were not found to be significant.

The difference between the analyses must be due to nonlinearities to insert variable declarations and to insert the contents between **begin ... end** statements, as these were the only differences between the plan analysis produced by the raters. In analysis 1, insertions of variable declarations and immediately following all **begin**s with their corresponding **end**s before filling in the content are counted as within-plan nonlinearities. Such actions occur often in Pascal, rarely in Basic, and never in PROLOG. Thus, it is not surprising that Pascal programmers make significantly more within-plan jumps in analysis 1.

To investigate whether preconditions were omitted during plan generation, we made a count of the nonlinearities to insert a base-case in PROLOG and to insert an initialization in Pascal and Basic. Such jumps were much more frequent in Pascal than Basic, and hardly occurred at all in PROLOG.

Summary of Results

1) There was no significant difference in the number of within and between-plan nonlinearities as would have been predicted by Rist's model.
2) Analysis 2 found a significantly greater number of within- than between-plan jumps. This was attributed to differences in the allocation of plans by the two raters.
3) There were more insertions of the base-case in Pascal than in Basic or PROLOG.

PROGRAMMING STRATEGIES

Assuming that the raters identified plans of the type described by Rist, these results show that programmers do not seem to use programming plans during generation in the manner suggested by Rist's model. Even our Pascal programmers, who used structured programming techniques, did not show evidence of plan generation. Does this mean that programming plans are not used for the task of program generation? A possible explanation for our results is that programmers neither possess nor use programming plans. In light of the evidence (presented above) for programming plans, we prefer a different explanation. We propose that theories of programming based on programming plans fail to capture the underlying causes of programmer behaviour. Expert programmers have the ability to make multiple representations upon a program (Pennington, 1987): for example, goal hierarchy, control flow, data flow, and conditional states. The representation they use reflects the strategies they have to employ when writing the program. Therefore the question we really want to ask is *what determines programming strategy?*

Programming plans as described by Soloway *et al.* reflect a hierarchical planning strategy. Stepwise refinement is merely the process of building a hierarchical plan, starting from a high-level goal and successively generating subgoals until a complete solution is reached. Soloway *et al.*'s programming plans are goal hierarchies, and thus represent the strategy of stepwise refinement. The use of an alternative strategy will reveal an alternative knowledge structure, a structure compatible with the actual strategy being used. Whether such knowledge structures become internalized as knowledge structures in long-term memory, is still an open question.

Recent studies of program comprehension (Widowski, 1986) and debugging (Vessey, 1988) support the view that programming strategies may play a larger role in programming skill than has previously been acknowledged. Vessey found that, for debugging, the processes programmers used to assimilate the structures contained in the program were more important than the knowledge structures they possessed prior to examining a program. Widowski identified two strategies used by experts in comprehending programs: a 'structure oriented strategy' and a 'variable oriented strategy'. The use of such strategies allows experts to perform significantly better than novices in reconstructing both stereotypical and non-stereotypical programs; results that could not be explained by plan-based theories.

The data in this experiment show a number of different programming strategies. The majority of Pascal programmers used the technique of stepwise refinement. Basic programmers seemed to use a more or less linear style of development, whilst our PROLOG programmers varied from the pure logic programmers to a hacking style of development. Such programming strategies do not always develop naturally; often programmers are taught a particular programming methodology such as structured programming. Such methodologies are usually supported by specialized programming notation and the programming support tools. The Pascal programming notation was specifically designed to support structured programming.

Why, if programming plans are used by structured Pascal programmers, do we not find evidence of plan generation in our results? We suggest that the task of translating from the plan structure to the linear structure of Pascal places far too high a mental load even on expert programmers, doing simple problems. In other words, the Pascal programming language fails to support plan generation. Thus, although the Pascal programmers may be using plans during generation, plan fragments may get lost from working memory. Evidence of working-memory load is seen in programmers' use of intermediate representations indicating actions still to be done. Thus, the notation is affecting the programming strategy.

Programming plans are dependent upon the programming strategy of a particular programmer. This in turn is influenced by the notation, taught strategies and the programming environment used during learning to program. As neither PROLOG nor Basic programmers adopt a hierarchical strategy, but tend towards a more opportunistic style of planning (Hayes-Roth and Hayes-Roth, 1979), we can expect to see the development and use of fundamentally different programming plans. What these plans would look like is a question that should be addressed by future research. Our results suggest that for Basic programmers, control structure is the most important representation, and for PROLOG programmers data flow. If data flow is the most important represent-ation, then we would expect the base-case to be the focal line. This may explain why PROLOG programmers never forget the base-case and almost always start by programming the base-case. However, as stated above, we do not think that programmers employ only one representation during planning. It is more likely that the demands of the notation and environment make one representation more useful, but programmers will make forays into other representations for certain coding tasks.

AN ALTERNATIVE PARADIGM OF STUDY

This chapter suggests that investigations of knowledge structures *per se* are misguided. A knowledge structure is tied to a certain task, carried out in a certain environment. Thus, rather than study the organization of knowledge, we should be studying the use of knowledge in a particular task context.

One way to tackle research in this context is to identify features of the external environment, and identify the role they play in programmer activity. Green (1990) has started to outline such an analysis: he identifies concepts such as role-expressiveness which determines how well a notation expresses the con-cepts used by the programmer. His analysis suffers, because it is not clear how the features he identifies interact to determine the programming strategy of a particular programmer. We would like to propose a study of programming strategy based on features of the notation and environment, that would serve to explain how the features of the external environment interact to determine programmer behaviour.

For such a study to succeed it must be intimately linked to the study of planning. We need to understand how the notation and the external environ-ment being used interact with the programmers' planning strategies. Gilmore (1986) suggests that it is not the notation *per se*, but how the structure of the notation affects the ease with which information can be extracted. Different tasks are going to require different mental operations and different notational struc-tures are going to be needed to support these different operations.

The study of planning in the context of an external environment proves to be a difficult issue. It pushes traditional theories of planning beyond their current scope (Young and Simon, 1987). In particular, the questions of planning using an external medium (for example, paper and pencil, a computer, etc.) must be addressed. The characteristics of the external medium will play a major role in determining the behaviour of the programmer (Schönflug, 1985); not only the features of the notation, but also the actions for operating on the notation. For example, if you want to see two separate and distant parts of your program at the same time, this is easier to achieve with a version on paper, than in a single window editor.

To understand the psychology of complex tasks such as programming, we need to consider planning strategies in particular task contexts. Theories of planning and problem solving have spent too long with their heads in the sand, ignoring the role the external world plays in determining behaviour. If psychology is going to make significant contributions both in theoretical and applied areas of research, we need investigations of how features of the external world determine behavioural strategies. Only then will we be able to produce artifacts that support effective task strategies.

REFERENCES

Adelson, B. (1981). Problem solving and the development of abstract categories in programming languages. *Memory and Cognition*, **9**, 422–433.

Anderson, J. R. (1983). *The architecture of cognition*. Harvard: Harvard University Press.

Atwood, M. E., & Ramsey, H. R. (1978). *Cognitive structures in the comprehension and memory of computer programs: An investigation of computer program debugging*. Technical Report SAI-78-054-DEN, Science Applications Inc., Englewood, Colorado.

Barfield, W. (1986). Expert–novice differences for software: implications for problem solving and knowledge acquisition. *Behaviour and Information Technology*, **5**, 15–29.

Bever, T. G. (1970). The cognitive basis for linguistic structures. In J. Hayes (ed.), *Cognition and the development of language*. New York: John Wiley.

Bobrow, D. G., & Collins, A. (1975). *Representation and understanding: Studies in cognitive science*. New York: Academic Press.

Davies, S. P. (1988). *The nature and development of expert knowledge in the comprehension of computer programs*. Unpublished manuscript, Department of Computer Science, Huddersfield Polytechnic.

Gammack, J. G. (1988). *Eliciting expert conceptual structure using converging techniques*. PhD thesis, University of Cambridge, UK.

Gilmore, D. J. (1986). *The perceptual cueing of the structure of computer programs*. PhD thesis, Department of Psychology, University of Sheffield, UK.

Gilmore, D. J., & Green, T. R. G. (1987). Are 'programming plans' psychologically real —outside Pascal? *Proceedings of INTERACT '87*. Stuttgart.

Green, T. R. G. (1990). Programs as information structures. In J-M. Hoc, T. R. G. Green, D. J. Gilmore & R. Samurcay (eds.), *The psychology of programming*. London: Academic Press.

Green, T. R. G., Bellamy, R. K. E., & Parker, J. M. (1988). Parsing–Gnisrap: a model of device use. In G. M. Olson, S. Sheppard & E. Soloway (eds.), *Empirical studies of programmers: second workshop*. New Jersey: Ablex.

Hayes-Roth, B., & Hayes-Roth, F. (1979). A cognitive model of planning. *Cognitive Science*, **3**, 275–310.

Michie, D. (1980). Expert systems. *Computer Journal*, **23**, 369.

Pennington, N. (1987). Stimulus structures and mental representations in expert comprehension of computer programs. *Cognitive Psychology*, **19**, 295–341.

Ratcliff, B., & Siddiqi, J. I. A. (1985). An empirical investigation into problem decomposition strategies used in program design. *International Journal of Man–Machine Studies*, **22**, 77–90.

Rist, R. S. (1986). Plans in programming: definition, demonstration and development. In E. Soloway and S. Iyengar (eds.), *Empirical studies of programmers*. New Jersey: Ablex.

Rist, R. (1987). Schema creation in programming. *Technical Report*. Yale University Psychology Department.

Schank, R. C., & Abelson, R. B. (1977). *Scripts, plans, goals and understanding*. Hillsdale, NJ: Erlbaum.

Schönflug, W. (1986). External information storage: an issue for the psychology of memory. In F. Klix & H. Hagendorf (eds.), *Human memory and cognitive capabilities, mechanisms and performance*. Holland: Elsevier Science Publishers.

Shneiderman, B. (1976). Exploratory experiments in programmer behaviour. *International Journal of Computer and Information Science*, **5**, 123–143.

Soloway, E., & Ehrlich, K. (1983). Empirical studies of programming knowledge. *IEEE Transactions on Software Engineering*, **5**, 595–609.

Suchman, L. (1985). *Plans and situated actions: The problem of human–machine communication*. New York: Cambridge University Press.

Vessey, I. (1988). Expert–novice knowledge organisation: an empirical investigation using computer program recall. *Behaviour and Information Technology*, **7**, 153–71.

Widowski, D. (1986). Comprehending and recalling computer programs of different structural and semantic complexity by experts and novices. In H-P. Willumeit (ed.), *Human decision making and manual control*. Holland: Elsevier Science Publishers.

Wilensky, R. (1983). *Planning and understanding*. Reading, MA: Addison-Wesley.

Winograd, T., & Flores, F. (1986). *Understanding computers and cognition: A new foundation for design*. New Jersey: Ablex.

Young, R. M., & Simon, T. (1987). Planning in the context of human–computer interaction. In D. Diaper & R. Winder (eds.), *People and computers III*. Cambridge: Cambridge University Press.

5

Statistical Computing: Individual Differences in Learning at Macroscopic and Microscopic Levels

A. J. K. GREEN
MRC Applied Psychology Unit, Cambridge

K. J. GILHOOLY
University of Aberdeen

INTRODUCTION

Learning may be viewed as a form of problem solving in which solvers aim to transform their competence from initial satisfactory levels to a desired level of proficiency. There are marked individual differences in the efficiency with which learning problems are tackled, and this chapter will focus on differences between faster and slower learners in strategic and tactical processes in the domain of statistical computing. The principal methodology used in the study reported here was protocol analysis.

In Ericsson and Simon's (1984) review of protocol analysis, many of the studies discussed involve the analysis of think-aloud protocols generated by subjects solving puzzle-like problems, such as the Tower of Hanoi and cryptarithmetic. For instance, Newell and Simon (1972) carried out a detailed analysis of protocols generated by subjects performing cryptarithmetic. The protocols were encoded as a series of productions that were executed to move from one knowledge state to the next. Such an analysis at the *microscopic* level yields much detailed information about the subject's search through the problem space. However, there are difficulties with coding schemes that focus exclusively on microscopic aspects of behaviour.

In particular, exclusive attention to microscopic details runs the risk of missing important events at a more *macroscopic* level. As Schoenfeld (1983, p. 348) notes:

'In analyzing human problem-solving, exclusive attention to the microscopic level may cause one to miss the forest for the trees; if the wrong strategic decisions are made, tactical ones are virtually irrelevant.'

Tactical decision making has been the focus of a number of protocol studies. Tactical decisions are 'local' and include those made within algorithms and heuristics, such as means–end analysis and hill-climbing. A tactical decision in statistical computing might be to select the command for analysis of variance rather than that for a t-test.

Strategic, or executive, decisions are very different. By their nature, they have a profound impact on the solution process. For example, an executive decision might be choosing to abandon a method not meeting with success and selecting a different method. Such a decision will greatly influence the effectiveness of search.

Schoenfeld (1980) notes that expert mathematicians are not only more able to solve mathematical problems than non-experts, but that they approach problems in qualitatively different ways. Schoenfeld (1983) argues that experts not only know more than novices but that they are better at managing their resources. When domain-specific knowledge is lacking, managerial skills are particularly important. The suggestion is that, in the process of becoming skilled, experts acquire managerial or executive skills. An expert can assume effectively the role of doer and observer. This raises questions about the acquisition of managerial skills. For example, do some novices approach a new learning situation with executive skills acquired in other domains? Could the presence, or absence of managerial decisions differentiate between good and poor learners tackling new complex problem areas such as statistical computing?

EXPERIMENT: LEARNING MINITAB

MINITAB (1982 edition) was used throughout this experiment. MINITAB is a general-purpose statistical computing system designed especially for students and researchers with little previous experience of computing. Data are entered into a 'worksheet' and analyses are carried out by means of various commands.

In the case of students with little knowledge of computing, MINITAB lends itself well to an examination of individual differences in learning. Any differences that arise between novice students must be attributed to the learning mechanisms brought to bear on the tasks. Also, MINITAB is an interesting domain for study because it is a real-world domain.

Subjects

Subjects were selected from students in their third year of a four-year honours psychology course. All students in this year are given an introductory course in MINITAB. At the beginning of their introductory MINITAB course, the third-year students completed a 33-item questionnaire on their computing background. From the class of 39, ten subjects (six females and four males) with the lowest computing background scores were asked to participate in the experimental sessions. Subjects were paid for their involvement.

Procedure

The MINITAB course comprised a series of three introductory lectures and five one-hour practicals. Students attended one practical a week for five weeks. During the practicals, subjects were given a handout containing worked examples and problems for them to attempt. Experimental sessions ran concurrently with the MINITAB course over a period of five weeks. A time limit of 55 minutes was imposed on each experimental session. During the experimental sessions, subjects were asked to think aloud as they attempted a series of tasks based on that week's MINITAB practical. They each had access to a copy of that week's handout describing how to perform the various operations and providing examples. Each subject was tested separately. The instructions to think aloud, which were taken from Ericsson and Simon (1984), asked subjects to tell the experimenter everything they were thinking from the time they first saw the question until they gave an answer. Subjects were asked not to plan out or try to explain what they said and were told that they would be prompted to think aloud should they be silent for a 15-second period. All subjects were given two practice tasks at the start of the first session in order to familiarize themselves with the think-aloud procedure. A session record of key presses made by each subject was also obtained. In this way, we were able to make use of both verbal and behavioural protocols.

When the results were analysed, both quantitative and qualitative aspects of performance were examined. Here, quantitative aspects are considered first.

Scoring

The MINITAB problems comprised two distinguishable components: data entry and manipulation, and the selection of a statistical technique. Each problem was decomposed into a data entry and manipulation component and/or a statistical component. Each of these components might demand that the subject carry out one or more operations. For example:

READ DATA INTO C1 TO C4
ONEWAY ON DATA IN C1 C2

This example requires that the subject carry out one data entry operation and one statistical operation. Thus, two points were awarded for a correct answer. A subject might receive one point if, in the example above, errors were made in entering data but the correct statistical test was applied, or vice versa. As the tests varied from week to week, so did allocatable points. Each individual was awarded two scores: a data-entry and manipulation score, and a statistical analysis score. Total performance over the five sessions was taken as the sum of the two scores. On the basis of overall performance, subjects were divided into the top five and bottom five learners.

Performance Statistics

Performance statistics are presented in Table 5.1. Faster learners obtained higher data-entry and manipulation scores ($F(1,8) = 13.18$, $p < 0.01$) and higher overall scores than slower learners ($F(1,8) = 18.51$, $p < 0.01$).

Table 5.1 Analysis of variance on performance statistics (percentage figures)

Score category	Fast learners $(N=5)$	Slow learners $(N=5)$	Group mean $(N=10)$	Range
Data entry and manipulation	83.8^a	52.3	68.1	26.9–92.3
Statistical analysis	74.4	60	67.2	50–83.3
Overall	78.4^a	56.8	67.6	40.3–83.9

^{a} $p < 0.01$.

Table 5.2 Mean error rate per session

Category	Fast learners $(N=5)$	Slow learners $(N=5)$
Data entry and manipulation	3.6	4.8
Statistical analysis	2.2	2.4
Overall	5.8	7.2

Errors were categorized as data-entry and manipulation errors or errors in statistical analysis. Examples of the former might be incorrectly adding two columns of data, or using a data-entry command inappropriately. Statistical errors were instances where the wrong statistical test was used. Data on error rates are presented in Table 5.2. There were no reliable differences between the two groups in the mean number of errors made of either category per session.

Finally, we considered the time taken by subjects to complete the tasks. Fast learners completed the tasks in an average of 27 minutes, which was faster than slower learners who took an average of 37 minutes ($F(1,8) = 11.03$. $p < 0.01$).

The Coding Scheme

A hierarchical coding scheme was developed to analyse the protocols. At the macroscopic level, learning *episodes* were considered. An episode was defined as a series of related behaviours, such as planning or implementation. Five clearly discernible types of episode were identifed; these were:

a) Understanding
b) Method finding
c) Planning
d) Implementation
e) Verification

An 'understanding' episode begins when the subject starts to read the question, and it includes re-reading and ingesting the problem conditions. If the solution attempt is not schema-driven, the next phase of solution is 'method finding'. During the method-finding episode, hypotheses may be generated, worked examples may be referred to, and analogies may be made between the problem and an example. Once an attempt has been made to formulate an appropriate perspective, a plan may be developed. The 'planning' phase includes goal formulation and the setting of local, short-range plans. Planning may lead directly into 'implementation', where an attempt is made to solve the problem. Implementation in this context comprises only executive episodes. The categorization of solution attempts is dealt with independently. Finally, once a solution attempt has been made, the next ideal phase is 'verification'. During the verification episode, the learner may describe and interpret the solution. In the case of statistical computing, the significance of the result may be ascertained.

Each episode comprised a set of tactical and executive processes. Only tactical processes were episode-specific. The tactical processes specific to 'understanding', 'method finding', 'planning' and 'verification' are listed below. Some, like *read* are self-explanatory, whilst others, like *probe*, require clarification. The less obvious categories are therefore explained. ('Implementation' is dealt with separately.) The abbreviated code is presented beside each process.

Tactical Processes

Understanding

Reading the question (*read*)

Re-reading the question (*rere*)

Noting conditions in the question (*note*)
(For example, noting that there are three columns of data to be entered.)

Method Finding

Probing (*prob*)
(For example, a subject might reflect upon whether the problem was an instance of one requiring the data to be entered in a particular way.)

Mapping (*map*)
(For example, a subject might compare the problem with a worked example and note the similarity or dissimilarity.)

Abductive hypothesis generation (*agen*)
(Subjects sometimes abduced a hypothesis when it, together with other assumptions already held, was consistent with some observation. Abductions were often inaccurate and incomplete and reflected the subject's desire to make sense of their experience. For example, a subject might abduce that the error message 'Incomplete row—re-enter' occurred as a result of the data not being properly aligned, rather than as a result of insufficient data entered. Abductive hypotheses, then, are erroneous hypotheses. For fuller descriptions of abduction and *ad hoc* reasoning, see Carroll and Mack (1984) and Carroll and Rosson (1987).)

Hypothesis generation (*hgen*)

Planning

Goal setting (*gset*)

Local planning (*locp*)
(This differed from goal setting in that an intention was formulated without a goal being explicitly stated.)

Verification

Describing the solution (*dess*)
(For example, the subject might note that the mean was 20.5.)

Interpreting the solution (*ints*)
(For example, a subject might infer significance and state that this meant that two groups did or did not differ.)

Inferring significance (*infs*)
(For example, a subject might infer that a probability value of 0.01 was significant.)

Executive Processes

Executive processes were found to be episode-independent. They fell into three categories and are listed below.

Evaluative Decisions

Evaluating progress, tactics or solution (*eval*)

Evaluating knowledge (*evalk*)
(For example, subjects frequently determined whether or not they knew a fact or procedure.)

These two types of evaluative decision should be either positive or negative.

Action Decisions

Revise tactics (*revt*)
(For example, such a decision to try a different approach might follow on from a negative evaluation of tactics.)

These decisions could be either implicit or explicit.

Checking Decisions

Recap (*rec*)
(For example, a subject might verbalize what s/he had just done.)

Referring to prompts (*refp*)

Standard check (*prin*)
(For example, subjects sometimes checked the accuracy of what they were doing by using the PRINT command.)

Error detection processes (*erd*)
(For example, subjects often noted errors, and tried to determine the cause of the error.)

Solution Attempts

The 'implementation' episodes were treated separately and considered in terms of solution attempts. It was evident that a single solution attempt might span one or more episodes. Seven types of solution attempt were identified in the protocols. These are listed below with their abbreviated code and an explanation of each.

Schema Activation (SA)

This approach was easily identified in protocols where subjects solved a problem with no search (that is, no method finding) and where the solution procedure was implemented after reading the problem statement.

Abductive Hypothesis Testing (AT)

This approach was identified in protocols where subjects abduced, and then subsequently tested, a hypothesis. The abduced hypothesis might immediately be tested, or there might be a short delay before proceeding to test.

Hypothesis Testing (HT)

Hypothesis testing was identified in protocols where a hypothesis was generated and tested. Like the previous category, it remains distinct from simple hypothesis generation because not all hypotheses were tested.

Trial and Error (TE)

The trial and error approach was characterized as an unstructured, random approach where each attempt to solve the problem seemed independent of any previous attempt. It was frequently preceded by comments such as 'I don't know what I'm doing', etc.

Repetition (RE)

Repetition was identified in protocols where the subject was clearly repetitively using either a command or a test. It was often preceded by comments such as 'I'll just do the same thing again'.

Copy (CO)

The copy approach differed from analogy (see below) in that it was not preceded by mapping. Thus, subjects using the copy approach would simply select an example and copy it, sometimes exactly, without determining whether that example was appropriate or not.

Analogy (AN)

Analogy, unlike copy, was always preceded by mapping. Subjects using this approach always evaluated a worked example before proceeding by analogy to solve the problem.

Analysis of Individual Differences

Encoder reliability was established by asking two independent encoders to code a number of protocols. Ten per cent of the set of MINITAB protocols, each coded at the three levels, were analysed by the independent encoders. In each instance, agreement was greater than 80%.

A principal concern was to identify those variables that best predicted learning. Which combination of predictor variables maximizes differences between good and poor learners? Can group membership be predicted at the macroscopic or microscopic levels, or both?

Thirty-six of the 50 protocols were included for analysis. Eleven fast learners' and three slow learners' protocols were discarded because their problem solving was schema-driven. Problem solving was defined as schema-driven if the subject proceeded from 'understanding' to 'planning' or 'implementation' with no 'method finding'. Schema-driven protocols gave no evidence for difficulty in problem solving. As anticipated, good learners' problem solving was schema-driven more often than poor learners' solving ($F(1,8) = 6.4$, $p < 0.05$).

Discriminant function analysis was the statistical technique used to determine which, if any, of the variables predicted group membership. Discriminant function analysis allows the researcher to study the differences between two or more groups of subjects with respect to several variables simultaneously. Our objective was to interpret the ways in which groups differ. Is it possible to discriminate between fast and slow learners on the basis of some set of characteristics, how well do they discriminate, and which variables are the most powerful discriminators?

Episode Variables as Predictors

Subjects' performance varied from session to session. Correlations between sessions ranged from -0.554 to 0.572. These were the only two of the ten correlation coefficients that were significant at the $p = 0.05$ level. None of the other correlations reached significance. Because of this, it was decided to treat data from each subject's experimental session independently. In this way, 36 cases were entered into the analysis.

No episode variables significantly discriminated between fast and slow learners.

Process Variables as Predictors

Data on tactical and executive processes were then used jointly in stepwise discriminant function analysis. Variables are entered into the stepwise analysis one at a time until a cutoff value for F is reached. In this instance, computation ceased at step 6. Group means are presented in Table 5.3.

A discriminant function with $\chi^2(6) = 26.53$ ($p < 0.01$) maximally separated good from poor learners' protocols. Results are presented in Table 5.4.

Three variables significantly discriminated between the two groups. Good learners re-read the question, abduced fewer hypotheses and (negatively) evaluated their knowledge less frequently than did poor learners. Classification results show that the discriminant function correctly classified 86.11% of cases.

Executive and tactical processes were then considered in relation to episodes. If executive processes are critical, then it might be anticipated that performance should be related to the presence of executive processes in learning episodes. To examine this, the proportion of episodes containing at least one executive process was calculated for each case: 18.6% of good learners' episodes contained at least one executive process, whilst 13.8% of poor learners' episodes contained an executive process ($F(1,34) = 4.21$, $p < 0.05$).

Individual executive processes were than analysed in more detail. One further concern was to consider possible differences in the ways in which learners responded to negative evaluations of tactics. That is, when a learner expressed little confidence in his or her tactics or decided that the approach was wrong,

Table 5.3   Group means for processes

Variable	Slow learners	Fast learners
Read	4.95	4.29
Rere	3.32	1.50
Prob	0.68	0.71
Exam	3.32	2.79
Map	0.86	1.43
Agen	1.82	0.21
Hgen	0.91	1.07
Gset	4.27	4.86
Locp	3.77	3.64
Dess	4.36	4.36
Ints	0.64	0.93
Infs	1.23	1.64
Eval	4.45	4.71
Revt	0.95	1.43
Erd	1.82	1.86
Prin	0.55	1.50
Rec	0.82	0.79
Evalk	5.50	2.43

Table 5.4 Results of discriminant function analysis of MINITAB processes

Predictor variable	Correlations of predictor variables with discriminant function	Univariate $F(1, 34)$
Evalk	0.548	13.795[a]
Agen	0.458	9.639[a]
Rere	0.417	7.995[a]
Prob	−0.229	0.428
Exam	−0.220	0.576
Revt	−0.127	2.303
Gset	−0.107	0.421
Erd	0.096	0.405
Infs	−0.087	0.351
Map	0.058	0.859
Prin	−0.054	3.536
Read	0.054	1.002
Hgen	−0.036	0.171
Locp	−0.030	0.268
Eval	0.020	0.726
Rec	0.014	0.861
Ints	0.005	0.653
Dess	0.001	0.438

Classification results

Actual group	Number of cases	Predicted slow	Predicted fast
Slow	22	18	4
Fast	14	1	13

[a] $p < 0.01$
Canonical $R = 0.758$
Eigenvalue $= 1.353$

what action was taken? One of two responses was possible. The learner might abandon the proposed action, or go ahead and execute the command. On 81.2% of occasions, slow learners went ahead and executed the move whilst only on 36.8% of such occasions did fast learners proceed with the move ($F(1,7) = 6.96$, $p < 0.05$). There were no differences in evaluation accuracy. Evaluation accuracy was assessed by comparing the subject's evaluation with an objective evaluation of the move. The objective evaluation was made by the first author. Fast learners were correct in their evaluations on 88% of occasions whilst slow learners were correct on 79% of occasions.

References to prompts and error messages were analysed separately. Since such references depend upon commands executed, a simple measure of attention paid to feedback was sought. This was obtained by determining whether mention was made of prompts and error messages received. Multiple references to the same prompt or error message were ignored. Analysis of variance showed that good learners attended more to feedback than did poor learners ($F(1,8) = 7.3$, $p < 0.05$).

Solution Attempts as Predictor Variables

Discriminant function analysis was carried out using the seven types of solution attempts as predicting variables. Group means are presented in Table 5.5. Computation ceased after six steps.

A discriminant function with $\chi^2(6) = 20.91$, ($p < 0.01$) maximally separated the protocols of good from poor learners. Results are presented in Table 5.6. The discriminant function correctly classified 85.71% of cases.

Table 5.5   Group means for attempt categories

Variable	Slow learners	Fast learners
TE	2.95	1.64
AT	0.90	0.21
CO	1.81	1.86
SA	3.57	6.00
RE	0.76	0.29
HT	0.14	1.29
AN	0.52	1.29

Table 5.6   Results of discriminant function analysis of MINITAB solution attempts

Predictor variable	Correlations of predictor variables with discriminant function	Univariate $F(1, 33)$
HT	0.380	4.800[a]
AT	-0.363	4.381[a]
SA	0.352	4.117[a]
TE	-0.347	2.698
AN	0.311	3.212
RE	-0.234	1.813
CO	0.015	0.796

Classification results

Actual group	Number of cases	Predicted slow	Predicted fast
Slow	21	19	2
Fast	14	3	11

[a] $p < 0.05$
Canonical $R = 0.708$
Eigenvalue $= 1.007$

DISCUSSION

Novice subjects were grouped according to their overall performance in solving statistical computing problems. What might explain the observed performance differences between faster and slower learners in the complex task used here?

Analysis of the think-aloud protocols provided information about qualitative factors discriminating amongst novice learners. In particular, stepwise discriminant analysis showed that none of the five types of episode predicted group membership. However, as Schoenfeld (1983) notes, it may be more appropriate to examine executive processes within episodes, and their effects on performance, rather than the episodes themselves.

Discriminant analyses of learning processes and solution attempts produced a number of interesting results. The analysis of *processes* showed highly significant discriminating power and revealed that three processes differentiated the two groups. Slow learners negatively evaluated their knowledge, abduced hypotheses and re-read the problem more frequently than did fast learners.

It is quite plausible that abducing hypotheses may be a cause rather than a symptom of poor performance. Carroll and Rosson (1987) describe learning as an active process in which the learner will often strike out into the unknown, putting together *ad hoc* theories. This would suggest that learners should make as much use of all available information, such as prompts and error messages, as possible. Consistent with this view, good learners attended more to feedback than did poor learners, although it is difficult to ascertain how exactly the respective groups made use of feedback.

It was hypothesized that executive processes might be disproportionately important in the early stages of skill acquisition. This would follow from Schoenfeld (1983) and Sternberg (1985), and is supported by the finding that a greater proportion of good learners' episodes are characterized by the presence of executive processes. Some more results lend further support to this hypothesis, showing that it may be necessary to consider what prompts and follows an executive decision. For instance, on a negative evaluation of a possible action, good learners were more likely to abandon it and look for another method. Slow learners, on the other hand, were more likely to go ahead with the action, even though their initial evaluation was quite accurate.

Comparing the present results with previous studies we note that the results of Thorndyke and Stasz (1980) can be interpreted in terms of a hierarchical framework, such as that previously outlined. Some of the ten 'learning bugs' which they identify seem to recur here. For instance, Thorndyke and Stasz found that poor learners in their map-learning study failed to make use of evaluation feedback and used ineffective procedures to try to learn map information. Also, they did not monitor their learning progress to help them to determine what map information to study next. Parallels in the present study are the lack of attention paid by poor learners to prompts and error messages, the use of processes such as probing and recapping that did not succeed in producing learning, and a general absence of executive processes.

The stepwise discriminant analysis of MINITAB solution attempts again showed highly significant discriminating power. Group means showed that fast learners attempted to solve problems by copying an example, activating an appropriate schema and hypothesis testing more frequently than did slow learners. Slow learners more often attempted to solve problems by testing abductive hypotheses. It is plausible that testing erroneous hypotheses may be a cause rather than a symptom of poor performance. Poor learners paid less attention to feedback than did good learners, which might in turn have caused them to abduce more hypotheses.

Protocol studies (see, for example, Carroll and Mack, 1984) seek to show an association between certain categories of behaviour and learning for problem-solving performance. The principal problem lies in determining whether the use of certain processes or strategies is a cause or a symptom of task performance. Using a hierarchical scheme, such as that developed and described here, enables the researcher to identify potentially critical processes and to examine the consequences of their use and misuse. In this way, inferences may be drawn about the factors influencing rate of learning.

CONCLUSIONS

Quantitative and qualitative analyses of performance show that novices differ, give some clues as to factors differentiating good from poor learners, and suggest directions for future research. A hierarchical approach to the analysis of think-aloud protocols lends insight into individual differences in learning. Distinguishing between executive and non-executive processes seems necessary. Carroll (1976, p. 31) notes: 'The assumption of an executive process... seems an intuitive necessity if one is to get the system in operation'. The real problem for hierarchical approaches lies in specifying in sufficient detail precisely how such a model of human information processing might operate. In what ways might executive processes operate on non-executive processes, and are executive processes internally or externally triggered? Current models of human information processing (see, for example, Barnard, 1985) offer a framework for cognition where specialized and functionally independent subsystems interact with each other. Processing capabilities are constrained by the characteristics of the subsystems, the processes involved and the interactions between subsystems. Whilst the approach does not explicitly deal with processing at the strategic level, the findings presented here are not incompatible with Barnard's model. There is clearly a general need to elaborate on the concept of control in cognition. Given that the development of automaticity has been invoked to explain the development of skilled performance (Schneider and Shiffrin, 1977), what are the mechanisms relating attention, awareness and executive control and how do they give rise to variations in performance?

REFERENCES

Barnard, P. (1985). Interacting cognitive subsystems: a psycholinguistic approach to short-term memory. In A. Ellis (ed.), *Progress in the psychology of language*, Vol. 2, London: Erlbaum.

Carroll, J. M. (1976). Psychometric tests as cognitive tasks: a new 'structure of intellect'. In L. B. Resnick (ed.), *The nature of intelligence*. Hillsdale, NJ: Erlbaum.

Carroll, J. M., & Mack, R. L. (1984). Learning to use a word processor: by doing, by thinking and by knowing. In J. C. Thomas & M. L. Schneider (eds.), *Human factors in computer systems*. Norwood, NJ: Ablex.

Carroll, J. M., & Rosson, M.B. (1987). Paradox of the active user. In J. M. Carroll (ed.), *Interfacing thought*. Cambridge, MA: MIT Press.

Ericsson, K. A., & Simon, H. A. (1984). *Protocol analysis*. Cambridge, MA: MIT Press.

Newell, A., & Simon, H. A. (1972). *Human problem solving*. Englewood Cliffs, NJ: Prentice-Hall.

Schneider, W., & Shiffrin, R. M. (1977). Controlled and automatic information processing: 1. Detection, search and attention. *Psychological Review*, **84**, 1–66.

Schoenfeld, A. H. (1980). Teaching problem solving skills. *American Mathematical Monthly*, **87**, 794–805.

Schoenfeld, A. H. (1983). Episodes and executive decisions in mathematical problem solving. In R. Lesh & M. Landau (eds.), *Acquisition of mathematical concepts and processes*. New York: Academic Press.

Sternberg, R. J. (1985). *Beyond IQ: A triarchic theory of human intelligence*. New York: Cambridge University Press.

Thorndyke, P. W., & Stasz, C. (1980). Individual differences in procedures for knowledge acquisition from maps. *Cognitive Psychology*, **12**, 137–175.

6

Talking About Cognitive Processes

DIANNE C. BERRY
University of Oxford

INTRODUCTION

Talking to oneself has long been considered to be a sign of madness. Yet despite this rather negative association, concurrent verbalization has become an established technique in both experimental and applied psychology. This chapter looks at how verbalization has been used in the literature and makes a distinction between studies that have employed the technique to reveal something about the way in which a particular task is performed and those that have used verbalization to affect the way a task is performed. It is suggested that in many areas the benefit of verbalization lies more with its potential biasing properties than with its ability to throw light on otherwise hidden thought processes. Experiments are reported which show that concurrent verbalization can actually play a crucial role in learning.

THE VALIDITY OF VERBAL REPORTS

More than a century ago Wilhelm Wundt defined psychology as the science of immediate experience and proposed to explore it by collecting verbal reports of observers trained in his special technique of introspection. It took less than fifty years for the American behaviourists to redefine psychology as the science of behaviour, citing the unreliability of introspection as one of the major reasons for abandoning consciousness as a scientific problem.

The debate over the validity of verbal reports has returned to the foreground in more recent years with influential statements by Nisbett and Wilson (1977) and Ericsson and Simon (1980, 1984). Nisbett and Wilson reviewed a large body of evidence from cognitive and social psychology and concluded that 'people appear to have little ability to report accurately on their cognitive processes'

Lines of Thinking, Volume 2 Edited by K.J. Gilhooly, M.T.G. Keane, R.H. Logie and G. Erdos
© 1990 John Wiley & Sons Ltd

(p. 246). They suggest that, rather than indicating an awareness of underlying causal processes, introspective reports consist of cause–effect type 'theories' which subjects construct in an attempt to explain their own behaviour.

Nisbett and Wilson's position has been criticized on both theoretical and methodological grounds (Smith and Miller, 1978; White 1982; and notably, Ericsson and Simon, 1980). In contrast to Nisbett and Wilson, Ericsson and Simon argue that 'verbal reports, elicited with care and interpreted with full understanding of the circumstances under which they were obtained, are a valuable and thoroughly reliable source of information about cognitive processes' (1980, p. 247). They suggest that there is an important difference between asking people to describe their thought processes and treating verbal protocols as a form of data from which underlying thought processes can be inferred.

Ericsson and Simon stress the need for, and put forward, an information processing model to account for the wide range of verbalization processes previously grouped together under the label 'introspection'. The authors distinguish between various types of verbalization procedure (for example, concurrent–retrospective, general–specific and primary–incidental) and outline the circumstances under which the different types of verbal report would be expected to be reliable and complete. The model specifies three levels of verbalization:

a) *level 1*, in which information is produced in the form in which it is heeded;
b) *level 2*, in which the information is heeded but normally encoded in a non-verbal form (e.g. imagery) and so must be translated for verbalization;
c) *level 3*, where the subject is asked to report selectively or induced to attend to information that would not normally be heeded.

These levels are clearly associated with increasing numbers of intervening cognitive processes between the information being heeded and it being verbalized.

Ericsson and Simon suggest that under a variety of circumstances verbal reports may omit information that subjects use to perform a task. Evidence of the nature of omissions is, however, consistent with the predictions of their model. The intermediate steps of immediate recognition processes and detailed steps of perceptual-motor processes are not generally recorded in long-term memory; hence they are not reported. Processes that have been so often repeated as to become automated are less often and less fully reported. When subjects give indications that they are working under a heavy cognitive load they tend to stop verbalizing or produce less-complete verbalizations. The contents of short-term memory can be obliterated; hence the omissions caused in reports by requiring subjects to perform intervening tasks concurrently with their verbal reporting. As far as retrospective reporting is concerned, Ericsson and Simon propose that inconsistent reports can be produced as a result of probes that are too general to elicit the information actually sought or as a result of subjects' use of inferential processes to fill out and generalize incomplete or missing memories. Ericsson and Simon claim that by using their model, many of the results from studies that are often cited against the use of verbalized information can be understood in terms of the methods used to collect and analyse the verbalizations.

The idea that verbal reports may or may not be useful sources of information depending on the conditions under which they are collected has received support from other researchers, including Kellogg (1982) and Byrne (1983). Kellogg, for example, presents evidence from a concept-learning paradigm to support the position that introspection can be either a valid or an invalid research tool depending on the demands of the experimental task. His experiments show that when concept learning relies solely on automatic frequency processing introspective reports are inaccurate, but when the nature of the task prompts intentional hypothesis testing introspective reports are accurate, revealing clues that subjects engage in a conscious hypothesis testing strategy.

It follows from Ericsson and Simon's model that some tasks are more inclined to give rise to accurate verbal reports than others. As Evans (1982) notes, problems of the sort studied by Newell and Simon (such as cryptarithmetic) are amenable to study by thinking-aloud protocols since they are comprised of a number of sub-problems which have verbal outputs. Recording the outputs of such intermediate stages facilitates construction of an overall picture of the problem-solving process: 'If, however, a thought process has no intermediate stages then the technique will not be helpful' (p. 237).

Broadbent and colleagues have studied performance on a number of tasks that fall into this latter category (Broadbent, FitzGerald and Broadbent, 1986; Berry and Broadbent, 1984, 1987a, 1988; Hayes and Broadbent, 1988). Berry and Broadbent (1984), for example, found that practice significantly improved ability to control complex computer-implemented systems, but had no effect on associated verbalizable knowledge. The tasks involved subjects having to reach and maintain target values of an output variable by varying a single input variable. In one version they took on the role of manager of a small factory and were required to reach and maintain a target level of output by varying the number of workers employed. Verbal knowledge was assessed by a series of post-task questions which asked about the relationships within the systems. Although such a technique is subject to methodological criticism, subsequent experiments found no evidence of accurate verbalizable knowledge using a range of retrospective and concurrent techniques. Moreover, there are some aspects of the results that would not be predicted by Ericsson and Simon's model. There was an overall negative correlation between control performance and questionnaire scores. People who were better at the task were actually significantly worse at answering the questions. Berry and Broadbent suggested that these tasks were normally performed in some implicit way with individuals not being verbally aware of the basis on which they were responding.

It is not sufficient, however, simply to demonstrate that some tasks give rise to accurate verbal reports while others do not. One must also identify the important criteria that distinguish the two types of task. More recent research has attempted to do this, with some degree of success (for example, Berry and Broadbent, 1988). Research in this area has also shown that tasks that do not lead to accurate verbal reports tend to be the ones that are more prone to bias by the introduction of some forms of reporting technique. This point will be returned to below.

THE USE OF VERBAL REPORTS IN APPLIED PSYCHOLOGY

The use of verbal reports, particularly protocol analysis, has been relatively widespread in many areas of applied psychology. Bainbridge (1979), for example, reviewed a set of studies looking at process control operators and argued that if we want to use verbal data we need to know what factors influence the way verbal reports are produced, so that we can minimize the distortions and maximize the validity of the evidence. Bainbridge surveyed several methods of obtaining verbal reports—such as system-state/action-state diagrams, questionnaires, interviews, static simulation and verbal protocols— and concluded that the validity of verbal reports depends closely on the method of collecting them. Different reporting techniques make it more or less difficult for the person involved to give a reliable report.

In recent years protocol analysis has been used as a technique for eliciting knowledge from human experts in order to develop expert or knowledge-based systems. Fox *et al.*, (1985), for example, employed protocol analysis as the primary elicitation technique in developing an expert system for the interpretation of immunological data obtained in the cell-surface phenotyping of leukaemia. They recorded their expert diagnosing cases of leukaemia from written laboratory records. (This is the normal clinical procedure; patients are never seen). Transcripts were made from the tapes and key statements were extracted, simplified and transformed into a set of if–then rules suitable for the expert system package. The authors suggest that protocols are a useful basis for starting to build a knowledge base, although they did not reflect certain kinds of knowledge, such as higher-order information about the structure of the task and information about the strategy for dealing with undiagnosable cases.

It has been suggested that an advantage of protocol analysis is that it gives access to information that would not be available from interviews or questionning. Gammack and Young (1984), for example, state that the merit of protocol analysis is that:

> 'it goes beyond what experts can explicitly tell you in a problem solving situation to permit inference of what knowledge they must be using but either cannot verbalize or are unaware of. By reconstructing the solution using inferred production system rules the experts' knowledge can be modelled. Such a method is particularly useful for eliciting procedures that experts use in problem solving which they may not be able to articulate.'

In order for protocol analysis to be effective, however, the knowledge engineer must be sufficiently acquainted with the task domain to understand the expert's task (note that this is different from being able to perform the task). If a simulation technique is being used it is necessary to ensure that a representative sample of tasks has been selected. Similarly, if the expert is being studied in his or her natural setting then behaviour must be recorded for a sufficiently long period of time to cover a representative sample of activities. This is obviously very time-consuming. Burton *et al.* (1987) carried out a formal evaluation of various knowledge elicitation techniques including protocol analysis. They found that protocol analysis not only took longer to perform and analyse than comparable techniques, but it also yielded a substantially smaller amount of information. It is also the case that experts need experience at 'thinking aloud'. Not all experts are able to produce running commentaries. As Kidd and Welbank (1984) point out, non-professional experts, such as technicians, have particular difficulty with such techniques. It can be an even more alien process to them.

There are other problems with this type of assessment method, as would be predicted by Ericsson and Simon's model. Protocols are often incomplete. They may contain evidence about how knowledge is used but not about its full range. Such techniques cannot be used to establish the limits of an expert's knowledge. If something is not mentioned it does not mean that the expert does not know it. In many domains, providing a running commentary is a demanding secondary task. This is a particular problem where the task in question requires a great deal of mental effort. In this case protocols are likely to be particularly sketchy. Moreover, experts generally cannot verbalize as fast as they can reason. They may well leave out steps in the reasoning process. They may also omit things that seem obvious to them.

A final problem is that producing a running commentary can affect the way a task is actually carried out. If experts have difficulty describing the way in which they carry out a task, because of the nature of the knowledge involved, forcing them to produce a running commentary is likely to make them approach the task in a different, possibly more systematic, way. The line of reasoning chosen by an expert when asked to comment on his or her behaviour while solving a problem will therefore be different from when that same expert solves the same problem under more natural conditions. The biasing effects of concurrent verbalization are discussed in detail in the next section.

It is clear that in some situations verbal protocols can provide more information about an expert's knowledge than can be obtained by interview techniques. It is also clear, however, that protocol analysis will still leave many aspects of an expert's knowledge untapped. Although it is possible that knowledge engineers will be able to infer some of the more implicit aspects of an expert's knowledge from observing and recording their behaviour and commentary, this will only be the 'tip of the iceberg'. Where behaviour is particularly complex, knowledge engineers will stand little chance of isolating the sub-components and assessing exactly what the expert knows about each of these. They will only be able to observe the expert's behaviour as a whole.

THE BIASING EFFECTS OF VERBALIZATION

Most of the literature on verbalization has been concerned with the question of whether verbal reports accurately reflect underlying thought processes. Less attention has been paid to the question of whether the production of a verbal report has any effect on thought processes. Where the latter issue has been addressed, it tends to be in terms of the former; that is, the verbalization process distorts the reasoning process and this results in non-veridical verbal reports. The present chapter asserts, however, that the biasing effects of verbalization should not always be viewed in this negative way. An increasing number of studies support the view that concurrent verbalization can actually have beneficial effects on the way tasks are performed. Overt verbalization has, for example, been shown to result in more efficient solutions to the Tower of Hanoi problem (Gagne and Smith, 1962; Ahlum-Heath and Di Vesta, 1986), to improve concept learning (Bower and King, 1967) and to facilitate transfer from a 'concrete' to an 'abstract' version of the Wason Selection Task (Berry, 1983). Moreover, a recent line of work by the present author has taken advantage of the biasing properties of verbalization to show that it can actually play a very crucial role in learning. It does this by bringing into temporary memory at the same time the various critical factors involved in a particular decision.

Gagne and Smith investigated the effects of verbalization on the Tower of Hanoi problem. Subjects were required to state verbally a reason for each move at the time it was made, or to search for a general principle which could be stated verbally after the tasks were solved. The results showed that concurrent verbalization resulted in significantly improved performance. The advantage was present in the practice trials and was maintained on a final transfer task (on which verbalization was not required). In contrast, instruction to formulate a general principle had no beneficial effect on problem-solving performance. Gagne and Smith suggested that verbalization during the practice trials had the effect of making subjects think of reasons for moves, which facilitated their employment in successive problems.

Ahlum-Heath and Di Vesta also found a positive effect of verbalization on learning to solve the Tower of Hanoi problem. They looked at the effects of practice and verbalization (alone and in combination) and concluded that verbalization was most helpful during the initial flexible stages of learning to solve problems before the skill had become organized.

Bower and King examined the effects of concurrent verbalization in a concept learning study. Subjects were required to verbalize their hypotheses before classifying the stimuli. The number of irrelevant dimensions of the stimuli was varied, although the instructions indicated which two features were relevant to the solution in each case. The results showed that the verbalization requirement significantly improved performance (that is, the number of responses to criterion) but only for the first problem. Bower and King found that variation in the number of irrelevant features also affected the initial problem. They suggested that verbalizing hypotheses might help subjects ignore irrelevant attributes.

Berry (1983) looked at the effect of concurrent and retrospective verbalization on deductive reasoning performance. Subjects were required to solve a 'concrete' version of the Wason Selection Task. Following an initial trial they were provided with a minimal explanation of the correct solution. This improved performance on subsequent concrete trials, but there was no evidence of transfer to a logically equivalent abstract task. However, concurrent verbalization during the trials following the explanation (or post-verbalization following these trials) led to significantly higher scores on the abstract task.

Ericsson and Simon (1980, 1984) considered the question of whether the production of a verbal protocol significantly distorts normal thinking. They compared the performance of subjects with and without concurrent verbalization and concluded that, in most cases, performance was not significantly changed by having to produce a verbal report. They suggested that, when subjects articulate information which is already available to them (level-1 verbalization), thinking aloud will not change the course and structure of cognitive processes. Nor will verbalization under these conditions slow the processes down. When the information being processed in order to fulfil the main task is not verbal or propositional (level-2 verbalization), performance may be slowed and verbalizations may be incomplete, but the course and structure of the task performance processes will remain largely unchanged. It is only at the third level of verbalization (where the subject is asked to report selectively or is induced to attend to information that would not normally be heeded) that Ericsson and Simon suggest that ongoing cognitive processes will be directly affected by the verbalization requirement. The effects will be especially prominent if subjects are asked for information that would not normally be available to them during their performance of the task.

Ericsson and Simon's model tends to predict when, rather than state why, concurrent verbalization has effects on task performance. They do emphasize, however, that the relationship between the main task and the verbalization task is mutual. The predictions of the model can be used to test hypotheses about task processes, just as predictions from the latter can be used to test hypotheses about the model of verbalization: 'Once we have acquired confidence in the verbalization model, we find that differences between subjects in thinking aloud and silent conditions have implications for the processes that are being used to perform the main task' (Ericsson and Simon, 1980, p. 228).

INTERACTION WITH INSTRUCTIONS

A recent line of work by Berry and Broadbent (1984, 1987b, in press) has taken advantage of the biasing properties of verbalization to show that it can play a crucial role in learning to perform complex tasks. In all three studies a critical interaction was found between verbalization and the presentation of some form of verbal instruction or explanation. Berry and Broadbent (1984), for example found that detailed verbal instruction had no significant effect on ability to control the complex computer-implemented systems described above. It cannot be argued that the instructions were not understood or remembered, however, as the instructed subjects scored significantly higher than the non-instructed subjects on the series of written post-task questions that asked about the relationships within the system. It was suggested that these tasks were normally performed in some implicit way. This meant that relevant verbal information could not easily be incorporated into task performance.

Performance did significantly improve, however, if subjects were required to verbalize concurrently throughout the trials following the verbal instruction. In contrast, verbalization without prior instruction had no significant effect on control performance or question answering. It was suggested that the instruction–verbalization combination was beneficial because the verbal instruction directed attention towards certain critical features of the task. The subsequent verbalization requirement kept attention on these salient features and irrelevant aspects were ignored. Bainbridge (1979) also proposed that certain types of verbalization might change the way in which a task is carried out by forcing concentration on critical task components.

Using a different type of task, Berry and Broadbent (1987b) again reported differing effects of verbalization on performance on a computer-assisted search task depending on whether or not relevant verbal information was at hand. The task was to determine which of a set of factories was responsible for polluting a river by testing the river for the presence or absence of various pollutants. Successful performance involved both selecting pollutants to distinguish between the factories and, given the answer to any pollutant test, making the necessary inferences about the remaining factories. Generally people tend to use a non-optimal exhaustive search strategy, making many unnecessary pollutant tests. Moreover, it has been shown that recommending to subjects which pollutants they should test for is of no benefit (Berry and Broadbent, 1986). Subjects perform at the same level when they receive the suggested pollutants as when they carry out the task unaided. It seems that they are not able to use the critical information gained from the suggestions in a successful way. They are not able to make the necessary inferences.

Berry and Broadbent (1987b) therefore implemented two different forms of explanation which conveyed to subjects the principle according to which the advice programme worked. (This was basically a binary split method, whereby the computer recommended a pollutant that was emitted by half of the factories under consideration at that time.) In the one case subjects were presented with a block text of explanation at the beginning of each of four trials. In the other case they were allowed to ask 'Why?' following the recommendation of each pollutant, and in return they were provided with a short explanation referring to the particular pollutant in question. The results showed that provision of the preliminary block explanation had no significant effect on task performance, whereas subjects who were allowed to ask why each computer recommendation was made performed significantly better on all trials. The former type of explanation was not totally ineffective, however. Subjects who were required to verbalize concurrently following the block explanation performed significantly better than subjects who were required to verbalize but who had not received any form of explanation.

Berry and Broadbent suggested that individuals need an explanation that applies directly to the pollutant being considered at the time at which the necessary inferences have to be made. The relevant information must be in some form of working memory at the critical time. It is not enough that the abstract principles should be present in a lasting declarative memory; they must also be temporarily activated at the moment they are needed in the task.

The lack of effect of the preliminary block explanation and the interaction with concurrent verbalization is in line with the earlier study with the computer control tasks. Berry and Broadbent (1984) attributed the lack of effect of the verbal instruction to the fact that the control tasks were normally carried out in an implicit way. There is no evidence, however, that the river pollution task is performed in an implicit way. People who are good at the task are also verbally aware of the basis on which they are responding. A recent study (Berry and Broadbent, in press) therefore looked at whether detailed verbal instruction has any effect on performance on the river pollution task. The instructions described the optimal way to carry out the task. The results showed that the verbal instruction had no significant effect on task performance, although it did lead to significantly higher post-task questionnaire scores. In contrast to the 1984 study, performance was positively correlated with question answering. A second experiment showed that subjects who were required to verbalize concurrently throughout the subsequent trials performed significantly better than those who received the instruction alone. Verbalization without prior instruction again had no significant effect on task performance or question answering.

It should be noted that the benefit of the instruction-verbalization combination was immediate. It was apparent on the initial trial and there was no further improvement across trials. It was not the case, however, that subjects simply learned four optimal pollutants and then tested for these on subsequent trials. Inspection of their performance protocols showed that no subjects tested for the same sequence of pollutants on all four trials. In fact, only a very small number of subjects even tested for the same initial pollutants on each trial.

To look further at the question of what is learned as a result of the instruction–verbalization combination, a third experiment presented subjects with a subsequent transfer task. Following the preliminary verbal instruction they were given two trials with the river pollution task during which they verbalized concurrently. They then carried out two trials with an isomorphic, but seemingly different, Estate Agent task. In this task subjects had to find the one property that matched a client's requirements by asking the computer whether or not the various features were required by the client. The results showed that subjects were able to transfer a successful working strategy to the superficially different Estate Agent task. The experience of the instruction–verbalization combination did not lead to a restricted form of learning that was solely in terms of selecting pollutants to eliminate the greatest number of factories. The process of verbalization did more than convert the knowledge into simple procedures that could be run off at the appropriate time.

Again, therefore, the disparity between the effects of verbal instruction on performance and question answering shows that it is not sufficient simply to have knowledge in some lasting declarative store. It must also be temporarily activated at the moment it is needed in the task. The processes that do this can only be built up by a history of episodes in which the relevant long-term knowledge has been activated at the correct instant. That is, the way to select a test must be explained or recalled at the moment of selecting tests, not at some other time. The benefit of concurrent verbalization here is that it brings into temporary memory at the same time the various critical factors in the decision. Once a certain level of performance has been reached, however, it is not necessary for people to keep verbalizing. Their knowledge is in such a form that they not only maintain a high performance level when they stop verbalizing, but they are also able to transfer the general principles to a related, but seemingly different, task.

It should be noted that verbalization without prior instruction or explanation had no effect on performance or question answering in any of these studies. It was not the case that these subjects failed to comply with the verbalization requirement, but rather that the content of their verbalizations was different. Although all subjects were asked to give reasons for decisions, those in the 'verbalization alone' conditions tended not to do this. Instead, they would talk at a more superficial level, often merely describing computer inputs and outputs. In contrast, subjects who had received the preliminary instruction or explanation tended to refer to this in their verbalizations.

It is clear that concurrent verbalization is not uniform in its effects and should therefore not be thought of as a single treatment. The effects of verbalization are likely to depend on such things as the nature of the task, the precise instructions given to subjects, and whether or not relevant verbal information is available on which the verbalizations can be based. It is likely that in other studies that have reported positive effects of verbalization (such as those of Gagne and Smith and Bower and King) that the key information was more readily available for verbalization. The verbalization requirement therefore again acted as some form of maintenance device, maintaining attention on the critical features of the task.

IMPLICIT AND EXPLICIT THINKING

As well as distinguishing between implicit and explicit knowledge, Berry and Broadbent (1988) also distinguished between implicit and explicit modes of learning. The two distinctions are related, although clearly not identical. As far as different modes of learning are concerned, Berry and Broadbent point out that in complex learning situations a learner has to acquire knowledge about the relationships between a number of variables, without necessarily knowing in advance what the key variables are. They suggest that there are two ways in which such learning can take place. First, a person encountering a complex task may observe the variables unselectively and attempt to store all of the contingencies between them. The correct factors as well as the incorrect ones will be stored and, ultimately after much experience, the person will retain a large number of condition–action links that will secure effective performance. It may well be hard to report so many links, however, or have confidence in any one of them. Use of this unselective or implicit mode is therefore unlikely to be associated with accurate verbalizable knowledge. It will also be relatively slow.

An alternative mode of learning is a selective or explicit one in which a few variables are selected and only the contingencies between these key variables are observed. Provided that the correct variables are selected this will be a fast and effective method of learning. It is also likely to result in a form of knowledge that can be made explicit because of the relatively small number of relationships involved. There are disadvantages associated with the selective mode, however. If the task involves many irrelevant variables and the wrong variables are selected for examination, this mode of learning will do badly compared with the unselective mode. Experiments have shown that inducing subjects to adopt an explicit mode of learning while performing tasks that would normally be carried out in an implicit way has a significant detrimental effect on performance.

The results from the verbalization studies can be incorporated into this framework by assuming that, irrespective of the nature of the task, complex instructions are not effective unless they are available and temporarily activated at the moment they are needed in the task. Concurrent verbalization serves this function. Verbalization is beneficial because it helps to bring into temporary memory the various different factors involved. If the nature of the task is such that it would normally be carried out in an implicit way, then the instruction–verbalization combination will inevitably induce a more explicit mode of learning.

Verbalization by itself will not necessarily affect an individual's mode of learning. As stated above, people can comply with a verbalization requirement without significantly altering the way in which they carry out a task. There are instances, however, when verbal reporting techniques can induce a more explicit mode of learning, with detrimental results. Berry (1984) found that completion of a written post-task questionnaire had a significant detrimental effect on subsequent control performance, if the tasks in question were normally performed in an implicit way. A detrimental effect was not found for tasks that are normally performed explicitly. It was suggested that the questionnaire induced subjects to adopt a more explicit hypothesis testing mode of learning that was not appropriate for the former type of task. It is therefore necessary to be especially cautious when asking people to produce verbal reports for tasks that would normally be performed in an implicit way.

CONCLUSIONS

This chapter has examined how verbalization techniques have been used in both experimental and applied psychology. As well as considering the validity of verbal reports, it has looked at the question of whether verbalization actually biases cognitive processing. Rather than viewing such biasing as a problem, however, it has been suggested that in some situations verbalization can actually play a crucial role in learning. Experiments have been reported which demonstrate that performance on complex control or search tasks is not affected by the presentation of detailed instructions or explanation, unless people are required to give reasons for decisions while performing the task. It is suggested that the benefit of verbalization in this situation is that it brings into memory at the same time the various critical factors in the decision.

REFERENCES

Ahlum-Heath, M. E., & Di-Vesta, F. J. (1986). The effect of conscious controlled verbalization of a cognitive strategy on transfer in problem solving. *Memory and Cognition,* **14**, 281–285.

Bainbridge, L. (1979). Verbal reports as evidence of the process operator's knowledge. *International Journal of Man–Machine Studies,* **11**, 411–436.

Berry, D. C. (1983). Metacognitive experience and transfer of logical reasoning. *Quarterly Journal of Experimental Psychology,* **35A**, 39–49.

Berry, D. C. (1984). Implicit and explicit knowledge in the control of complex systems. Unpublished D.Phil thesis, University of Oxford.

Berry, D. C. & Broadbent, D. E. (1984). On the relationship between task performance and explicit verbalizable knowledge. *Quarterly Journal of Experimental Psychology,* **36A,** 209–231.

Berry, D. C., & Broadbent, D. E. (1986). Human search procedures and the use of expert systems. *Current Psychological Research and Reviews,* **5,** 130–147.

Berry, D. C. & Broadbent, D. E. (1987a). The combination of explicit and implicit learning processes in task control. *Psychological Research,* **49,** 7–15.

Berry, D. C., & Broadbent, D. E. (1987b). Explanation and verbalization in a computer assisted search task. *Quarterly Journal of Experimental Psychology,* **39A,** 585–609.

Berry, D. C., & Broadbent, D. E. (1988). Interactive tasks and the implicit–explicit distinction. *British Journal of Psychology,* **79,** 251–272.

Berry, D. C., & Broadbent, D. E. (in press). The role of instruction and verbalization in improving performance on complex search tasks.

Bower, A. C., & King, W. L. (1967). The effect of number of irrelevant stimulus dimensions, verbalization and sex on learning biconditional classification rules. *Psychonomic Science,* **8,** 453–454.

Broadbent, D. E., Fitzgerald, P., & Broadbent, M. H. P. (1986). Implicit and explicit knowledge in the control of complex systems. *British Journal of Psychology,* **77,** 33–50.

Burton, A. M., Shadbolt, N. R., Hedgecock, A. P., & Rugg, G. (1987). *A formal evaluation of knowledge elicitation techniques for expert systems.* Report on Alvey project IKBS 134, July 1987.

Byrne, R. (1983). Protocol analysis in problem solving. In J. St. B. T. Evans (ed.), *Thinking and reasoning: psychological approaches.* London: Routledge and Kegan Paul.

Ericsson, K. A., & Simon, H. A. (1980). Verbal reports as data. *Psychological Review,* **87,** 215–251.

Ericsson, K. A., & Simon, H. A. (1984). *Protocol analysis.* Cambridge, MA: MIT Press.

Evans, J. St. B. T. (1982). *The psychology of deductive reasoning.* London: Routledge and Kegan Paul.

Fox, J., Myers, C., Greaves, M., & Pegram, S. (1985). Knowledge acquisition for expert systems: experience in leukaemia diagnosis. *Methods of Information in Medicine,* March, 1–8.

Gagne, R., & Smith, E. (1962). A study of the effects of verbalization on problem solving. *Journal of Experimental Psychology,* **63,** 12–18.

Gammack, J., & Young, R. (1985). Psychological techniques for eliciting expert knowledge. In M. Bramer (ed.), *Research and development in expert systems.* Cambridge: Cambridge University Press.

Kellogg, R. T. (1982). When can we introspect accurately about mental processes. *Memory and Cognition,* **10,** 141–144.

Nisbett, R. E., & Wilson, T. D. (1977). Telling more than we can know: verbal reports on mental processes. *Psychological Review,* **84,** 231–279.

Smith, E. R. & Miller, F. D. (1978). Limits on perception of cognitive processes: a reply to Nisbett and Wilson. *Psychological Review,* **85,** 355–362.

White, P. A. (1980). Limitations on verbal report of internal events: a refutation of Nisbett and Wilson and of Bem. *Psychological Review,* **87,** 105–112.

7

Working Memory and Modes of Thinking: A Secondary Task Approach

ROBERT H. LOGIE

ALICE F. S. SALWAY
University of Aberdeen

INTRODUCTION AND REVIEW

There is widespread interest in human use of complex equipment, such as computer-based systems, and a continuing need for understanding human capacity for strategy development, reasoning, and problem solving. For any given task, differing demands are imposed on an individual by learning, by task performance once expertise is attained, and by problem solving, whether problems arise from errors or as a normal task requirement.

One approach to an understanding of human thinking in this domain is to consider the notion of mental load. It conveys the idea that some limited mental resource is employed in the performance of a task, but without the means to specify the nature of that resource or the way in which it interacts with task difficulty.

Resource Theory

A simple view might characterize mental resource as a single, yet flexible, facility of limited capacity (see, for example, Broadbent, 1958; Norman, 1968). As demands on the mental resource exceed the predetermined limit, so the performance of the individual on the task will tend to deteriorate. However, there are numerous examples of effective simultaneous performance of multiple tasks, some of which are quite complex (for example, walking and talking). The single-resource view might suggest that dual-task performance is made possible by time-sharing the tasks, and that the performance of each task will be

Lines of Thinking, Volume 2 Edited by K.J. Gilhooly, M.T.G. Keane, R.H. Logie and G. Erdos
© 1990 John Wiley & Sons Ltd

unimpaired as long as the resources required of the combined tasks do not exceed the total resources available. However, this is not sufficient since the nature of the tasks is crucial. It is possible to drive a car while talking to others, but extremely difficult to read while holding a conversation.

More recently, there has been a rather more sophisticated approach that involves the concept of multiple resources (Navon, 1987; Wickens, 1984). The argument here is that there are several specialized resources on which an operator may draw, with assignment of a particular resource determined by the nature of the task. Thus the concurrent performance of two dissimilar tasks is facilitated, since each will require a different resource. Similar tasks will require similar resources, thereby leading to inefficient performance when such tasks are concurrent. Navon and Gopher (1979) suggest there may be also a processing overhead or a 'cost of concurrence'; that is, when two tasks are performed together, the overall load may be greater than the sum of the loads imposed by each task performed singly. Several authors have suggested that this extra demand may reflect the operation of an 'executive time-sharer' (see, for example, Hunt and Lansman, 1982; McLeod, 1977). However, attempts to specify the nature of this 'executive' have been somewhat unsuccessful (Logan and Cowan, 1984). Logan (1985) has pointed out that there is a problem in attempting to identify the executive resource, and to separate its effects from those of its subordinates.

Task Difficulty

A further issue is how task difficulty might be measured independently of task performance. Asking an operator to provide a subjective assessment results in problems of subjective scaling and response biases (Moray, 1982). A requirement to assess task difficulty may change the nature of the task or how it is performed (Nisbett and Wilson, 1977). Finally, subjective ratings of difficulty when tasks are performed singly appear to be poor predictors of mutual interference when two tasks are performed together (Logie et al., 1989).

The problems in assessing mental workload are compounded in situations which reflect more closely tasks encountered outside the laboratory; for example, in complex thinking and problem solving in certain occupations. Tasks are not clearly specified and performance often comprises several components: development of strategies, reasoning and problem solving, memory load and the control of actions.

Working Memory

Resource theory has its roots in theories of selective attention. A parallel development has occurred in the study of working memory. Working memory refers to the temporary storage and manipulation of information, with implications for a wide range of everyday tasks as well as laboratory studies of short-term storage (Baddeley and Hitch, 1974). Working memory is thought to comprise a central executive that is responsible for reasoning, decision making and coordinating the activities of two subordinate systems: the articulatory loop, thought to be a speech-based system to provide temporary storage of verbal material, and the visuo-spatial sketch pad, thought to provide temporary storage for visual and/or spatial material and to be involved in active visualization.

Evidence for the role of the central executive is scant, although there is some evidence for it being involved in coordinating dual-task activity (Baddeley *et al.*, 1986). However, its hypothesized characteristics bear a striking resemblance to the 'executive' that has proved equally elusive in the literature on selective attention and multiple resources.

Working Memory Methodology

Dual-task methodology is applied widely in the working memory literature, as in resource theory. However, working memory provides a functional model for the organization of the resources involved, and this model is based on several different paradigms. For example, immediate, verbal, serial recall is characterized by a difficulty in recall of items that are phonologically similar (Conrad, 1964) and more difficulty in recall of longer words (Baddeley, Thomson and Buchanan, 1975). In addition, there are a number of interactions between these effects and articulatory suppression (concurrent articulation of an irrelevant word), (Baddeley, Lewis and Vallar, 1984). The strength of this approach is that the resulting model of the 'articulatory loop' is based on converging evidence from a number of different paradigms. A similar approach has been taken in the investigation of the visuo-spatial sketch pad (Logie and Baddeley, 1989).

The concept of working memory has been fruitful in providing an understanding of temporary storage of information as it is required in laboratory memory tasks, and in a number of everyday tasks such as reading (Baddeley and Lewis, 1980; Daneman and Carpenter, 1980) and counting (Hitch, 1978; Logie and Baddeley, 1987). A recent development has been to explore the role of working memory in tasks involving temporary storage of complex information or information from several sources as might be required in studies of mental workload.

Working Memory and Mental Load

Logie *et al.* (1989) have used dual-task methodology to study the role of working memory in learning and performing a complex computer game known as Space Fortress (Mane and Donchin, 1989). Unlike previous studies of working memory, the main task involved strategy development and deployment as well as perceptual-motor control, and verbal and visual short-term storage. The main task was performed with a range of secondary tasks, and the degree and the nature of the mutual impairment in performance was assessed. The secondary tasks were chosen on the basis of the existing literature such that their memory and processing demands were relatively well known. For example, one secondary task, articulatory suppression, is known to make heavy demands on the articulatory loop, and minimal demands on other components of working memory. The extent to which concurrent articulation of an irrelevant word interferes with or is impaired by performance on Space Fortress gives an indication of the involvement of the articulatory loop in primary task performance.

A range of secondary tasks were involved, and subjects were tested on both single and on dual-task performance at three different levels of expertise on the Space Fortress task. Highly trained game performance was affected when subjects were required to generate concurrent, paced responses such as articulatory suppression or regular foot tapping, and by concurrent general working-memory loads (Daneman and Carpenter, 1980), but not when they were required to produce a vocal or a tapping response to a secondary stimulus. There appeared to be no distinction between the impairment resulting from a secondary visuo-spatial memory load (remembering locations on a map) or from a verbal memory load (remembering the location of words in a poem). In contrast, novice performance on Space Fortress was largely unaffected by concurrent, paced responses. As with expert performance, a concurrent visuo-spatial or verbal memory load resulted in an impairment of primary task performance. However, unlike expert performance, novice performance was affected more by a concurrent visuo-spatial load than by a verbal load.

The differential effects of visuo-spatial and verbal loads were interpreted by suggesting that visuo-spatial resources were required by novices to master the perceptual-motor aspects of the game, which became automated and relied less on specialized visuo-spatial resources with increasing expertise.

A more detailed analysis was also feasible in that a large number of parameters of Space Fortress performance were recorded. These could be classified broadly as involving a verbal memory load, a strategic load, a visual-perceptual load, and control of response output. It was possible to examine the effect of different secondary tasks on different game components, rather than on overall game performance. Results suggested that the nature of the secondary task was important in determining which game components would be disrupted.

The role of the central executive in expert Space Fortress performance received support in a study by Fabiani et al. (1988). In this study a further secondary task was introduced, involving random generation of single letters from the alphabet. Baddeley (1966, 1986) argues that it requires execution of strategies, as should reflect the operation of a central executive, although its characteristics as a secondary task are relatively unexplored. The general pattern of secondary-task disruption was broadly similar to that found in the earlier studies. However, random generation produced by far the greatest impairment in subjects with a moderate amount of training on Space Fortress, in comparison with the effects of the other secondary tasks. At the time of writing, a more detailed analysis is in progress.

From these studies it appears that the pattern of dual-task performance can be used to interpret, within a coherent theoretical framework, the nature and relative importance of each of a number of specialized resources required in a primary task.

Dual Tasks and Mental Rotation

Our current research is geared towards further development of this approach. The study of Space Fortress is continuing to be fruitful. However, by its very nature a number of different mental resources are required in its execution. It appears that all three components of working memory are involved to a greater or lesser extent at different stages of training. Where we have a primary task that is likely to place heavy demands on fewer mental resources, we ought to be able to predict which of a number of particular secondary tasks would interfere. Thus we have chosen to study performance of a task that has been reported previously in the literature, and which may rely more heavily on the visuo-spatial and central executive components; namely, the Cooper and Podgorny (1976), mental transformations and visual comparisons task.

In this task the subjects were required to discriminate between a standard shape and a set of probe shapes which varied in similarity to the standard. The task has two stages, each requiring a response from the subject: preparation for the presentation of the probe (which Cooper and Podgorny suggest involves mental rotation), and the discrimination of the probe from an internal representation of the standard.

It seemed likely that the relative involvement of the working memory components would differ across the two stages of the task, which in turn may differ qualitatively in their processing requirements (Cooper, 1982). The various levels of orientation, and of similarity of the probes to the standard, may also show differential involvements of working memory components. At a general level, we would expect that secondary tasks involving visuo-spatial resources and those involving 'central executive' type resources would interfere with such a task, but that there would be little interference from secondary tasks involving the articulatory loop or repeated generation of a response.

A second, but equally important purpose of the study was to highlight aspects of this dual-task approach which require further development.

THE METHOD

Primary Task

The standard stimulus was an eight-point, random, angular shape (Cooper, 1975). Four probes were chosen from the set developed by Cooper and Podgorny (1976) (see Figure 7.1). Probe one was the standard shape. Probes two and three differed in similarity to the standard. Probe four was a reflection of the standard shape. The probes were presented in four rotations: $0°$, $45°$, $180°$ and $270°$ clockwise from the standard's orientation.

The stimuli were presented on a monochrome monitor approximately one metre from the seated subjects. Each stimulus filled an area approximately 5×3 cm. An Apple IIe microcomputer was used to present the stimuli and record the subjects' responses.

The standard was displayed for 3000 ms, followed in the same location by an orientation cue, in the form of an arrow. The arrow was oriented at $0°$, $45°$, $180°$

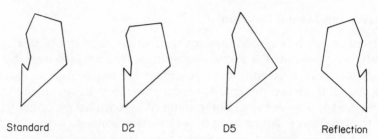

| Standard | D2 | D5 | Reflection |

FIGURE 7.1 Probe stimuli, shown in the standard (zero degrees) orientation.

or 270° from the orientation of the standard and remained on the screen until the subjects indicated that they had completed their 'preparation' for the probe by pressing a button with the non-preferred hand. Next the probe was presented in the orientation cued by the arrow, and remained on the display until the discriminative response was made, by pressing a button for 'same as standard' or 'different from standard'. After a blank screen of approximately 1000 ms this schedule was repeated for 24 trials. Same and different probes appeared equally often in a random sequence.

Secondary Tasks

For each secondary task, subjects were to generate secondary task responses at a rate of two per second. This speed was demonstrated using a metronome before each trial, but with no external pacing when the task was performed. In each case inter-response intervals were recorded and, where appropriate, responses were tape-recorded.

We investigated the possible role of the central executive with random generation. Subjects were required to generate a random series of digits, by saying aloud numbers between 0 and 9. The possible involvement of the articulatory loop was investigated by using articulatory suppression. This involved continuous spoken repetition of the word 'go'. This task was also used to gauge whether the effects of random generation could be attributed to the requirement to produce repeated vocal output.

The role of the visuo-spatial sketch pad was studied with a technique known as spatial suppression, where the subjects sequentially tapped four square metal plates with a stylus (Farmer, Berman and Fletcher, 1986). Repeated tapping with the stylus of the same plate constituted a secondary task to investigate the effects of response production at a preset rate. This task could be used to gauge whether any disruptive effects of the spatial suppression secondary task could be attributed to a requirement to generate a repeated motor response.

Procedure

Subjects (10 male and 14 female, aged 18 to 25 years) were run individually for three one-hour sessions on three consecutive days. Presentation order of the secondary tasks was counterbalanced across four subject groups. The first session involved two part tasks, the 'rotate task' and the 'compare task'. In the rotate task subjects were asked to remember each presentation of the standard shape, and to rotate it until it was imagined in the orientation indicated by the arrow cue, at which point they pressed a response key. The shape was then shown in the correctly rotated position. In the compare task, the presentation of the standard shape was followed in the same orientation by one of the probe set. The subject responded as to whether the second shape differed from the first. Next the full primary task was performed twice, for practice.

Sessions two and three shared similar procedures, except that for any given subject, the secondary tasks differed between sessions. The rotate task was performed, followed by primary task alone, secondary task alone (3 minutes), dual-task, three-minute rest, further secondary tasks alone (3 minutes), dual-task and primary task alone.

The levels of performance under dual-task conditions must be considered in relation to a baseline of optimal performance on the separate tasks performed alone. Since two experimental sessions were involved, practice effects are likely to occur. Therefore we decided to measure single-task performance at the start and end of each session, and to produce average control values for each subject, for each session. Control performance was measured on each secondary task performed alone, prior to its combination with the primary task. Thus each subject was used as their own control. The main measure of dual-task disruption of the primary task was in the form of the percentage difference in performance between the primary task performed alone and the primary task performed with one of the secondary tasks. This has the effect of removing variance due to differences in the overall performance of individual subjects.

Results

The median preparation times for each angle of orientation cue, and each probe type, were obtained from each subject's primary-task data. Medians were used since outliers were fairly common. Percentage differences from control values were then calculated for the dual-task performances, where control was the mean of the medians of the two single-task performance conditions in the relevant experimental session.

Primary Task Data

The 'preparation time' control data were subjected to a three-way mixed ANOVA, with factors of 'group', 'session' and 'angle'. There was a significant main effect of session ($F(1,20) = 58.15$, $p < 0.01$), but no effect of angle or group (see Figure 7.2a). The percentage difference data were subjected to a similar analysis, with factors of 'group', 'secondary task' and 'angle' (Figure 7.2b). The effect of secondary task was highly significant ($F(3,60) = 26.9$, $p < 0.01$) and interacted with group ($F(9,60) = 2.71$, $p < 0.05$). *Post hoc* comparisons with the Newman–Keuls test suggested that the articulatory suppression and tapping conditions were not different from control or from each other, but all other differences between pairs were significant at $p = 0.05$. The angle factor was also

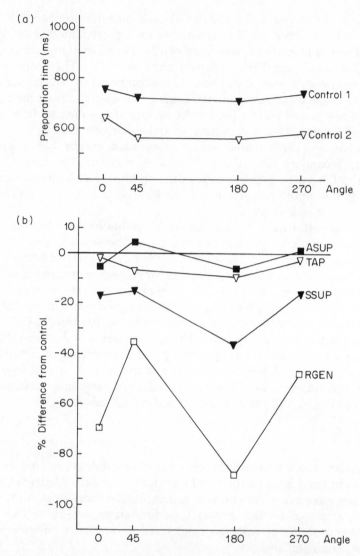

FIGURE 7.2   Preparation times, by angle of cue. (a) Control primary task performance by session—median preparation times averaged over subjects. (b) Dual-task performance by task—percentage difference from control preparation times, averaged over subjects.

significant ($F(3,60) = 4.48$, $p < 0.01$), with two significant comparisons ($45°$ versus $180°$ and $270°$ versus $180°$).

The 'discriminative reaction time' control data by probe type were subjected to a three-way mixed ANOVA, with factors of 'group', 'session' and 'probe type' (see Figure 7.3a). There were significant main effects of session ($F(1,20) = 4.62$, $p < 0.05$), and of probe type ($F(3,60) = 3.96$, $p < 0.05$). *Post hoc* comparisons suggested that the reflected probe did not differ from the D2 probe, and that the standard did not differ from the D5 probe, but that all other comparisons were significant at $p = 0.05$.

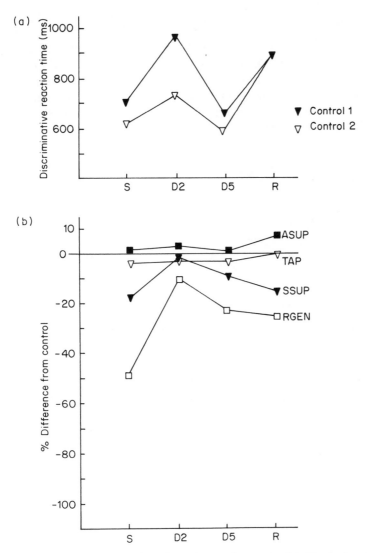

FIGURE 7.3 Discriminative reaction time, by probe type. (a) Control primary task performance by session—median reaction times averaged over subjects. (b) Dual-task performance by task—percentage difference from control reaction times, averaged over subjects.

A similar analysis was carried out with 'group', 'secondary task' and 'probe type' as the factors (Figure 7.3b). A significant main effect of secondary task was found ($F(3,60) = 20.7$, $p < 0.01$), and this interacted with group ($F(9,60) = 3.60$, $p < 0.05$), although there was no main effect of group. There was also a significant main effect of probe type ($F(3,60) = 2.76$, $p < 0.05$), and this factor interacted with secondary task ($F(9,180) = 2.09$, $p < 0.05$).

One-way ANOVA tests were carried out across all levels of these two interacting factors, to test for simple main effects. For probe type the following effects were significant: standard ($F(3,69) = 15.64$, $p < 0.01$), D5 ($F(3,69) = 10.23$, $p < 0.01$) and reflection ($F(3,69) = 5.97$, $p < 0.01$).

In the tests for simple main effects of the secondary tasks, two were significant: spatial suppression ($F(3,69) = 3.06$, $p < 0.05$) and random generation ($F(3,69) = 3.27$, $p < 0.05$). Where significant simple main effects were found, Newman–Keuls tests were performed to examine the comparisons among means. With the standard and the D5 probes, the comparison for spatial suppression and articulatory suppression was significant, as was the com-

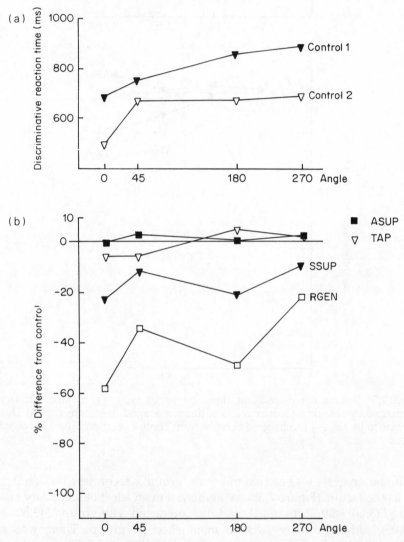

FIGURE 7.4 Discriminative reaction time, by angle of probe. (a) Control primary task performance by session—median reaction times averaged over subjects. (b) Dual-task performance by task—percentage difference from control reaction times, averaged over subjects.

parison of random generation and spatial suppression. The spatial suppression and articulatory suppression comparison was significant across the reflected probe. The comparison between the effects of random generation and of spatial suppression was significant for the standard probe and for the D2 probe.

An ANOVA test was performed on the control data, for discriminative reaction time by probe angle, with factors of 'group', 'session' and 'angle' (see Figure 7.4a). There were no significant interactions. There were significant main effects of session ($F(1,20) = 22.43$, $p < 0.01$) and of angle ($F(3,60) = 7.9$, $p < 0.01$). Pairwise comparisons suggested that the $270°$ data did not differ from those for $180°$, but all other comparisons were significant.

The main effect of 'secondary task' was significant ($F(3,60) = 23.5$, $p < 0.01$). *Post hoc* comparisons found that the articulatory suppression and tapping conditions did not produce significant disruption, but all other differences between pairs of means were significant. The effect of angle was also significant ($F(3,60) = 2.90$, $p < 0.05$). A Newman–Keuls test showed the only significant comparison to be between $270°$ and $0°$.

There was no effect of secondary task on the number of errors made in the discriminative response.

Secondary-Task Data

The difference from control for subjects' mean inter-response intervals was tested using a *t*-test for each secondary task. The characteristics of the data indicated that means were appropriate. The results are shown in Table 7.1. To be consistent with the reporting of data for the primary task, a negative sign in the table indicates an *increase* from control values.

Articulatory suppression and spatial suppression were not significantly different from control levels. Tapping and random generation responses were significantly faster under dual-task conditions ($t = 2.66$, $p < 0.05$ and $t = 2.07$, $p < 0.05$ respectively).

Table 7.1 Secondary task inter-response interval data: Single-task (control) means and variances (ms) averaged over all subjects, with changes in performance under dual-task conditions (percentage difference from control) shown in brackets

Secondary task	Means	Variances
Articulatory suppression	577(+1.9)	7565(−8.2)
Tapping	500(+4.4)[a]	1359(−885.7)[a]
Spatial suppression	508(−0.3)	9709(−182.0)[a]
Random generation	677(+5.0)	161892(+2.7)

[a] *t*-test (2-tailed) significant at $p = 0.05$.

The difference from control for variances in the inter-response intervals was tested for each secondary task, using t-tests. The results are shown in the table. Articulatory suppression and random generation were not significantly different from control. Tapping was significantly more variable under dual task conditions ($t = 2.19$, $p < 0.05$), as was spatial suppression ($t = 2.77$, $p < 0.05$).

The redundancy of the sequences produced in the random generation conditions was examined. Four indices of randomness were calculated using the first 100 responses from each sequence: H_1 for single digits, H_1 for digrams (or digit pairs), H_2 (Attneave, 1959), and the RNG index (Evans, 1978). The possible increase in redundancy between single- and dual-task conditions was tested using t-tests on these indices. The only index to show a significant difference was H_1 for diagrams, $t = 1.70$, $p < 0.05$.

The significant decrease in H_1 for digrams indicates that the production of pairs of digits becomes less random in the dual-task condition. That is, the redundancy has increased in dual-task conditions where we consider generation of two consecutive digits.

DISCUSSION

The main aim of this study was to investigate the general usefulness of dual-task methodology within the context of working memory. We chose to study a task which arguably might involve both the central executive and the visual-spatial components of working memory. It is clear that the control data shown in Figure 7.2 do not show the linear increase in preparation time that would be expected if the subjects were 'mentally rotating' their image of the standard shape during this period. The control data on discriminative response time in Figures 7.3 and 7.4 show a pattern that is rather closer to that reported by Cooper and Podgorny (1976): when the response times are broken down by type of probe, the times are very similar. When the response times were considered by angle, there was a tendency for an increase in response time as the probe orientation increased in a clockwise direction from the vertical, suggesting some form of mental rotation during the discrimination phase. Whatever subjects were doing in the preparation part of the experiment, they appear to have produced the same pattern, and order of magnitude of discriminative responses, as did Cooper and Podgorny's subjects.

Differences in the procedures used by Cooper and Podgorny and by ourselves might account for the lack of an effect of angle on preparation time. For example, only one standard shape was used in our study, in contrast to the five used in the original study. It is also difficult to specify the criteria used by subjects to assess whether or not they were 'prepared'.

The major thrust of the study was whether a dual-task approach could provide an account of the underlying cognitive processing that is involved in performance under these conditions. Whatever the processes of the subjects' interactions with the primary task, the dual task techniques should allow us to examine which components of working memory were involved in task performance.

The control data show that faster response times were obtained in the final experimental sessions, and this was attributed to practice effects. The study highlighted the importance of allowing for learning during the course of the study (Braune and Wickens, 1986; Logie *et al.*, 1989). Therefore the improvement in control times over the course of the experiment vindicated the use of control performance from the same experimental session as the dual task performance being considered.

The preparation time and discrimination time data suggest that the different secondary tasks had a differential effect on performance. Neither articulatory suppression nor tapping had a disruptive effect, while the effects of spatial suppression and of random generation differed from each other, and from baseline. It is well established that articulatory suppression has a reliable disruptive effect on verbal short-term memory (see, for example, Baddeley, Lewis and Vallar, 1984). Therefore the lack of an effect of articulatory suppression suggests that subjects did not rely on verbal short-term memory in either stage of the primary task. There is evidence that repeated tapping disrupts the production of fast, highly controlled motor responses (Logie *et al.*, 1989). The lack of such a disruption suggests that the motor output control required to make a secondary response was not an important component of the primary task.

The disruption in performance attributable to spatial suppression indicates that this task shares mental resources with performance of the main task. The lack of an effect by concurrent tapping further suggests that any effect of spatial suppression is not simply due to generating a repeated motor response. The working-memory dual-task literature has demonstrated that performance disruptions by a concurrent spatial task are indicative of the shared need for specialized visuo-spatial functions of short-term memory (Baddeley and Lieberman, 1980; Farmer, Berman and Fletcher, 1986). This finding is consistent with the involvement of such a visuo-spatial function in both phases of the task, despite the apparent lack of evidence for mental rotation in the 'preparation' phase.

A much larger disruption of the primary task was produced by random generation. The theoretical implications of this are unclear, since the relationship is uncertain between the random generation task and the functioning of the central executive. For example, it is surprising that the random generation task itself was not more disrupted under dual-task conditions. It could be argued that the large effect on the primary task was due to more emphasis being given to the secondary task (Pew, 1979), resulting in very little decrement in random generation. This allocation bias may act as a confounding factor which elevates the performance decrements on the primary task, and could also lead to false conclusions being drawn from the patterns of disruption. Possibly tasks which purport to involve central-executive processing would have the potential for directing attention in this way. Alternatively the indices of random generation performance may not be sufficiently sensitive to assess performance under these conditions.

The patterns of disruption shown across the probe types for the different secondary tasks (Figure 7.3) suggest that spatial suppression and random generation seem to result in similar functions. This might indicate that the two secondary tasks involve similar resources, to different degrees. There is reasonable support in the literature for the specific effects of spatial suppression. This is not true of random generation, and its use as a secondary task is clearly not straightforward. It is clearly an area for further development.

CONCLUSIONS

Our initial intention was to explore further the use of dual tasks within the context of working memory, in the investigation of tasks that are likely to require several working-memory components for successful performance. Our initial studies using Space Fortress suggested that this approach was likely to be fruitful, but that it required considerable development before it might be generally applied. The study of a 'mental rotation' task provided some support for the use of this technique in investigating whether tasks appear to require specifically visuo-spatial or verbal resources. In this sense the results are relatively clear. However, the study was particularly useful in highlighting areas of this work, such as characterizing the secondary tasks, which require careful development.

REFERENCES

Attneave, F. (1959). *Applications of information theory to psychology*. New York: Holt.

Baddeley, A. D. (1966). The capacity for generating information by randomization. *Quarterly Journal of Experimental Psychology*, **18**, 119–129.

Baddeley, A. D. (1986). *Working memory*. London: Oxford University Press.

Baddeley, A. D., & Hitch, G. (1974). Working memory. In G. H. Bower (ed.), *The psychology of learning and motivation*, Vol. 8 (pp. 47–90).

Baddeley, A. D., & Lieberman, K. (1980). Spatial working memory. In R. Nickerson (ed.), *Attention and performance*, Vol. 8. Hillsdale, NJ: Erlbaum.

Baddeley, A. D., & Lewis, V. J. (1980). Inner active processes in reading: the inner voice, the inner ear and the inner eye. In A. M. Lesgold & C. A. Perfetti (eds.), *Interactive processes in reading* (pp. 107–129). Hillsdale, NJ: Erlbaum.

Baddeley, A. D., Lewis, V. J., & Vallar, G. (1984). Exploring the articulatory loop., *Quarterly Journal of Experimental Psychology*, **36**, 233–252.

Baddeley, A. D., Logie, R. H., Bressi, S., Della, Sala, S., & Spinnler, H. (1986). Dementia and working memory. *Quarterly Journal of Experimental Psychology*, **38A**, 603–618.

Baddeley, A. D., Thomson, N., & Buchanan, M. (1975). Word length and the structure of short-term memory. *Journal of Verbal Learning and Verbal Behavior*, **14**, 575–589.

Braune, R., & Wickens, C. (1986). Time sharing revisited: test of a componential method for the assessment of individual differences. *Ergonomics*, **29**, 1399–1414.

Broadbent, D. E. (1958). *Perception and communication*. London: Pergamon Press.

Conrad, R. (1964). Acoustic confusions in immediate memory. *British Journal of Psychology*, **55**, 75–84.

Cooper, L. A. (1975). Mental rotation of random two-dimensional shapes. *Cognitive Psychology*, **7**, 20–43.

Cooper, L. A. (1982). Strategies for visual comparison and representation: individual differences. In R. J. Sternberg (ed.), *Advances in the psychology of human intelligence*, Vol. 1 (pp. 77–124). Hillsdale, NJ: Erlbaum.

Cooper, L. A., & Podgorny, P. (1976). Mental transformations and visual comparison processes: effects of complexity and similarity. *Journal of Experimental Psychology: Human Perception and Performance*, **2**, 503–514.

Daneman, M., & Carpenter, P. A. (1980). Individual differences in working memory and reading. *Journal of Verbal Learning and Verbal Behavior*, **19**, 450–466.

Evans, F. J. (1978). Monitoring attention deployment by random number generation: an index to measure subjective randomness. *Bulletin of the Psychonomic Society*, **12**, 35–38.

Fabiani, M., Buckley, J., Gratton, G., Coles, M., Donchin, E., & Logie, R. (1988). *The training of complex task performance*. Technical report CPL 88-1, University of Illinois.

Farmer, E. W., Berman, V. F., & Fletcher, Y. L. (1986). Evidence for a visuo-spatial scratch pad in working memory. *Quarterly Journal of Experimental Psychology*, **38A**, 675–688.

Hitch, G. J. (1978). The role of short-term working memory in mental arithmetic. *Cognitive Psychology*, **10**, 302–323.

Hunt, E., & Lansman, M. (1982). Individual differences in attention. In R. J. Sternberg (ed.), *Advances in the psychology of human intelligence, Vol. 1*. Hillsdale, NJ: Erlbaum.

Logan, G. D. (1985). Skill and automaticity: relations, implications and future directions. *Canadian Journal of Psychology*, **39**, 367–386.

Logan, G. D., & Cowan, W. B. (1984). On the ability to inhibit thought and action: a theory of an act of control. *Psychological Review*, **91**, 295–327.

Logie, R. H., & Baddeley, A. D. (1987). Cognitive processes in counting. *Journal of Experimental Psychology: Learning, Memory, and Cognition*, **13**, 310–326.

Logie, R. H., & Baddeley, A. D. (1990). Imagery and working memory. In P. Hampson, D. Marks & J. Richardson (eds.), *Imagery: Current developments*. London: Routledge and Kegan Paul.

Logie, R. H., Baddeley, A. D., Mane, A., Donchin, E., & Sheptak, R. (1989). Working memory and the analysis of a complex skill by secondary task methodology. *Acta Psychologica*, **71**, 53–88.

McLeod, P. (1977). A dual task response modality effect: support for multi-processor models of attention. *Quarterly Journal of Experimental Psychology*, **29**, 651–667.

Mane, A., & Donchin, E. (1989). The space fortress game: a description. *Acta Psychologica*, **71**, 17–22.

Moray, N. (1982). Subjective mental load. *Human Factors*, **23**, 25–40.

Navon, D. (1987). The role of outcome conflict in dual-task interference. *Journal of Experimental Psychology: Human Perception and Performance*, **13**, 435–448.

Navon, D., & Gopher, D. (1979). On the economy of the human-processing system. *Psychological Review*, **86**, 214–255.

Nisbett, R. E., & Wilson, T. D. (1977). Telling more than you know: verbal reports on mental processes. *Psychological Review*, **84**, 231–259.

Norman, D. A. (1968). Toward a theory of memory and attention. *Psychological Review*, **75**, 522–536.

Pew, R. W. (1979). Secondary tasks and workload measurement. In N. Moray (ed.), *Mental workload* (pp. 23–28). New York: Plenum.

Wickens, C. (1984). Processing resources in attention. In R. Parasuraman & D. R. Davies (eds.), *Varieties of attention* (pp. 63–102). New York: Academic Press.

Part II

Emotion and Thinking

Emotion and Thinking

FRASER N. WATTS
MRC Applied Psychology Unit, Cambridge

Recent years have seen an upsurge of interest in the study of emotion from the standpoint of cognitive psychology. The questions that have been considered include the following: Do emotional responses occur without any prior cognitive appraisal? What is the relationship between cognitive and emotional development in infants? Can a theory of emotion be cast in terms of computational modelling? What are the cognitive processes associated with abnormal emotional states?

Contributions to these and other questions that arise on the cognition–emotion interface can be found in the journal, *Cognition and Emotion*, first published in 1987. The following four chapters are concerned with work on the interface of emotion and *thinking*, though it may be helpful to see this as part of the broader current concern with the cognition–emotion interface.

Like most areas of psychology, the study of thinking has shown an increasing concern with applied work. Work on emotion represents one of the main current attempts at applied work on thinking, though there are others such as work on the interface of thinking and computational psychology.

There may be some surprise that work should be attempted on the interface of emotion and thinking, in view of the frequently stated assumption that there is an antithesis between emotion and thinking, or that emotion is inherently irrational. This is the issue considered by Oatley in the first chapter in this section. To consider the question of whether thinking is inherently irrational, it is necessary to have a considered view of the nature of rationality. Oatley suggests that it is not so much 'a property of thought' as 'a standard by which thought or action can be judged'. The case that Oatley makes out is that emotions are functional and adaptive. They provide 'a clever biological solution' to common problems to which careful, conscious thought is not a helpful approach.

The next two chapters, by Conway and by Watts, are concerned with the application of the psychology of concepts to understanding emotion. Conway is concerned with concepts of emotion itself; Watts with concepts of a particular class of objects which give rise to emotion.

A central hypothesis in Conway's work is that emotion words are represented in terms of exemplars, and that these exemplars commonly take the form of autobiographical memories of experiences related to the emotion concerned. This hypothesis, of course, draws on general recent work in the psychology of thinking concerned with the representation of conceptual categories by exemplars, though emotion concepts may be distinctive in the extent to which they are represented by autobiographical exemplars. In the experimental paradigm that Conway uses, subjects are required to generate as quickly as possible an image of what the emotion concept refers to. This approach has considerable promise for the investigation of the cognitive representation of emotion.

Watts is concerned with the conceptual representation of a specific class of emotion-generating objects, the representation of spiders in spider phobics. The central hypothesis is that the conceptual representations of emotion-arousing objects are highly cohesive, a view that is similar to Peter Lang's assumption that the 'emotion prototype' is highly coherent. Watts examines this in terms of the correlations between phobics' ratings of spider exemplars on various spider attributes. The cohesiveness of phobic categories is reflected in high intercorrelations between attributes, and especially in the correlations between ratings on specific attributes and general typicality ratings. Watts relates this to the way in which highly emotional stimuli are processed, suggesting that there is a relationship between the cohesiveness of the concept and a lack of differentiation in the processing of phobic stimuli.

The final chapter by Power is concerned with a topic which has been important in clinical research on emotional states, the identification of cognitive characteristics which predict the development of emotional disorders and which can therefore be regarded as embodying vulnerability to them. Power's chapter reports preliminary research on a novel and promising paradigm designed to identify aspects of the cognitive structure relevant to vulnerability to depression. Priming effects were used as an index of the cognitive structure. The primes were names of positive or negative life events, and the target stimuli were positive or negative trait words that subjects were required to rate for self-descriptiveness. The data from this paradigm presented here are consistent with other indications that experimental paradigms are useful in investigating aspects of cognitive processes that are relevant to emotional vulnerability.

These four chapters provide a broad sample of work that is currently being done on the interface of emotion and thinking. However, they do not exhaust the possible approaches. For example, one well-established line of work not represented here concerns the effects of emotional states on judgemental processes. There is clear evidence that judgements are biased by emotional state, but there are more subtle effects to investigate such as the 'overgeneralization' from negative instances which is an important feature of Beck's theory of depression.

Work on emotion and thinking constitutes a relatively new research field, and it is difficult to predict what its ultimate scientific contribution will be. However, early results are sufficiently promising to hope that it will make a useful contribution to both its parent fields. We can hope both that our understanding of emotion will be enriched by studying the role of thinking in emotion in the ways represented in these chapters, but also that the study of thinking will be enriched by examining how far generalizations based on neutral material hold up when emotional thinking is studied.

8

Do Emotional States Produce Irrational Thinking?

KEITH OATLEY
University of Glasgow

INTRODUCTION

In this chapter I shall discuss the common folk theory that emotions are irrational, in contrast to thinking which is rational. There is no question about what is meant: when experiencing compelling emotions people often act with consequences that can be foreseen, but which are contrary to some of their apparently most important purposes. In one recent example, a politician running for the American presidency was observed with a woman to whom he was not married. This discovery crushed his hopes for nomination.

Observations reported in the academic literature support the idea that strong emotions make one irrational. Tyhurst (1951) found that during fires or floods only some 15% of people behaved in an organized way. About 70% showed a mixture of organized and disorganized behaviour, and some 15% became completely disorganized, running around screaming or becoming aimless. In battle only a small proportion of soldiers fight: Marshall (1978), interviewing Second World War personnel, found that 15% of men had fired their weapons during battles, with this proportion rising to 25% in the best units. In most actions about 80% of the troops could have used their weapons.

When seriously upset, people may be unable to act sensibly. A parent when depressed may neglect children (Pound *et al.*, 1985), or when angry or anxious may hurt or scold them in ways that clearly do not benefit anyone.

That emotions may make us involuntarily irrational is seen in the cultural practices of law. To kill someone in cold blood, with malice aforethought or while carrying out a robbery, is more heinous, and carries more severe penalties, than to kill in anger or jealousy, in the heat of passion.

The conclusion that there is often something irrational about emotions

---

Lines of Thinking, Volume 2   Edited by K.J. Gilhooly, M.T.G. Keane, R.H.Logie and G. Erdos
© 1990 John Wiley & Sons Ltd

therefore need not be laboured. Emotion implies a degree of compulsion in our thinking and action (see, for example, Frijda, 1988). If voluntary actions are the means by which we change the world, emotions are among the events that change us. They were defined by Descartes as passions for this reason. This passivity has often been attributed to biochemical causes, to instincts, to the autonomic nervous system, and to other non-conscious processes.

The usual contrasting assumption is that thought is rational. The emblem of rationality is a technical plan, such as might be embodied in a computer program, which has a single goal to which everything relevant is assimilated, and which is executed in a perfectly known world.

The twentieth century Western distrust of emotions is no doubt related to Plato's articulation of the idea that emotions can distort truth. Both in ancient times and today, influential schools of thought have elaborated the idea that the emotions are the principal cause of human suffering. Coming after Plato and Aristotle, the Stoics took up this idea, regarding emotions as diseases of the soul, to be cured by proper thinking.

DO EMOTIONS HAVE FUNCTIONS?

I suggest that the question of whether emotions are irrational can only be answered if we decide whether or not they have functions.

The functional argument is that emotions have a role in cognition. According to the theory of Oatley and Johnson-Laird (1987), they have a function in the planning of our actions. They are concerned in managing cognitive organization where there are multiple goals and where our models of the world are imperfect.

The contrary argument, that emotions are non-functional, takes two principal forms: that emotions are disorganizations, and that they are vestiges of behaviour which once were functional but are so no longer.

Emotions as Irrational: 1. Physiological Intrusion

A common type of theory is that strong emotions disorganize voluntary behaviour and thinking. Attention can become narrowly focused, action can become stereotyped and compulsive.

Many theories of emotion are based on this view. It can be illustrated by the influential theory of Cannon (1927). As he put it, impulses from the thalamus reaching the cortex contribute the glow and colour of emotional experience in otherwise neutral cognitive states. He also argued that normally the thalamus is under a degree of inhibition by the cortex. Emotional expressions of high intensity are seen if this inhibition is removed, surgically as in the sham rage of decorticated cats, or pharmacologically as in the aggressiveness or senti-mentality of drunkenness. The explanation of the strong emotions of infancy and childhood is that the cortex has not yet achieved its adult level of inhibitory control. The idea also explains the involuntariness of emotions in terms of 'powerful impulses originating in a region of the brain not associated with cognitive consciousness... [which] explain the sense of being seized, possessed, of being controlled by an outside force and made to act without weighing of the consequences'.

It is clear that there are many instances in which strong emotions are disorganizing, especially when seen from an outsider's viewpoint. These are important data to be explained. What is required, however, are explanations in terms of psychological processes. Theories such as 'Involuntary emotional behaviour occurs because of intrusions of unchecked compelling influences' do no more to explain the phenomena than did the doctor in one of Molière's plays who sagely explained that the action of opium in inducing sleep was due to its 'dormitive potency'.

Nevertheless, the idea has given rise to many observations, in which factors such as arousal or pharmacological states are manipulated, and behaviour influenced by this non-rational input is measured. For example, changing the level of arousal was studied in the most influential piece of psychological research on emotion in recent times: Schachter and Singer's (1962) study of the idea that emotion is arousal, such as that produced by an injection of adrenaline, plus an attributional labelling.

Shachter's theory has not been widely confirmed (see, for example, Reisenzein, 1983); but to the extent that its tenets can be maintained, we may conclude that, where arousal contributes to judgement, and is induced by apprehension of heights, by drugs, by physical exercise, by bogus feedback of autonomic arousal etc., its effects are irrational. They depend on processes other than reason that disorganize or reorganize it in non-rational ways.

Oatley and Johnson-Laird's (1987) theory is no different in this respect. Emotions are based on what we call non-propositional signals, which can sometimes be triggered by events that have nothing to do with evaluation of the outside world (e.g. by drugs). To this extent, we agree that emotions allow a special type of irrationality. We do not, however, suppose that this irrationality is a central characteristic of the emotion system. Rather, it arises because the triggering processes can affect the system outside its usual range of operation, just as a perception of light can be induced by pressing on the side of the eyeball in the dark. Normally, emotions are triggered appropriately in situations that have been evaluated in relation to goals.

Emotions as Irrational: 2. Behavioural Vestiges

The most venerable version of the theory that at least some aspects of emotion are non-functional is Darwin's (1872). He argued that emotional expressions occur even though 'they may not be of the least use' (p. 28). Otherwise, of course, we would say that the behaviour was rational, adaptive, functional.

Darwin was mainly concerned with the following kind of problem. Whereas some behaviour, such as avoiding a poisonous snake, is functional in some circumstances, it also occurs inappropriately. Here is a typical Darwinian observation:

'I put my face close to the thick glass-plate in front of a puff-adder in the Zoological Gardens, with the firm determination of not starting back if the snake struck at me;

but, as soon as the blow was struck, my resolution went for nothing, and I jumped a yard or two backwards with astonishing rapidity. My will and reason were powerless against the imagination of a danger which had never been experienced.'

Darwin amassed evidence of bodily activity which was, on occasion, superfluous to efficient action: tears that do not function to lubricate the eyes, piloerection which adds nothing to the skill of an attack, dogs wagging their tails which seems to have no relation to the purpose of their other activity, laughter which seems not to improve the execution of any task. He argued that all of these have an element of the functionless. He would have been fascinated by the facial expressions of people talking on the telephone.

Darwin explained these effects by three principles. First there is habit which may derive from infancy and be inherited from previous generations. Thus crying, he supposed, is the vestige of a habit of screaming established in childhood, and only partly inhibited in adult life. (Darwin was Lamarkian in his idea that habits practised over a number of generations can be inherited.) Secondly, there is the principle of antithesis in which we sometimes do the opposite of an action prompted by habit, as when we shrug rather than hitting someone with whom we are angry. Thirdly, there are effects that occur because nerve force may be generated in excess, and flows into channels not strictly necessary for behaviour.

The theory, as he said, 'confirms to a certain limited extent the conclusion that man is derived from some lower animal' (p. 365), and it confines emotional expressions to the class of not yet dead fossils.

Vestiges or Automatic Behaviour Mechanisms?

I would like to distinguish two aspects of Darwin's theory. One is the idea that emotions are vestiges of an animal and infantile past. The second, which is not easy to disentangle from the first, is conceptually very different. It is concerned with how automatic behaviour mechanisms might have been installed during evolution, how they might be triggered, and how modifying such mechanisms for special cases might not be advantageous.

Darwin's research, in its first aspect, takes emotional expression as evidence for the theory of evolution, and regards emotions as vestiges that are no longer always functional. If evolution is a process in which new anatomical, physiological and behavioural forms are generated, emotional expressions are undiscarded behavioural debris from this process. They linger, just as do anatomical vestiges such as the small bones at the base of the human spine, the remains of a tail. This is a paradigm idea of emotions as irrational.

The second aspect of Darwin's work is more nearly a theory of emotional expression as such. It can be seen in terms of problems of function of behavioural mechanisms, and expressed as follows. Darwin concentrates on a kind of behavioural mechanism, the habit. Habits are useful, and are built up by repetition to become automatic; and, according to Darwin, they can be inherited. We now commonly distinguish automatic processes that are instinctual from those that are learned, and make the sharp separation of the Weissman doctrine, that adaptations made by the individual cannot be passed on genetically.

In terms of a computational metaphor, we might talk of both genetically specified and individually acquired mechanisms as procedures that had been compiled, and in terms of knowledge embedded in procedures. It is a useful property that such a mechanism is not accessible to alteration. Such procedures may be invoked by eliciting conditions for which they were designed. The difficulty is that for such a mechanism to work well in its designed setting, it will also be invoked by similar, but slightly different patterns; for example, by a 'desire or sensation' in circumstances other than those for which it was designed.

It is advantageous to compile plans as habits, storing sequences that have been practised, for later use. But with such an advantageous mechanism, sometimes the triggering circumstance will not be discriminated accurately by the relatively simple recognition device that such mechanisms must have to maintain the advantages of needing no thought. Darwin's experience with the puff-adder at the zoo had nearly all the characteristics of a situation in which it would be a very good idea to spring backwards. The apparent inappropriateness is really due to a limitation in the discriminative ability of the recognition mechanism failing to take into account the plate glass; it is not a defect in the idea of compiled action sequences.

Time enters the analysis with the realization that behavioural mechanisms have inertia. It takes time to generate good plans. One might not want to modify an elaborately compiled plan just because in a particular instance this would be rational.

A slightly different interpretation is in terms of optimizing multiple constraints. If in evolution many different constraints are being satisfied, then not all of them can be fulfilled adequately and simultaneously in any one solution (for example, in any one species). There will be conflicts, and hence tradeoffs of various kinds. For example, anatomical size may be an advantage for some purposes, such as speed of locomotion, but it requires increases in the strength of bones and hence in weight. Human bones are sometimes broken, and human backs often give trouble. One might therefore argue that certain size–strength–weight problems have not been optimized for humans, at least in some situations. Emotional expressions may also indicate that multiple constraints have not been optimized for all circumstances. Emotions may be related to the idea of human agents pursuing many goals. Clashes, tradeoffs and conflicts occur, and give rise to dislocations of functioning, which seem to be a nuisance.

Neisser (1963) drew attention to this aspect of our mental lives in his paper comparing minds to computers. When developing computer programs side effects are best minimized. Traces of previous versions of the program should be eliminated immediately they are superseded, since their continued existence will cause inefficiency, and make the rational structure of the program more difficult to understand. But human beings ordinarily are not faced with the same task as the programmer. The programmer typically develops a rational solution to a single technical task in a limited domain. By contrast, we as human beings have to develop new pieces of program as we go along. These new developments have to meet current contingencies about which we have not been informed by our genetic start-up program, and they also have to serve as bases for future developments that we cannot foresee.

The phenomena that Darwin studied are ambiguous as to their interpretation as vestiges or as problems of optimization in an organism that changes in its own lifetime. The alternative in which Darwin was most interested was that emotional expressions are vestiges of a bestial or infantile past. It has been seriously misleading. Unintentionally it has strengthened an incorrect folk theory already present in our culture. Darwin's aim, of course was to see continuity between ourselves and other animals, and between adults and infants. Assimilated with the stock of other cultural ideas, however, his idea has become not one of continuity but contrast. Bestiality and infantility are the opposite of adult human rationality. And when supposed vestiges occur they are best denounced as inappropriate to our higher, adult life—or at least to the life of slightly less than 50% of us, the males: Grown up men do not cry.

Such arguments need to be answered. The answer, I think, is as follows. The idea that emotions are vestiges, the most serious of the non-functional arguments, is countered by saying that emotions do indeed have an evolutionary history, but so also do thinking and walking. Darwin tried to persuade his readers of the veracity of evolutionary theory, and was perhaps over-enthusiatic about some phenomena he took to be evidence of it. For those who now accept evolution, there is no reason to doubt that emotions may indicate some of the history of our species. But there is also no reason why, among mammals, emotional expressions should have been shielded from selection pressures to furnish a museum of evolutionary fossils. On the contrary, since emotional expressions—and presumably the underlying emotions—are more widespread among mammals than thinking or upright walking, they must have an important and continuing function.

Let us now turn to the other side of the antithesis 'the heart or the head' to see how far thought is, indeed, rational, in the sense that is commonly assumed.

WHAT IS RATIONALITY?

In its usual sense, rationality means possessing reason or being based on reason. If reason implies deriving conclusions by conscious thought, irrationality means decision without due thought, or action uninfluenced by thought.

If we were to accept such a definition, then, to the extent that emotions are involuntary, they are irrational. But that is almost tautology. We need a less superficial understanding. One such is provided by the idea that rationality implies inferences made validly from premises to a conclusion. With this more informative definition, one can see the term being used of beliefs, and of actions.

A pervasive idea about the nature of thinking, that sets it apart from emotions, is that it depends on a mental logic. If this were true, rationality could be understood in terms of whether a belief or conclusion followed from laws of logic. Beliefs derived without following such laws would then be irrational.

Johnson-Laird (1983) has shown that there are considerable difficulties with such a doctrine. For instance, human thinkers including professional scientists and mathematicians often make mistakes, some of which are grossly illogical. There are many demonstrations of this. Two well-known series are by Wason (1960, 1966) particularly on confirmation bias in which people irrationally attend to evidence that will confirm current hypotheses while ignoring potentially refuting evidence, and by Kahneman and Tversky (Kahneman, Slovic and Tversky, 1982) in which people make large mistakes in estimating probabilities.

Rather than seeing such instances as indicating that the brains of some or all of us have been miswired, we can see these instances as a clue—the clue is that our intuitions are better at some things than others, and that where we are not good we can use cultural amplifiers. Among the areas in which our naive psychology is not good are generating potentially refuting hypotheses (the issue in Wason's 1960 experiment,) formal logic (the paradigm for Wason's 1966 experiment), and probability theory (the reference point for most of Kahneman and Tversky's experiments). In these areas it has required many clever people preoccupied with a narrow range of problems to invent the necessary pieces of theory, and for the rest of us to take part in programmes of careful learning of procedures which will allow us to reason validly in those delimited areas of scientific experimentation, formal logic, and probability theory. Just as pencils and paper are prostheses for our memory, and telescopes extend our senses, such pieces of theory are cultural prostheses which we can adopt if they become important for us, and which allow us to think in ways that we have not been genetically adapted to. Without this learning, we are irrationally triggered into wrong responses.

Criteria for Rationality of Belief

Characterizing rationality of belief is difficult (see, for example, Wason, 1983; Baron, 1985). The fact that we listen to each other's arguments, however, suggests that the goal of characterizing it may be approached. Rationality is an ideal to be aimed at, perhaps a description of heuristic procedures for search of various kinds as Baron suggests: Individuals may only approach it.

The most neglected fact about rationality is that it is a social phenomenon. When one person gives up the search on a problem, others can continue. When one scientist is (irrationally) convinced of the truth of a hypothesis, another can suggest refutations. As one set of people with their hearts pounding imagine that this time the roulette wheel may do as they desire, others can search for principles of probability, and so on.

Irrationality is not especially characteristic of emotions. Many examples of irrational thinking are unemotional. When thinking emotionally people sometimes terminate search too quickly, or fail to consider alternatives, just as they do when thinking unemotionally. Perhaps further research will show that premature termination of search is more marked when thinking under the press of some emotions in some situations.

A More Productive Contrast

This now brings us to a productive contrast between emotional and unemotional thinking. When experiencing an emotion it is typically the individual who has to generate a practical solution for his or her action. With the dysphoric emotions we each have to generate a solution to a problem which is new to us on that occasion. On the other hand, when thinking unemotionally we can usually draw on cultural experience, practised skills, and a range of aids. The non-emotional thinking that is offered as the paradigm of rationality is largely thinking about rational solutions to defined and soluble scientific and technical problems, assisted by methods that have become the potential cultural property of us all.

When problems of any kind are new to us, we often get them wrong, if indeed they have correct solutions. Emotional thinking seems more irrational than non-emotional thinking because it is applied by the individual to new problems, some of which do not have solutions.

Could the Confirmation Bias be Advantageous?

A clue to escaping from the difficulties of understanding rationality and human fallibility comes from considering not belief, but action. Perhaps we can derive from the theory of action a clue as to why the confirmation bias exists. Rather than being a mental defect, it may emerge from a mechanism that continues looking for evidence that will allow a plan to continue once started. There are considerable costs of starting up a different plan once a plan has been embarked upon. What appears as a defect in thinking may be a positive attribute of planning that allows us to concentrate on what we are doing, looking for positive information to allow us to continue, rather than taking negative evidence as an instigation to interrupt what we are doing and start up some quite different plan. In evolution, back-tracking may have been selected against. In an uncertain environment single disconfirmations may mean little. Situations where a single contrary indication to a scheme is significant may have been rare until science and technology became preoccupations of society. Indeed they are still rare now.

Why Humans Seldom Attain Rationality

Just as people can hold irrational beliefs it is clear that human plans often go wrong. If there were a kind of reasoning that could construct perfect plans, or a mechanism that would enact them without error, we humans do not have it.

There are two main reasons. First, models of the ordinary world are not perfect. Within delimited domains they can be better or worse, more or less useful for specific purposes. There is also a hint of paradox. To be rational implies not being necessarily right, but being prepared to be wrong. A rational belief, like a scientific theory, is corrigible. Secondly, most plans do not run smoothly, since as well as incomplete knowledge there are likely to be multiple goals, and hence potential conflicts. Even the idea of optimal solutions or compromises can become problematic, since goals may be incommensurable. In the example of the American politician's illicit sexual relationship, there may have been no rational solution, since there is not necessarily a metric by which the goals of a relationship can be compared with those of a career, even when questions of uncertainty about the outcomes of his various choices are not considered.

One can rightly maintain that thinking has a voluntary quality, that conclusions drawn by conscious thought may change in response to evidence, and that thought contrasts with processes that are somewhat involuntary, as emotions are. Behaviour and thought can only be seen as rational or otherwise in relation to some specific domain. If any human activity had the quality of rationality more generally it would be the social activity of critical discussion, not the private activity of individual thought.

Thus the general idea of rationality can only be rather loosely indicated, perhaps in terms of what information is necessary to a mental model for particular problems or plans. Thinking is not governed by any process that enables reasoning to valid conclusions independently of context. And we cannot construct perfect plans for all situations. Rather, reasoning and planning depend on making models which are more or less fallible and mirror more or less well some specific aspects of the world.

If this analysis is correct, the dichotomy of reason versus emotion dissolves. Rationality is hard to attain. It needs knowledge, experimentation, learning of skills, critical discussion, time, the opportunity to make mistakes, the possibility of social interaction; and it is only attained in limited domains. Thinking and action under the influence of an emotion do have qualities different from thinking and planning without emotional influence—but the difference is not that emotions are irrational and thinking rational.

Both emotional and non-emotional thinking typically relate to plans of action which are constructed and enacted with respect to goals. Although people caught up in emotions often behave irrationally, this is not insightfully described by saying that their behaviour has come under the control of some non-rational process, perhaps generated by primitive regions of the brain, whereas at other times a cortical logic engine makes rational decisions.

Usually an emotional state, related to a meaningful event that elicited it, is characterized by:

a) a subset of goals becoming salient;
b) some of these goals being linked with default plans that have been selected and consolidated during evolutionary or individual history;
c) differential attention to different aspect of evidence relevant to these plans; and
d) the possibility of invocation of new plans, which like any new plans will be liable to mistakes.

If we leave aside instances of emotional states being induced by a drug or the like, we can compare actions prompted by emotions and those directed by thinking. When an emotional action does not seem voluntarily intended, or does not achieve an advantageous end, it is explicable in terms of the goals and knowledge invoked in the mechanisms that direct action. In an emotional action, some goals may be unconscious. Some plans may have been compiled, and the knowledge embodied in them may be procedural, not declarative. They may have been socio-culturally or biologically determined, and they may be triggered inappropriately. But there is nothing about this description that makes the process necessarily less rational then deliberative thinking, or skilled action, since here too processes by which inferences are drawn are unconscious, mental models may be inadequate, search may terminate too soon, decisions or action sequences may be triggered inappropriately, and so on.

A full explanation of an action will refer to the tacit or explicit knowledge on which it is based. Rationality depends on how widely and appropriately these knowledge bases are used, and this is true both in emotional and non-emotional instances.

REPLACING THE DICHOTOMY OF REASON VERSUS EMOTION

There are indeed differences between thinking under the influence of an emotion, and thinking deliberatively, for instance when constructing a plan, or trying to solve an intellectual problem. There is no basis, however, for assuming that emotions are distinctively and inherently irrational, while non-emotional thinking is inherently rational. This is the wrong distinction, a relic of a folk theory which in this case was false.

A better basis for understanding the irrational in human belief and action is that human beings can hardly ever be wholly rational, because the world is largely unknowable, and goals often not only conflict but may be incommensurable. We can, perhaps should, strive for rationality. But we attain it only in defined circumstances, which correspond quite closely to the technical. Rationality can sometimes be attained in limited stationary domains (for example in certain branches of mathematics, in games like chess, or in technical plans such as those of a car-assembly robot). Moreover these are not cases in which a lone thinker comes individually, and *de novo*, to a rational conclusion. They have been culturally elaborated over years or centuries, until rational modes of thought have been elaborated, their properties explored by many people, and passed on by education. Rationality implies the possibility of having explored the implications of all possible mistakes.

The idea of planning helps shift the emphasis from men as rational beings to people as cognitive beings. Cognitive theory holds that an actor acts from knowledge. The difference from the eighteenth-century idea of rationality is that we are now more aware that knowledge may be fallible, and that much of it is tacit and not available to consciousness.

To refer to irrational and mistaken thought or behaviour is to imply that, from some perspective other than the actor's, a thought or action is questionnable, and therefore that a knowledge base, or the actor's use of it, could be improved, goals changed, or an action sequence replanned.

Rationality is not a property of thought. It is a process of converging on solutions, or alternatively a standard by which thought or action can be judged when one knows a great deal about the domain in question, a standard to which thought or action can aspire.

To answer the question in the title of this chapter: Emotional states do sometimes produce irrational thinking—but thinking is quite capable of being irrational when it is unemotional. Irrationality is not a defining characteristic of emotions, though emotions often constrain thinking to a limited number of considerations.

The appropriate way to see emotions is not as irrational elements in our lives, but as a clever biological solution to problems with which we are often confronted that have no fully rational solutions.

REFERENCES

Baron, J. (1985). *Rationality and intelligence.* Cambridge: Cambridge University Press.

Cannon, W.B. (1927). The James–Lange theory of emotions. *American Journal of Psychology,* **39**, 115–124.

Darwin, C. (1872). *The expression of emotions in man and the animals.* Reprinted Chicago: University of Chicago Press, 1965.

Frijda, N. H. (1988). The laws of emotion. *American Psychologist,* **43**, 349–358.

Johnson-Laird, P. N. (1983). *Mental models: Towards a cognitive science of language, inference and consciousness.* Cambridge Cambridge University Press.

Kahneman, D., Slovic, P., & Tversky, A. (1982). *Judgement under uncertainty: Heuristics and biases.* Cambridge: Cambridge University Press.

Marshall, S. L. A. (1978). *Men against fire.* Gloucester, MA: Peter Smith.

Neisser, U. (1963). The imitation of man by machine. *Science,* **139**, 193–197.

Oatley, K., & Johnson-Laird, P. N. (1987). Towards a cognitive theory of the emotions. *Cognition and Emotion,* **1**, 29–50.

Pound, A., Cox, A. D., Puckering, C., & Mills, M. (1985). The impact of maternal depression on young children. In J. E. Stevenson (ed.), *Recent research in developmental psychopathology.* Oxford: Pergamon.

Reisenzien, R. (1983). The Schachter theory of emotion: two decades later. *Psychological Bulletin,* **94**, 239–264.

Schachter, S., & Singer, J. (1962). Cognitive, social and physiological determinants of emotional state. *Psychological Review,* **69**, 379–399.

Tyhurst, J. S. (1951). Individual reactions to community disaster. *American Journal of Psychiatry,* **107**, 764–769.

Wason, P. C. (1960). On the failure to eliminate hypotheses in a conceptual task. *Quarterly Journal of Experimental Psychology,* **11**, 92–107.

Wason, P. C. (1966). Reasoning. In B.M. Foss (ed.), *New horizons in psychology,* Harmondsworth: Penguin.

Wason, P. C. (1983). Reason and rationality in the selection task. In J. St. B. Evans (ed.), *Thinking and reasoning: Psychological approaches.* London: Routledge and Kegan Paul.

9

Conceptual Representation of Emotions: The Role of Autobiographical Memories

MARTIN A. CONWAY
Lancaster University

INTRODUCTION

When a person processes a word naming an emotion, what kinds of knowledge are activated? Conway & Bekerian (1987a) found that one type of knowledge which becomes available when processing emotion words is that of memories for experienced events. For example, when listing attributes of emotional situations subjects recalled emotional experiences which they had either directly experienced or been told about, and then abstracted attributes from these memories (Conway and Bekerian, 1987a, experiment 3). Similarly, when imaging emotional situations, subjects' images largely comprised autobiographical memories of emotional experiences (Conway and Bekerian, 1987a, experiment 7). In general, Conway & Bekerian found that autobiographical memories were spontaneously retrieved across a range of tasks in which subjects processed emotion words.

One interpretation of these findings is that the conceptual representation of emotions in memory is in terms of experienced events. That is to say, words naming emotions are represented by *examples* of emotional experiences, and these examples provide the knowledge on which conceptual models of emotions are based. Exemplar or instance models of conceptual representation have been proposed before, most notably by Medin and Schaffer (1978) and Medin and Smith (1981), and have been reviewed by Smith and Medin (1981). One type of exemplar model proposes that concepts are represented by exemplars and by subsets of exemplars. For example, an emotionally complex experience might be directly represented as an instance of the concept 'emotion'. More identifiable emotional experiences might be represented in subsets of exemplars which instantiate particular types of emotional experience (for example, all *anger* experiences might be represented in a subset) and instantiate the concept of emotion generally.

This exemplar model does not, however, exclude abstract knowledge, and Smith and Medin (1981) consider a number of ways in which abstract knowledge might supplement exemplar-based knowledge structures. Conway and Bekerian (1987a) found that abstract knowledge in the form of descriptions of typical emotional situations could be used to prime the recognition of emotion words and the retrieval of emotional experiences. In the case of emotions, then, abstract knowledge may take the form of specification of potential situations in which a person might experience a specific emotion. Certainly, literature, television, and other media sources constantly present such situations and, perhaps, abstract conceptual knowledge of emotions is primarily culturally determined. Thus, a person who has never attended a funeral of someone they were close to may, nonetheless, have considerable knowledge of the emotional features of such an event.

The exemplar model of conceptual representation considered above postulates that when people process emotion words they retrieve autobiographical memories of related experiences and/or schematic representations of emotional situations. One question of some importance for this exemplar model is: Which type of knowledge—autobiographical or schematic—is automatically activated when a person processes an emotion word? The experiments reported in the remainder of this chapter investigated this question.

FIRST EXPERIMENT

In order to examine the spontaneous retrieval of emotional knowledge, an image-generation task was employed. Subjects were to be presented with words and phrases naming common objects, activities and feelings, and in response to each stimuli subjects were required to bring to mind an image of whatever they took that word or phrase to refer. Image generation times (IGTs) were recorded and subjects provided a number of judgements of each image. One of the judgements made by subjects specified the type of image (TOI) they had brought to mind, and three classes of TOI were employed:

a) *Autobiographical memories* referred to images which were based on experienced events which the subject could accurately date (to the nearest month).

b) *Generic images* referred to images which were based on experienced events but which subjects could only date to a lifetime period (see Conway and Bekerian, 1987b) and which were abstracted from specific experiences.

c) *Semantic images* referred to images which were not in principle datable and which represented knowledge not directly based on any specific experience or set of experiences.

For further discussion of these TOIs, see Brewer (1986) and Conway (1990).

Four classes of concepts were employed:

1) *Taxonomic categories* naming categories of objects (furniture, vegetables, clothing, etc.) were selected to represent common everyday objects.

2) *Goal-derived categories* naming other common groupings of objects and activities (birthday presents, things to take on holiday, farm animals, etc.) were selected because these concepts may be represented in terms of schemata (Barsalou, 1985; Conway, 1990).

3) *Emotion words* (anger, love, fear, grief, etc.) were taken from Conway and Bekerian (1987a).

4) *Short phrases* naming common occupational roles (hospital worker, television presenter, manual worker, etc.) were used as it was reasoned that these concepts may also be closely associated with autobiographical memories.[*]

If emotions are represented in memory by exemplars in the form of memories of specific experiences, then it should be the case that more autobiographical memories than other types of images are spontaneously recalled when subjects image the referents of emotion words. If emotions are a 'special' case of conceptual representation by autobiographical memories, then more memories should be spontaneously retrieved to words naming emotion concepts than to words naming other types of concepts. The distribution of TOIs should correspond to the IGT measure in that, when a concept is dominated by a particular type of knowledge, then that knowledge should be highly available and therefore should be retrieved quickly (Barsalou, 1982).

The Method

Subjects and Design

There were 17 subjects, ten women and seven men, aged between 27 and 42 years. A within-subjects design was employed, and the main independent variable was concept-class of which there were four levels: 'taxonomic categories', 'goal-derived categories', 'emotions' and 'person categories'. Each concept-class was represented by eight items naming categories in that class. Subjects generated an image of whatever they took a concept to refer to and did so as quickly as possible. The dependent variables were TOI and IGT (measured in milliseconds).

Procedure

The experiment was run on a BBC Acorn plus Torch Z80 microcomputer. Subjects were tested individually, each being seated at a table containing a monitor, a response key and a response booklet. Written instructions described the procedure and provided examples of images (previously collected in pilot studies) classified by TOI. Subjects were told that when they pressed the response key to initiate a trial the word *Ready* would appear in the centre of the screen. This warning signal would be automatically blanked from the screen and replaced by a word or short phrase naming a common everyday concept.

---

[*]A full list of the stimuli is available from the author on request.

Subjects were instructed to bring to mind an image of whatever they took the concept to refer to and to do so as quickly as possible. Subjects were led to believe that speed of image generation and not TOI was the principal measure of interest. When a subject had generated an image he or she pressed the response key and the stimulus was blanked from the screen. The IGT was taken as the time between the stimulus appearing on the screen and the key being pressed. The subject then turned to the response booklet and completed a number of ratings of their image. Each trial followed the same procedure. Subjects also completed eight practice trials under close supervision and the procedure was reviewed during the practice trials. Additional instructions informed subjects of what to do if no image came to mind—mark 'X' in the response booklet and then proceed to the next trial. On completion of the trials all subjects took part in a post-experimental interview in which they described some of their images.

Results and Discussion

Table 9.1 shows the percentage distribution of TOIs by concept class. These data were analysed in an ANOVA test in which concept-class and TOI formed the main variables. The principal finding was that of a significant interaction of TOI with concept class ($F(6,102) = 9.1$, $p < 0.01$). Images generated to 'taxonomic' categories were equally likely to be autobiographical memories, generic images, or semantic images, suggesting a heterogeneous knowledge base for these concepts. Images generated to 'person' categories were dominated by generic images and autobiographical memories, and semantic images rarely spontaneously came to mind. For 'emotions' and 'goal-derived' categories, however, autobiographical memories formed the dominant image type and other types of knowledge were rarely employed in image generation for these concepts. Emotion categories and goal-derived categories might then be represented by exemplars in the form of autobiographical memories, and this lends some support to the proposal that emotion concepts are represented in memory by instances of emotional experiences.

Mean image-generation times are presented in Table 9.2. The IGTs were analysed by an identical ANOVA test to that described above; but because of the inherently unbalanced nature of the design (subjects were free to base their images on any type of knowledge) there were a number of missing cases in all

Table 9.1 Percentage distribution of type of image in the first experiment

Category	Autobiographical memories	Generic images	Semantic images
Taxonomic	33.8	36.8	29.4
Goal-derived	53.0	23.5	23.5
Emotions	59.5	27.2	13.3
Persons	26.4	52.3	21.3
Means	43.2	34.9	21.9

Table 9.2   Retrieval times of type of image in the first experiment

Category	Autobiographical memories	Generic images	Semantic images
Taxonomic	2253	2302	2278
Goal-derived	2313	2321	2960
Emotions	2528	2031	4478
Persons	2367	2571	2818
Means	2365	2306	3133

cells of the design. For the purposes of analysis, missing cases were replaced using an algorithim taken from the GENSTAT manual (Alvey *et al.*, 1983, section 7.1; see Conway, 1990, for further details). Table 9.2 however, presents the unadjusted means. A significant main effect of TOI was observed ($F(2,31(1)) = 6.24$, $p < 0.01$), and autobiographical memories and generic images were generated equally quickly and both of these image types were generated reliably more quickly than semantic images. There was no significant main effect of concept class, but a significant interaction of TOI with concept class was observed ($F(6,70(26)) = 4.7$, $p < 0.01$). This arose because semantic images generated to emotion concepts were significantly slower than all other IGTs shown in Table 9.2.

These effects of IGT, then, all related to the very slow semantic image generation to emotion words. This suggests that emotion concepts are not at all associated in memory with non-experiential, depersonalized knowledge (Brewer, 1986), but other classes of concepts are associated, at least to some extent, with this type of knowledge. Overall the findings indicate that emotion concepts are represented by memories of specific experiences and to a lesser extent by generic knowledge, but are not represented by abstract depersonalized knowledge.

SECOND EXPERIMENT

In order to explore the association between autobiographical memories and emotion concepts in further detail, a second image-generation experiment was conducted. In this experiment words directly naming emotions were not used, but rather words varying in their rated emotionality (Rubin and Friendly, 1986) were employed. An attempt was also made to vary the degree of self-reference of the stimuli, and five classes of concepts were constructed. The first class comprised concepts denoting positive personality traits 'confident', 'loyal', 'capable', etc.) and these are referred to as self-positive (SPOS) concepts; the second class referred to self-negative (SNEG) concepts ('greedy', 'moody', 'vain', etc.); the third class referred to self-neutral (SNEUT) concepts ('justice', 'freedom', 'miracle', etc.); a fourth class also denoted self-neutral concepts but which were also rated as being low in imagability (LIM) ('hour', 'history', 'custom', etc.). Finally, a fifth class of words denoted concepts which were rated as being highly emotional (EMO); examples of these were 'devil', 'power', 'genius', etc.

Note that all the words were rated as being highly abstract and, with the exception of LIM words, as being highly imagable. The main purpose of the experiment was to investigate whether it was the self-reference of the concepts which led to their instantiation as autobiographical memories, or just their emotional qualities, or some combination of the two. A second, more general, purpose was to examine the type of knowledge base drawn on when imaging these more abstract concepts.

The Method

The method was the same as for the first experiment, with the following exceptions: there were 16 subjects, ten women and six men, aged between 21 and 50 years, and there were five concept-classes (SPOS, SNEG, SNEUT, LIM and EMO).

Results and Discussion

The analyses were the same as those conducted in the first experiment. Table 9.3 shows the percentage distribution of TOI across concept-classes. There was a significant interaction of TOI with concept class ($F(8,120) = 4.84$, $p < 0.01$). Reliably more autobiographical memories were spontaneously recalled to SPOS and SNEG concepts than to the other three concept classes ($F(4,60) = 3.88$, $p < 0.01$). Within SPOS and SNEG, however, there were equal numbers of autobiographical memories, generic images, and semantic images ($F < 1$ in both cases). The concept-classes, SNEUT, LIM and EMO were dominated by semantic images and these classes had significantly more semantic images than SPOS and SNEG ($F(4,60) = 10.42$, $p < 0.01$). This distribution of TOI indicates that emotional concepts may be represented by abstract depersonalized knowledge and, perhaps, it is the degree of self-relevance of a concept which determines whether or not it will be represented by autobiographical memories.

Table 9.3 Percentage distribution of type of image in the second experiment

Category	Autobiographical memories	Generic images	Semantic images
Self-positive (SPOS)	36.7	28.1	35.2
Self-negative (SNEG)	39.1	28.9	32.0
Self-neutral (SNEUT)	23.4	21.9	54.7
Neutral (LIM)	25.8	24.2	50.0
Emotional (EMO)	22.6	18.0	59.4
Means	29.5	24.2	46.3

The IGT data, however, suggested a slightly different interpretation. There were no significant effects of IGT, although TOI approached significance ($F(2,30) = 2.863$, $p < 0.073$). Mean IGTs for autobiographical memories were 5874 ms, for generic images the mean was 7844 ms, for semantic images the mean was 8061 ms, and only autobiographical memory IGTs differed reliably from semantic image IGTs ($t(80) = 3.6$, $p < 0.01$). In fact, these IGTs were highly variable and the standard error of differences of means for the TOI contrasts was 2128 ms—thus, mean IGT differences had to be in excess of 2000 ms in order to approach significance. Post-experimental interviews with the subjects indicated that all subjects had experienced some difficulty in *constructing* their images and, unlike with subjects in the first experiment, images rarely 'popped' into mind. Thus, it seems that these abstract concepts were not represented in memory by more or less discrete knowledge structures amenable to image generation but, rather, that representations were constructed on-line in order to satisfy the experimental task of imaging the concept. The marginally faster IGTs for autobiographical memories appeared to reflect the retrieval, rather than construction, of an image.

THIRD EXPERIMENT

The findings of the second experiment suggested that it was not the emotional quality of a concept which determined whether that concept would be represented by autobiographical memories, but rather that it was the degree of self-relevance of the concept. Perhaps, self-concepts are directly represented by memories of instantiating experiences. This final experiment contrasts imaging 'emotion' concepts and personality traits which differ in their rated self-relevance.

The Method

In the first phase of the experiment a group of subjects rated the self-relevance of various personality traits. Three months later 19 subjects returned and took part in an image-generation experiment similar to the first experiment, with the following exceptions: there were four concept classes, 'emotions' (EMO), 'high self-relevant traits' (HS), 'low self-relevant traits' (LS), and traits which were not self-relevant (NOTS). The personality traits were selected on the basis of each subject's ratings in the first phase of the experiment.

Results and Discussion

Table 9.4 shows the percentage distribution of TOI across the concept classes and the interaction of TOI with concept class was significant ($F(6,108) = 10.5$, $p < 0.01$). Reliably more autobiographical memories were spontaneously retrieved to emotion concepts than personality traits varying in their self-reference ($F(2,36) = 32.74$, $p < 0.01$). High self-relevant traits were dominated by generic images ($F(2,36) = 3.71$, $p < 0.05$), whereas LS and NOTS traits showed no differences in TOI. These findings strongly suggest that words

Table 9.4 Percentage distribution of type of image in the third experiment

Category	Autobiographical memories	Generic images	Semantic images
Emotions (EMO)	63.2	24.3	12.5
Highly characteristic (HS)	30.9	46.0	23.1
Marginally characteristic (LS)	41.4	32.2	26.4
Not characteristic (NOTS)	27.6	35.5	36.9
Means	40.8	34.5	24.7

naming emotions are instantiated in memory by memories of specific emotional experiences, whereas other concepts appear to be represented by more depersonalized knowledge.

A significant main effect of TOI on IGT was also observed ($F(2,35(1)) = 7.3$, $p < 0.01$), and autobiographical memories (3843 ms) were retrieved more quickly than generic images (5066 ms) ($t(35) = 2.87$, $p < 0.05$), which in turn were generated reliably more quickly than semantic images (7245 ms) ($t(35) = 2.41$, $p < 0.05$). This finding, in conjunction with subjects' comments in the post-experimental interviews, indicated that autobiographical memories 'popped' into mind whereas generic and semantic images required more extended processing.

GENERAL DISCUSSION

The striking finding to emerge in these studies was that, when subjects generated images of the referents of emotion words, more than 60% of their images took the form of autobiographical memories. This preponderance of spontaneously retrieved autobiographical memories was not evident in images to other types of concepts, where it was found that abstract concepts were dominated by semantic images and that self-referring personality traits were dominated by generic images.

One explanation of these findings is as follows. When a subject is presented with a word and instructed to image whatever the word refers to, an automatic memory search for suitable *prestored* knowledge is conducted. If a concept is represented in memory by some more or less discrete knowledge structure which can be instantiated in an image, then this is retrieved and imaged. The dominance of the conceptual representation for a class of concepts by a certain type of knowledge will be reflected in the TOIs reported. Thus, as autobiographical memories dominated TOI for emotion concepts (but did not dominate for most other classes of concepts), it can be concluded that the representation of emotion concepts is primarily in terms of memories of emotional experiences. Moreover, when appropriate prestored knowledge is directly accessed, a fast IGT will result, compared with the IGT when direct retrieval and generation is not possible. In this latter case additional processing must be undertaken, perhaps, involving computation of possible features of the image and/or extended memory search for appropriate knowledge (cf. Kahneman and Miller, 1986).

In the second and third experiments which employed abstract concepts, the IGTs for non-emotion words suggested that subjects *constructed* images in order to comply with the experimental task (Conway, 1990, provides further evidence supporting this point). In contrast, the faster IGTs to emotion words suggest that for these concepts there was little on-line construction of images, but rather that knowledge was directly accessed and instantiated as an image. In the first experiment, however, images may have been computed when subjects generated semantic images to emotion words, and this may account for the lengthy IGTs observed in this condition. The fast IGTs in all other conditions in the first experiment suggest that, generally, direct retrieval may have mediated image generation and that, indeed, different classes of concepts are represented in memory by different types of knowledge.

In the present studies a small percentage of emotion concepts did not lead to the spontaneous retrieval of autobiographical memories. Clearly, a person who has not experienced 'grief' cannot represent this concept by a memory of an experience; and in this case the emotion concept may be represented by less personal knowledge, possibly by knowledge gained vicariously. Conway and Bekerian (1987a) found that images of the emotion 'jealousy' often took the form of vignettes abstracted from a popular television series, and in the present studies subjects' self-reports in the post-experimental interviews provided further evidence for this. These types of images were usually classified by subjects as being generic (although they comprised only a small part of this TOI). It does not, of course, follow that these exemplars will be retrieved any less slowly than autobiographical memories. If they are prestored with the concept and usually retrieved when the concept is accessed, then they too should give rise to fast IGTs (Barsalou, 1982; Conway, 1987; Conway, 1990).

The present findings indicate that emotion concepts are represented in memory by exemplars and the exemplars are primarily autobiographical memories of emotional experiences. Emotion exemplars can also take the form of generic knowledge, but this is comparatively rare and even less frequently observed in the present experiments was the computation of emotional knowledge. Finally, two additional findings suggest that emotion exemplars may have a special status in the conceptual representation of emotions. Firstly, Conway (1990) found, in an autobiographical memory retrieval experiment, that memories retrieved to emotion concepts (identical to those used in the first experiment in the present study) were significantly older than memories retrieved to personality traits and other types of concepts. Secondly, Conway and Bekerian (1987c) found that memories of emotional experiences were nearly always associated with significant life-events (see also Bekerian and Conway, 1988), and that retrieval of personally insignificant events which were also emotional rarely occurred. Taken together these findings indicate that, when memories of emotional experiences are accessed, the memories are ones which are well established in memory and relate to events of high personal significance.

It is proposed that these emotional memories constitute *focal episodes* which represent the core meanings of emotion concepts. Possibly, emotion experiences become focal instances of an emotional concept by some process of socialization. This could occur in adult/child interactions and/or through cultural sources of knowledge (de Sousa, 1987). One implication of this is that people within a culture (and, perhaps, within a particular generation within a culture) will tend to have similar focal episodes representing the core meaning of emotional concepts, and so there should be some normative aspects of emotion concepts (Conway and Bekerian, 1987a). As emotion concepts are represented by exemplar experiences which will be idiosyncratic to individuals, there will, of course, be marked individual differences in meanings of particular emotion concepts held by specific individuals.

Finally, the focal-episode model is compatible with the processing account of exemplars proposed by Smith and Medin (1981). Thus, an experience will be classified as being of a specific emotion to the extent that it retrieves some criterial number of focal episodes or properties from focal episodes. However, some—perhaps many—experiences will retrieve prestored knowledge across a range of focal episodes; for instance, an experience might retrieve focal episodes of 'love, 'anger', and 'depression'. These complex emotional experiences will be classified as *emotional*, because of the retrieval of focal emotional episodes, but will not be classified as being of a specific nameable emotion. Such experiences are, perhaps, represented as direct exemplars of the concept *emotion* rather than being represented in a subset of instances exemplifying a specific type of emotional experience.

In summary, the findings of the present studies suggest that emotion concepts may be represented by exemplars in the form of autobiographical memories of emotional experiences. Certain experiences will form focal episodes which represent the core meaning of the concept, whereas more emotionally complex experiences will instantiate aspects of the general concept 'emotion'. It is proposed that experiences are classified as emotional and as being of a specific emotion to the extent to which they retrieve memories of focal or more complex emotional episodes.

REFERENCES

Alvey, N. G., *et al.* (1983). *GENSTAT: a general statistical programme*. The Numerical Algorithms Group, Oxford.

Barsalou, L. W. (1982). Context-independent and context-dependent information in concepts. *Memory and Cognition*, **10**, 82–93.

Barsalou, L. W. (1985). Ideals, central tendency, and frequency of instantiation. *Journal of Experimental Psychology: Learning, Memory and Cognition*, **11**, 629–654.

Bekerian, D. A., & Conway, M. A. (1988). Everyday contexts. In G. Davies & D. Thomson (eds.), *Context in memory: memory in context*. Chichester: John Wiley.

Brewer, W. F. (1986). What is autobiographical memory? In D. C. Rubin (ed.), *Autobiographical memory*. Cambridge: Cambridge University Press.

Conway, M. A. (1987). Verifying autobiographical facts. *Cognition*, **25**, 39–58.

Conway, M. A. (1990). Autobiographical memory and conceptual representation. Manuscript under review.

Conway, M. A., & Bekerian, D. A. (1987a). Situational knowledge and emotions. *Cognition and Emotion*, **1**, 145–191.

Conway, M. A., & Bekerian, D. A. (1987b). Organization in autobiographical memory. *Memory and Cognition*, **15**, 119–132.

Conway, M. A., & Bekerian, D. A. (1987c). Characteristics of vivid memories. In M. M. Gruneberg, P. E. Morris & R. N. Sykes (eds.), *Practical aspects of memory: current theory and research*, Vol. 2, (pp. 519–524). Chichester: John Wiley.

de Sousa, R. (1987). *The rationality of emotion*. London: MIT Press.

Kahneman, D., & Miller, D. T. (1986). Norm theory: comparing reality to its alternatives. *Psychological Review*, **93**, 136–153.

Medin, D. L., & Schaffer, M. M. (1978). Context theory of classification learning. *Psychological Review*, **85**, 207–238.

Medin, D. L., & Smith, E. E. (1981). Strategies in classification learning. *Journal of Experimental Psychology: Human Learning and Memory*, **7**, 241–253.

Rubin, D. C., & Friendly, M. (1986). Predicting which words get recalled: measures of free recall, availability, goodness, emotionality, and pronunciability for 925 nouns. *Memory and Cognition*, **14**, 79–94.

Smith, E. E., & Medin, D. L. (1981). *Categories and Concepts*. Cambridge, MA: Harvard University Press.

10

The Cohesiveness of Phobic Concepts

FRASER N. WATTS

MRC Applied Psychology Unit, Cambridge

INTRODUCTION

Recent work on the structure of categorical concepts has emphasized that they are much more variable than used to be supposed (Smith and Medin, 1981; Medin and Smith, 1984; Neisser, 1987). Barsalou (1982, 1987) has formulated this by saying that different concepts can represent the same category on different occasions, and that the process of constructing concepts to represent categories is one that is highly dependent on the context.

My purpose in this chapter is to consider the role of emotion as one of the contextual factors that influences the kind of concept with which a category is represented. This is a large and under-explored topic, so to narrow things down to manageable proportions I shall confine myself to the emotion of fear as it occurs in the context of simple animal phobias such as phobias of spiders, dogs or snakes. I leave to one side whether concepts associated with other emotions have similar properties. If emotion affects categorical concepts at all, this seems a promising place to look. In animal phobias, the emotional reactions are powerful, reliable (that is, relatively independent of other situational factors) and long term, in many cases over a lifetime.

Another advantage is that it is relatively straightforward to compare the concept that an animal phobic has of a particular animal with the concept of a non-phobic. Some categories of emotion-producing situations are likely to be so specially constructed that the categories do not exist at all for the bulk of the population. For example, a particular individual may have a category of social situations in which he is likely to feel humiliated. To most people, the exemplars of such a category might appear to have almost nothing in common. In this, they would be analogous to the 'goal-directed' categories that Barsalou has studied. In contrast, though spider phobics may have particular kinds of spider concept, everyone has some kind of concept of a spider. The category concerned is basically a common, taxonomic one, though for phobics it may have particular properties.

A disclaimer that needs to be made early on is that I am not necessarily suggesting that emotion affects categorical concepts in any unique way. Phobic concepts may have properties which are similar to concepts of other objects which have important personal significance, even though they do not elicit emotion. My guess, though I know of no relevant data, is that categorical concepts in which powerful evaluative reactions are involved are likely to have similar properties, whether or not emotion is involved.

THE ROLE OF CORRELATED ATTRIBUTES IN CATEGORICAL CONCEPTS

A theory of categorical concepts that was popular ten years ago was that concepts are based on the correlations between attributes in the natural environment (Rosch, 1978). The idea was that the world is divided into clusters of correlated attributes that 'cut the world at its joints' and form natural categories. Taxonomic categories, such as spiders, were seen as preserving these attribute clusters, thus making maximal use of the correlational structure of the environment.

Various doubts have subsequently been put forward about this theory. One is that it is not clear how correlations are selected and analysed to generate clusters (Keil, 1981). Another problem, pointed out by Barsalou (1985), and one particularly germane to the topic of this chapter, is that the correlations that people perceive as existing between attributes are not necessarily those that really exist in the natural environment. One clear demonstration of this is the phenomenon of 'illusory correlation' that Chapman and Chapman (1969) have demonstrated in the field of clinical judgement. Subjects who were presented with a series of case descriptions, together with a drawing from each case, perceived correlations between drawings and clinical characteristics that reflec-ted their theoretical assumptions but had no basis in the actual data.

Perceived correlations between attributes may not reflect the structure of nature, but they are probably nevertheless significant for the person concerned. The hypothesis that guided the research to be reported here is that spider phobics perceive spider attributes as being unusually highly correlated. Thus, if a putative spider exemplar is seen as being 'spidery' on one attribute it will tend to be seen as spidery on other attributes too. To put it another way, it is hypothesized that phobics do not apply spider attributes to exemplars as uniquely and discriminately as do controls.

This hypothesis might be formulated in terms of phobics having a relatively 'simple' conceptual structure. Landau (1980) has provided convergent evidence for this hypothesis using a different paradigm (a listing methodology) in a study of dog phobics. Both a highly correlated attribute structure and poverty of attribute listings have been taken as indices of cognitive simplicity. He predicted that dog phobics would be able to list relatively few examples of dogs and relatively few dog attributes. The trend was in the predicted direction in both cases, but was significant only for dog examples, and here the interpretation was complicated by the fact that dog phobics also listed fewer examples of mammals.

The methodology is not a powerful one, but the results are at least broadly consistent with the claim that phobics perceive spider attributes as being relatively highly correlated.

The First Study

The technique used for studying correlations between attributes was based on the repertory grid technique of George Kelly (1955). Subjects were supplied with a standard set of eight spider attributes (constructs) spanning descriptive and evaluative features ('large-bodied', 'hairy', 'dark', 'fast-moving', 'long-legged', 'frightening', 'unpleasant', 'easy to deal with'). The exemplars (elements) were presented in picture form as it was thought that subjects would not all be sufficiently familiar with species names. For each construct, subjects rank-ordered ten colour pictures of different spiders for how much they exemplified the attribute concerned. The task was completed by a group of 35 spider phobics recruited by newspaper advertisement, and 18 non-phobic controls from the Applied Psychology Unit Panel subjects.

The data have been reported in outline elsewhere (Watts and Sharrock, 1985), though they are here analysed in more detail and set in a new theoretical context. An analysis of variance was run on the rankings obtained, with the elements as a repeated measures factor. The coefficient of concordance, w, was used as an index of the overall degree of correlation between attributes for each subject. This index is linearly related to the mean correlation between attributes. Concordance was significantly higher in phobics ($x = 0.46$; SD $= 0.16$) than controls ($x = 0.37$; SD $= 0.14$) using a 5% significance level on a two-tailed t-test. Phobics thus perceived spider attributes as being more highly correlated across spider exemplars than did controls. This was substantiated by a significant correlation within the 35 spider phobics tested between their preoccupation with spiders as assessed by a questionnaire and the index of concordance ($r = 0.32$, $p < 0.05$).

The groups did not differ in verbal intelligence and there was no correlation between verbal intelligence and concordance. The between-group difference in concordance thus cannot be attributed to a difference in intellectual ability.

It should be noted that no assumption is being made about how well the correlational structures derived from phobics and controls map on to the structure of correlations in the real world. Phobics might be assuming more correlational structure than actually obtains. Alternatively, controls might be insensitive to the correlational structure of spider attributes in the environment.

Fresh analyses of these data have recently been conducted using a breakdown of attributes into descriptive and evaluative ones. There were five descriptive attributes (dark, hairy, large-bodied, long-legged and fast-moving) and three evaluative/goal-directed attributes (unpleasant, frightening, easy to deal with). Independent raters agreed on this classification. There was a clear tendency for correlations between pairs of descriptive attributes to be higher in phobics than in controls. The same tendency was equally apparent for correlations between pairs of one descriptive and one evaluative attribute. However, the tendency did not apply to the correlations between pairs of evaluative attributes—though,

Table 10.1 Mean z-transformed correlations between types of attributes

	Phobics	Controls
Descriptive × descriptive	0.48	0.37
Descriptive × evaluative	0.74	0.67
Evaluative × evaluative	0.93	1.0

with only three such correlations, this has to be treated very cautiously. (The z-transformed correlations are given in Table 10.1). Thus, in controls, the evaluative response to spiders is internally coherent but more independent of neutral, descriptive features. Descriptive features are also more independent of each other in controls.

The dichotomization into evaluative and descriptive attributes glosses over some subtleties. Among evaluative attributes, 'frightening' and 'unpleasant' were more 'central' (had higher correlations with other attributes) in the phobic group. However, 'easy to deal with', uniquely among the eight attributes studied, was higher in the control group. This may reflect the fact that controls are better able than spider phobics to give accounts of how they would actually deal with a spider (Watts, Sharrock and Trezise, 1986). Descriptive attributes also do not all show the same pattern of differences between groups. The three that show most clearly the pattern of higher correlations with other attributes in phobics than controls are 'dark', 'hairy' and 'fast'. The two size attributes show smaller between-group differences, 'large' being relatively central in the categories of both groups, and 'long-legged' being relatively independent of other attributes in both groups.

Despite the fact that spider attributes are generally more highly correlated in phobics, the structure of the spider category is basically similar to that found in controls. This was assessed by computing centrality values for each attribute (that is, the mean z-transformed correlations of each attribute with every other attribute). The resulting centrality values are given in Table 10.2. There is remarkable similarity in the relative centrality of these various attributes in the categorical concepts of phobics and controls. The Pearson correlation between

Table 10.2 Centrality values for each attribute

	Phobics	Controls
Frightening	0.83	0.77
Unpleasant	0.75	0.65
Hairy	0.71	0.52
Easy to deal with	0.67	0.76
Large-bodied	0.60	0.52
Dark	0.57	0.38
Fast-moving	0.40	0.15
Long-legged	−0.13	0.05

the two sets of values is 0.92 ($p < 0.001$). It is clear that, in both groups, evaluative attributes tend to be the most central (that is, to have the highest correlations with other attributes).

It remains an outstanding question whether the pattern of higher correlations between attributes found in the phobic group is specific to spider attributes. Animal phobics generally do not show a range of other psychopathology beyond their specific animal phobia, though the possibility cannot be ruled out that they have a general tendency to perceive the attributes associated with a variety of categories as being relatively highly correlated. There is evidence, reviewed by Button (1983) derived from more conventional repertory grids with individual people as the exemplars/elements, that people with emotional disorders tend to perceive attributes/constructs as being relatively highly correlated. However, even here, it seems that the tendency is largely one that relates specifically to attributes/constructs concerned with the subjects' emotional problems. For example, Winter (1983) found that the tendency for attributes to be relatively highly correlated in a mixed group of neurotic subjects applied particularly to attributes related to personal symptoms, and may have been confined to such attributes.

THE GRADED STRUCTURE OF PHOBIC CATEGORIES

A major focus of interest in research on categorical concepts over the last decade has been their graded structure. It will help to focus the concerns of this chapter to proceed to consider how phobics perform on tests of graded structure. Where attributes are perceived to be relatively highly correlated, the graded structure of categories will be more nearly unidimensional. Exemplars which are perceived as being atypical on one attribute will tend to be seen as atypical on other attributes too. Clearly, this is more true of phobics' than controls' spider categories.

Relatively unidimensional categories may be found to have a steep graded structure, though this is not a necessary deduction. Phobics may thus show a steeper graded structure for spiders than do controls. For example, it might be predicted that, though 'daddy-long-legs' would be given borderline typicality ratings as spiders by non-phobics, they would not be accepted as spiders at all by phobics.

Another hypothesis would be that phobics would show higher correlations between attribute ratings and typicality ratings. This would be consistent with the finding of higher perceived correlations between attributes already reported. Indeed correlations between typicality ratings and other attributes may be a particularly sensitive index of the cohesiveness of phobic categories.

It would be particularly interesting to examine whether both descriptive and evaluative attributes show equally strong correlations with typicality ratings in phobics. This question is somewhat similar to the one that Barsalou (1985) has examined recently concerning the relative relationship of 'ideal' instances (which are comparable to evaluative attributes) to category structure in common taxonomic categories and goal-derived categories. It might be suggested that, for phobics, the spider category is not just a common taxonomic one but, because of the need to avoid or escape from spiders, is also a goal-directed category. In fact, Barsalou found, contrary to what might have been expected, that ideals were no more closely related to typicality in goal-directed than in common taxonomic categories.

The Second Study

We have recently conducted a further small-scale study of spider categories in phobics with two main objectives. One was to obtain some preliminary typicality data. The other was to remedy the lack of a control category in the first study. The second study was similar in many ways to the first, but included the following modifications:

a) Both spider and beetle categories were studied, with an increased number of exemplars in each (16). Six exemplars were used in each category that strictly fell outside the category concerned but were in many respects similar. Again, all exemplars were represented by pictures taken from the Audubon Society Field Guide to North American Insects and Spiders (Milne and Milne, 1980).

b) The same categories were used as before for both spiders and beetles, except that (i) 'long-legged' was replaced by 'thick-legged' (because in the first study it had been unrelated to other attributes in both groups), (ii) 'easy to deal with' was replaced by 'difficult to deal with' (so that the evaluative attributes were all negatively balanced), and (iii) 'hairy' was replaced, for *beetles only*, by shiny (all other attributes seemed to apply as well to beetles as to spiders).

c) Typicality ratings were obtained using the question devised by Barsalou (1985) of how 'good an example' an exemplar was of its category.

d) Rankings were replaced by 9-point ratings in which subjects arranged the exemplars under guide cards labelled 1 to 9. Ratings were used for typicality because there was particular interest in the shape of the distribution obtained; they therefore also used for the other attributes to facilitate examination of the relationship between typicality ratings and other attributes.

Six phobic and six control subjects were run, selected as before. The order of spider and beetle ratings was counterbalanced. Within each animal category, the order in which the nine attributes was presented was randomized. Data will be presented first on correlations between attributes, and then on typicality ratings.

To examine the general level of correlation between attributes, the matrix of Pearson correlations between attribute ratings that was obtained for each subject was transformed to a matrix of z scores. The six matrices in each of the four cells of the design (phobics' matrices for spiders and for beetles; controls' matrices for spiders and for beetles) were then averaged. Analyses were conducted on these averaged matrices. (All the correlations reported below are z-transformed.)

There was once again a trend for spider attributes to be more highly correlated on average in phobics (0.76) than in controls (0.66), though it did not reach significance. However, the number of subjects was much smaller than in the first study, and ratings may have proved less sensitive than rankings. Correlations between attributes were generally lower for the beetle category than for the spider category, but there was no comparable trend for them to be higher in phobics (0.48) than in controls (0.47). A two-way analysis of variance (groups × categories) produced a significant main effect of categories ($F(1,70) = 25.7$, $p < 0.001$), but the groups by categories interaction was not significant ($F(1,70) = 1.1$). Individual attributes again showed somewhat different patterns.

'Dark' as before, was the attribute that differed most between groups, being more highly correlated with other spider attributes in phobics (0.45) than in controls (0.19) ($t = 2.61$, $p < 0.05$). In contrast, the trend was for 'dark' to be *less* highly correlated with other attributes in spider phobics (0.38) than in controls (0.51). Linguistically, dark is an example of a 'double-aspect' term referring both to a physical and a moral/psychological quality. It may thus be particularly sensitive to the effects of phobic status.

As in the first study it was found that phobics and controls showed strong agreement about the relative centrality of the various attributes to the spider category (as indexed by the averaged z-transformed correlation of each attribute with all other attributes). The values are given in Table 10.3. Phobics and controls showed a similar pattern of values; the Pearson correlation between them being 0.84, ($p < 0.01$). It is substantially the same pattern as was found before, though changes in wording of two of the attributes prevents this being tested empirically.

The present study also allowed similar centrality indices for the beetle category to be examined, and these are also given in Table 10.3. The Pearson correlation between phobics and controls was 0.96 ($p < 0.001$). Evaluative attributes are clearly as central to the beetle category as they are to the spider category, so there is evidently nothing unique to spiders about this. There was also substantial similarity between the spider and beetle categories in the relative centrality of the various *descriptive* attributes, somewhat more so for phobics than controls —though the small number of descriptive attributes only permits possible trends to be indicated. Perhaps, for phobics, the structure of the spider category is so firmly established and dominant that it is used in the construal of other related categories such as beetles.

Table 10.3   Centrality values (second study)

	Spiders		Beetles	
	Phobics	Controls	Phobics	Controls
Unpleasant	1.28	1.13	0.84	0.89
Frightening	1.27	1.11	0.86	0.85
Difficult to deal with	1.24	1.06	0.87	0.93
Thick-legged	0.66	0.71	0.46	0.25
Large-bodied	0.50	0.58	0.28	0.39
Hairy	0.49	0.46	0.26	0.42
Dark	0.45	0.19	0.38	0.51
Fast-moving	0.23	0.30	0.28	−0.15

TYPICALITY RATINGS

The typicality ratings of spiders by phobics showed a tendency to use the extremes of the scale (both very typical and very atypical), reflecting a steeper graded structure. However, this was less pronounced than had been expected, and did not reach significance. Nevertheless, the trend was for phobics (cf. controls) to allocate more exemplars to both extreme categories in their typicality ratings of spiders (very typical: 4.7 cf. 3.0; very atypical 2.3 cf. 1.7). For beetles, there are hardly any differences at all between groups (very typical: 3.2, 3.0; very atypical 0.8). There is thus a non-significant trend towards the predicted steep graded structure for spiders in phobics. However, there was also a good deal of within-group variability in the extent of the phenomenon; it was not possible to track down the source of this with the measures available.

It had been predicted that the typicality ratings of spiders by phobics would show stronger correlations with other attributes, and the question was also raised of whether this would apply particularly to evaluative attributes rather than descriptive ones. Here the results were more encouraging. (All the correlations that follow are again z-transformed).

There was a clear and significant tendency for the typicality ratings of spiders to be more highly correlated with other attribute ratings in phobics than in controls (see Table 10.4). This was somewhat stronger for correlations with evaluative attributes than with descriptive attributes (0.50, 0.34), but there were too few evaluative attributes to test this interaction.

The relationship between typicality ratings and other attributes in beetles was very different (see Table 10.4). There was no difference between groups as far as the average correlation with descriptive attributes was concerned. Correlations between typicality and evaluative attributes were actually higher in controls than in phobics, though this was largely due to one phobic who produced a strong, negative correlation; that is, the least typical beetles were rated as frightening, unpleasant and difficult to handle.

Thus, though this small-scale study did not replicate the general tendency for spider attributes to be more highly correlated with each other (except for 'dark), it produced clear evidence that typicality ratings are more closely linked to other spider attributes in phobics than in controls. This means that phobics' concept of

Table 10.4 Z-transformed correlations of typicality ratings with attribute rating.

	Phobics	Controls
Spiders		
All attributes	0.71	0.40
Descriptive attributes	0.50	0.34
Evaluative attributes	1.06	0.51
Beetles		
All attributes	0.14	0.37
Descriptive attributes	0.24	0.22
Evaluative attributes	−0.02	0.62

a 'good example' of a spider is more clearly defined than for controls. Typicality judgements are in some ways the most abstract judgements that people can make about a spider. They also seem to be the ones that, more clearly than any other, embody the cohesiveness of phobics' spider categories.

That typicality tends to be more strongly linked to evaluative than to descriptive attributes is not surprising. It has been a repeated finding of the research reported here that evaluative attributes are the most central ones in the categories studied. It is also the case that (a) evaluative judgements have high internal coherence as reflected by the very high correlations of evaluative attributes with each other, and (b) descriptive attributes generally correlate more highly with evaluative attributes than with each other. Evaluative attributes (the negative ideal of a spider) are in some sense the core of the concepts for all subjects, but it is the sense of spider typicality that is unusually well articulated in phobics.

IMPLICATIONS OF CATEGORY STRUCTURE FOR EMOTIONAL ADAPTATION

In the final section of this chapter, implications of the results for phobics' reactions to spiders will be considered. I shall focus on what, for simplicity, will be called the high *cohesiveness* of phobics' concepts of spiders. This has two main facets:

a) the tendency, found more clearly in the first than the second study, for descriptive attributes to correlate more highly, both with each other and with evaluative attributes, in phobics than in controls; and

b) the stronger relationship of typicality ratings to other attributes, especially evaluative attributes, found in the second study.

The argument that will be deployed is in some ways similar to one that Peter Lang has made concerning the representation of phobic objects in the conceptual structure. He has referred to this as the 'emotion prototype' (see Lang, 1984; Lang, 1985; Watts and Blackstock, 1987; Lang, 1987). Lang's notion of an emotion prototype goes beyond the kind of categorical concepts that have been considered here and includes, not only stimulus features, but also what he terms 'response' and 'meaning' features. He has argued that, in phobics, emotion prototypes have high 'coherence'. By this he means partly that the three levels of the emotion prototype (stimulus, response and meaning levels) are relatively tightly connected, but also that the various components of each individual level operate coherently. For example, he has accumulated a good deal of evidence that, in phobics, the various components of the response level (physiological, behavioural and verbal) operate together particularly closely. It is also part of his theory—though he has offered less direct evidence for it—that the stimulus level is also internally coherent. The data presented in this chapter support this component of his theory.

An inference which he has drawn from the coherence of the phobic prototype is that relatively few stimulus features are required to activate the emotion prototype as a whole. Perhaps, where people have phobic concepts with high cohesiveness, there is scope to infer attributes which have not been directly observed. Alternatively, where links between attributes and typicality are unusually strong, a descriptive attribute can more readily activate an abstract judgement of high spider typicality. The data offer stronger support for the latter possibility.

Highly cohesive phobic concepts can have adaptive value. It can permit people to achieve, relatively quickly, a fully specified representation of an emotional stimulus such as a spider. This will in turn permit the kind of quick and synergistic reaction which is often adaptive in emotional situations. This point is consistent with Oatley and Johnson-Laird's (1987) theory that the adaptive value of emotions lies in bringing about a rapid change in a person's mode of processing.

However, there are also drawbacks in having a highly cohesive emotional category. If phobic attributes are inferred on the basis of an assumed correlational structure and with minimum observation, people can reach the view that they are confronted with a frightening object on the basis of very limited detailed inspection. This can have maladaptive consequences of two kinds. It may prevent subjects from making detailed observations of the phobic stimulus, some of which might mitigate their negative emotional reactions. Secondly, the failure to encode the actual detailed features of the stimulus adequately is likely to interfere with the habituation process which probably underlies the well-established fact that systematic observation of a phobic stimulus leads to anxiety reduction (Watts and Blackstock, 1987). The evidence (Watts and Blackstock, 1987) suggests that impoverished observation is particularly deleterious as far as long-term anxiety reduction is concerned.

In this way, emotional reactions to a phobic stimulus can 'take on a life of their own', in which actual observations of the phobic object play a small part and there is relatively little scope for adaptive processes of change to get to work. Though no claims can be made about the role of conceptual cohesiveness in the development of phobic reactions, it seems likely that it contributes to the maintenance of phobias.

REFERENCES

Barsalou, L. W. (1982). Context-independent and context-dependent information in concepts. *Memory and Cognition*, **10**, 82–93.

Barsalou, L. W. (1985). Ideals, central tendency, and frequency of instantiation as determinants of graded structure in categories. *Journal of Experimental Psychology: Learning, Memory and Cognition*, **11**, 629–649.

Barsalou, L. W. (1987). The instability of graded structure: implications for the nature of concepts. In U. Neisser (ed.), *Concepts and conceptual development: Ecological and intellectual factors in categorisation*. Cambridge: Cambridge University Press.

Button, E. (1983). Personal construct theory and psychological well-being. *British Journal of Medical Psychology*, **56**, 313–321.

Chapman, L. J., & Chapman, J. P. (1969). Illusory correlation as an obstacle to the use of valid psychodiagnostic signs. *Journal of Abnormal Psychology*, **74**, 272–280.

Kelly, G. (1955). *The psychology of personal constructs*. New York: W. W. Norton.

Keil, F. C. (1981). Constraints on knowledge and cognitive development. *Psychological Review*, **88**, 197–227.

Landau, R. J. (1980). The role of semantic schemata in phobic word interpretation. *Cognitive Therapy and Research, 4*, 427–434.

Lang, P. J. (1984). Cognition in emotion: concept and action. In C. E. Izard, R. J. Zajonc & J. Kagan (eds.), *Emotions, cognition and behaviour*. Cambridge: Cambridge University Press.

Lang, P. J. (1985). The cognitive psychophysiology of emotion: fear and anxiety. In A. H. Tuma & J. Maser (eds.), *Anxiety and the anxiety disorders*. Hillsdale, NJ: Erlbaum.

Lang, P. J. (1987). Image as action: a reply to Watts and Blackstock. *Cognition and Emotion, 1*, 407–426.

Medin, D. L., & Smith, E. E. (1984). Concepts and concept formation, *Annual Review of Psychology, 35*, 113–138.

Milne, L., & Milne, M. (1980). *The Audobon Society field guide to North American insects and spiders*. New York: Knopf.

Neisser, U. (1987). *Concepts and conceptual development: Ecological and intellectual factors in categorisation*. Cambridge: Cambridge University Press.

Oatley, K. J., & Johnson-Laird, P. N. (1987). Towards a cognitive theory of emotions. *Cognition and Emotion, 1*, 29–50.

Rosch, E. (1978). Principles of categorisation. In E. Rosch & B. B. Lloyd (eds.), *Cognition and categorization*. Hillsdale, NJ: Erlbaum.

Smith, E. E., & Medin, D. C. (1981). *Categories and concepts*. Cambridge, MA: Harvard University Press.

Watts, F. N., & Blackstock, A. J. (1987). Lang's theory of emotional imagery. *Cognition and Emotion, 1*, 391–405.

Watts, F. N., & Sharrock, R. (1985). Relationships between spider constructs in phobics. *British Journal of Medical Psychology, 58*, 149–153.

Watts, F.N., Sharrock, R., & Trezise, L. (1986). Detail and elaboration in phobic imagery. *Behavioural Psychotherapy, 14*, 115–123.

Winter, D. A. (1983). Logical inconsistency in construct relationships: conflict or complexity? *British Journal of Medical Psychology, 56*, 79–87.

11

A Prime Time for Emotion: Cognitive Vulnerability and the Emotional Disorders

M. J. POWER
MRC Social Psychiatry Unit, London

INTRODUCTION

The increasing pre-eminence of the cognitive approach in psychology and the parallel development of the cognitive therapies has led to the question of cognitive vulnerability to emotional disorders. One of the critical issues is whether there are particular cognitive characteristics that increase an individual's risk for disorders such as anxiety and depression. The initial attempts to address this issue focused on self-report measures. For example, the influence of Beck's (e.g. 1976) cognitive therapy has led to the development of a number of self-report measures which include the following: the Dysfunctional Attitude Scale (DAS) which measures extreme or negative beliefs (Weissman and Beck, 1978); the Automatic Thoughts Questionnaire (ATQ) which measures the occurrence of negative thoughts (Hollon and Kendall, 1980); and the Hopelessness Scale (HS) which measures pessimism about the future (Beck *et al.*, 1974). (See Segal and Shaw, 1988, for a review of these and other self-report measures.)

The initial results with scales such as the DAS, ATQ and HS were very promising and showed that during episodes of depression or anxiety patients scored significantly higher than controls; that is, they were found to subscribe to more extreme or negative beliefs, they reported more negative automatic thoughts, and they expressed more pessimism about the future (see Table 11.1). However, as studies began to accumulate with individuals who had recovered from episodes of depression, it emerged that these individuals reverted to normal or near-normal levels on these scales. If it is borne in mind that in some of these studies the patients were not fully recovered and that the experience of an episode of depression or anxiety could potentially lead to residual increases

Lines of Thinking, Volume 2 Edited by K.J. Gilhooly, M.T.G. Keane, R.H. Logie and G. Erdos
© 1990 John Wiley & Sons Ltd

Table 11.1 Mean values obtained by patients with emotional disorders on the DAS, the ATQ and the HS

	Episode	Recovery	Control
Dysfunctional Attitude Scale	$151.1(N = 9)$	$124.3(N = 7)$	119.4 ± 27.1^c
Automatic Thoughts[a] Questionnaire	$95.6(N = 7)$	$60.9(N = 4)$	48.6 ± 10.9^d
Hopelessness[b] Scale	$11.4(N = 4)$	$4.6(N = 3)$	4.1 ± 3.1^e

N = Number of studies on which each value is based; these are taken from the tables presented by Segal and Shaw (1988), with the following additions:
  [a] Harrell and Ryon (1983); Hollon and Kendall (1980)
  [b] Wilkinson and Blackburn (1981).
The values for the controls are from the following studies:
  [c] Weissman (1979)
  [d] Hollon and Kendall (1980)
  [e] Wilkinson and Blackburn (1981)

on the scales anyway, then the failure to find a stable vulnerability factor is all the more surprising.

The failure to find stable vulnerability factors has led to a number of different responses. From the theoretical point of view, Beck and his colleagues (see, for example, Beck *et al.*, 1979) proposed that between episodes of depression the dysfunctional schemata become latent and that they are only activated by the appropriate stressors. Although this interpretation has been widely accepted, it is *post hoc* and it ignores a number of other possibilities. Before the latency interpretation is accepted, at least three other options must be thoroughly investigated.

First, it is possible that the derivation of a single measure from scales such as the DAS may be too insensitive to pick up residual extreme or negative beliefs that remain only for the individual's most overvalued role or goal (cf. Reda *et al.*, 1985). To obviate this problem, sub-scaled versions of the scales could be derived either statistically or conceptually; thus at the MRC Social Psychiatry Unit we are currently developing a sub-scaled version of the DAS which consists of items which address issues about dependency, achievement and self-control, the results of which we hope to report in due course.

Second, self-report questionnaires that contain hedonically toned items may be subject to a number of response-bias and mood-congruency effects (see, for example, Williams, 1984); thus, the existence of a negative mood during depression may bias the individual towards subscribing to negative items, whereas the normal state of positive self-regard may bias the individual towards subscribing to positively toned items. One way to avoid this problem is to employ measures that are less transparent to the respondent. For example, there is some evidence that the Cognitive Failures Questionnaire (CFQ) (Broadbent *et al.*, 1982), which is a self-report measure of everyday failures of memory, action and perception, may provide a stable vulnerability measure of susceptibility to anxiety and obsessional disorders (Gordon, 1985; Power, 1988). The CFQ consists of items such as 'Do you bump into people?' and 'Do you fail to notice signposts on the road?', which are less obviously hedonically toned (though depending on who it was you bumped into or which signpost you failed to notice you could end up with other major problems instead).

The third option, and the one that will be focused on for the rest of this chapter, is that experimental cognitive paradigms need to be developed which assess both automatic and controlled processes. In many respects, it is no surprise that problems have arisen with the self-report approach to vulnerability, because self-reports focus on controlled processes rather than on automatic processes. Nisbett and Wilson (1977) argued that the individual has no access at all to underlying or automatic processes, though it would seem more likely that the penetrability of automatic processes varies across modalities (see, for example, Dixon, 1981). Nevertheless, even a limited access to underlying processes means that the individual can only present the current 'best model' which will not always represent the true state of affairs. A good example of this partial dissociation between automatic and controlled processes comes in fact from the clinical literature on anxiety. Following Lang's (e.g. 1979) three-systems theory of anxiety, it has been clear that the anxious individual need not be anxious according to self-report, yet may display physiological and behavioural evidence of anxiety. The moral is that it is necessary to develop tasks that address both the automatic and controlled aspects of cognitive vulnerability rather than focus on self-report measures alone.

A TASK TO MEASURE AUTOMATIC AND CONTROLLED PROCESSES

The need for the development of tasks that can assess both automatic and controlled processes in the emotional disorders has begun to receive consideration (see Williams *et al.*, 1988, for a review). For example, one such task that has proven useful with phobic and other patients is the so-called 'emotional stroop' (Watts *et al.*, 1986), in which the ink colours have to be named for words with a relevant emotional content. Following a suggestion of Gordon Bower's (1986) the particular paradigm that we chose to adapt for the study of cognitive vulnerability was the priming paradigm. Although most studies of priming have been designed to investigate word recognition and have combined priming with a lexical decision task (the decision about whether a string of letters is a word or a non-word), Bower summarized a wide range of other priming effects and suggested that the technique could be a useful one with which to investigate the emotional disorders.

Two initial studies that combined priming with a lexical decision task failed to find any significant effects in relation to mood. Clark *et al.* (1983) found no effect of mood induction on lexical decision times for pleasant and unpleasant words in a student sample. This lack of effect on lexical decision times was replicated with a sample of depressed inpatients by MacLeod, Tata and Mathews (1987). Not surprisingly, therefore, researchers are now being warned off the lexical decision paradigm (Williams *et al.*, 1988). However, the lexical decision task may be too low-level and insufficiently ego-involving to be sensitive to the priming effects that would be predicted to occur in the emotional disorders. But before the rationale behind the modified priming task that we are currently developing is presented, it is first necessary to digress in order to consider the model of depression for which the chosen form of the task provided an analogue.

A SOCIAL–COGNITIVE THEORY OF DEPRESSION

Together with Lorna Champion we have been working to develop a social–cognitive theory of depression (Champion and Power, 1990; Power and Champion, 1986; Power, 1987). This theory takes as its starting point a number of the proposals presented by Oatley and Bolton (1985).

The model is intended to be most applicable to the first episode of unipolar depression. As shown in Figure 11.1, the individual who is vulnerable to depression is likely to be characterized by one overvalued role or goal, whereas in contrast other roles and goals are considerably undervalued. Recent work by Lam and Power (1990) provides evidence of this pattern. A second characteristic of the vulnerable individual is what we have called the ambivalent self; namely, the vulnerable individual is proposed to have both extreme positive and extreme negative attitudes to the self. From a developmental perspective, however, we would consider that both the overvaluation of a single goal or role and the presence of an ambivalent model of the self derive from problems in the early relationship between the child and the main caretaker (see Champion and Power, 1990). So long as the vulnerable individual pursues the overvalued role or goal, the positive model of the self is superordinate; the individual maintains positive self-esteem to an extent that may sometimes border on the grandiose, but which often contains a strong undercurrent of self-criticism. The problem arises, of course, when such an individual experiences a negative life event that either threatens or leads to the loss of the overvalued role or goal; under these circumstances the normal mood and esteem repair processes break down and the negative part of the ambivalent self becomes predominant. Because the individual has no other valued role or goal, or because of the lack of availability of roles or goals that might be valued, the ensuing state of depression may be maintained by both personal and social factors.

Figure 11.1 also presents the proposed sequence for non-vulnerable individuals. For such an individual, the experience of a negative life event may

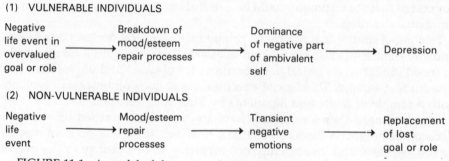

FIGURE 11.1   A model of depression based on Champion and Power (1990).

lead to the loss of a valued role or goal. This loss is also accompanied by feelings of sadness and dysphoria, which will increase according to the extent of the loss. However, the non-vulnerable individual will be protected by a combination of continuing positive self-esteem despite the significance of the loss and the availability of replacements for the lost goal or role. The negative emotions experienced will therefore not be accompanied by the self-criticism that Freud (1917) identified as the main difference between mourning and melancholia, so that these emotions will be more transient.

The first question that we wished to address with a modified priming task was whether an analogue of this theory could be set up that could reveal the mood and esteem repair processes in non-vulnerable individuals, and which would be sensitive to the possible breakdown of these processes in vulnerable individuals.

OUTLINE OF PRIMING STUDY

In order to provide an analogue of the theory presented in the last section, together with Chris Brewin we devised a priming task in which the priming stimuli consisted of the names of positive and negative life events and the targets consisted of positive and negative trait words for which the subject's task was to decide whether or not they were self-descriptive (see Figure 11.2).

Two categories of life events were chosen to reflect the dominant themes that have been identified in the depression literature (see, for example, Arieti and Bemporad, 1978); namely, interpersonal or role-related events which typically involve the loss or gain of a significant relationship, and achievement or goal-related events which involve the loss or gain of an important ambition. A third category of life event was also included to provide a further control. This category consisted of events that threaten the background goal of self-survival,

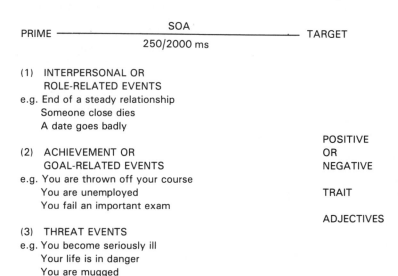

FIGURE 11.2 Outline of the priming study.

which Oatley and Johnson-Laird (1987) have argued are anxiety-related rather than depression-related events. These events are much less likely than the role- and goal-related events to be challenges to the individual's self-esteem. Both positive and negative versions of these three categories of events were constructed.

The self-referent adjective task was chosen because of the problems outlined earlier with the lexical decision task. The adjective task has proven useful in the investigation of mood effects on memory (Derry and Kuiper, 1981), it is ego-involving, and it should potentially be sensitive to fluctuations in the individual's mood.

The stimulus onset asynchrony (SOA) times between the prime and the target stimuli were chosen on the basis of Neely's (1977) original study of facilitatory and inhibitory processes in the lexical decision task. A short SOA of 250 ms was chosen, because Neely had found only automatic facilitatory effects at this speed. A second condition with an SOA of 2000 ms was also used for which Neely obtained both facilitatory and inhibitory effects. The predictions for the study were that at 250 ms facilitation effects should be found for positive adjectives following positive events and for negative adjectives following negative events. However, the esteem-threatening role and goal events at 2000 ms should lead to inhibition being obtained for the negative adjectives that followed negative primes if the subjects had brought into play the mood and esteem protective mechanisms. One note of caution for these predictions was that, in contrast to Neely, the primes used in this study consisted of phrases such as 'You fail an important exam' rather than single words; thus, different time courses for facilitation and inhibition might be obtained.

The preliminary analyses of a sample ($N = 49$) of non-depressed male and female undergraduate students that we have tested have shown a number of effects (Power and Brewin, 1990). Table 11.2 shows the uncorrected reaction times for each condition. These times are based on both the 'yes' and 'no'

Table 11.2   Uncorrected mean reaction times in seconds for priming study ($N = 49$)

	250 ms		2000 ms	
	Positive adjectives	Negative adjectives	Positive adjectives	Negative adjectives
1) Interpersonal + achievement events				
Positive event	1.203	1.256	1.201	1.242
Negative event	1.221	1.245	1.219	1.355
2) Threat events				
Positive event	1.165	1.274	1.148	1.292
Negative event	1.190	1.288	1.249	1.172

responses: the results were analysed in the form of a bivariate MANOVA test which included both the reaction times and the proportion of 'yes' responses as two dependent variables. Unless otherwise stated, only significant results for the reaction time analyses are presented.

Facilitation effects of positive events for positive adjectives (as compared to positive adjectives that followed negative events) were found at both SOAs for the threat events, and at the short SOA for the achievement events, but did not achieve significance at the long SOA for the interpersonal events ($F(1,48) = 1.73$). More interestingly, however, for the negative adjectives that followed negative events inhibition effects of an average of 110 ms were found for interpersonal and achievement events in the comparison of short and long SOAs, but in contrast the threat events showed a 116 ms facilitation effect for the equivalent comparison (see Table 11.2). Although we will need to run 'no prime' conditions before the facilitatory and inhibitory effects can be fully interpreted, these results suggest that, as predicted, normal subjects protect themselves against esteem-challenging negative events; this effect is revealed by the appearance of slower reaction times to negative adjectives at longer SOAs. In contrast, threat events which do not challenge self-esteem show facilitation effects at the longer SOAs.

During the running of the priming study, data were collected from a small sample of nine students who scored in the mild to moderately depressed range on the Beck Depression Inventory. These subjects showed a similar facilitation effect to the non-depressed subjects, with the threat events followed by negative adjectives at the longer SOA. However, they did not show an inhibition effect for the achievement and interpersonal events but again showed a small facilitation effect of an average of 18 ms. Therefore, the normal inhibition effect became a small facilitation effect for this small sample of dysphoric students, in line with the prediction made earlier that the normal mood- and esteem-repair processes break down in depression. This finding must be treated cautiously, though, until it is replicated with a larger sample of depressed subjects rather than with dysphoric students. Nevertheless, it is a good omen that the priming task may be useful in the assessment of cognitive vulnerability.

FURTHER COMMENTS AND CONCLUSIONS

In the theory of emotion developed by Oatley and Johnson-Laird (1987), one of the main functions of consciousness is considered to be the assignment of priority in a system of multiple goals and plans that are represented in modular independent automata. One of the crucial roles of emotion within this theory is to enable the system to switch priorities rapidly as appropriate; the presence of emotion may then serve to maintain this new goal or plan as priority until the situation has been resolved. One of the additional characteristics of automatic modular processes may be the occasional output into consciousness of information about their current state, which the individual experiences as interruptions to concentration, automatic thoughts, daydreaming, or whatever. It has been argued elsewhere that a proneness to such interruptions could possibly underly the relationship between cognitive failures and vulnerability to stress (Power,

1988). But whether or not the individual is vulnerable, one of the tasks for consciousness is to consider the status of this information and then decide whether to facilitate further processing or inhibit the automatic interruptions and continue with the current priority goal or plan. To give a minor example, an individual who is driving along a motorway will automatically experience intrusions into consciousness about the current state of stomach and bladder; initially these intrusions will not be considered sufficient to warrant an interruption of driving, though eventually the priority goal may well have to be set aside in order to satisfy these needs.

The priming study that has been outlined above attempts to present an analogue of this model. That is, the positive and negative primes are similar to the products of automatic processes entering consciousness which then receive either facilitatory or inhibitory processing. If one of the goals of consciousness is to maintain a mood and state of self-esteem that is congruent with the current model of the self—that is, a state of mild positive self-regard in normal individuals—then information which is esteem- or mood-threatening will be consciously inhibited in order to protect this state. The preliminary results that we have obtained with the priming task illustrate how these facilitatory and inhibitory processes may combine in normal individuals. Although the sample of dysphoric students was very small, their results at minimum show that the task may now be fruitfully extended to studies of currently depressed and recovered depressed individuals.

REFERENCES

Arieti, S., & Bemporad, J. (1978). *Severe and mild depression: The psychotherapeutic approach.* London: Tavistock.

Beck, A. T. (1976). *Cognitive therapy and the emotional disorders.* New York: Meridian.

Beck, A. T., Rush, A. J., Shaw, B. F., & Emery, G. (1979). *Cognitive therapy of depression: A treatment manual.* New York: Guilford Press.

Beck, A. T., Weissman, A., Lester, D., & Trexler, L. (1974). The measurement of pessimism: the Hopelessness Scale. *Journal of Consulting and Clinical Psychology,* **42,** 861–865.

Bower, G. H. (1986). Prime time in cognitive psychology. In P. Eelen & O. Fontaine (eds.), *Behavior therapy: Beyond the conditioning framework.* Hillsdale, NJ: Erlbaum.

Broadbent, D. E., Cooper, P. F., Fitzgerald, P., & Parkes, K. R. (1982). The Cognitive Failures Questionnaire (CFQ) and its correlates. *British Journal of Clinical Psychology,* **21,** 1–16.

Champion, L. A., & Power, M. J. (1990). Cognitive approaches to depression: towards a new synthesis.(Submitted for publication.)

Clark, D. M., Teasdale, J. D., Broadbent, D. E., & Martin, M. (1983). Effect of mood on lexical decisions. *Bulletin of the Psychonomic Society,* **21,** 175–178.

Derry, P. A., & Kuiper, N. A. (1981). Schematic processing and self-reference in clinical depression. *Journal of Abnormal Psychology,* **90,** 286–297.

Dixon, N. F. (1981). *Preconscious processing.* Chichester: John Wiley.

Freud, S. (1917). Mourning and melancholia. In *The Pelican Freud Library,* Vol. 11. Harmondsworth: Penguin (1984).

Gordon, P. K. (1985). Allocation of attention in obsessional disorder. *British Journal of Clinical Psychology,* **24,** 101–107.

Harrell, T. H., & Ryon, N. B. (1983). Cognitive–behavioral assessment of depression: clinical validation of the Automatic Thoughts Questionnaire. *Journal of Consulting and Clinical Psychology*, **51**, 721–725.

Hollon, S. D., & Kendall, P. C. (1980). Cognitive self-statements in depression: development of an Automatic Thoughts Questionnaire. *Cognitive Therapy and Research*, **4**, 383–395.

Lam, D., & Power, M. J. (1990). A questionnaire designed to assess roles and goals: a preliminary study. (Submitted for publication.)

Lang, P. J. (1979). A bio-informational theory of emotional imagery. *Psychophysiology*, **16**, 495–512.

MacLeod, C., Tata, P., & Mathews, A. (1987). Perception of emotionally valenced information in depression. *British Journal of Clinical Psychology*, **26**, 67–68.

Neely, J. H. (1977). Semantic priming and retrieval from lexical memory: the roles of inhibitionless spreading activation and limited capacity attention. *Journal of Experimental Psychology: General*, **106**, 226–254.

Nisbett, R. E., & Wilson, T. D. (1977). Telling more than we can know: verbal reports on mental processes. *Psychological Review*, **84**, 231–259.

Oatley, K., & Bolton, W. (1985). A social–cognitive theory of depression in reaction to life events. *Psychological Review*, **92**, 373–388.

Oatley, K., & Johnson-Laird, P. N. (1987). Towards a cognitive theory of emotions. *Cognition and Emotion*, **1**, 29–50.

Power, M. J. (1987). Cognitive theories of depression. In H. J. Eysenck & I. Martin (eds.), *Theoretical foundations of behavior therapy*. New York: Plenum.

Power, M. J. (1988). Cognitive failures, dysfunctional attitudes, and symptomatology: a longitudinal study. *Cognition and Emotion*, **2**, 133–143.

Power, M. J., & Brewin, C. R. (1990). Self-esteem regulation in an emotional priming task. *Cognition and Emotion*, (in press).

Power, M. J., & Champion, L. A. (1986). Cognitive approaches to depression: a theoretical critique. *British Journal of Clinical Psychology*, **25**, 201–212.

Reda, M. A., Carpiniello, B., Secchiaroli, L., & Blanco, S. (1985). Thinking, depression, and antidepressants: modified and unmodified beliefs during treatment with amitriptyline. *Cognitive Therapy and Research*, **9**, 135–144.

Segal, Z. V., & Shaw, B. F. (1988). Cognitive assessment: issues and methods. In K. S. Dobson (ed.), *Handbook of cognitive–behavioural therapies*. London: Hutchinson.

Watts, F. N., McKenna, F. P., Sharrock, R., & Trezise, L. (1986). Colour naming of phobia related words. *British Journal of Psychology*, **77**, 97–108.

Weissman, A. N. (1979). *Assessing depressogenic attitudes: A validation study.* Unpublished thesis, University of Pennsylvania.

Weissman, A. N., & Beck, A. T. (1978). Development and validation of the Dysfunctional Attitude Scale: a preliminary investigation. Paper presented at the meeting of the American Educational Research Association, Toronto.

Wilkinson, I. M., and Blackburn, I. M. (1981). Cognitive style in depressed and recovered depressed patients. *British Journal of Clinical Psychology*, **20**, 283–292.

Williams, J. M. G. (1984). *The psychological treatment of depression: A guide to the theory and practice of cognitive behaviour therapy*. London: Croom Helm.

Williams, J. M. G., Watts, F. N., MacLeod, C., & Mathews, A. (1988). *Cognitive psychology and emotional disorders*. Chichester: John Wiley.

Part III

Creative Processes

Creativity

GEORGE ERDOS
University of Newcastle upon Tyne

Creativity is one of the classic examples of psychology's 'fuzzy' concepts. Its meaning ranges from innovation to divergent thinking, including such concepts as ideational fluency, imagination, originality, lateral thinking, and so on. Its definition usually includes a sense of originality, uniqueness, or unusualness. While most psychologists agree that creativity is not a unitary trait and that non-cognitive factors are involved in the creative process, there is agreement that creativity is part of cognition and thinking. There are a number of reasons for this, one being that creativity entails symbolic representation and a mental manipulation of these symbols. Further, whether or not a product—which can be an idea or an object—is deemed to be original is based on social convention. In addition to the criterion of novelty, usefulness enters the picture, otherwise the idea may be viewed as merely eccentric. In order for an idea or product to be creative, it has to advance our understanding of the world or it has to overcome existing problems. For this to happen, the creative thinker has to be aware that the problem which requires a novel solution exists. This, in turn, makes sufficient grasp of the contents of a knowledge domain a prerequisite, before creative solutions in that domain can be offered. For a concise coverage of the prevailing issues in creativity see, for example, Gilhooly (1988) or Halpern (1984).

It has entered psychology's folklore that research into creativity received a great boost with the launch of the first Sputnik (Vernon, 1970). The Cold War has subsided since then, but new challenges, some of them global (such as pollution), some of them regional (such as famine), have emerged which require novel solutions. The question as to what fosters creativity in both individuals and in social systems is as valid as it was in the 1950s and it is a question which we neglect at our peril.

The following four chapters of this volume deal with creativity. They are quite wide-ranging in their coverage and their research methodology, giving a fair picture of the diversity within the field. They range from a conceptual analysis of artificial intelligence as an enhancer of human creativity (Sleeman), to an empirical investigation of the possible increase of creative production through a training in meaning dimensions and analogies (Kreitler and Kreitler). They also include a qualitative analysis of the work of two creative artists as support for Merleau–Ponty's Embodyment Theory (Haworth), and the proposal of an evolutionary perspective on creativity (Gear).

While on the surface these papers seem quite disparate, they share a common conceptualization of creativity. Furthermore, all four of them address tacitly or explicitly one of the central conundrums of psychology and philosophy; namely the relationship between the world and its symbolic representation in humans. Creativity involves the manipulation of this symbolic representation and its rearrangement into a novel form.

Sleeman discusses the interaction between 'artificial intelligence', including knowledge-based systems, and cognition. (For a concise discussion of AI see, for example, Best (1986), and for a more detailed coverage see Michie and Johnston (1985), O'Shea and Eisenstadt (1984) and Boden (1987).) Sleeman points out that one way in which new developments in this field can enhance human creativity is by shifting some of the tedious, routine work required for scientific progress to machines and thus leaving more time for creative thought. For a system to be intelligent it has to be able to learn and thus to refine its existing knowledge base. Sleeman compares human and machine knowledge acquisition. His central thesis is 'that the system's knowledge should be used to highlight inconsistencies in its knowledge base, and, given highly focused information, the creativity of the human can often *resolve* such ambiguities.'

Gear argues that creative expression serves an adaptive role through evolution by enabling the channelling of surplus energy into a safe outlet. She maintains that environmental pressures played an important role in the evolution of both creative persons and creative processes and that physiological factors have an important influence on the development of creativity. This links in closely with Gear's theorizing about perception and the evolution of style (Gear, 1989).

Haworth discusses the nature of pre-reflexive thought and creativity within Merleau-Ponty's Embodyment Theory. Merleau-Ponty, a contemporary phenomenologist philosopher, explored the origins of perceptual knowledge and consciousness. He maintains that we obtain primary knowledge of the world through our body. He distinguishes between *primary meaning*, which is reached through coexisting with the world and is brought about mainly by pre-reflexive thought, and *intellectual meaning* reached through analysis (Merleau-Ponty, 1962, 1964).

Haworth maintains that the process of embodyment involving pre-reflexive and reflexive thought plays an important role in artistic creativity—an Embodyment Theory of Art. In support of his ideas Haworth discusses contemporary print-making as an example and provides an analysis of the work of two printmakers, Michael Rothenstein and Alan Green, based on interviews with these artists and their own writings.

Kreitler and Kreitler provide a theoretical and empirical investigation of the role of cognitive factors in creativity. This work is closely tied to their theory about the nature of meaning and symbolism (Kreitler, 1986; Kreitler and Kreitler, 1985). They consider cognition as an interactive system with regard to meaning. Cognition processes meaning, but its processing is codetermined by the meaning it processes. In this respect this work can be taken as the natural development of the 'new look' in perception. Kreitler and Kreitler show that a frequent application of meaning variables has an enhancing impact on creative performance.

If one wishes to generalize from these four papers to the field of creativity, then it seems that the study of creativity is going through a similar shift of emphasis to that of intelligence: namely, moving away from the psychometric approach and towards a dynamic process approach. While striving towards measurements of the extent of individual differences in creative ability and the prediction of future creative potential is a legitimate undertaking, sufficient criticism of the limitations of this approach has been voiced to make one cautious. There seems to be a serious problem about the validity of tests of creativity when it comes to predicting future creative achievement in a given domain. Furthermore, the psychometric approach yields little information about the processes involved in creative thinking. Thus the rapid development of artificial intelligence should provide a useful test-bed for the dynamic process theories of creativity.

REFERENCES

Best, J. B. (1986). *Cognitive psychology*. St. Paul: West Publishing Co.
Boden, M. (1987). *Artificial intelligence and natural man*. (2nd edn.), Cambridge, MA: MIT Press.
Gear, J. (1989). *Perception and the evolution of style: A new model of mind*. London: Routledge.
Gilhooly, K. J. (1988). *Thinking: Directed, undirected and creative*. (2nd edn.). London: Academic Press.
Halpern, D. F. (1984). *Thought and knowledge: An introduction to critical thinking*. Hillsdale, NJ: Erlbaum.
Kreitler, S. (1986). *The psychology of symbols*. Tel Aviv: Papirus.
Kreitler, S., & Kreitler, H. (1985). The psychosemantic foundations of comprehension. *Theoretical Linguistics*, **12**, 185–195.
Merleau-Ponty, M. (1962). *Phenomenology of perception*. London: Routledge and Kegan Paul.
Merleau-Ponty, M. (1964). *The primacy of perception*. Evanston: North Western University Press.
Michie, D., and Johnston, R. (1985). *The creative computer*. Harmondsworth: Penguin Books.
O'Shea, T., and Eisenstadt, M. (1984). *Artificial Intelligence: Tools, techniques and applications*. New York: Harper and Row.
Vernon, P. E. (ed.), (1970). *Creativity*. Harmondsworth: Penguin Books.

12

Artificial Intelligence and the Enhancement of Human Creativity†

D. H. SLEEMAN
King's College, Aberdeen

INTRODUCTION

Since its inception, Artificial Intelligence has been a dynamic interdisciplinary activity which has pursued a range of high-level objectives, including:

a) building intelligent artifacts
b) encoding in machine manipulatable form (the whole of) human expertise; and
c) understanding human cognition.

Besides pursuing these lofty goals, the field has also developed a range of new representational and programming techniques; these are essentially the building blocks of today's AI technology, and are summarised in Figure 12.1.

Using AI to Enhance Human Creativity

Here, I wish to characterize systems at three levels. Firstly, one might argue that simply because much *routine* calculation is undertaken by a computer system then this should enable the user to spend his or her time more creatively. For instance, few social scientists now carry out statistical procedures by hand; this should give them much more time to *interpret* the results.

†This chapter has the same title as the author's BCS Jubilee lecture. This is a new presentation, but there is considerable overlap in the material covered.

I am particularly grateful to my research group for allowing me to draw upon their systems and thinking: Susan Craw (KRUST); Sunil Sharma (REFINER); Neil Gray and Martin Stacey (Theory Refinement); Meg Korpi and Sunil Sharma (the 'Thinking' study); and Ian Ellery and Haym Hirsh (INFER*).

Lines of Thinking, Volume 2 Edited by K.J. Gilhooly, M.T.G. Keane, R.H. Logie and G. Erdos
© 1990 John Wiley & Sons Ltd

```
*   Search (Systematic & Heuristic Search)
*   Representational Schemas
      —Predicate Calculus
      —Production Rules
      —Semantic Networks
      —Frames
      —(Data-Structure of LISP & PROLOG)
*   Inference Techniques
*   Learning
*   Natural Language Understanding
*   Perception
*   Programming Languages & Environments
```

FIGURE 12.1   Principal techniques developed by AI.

Secondly, there are several examples of systems where the human and the machine work cooperatively on a task, (such systems are often called 'Aides' or 'decision support systems'). An example is the writer's workbench described by Frase (1980), where the system highlights spelling, syntax and pragmatic errors found in a passage; however, the user decides *whether* to accept the advice. Similarly, a chemist's workbench has been implemented; its facilities include the ability to define functions and then to apply them to all compounds held in the program's database (Rouvray, 1986). The results of the several functions are then plotted graphically, thus allowing the scientist, one hopes, to have new insights.

Thirdly, there are systems which are able to solve 'creative' tasks completely. For example, using AI's search techniques programs have been implemented which can suggest synthesis paths for complex organic molecules; indeed, Sridharan (1973) reports having produced synthesis paths which absorbed the efforts of teams of chemists over a period of many years.

Most of the discussion in this chapter will be about Aides; Figure 12.2 gives an overview of some of the (desired) facilities of such systems.

Over the last decade computers have provided numerical computation to support the professional's activities.
Now, it is becoming possible to provide help with symbolic reasoning:
—CHANGE OF PERSPECTIVES
—TRANSFORMATIONS
—ALGEBRAIC SIMPLIFICATIONS
—KNOWLEDGE REFINEMENT
Computationally very demanding but possible because of dramatic development in hardware, and drop in cost.

FIGURE 12.2   The characteristics of Aides.

An Overview of the Chapter

As noted earlier, one of AI's grandiose objectives is to encode (the whole of) human expertise and knowledge. Some very small parts of this have now been 'captured' in 'knowledge bases', and so it seems that the (semi-) automatic refinement of such knowledge bases is a legitimate topic for this chapter. I then go on to discuss systems which infer scientific laws and refine theories. The section entitled 'Shortcomings of current machine learning approaches' discusses difficulties which inhibit the use of refinement, and machine learning in general; namely the need to specify in advance the set of descriptors which the learning algorithm will use. I describe an experimental study to determine how humans categorize a series of natural concepts.

A major theme that runs through the chapter is the necessity, in complex problem-solving tasks, for the human and the machine to act cooperatively. Unaided, the human often fails to consider possible solutions. Unaided, the computer's incomplete and inconsistent knowledge base will be inadequate to solve complex tasks. My central thesis is that the system's knowledge should be used to highlight inconsistencies in its knowledge base, and, given highly focused information, the creativity of the human can often *resolve* such ambiguities.

SYSTEMS WHICH ATTEMPT TO REFINE EXISTING KNOWLEDGE BASES

As I have argued elsewhere (Sleeman, 1987), key issues for Intelligent Systems are:

1) how to make sense of previously unencountered behaviour;
2) how to cope with missing knowledge;
3) how to communicate effectively with the human user once the system has decided the information to be communicated.

Humans have well-established strategies for each of these. In this section, we shall be concentrating on refining existing knowledge bases, and so how humans cope with the first two issues are pertinent to this discussion. In such circumstances humans use analogies, negative inference and 'island building'.

Learning Apprentice Systems or Knowledge-Based Refinement Systems

'Traditionally', a knowledge base (KB) is produced as a result of interactions between the domain expert and knowledge engineer. This process is complex, but has been stylized as three reasonably discrete phases (Jackson, 1986). In the first phase, the domain expert tells the knowledge engineer about the main concepts in the domain; and the knowledge engineer explains the facilities provided by the expert systems (ES) tool; in the second phase, the expert works a variety of specific tasks and the knowledge engineer attempts to encode these in some representation available in the ES tool; in the third phase, the expert and the knowledge engineer together attempt to use the expert system to solve the tasks discussed in phase two, and then subsequently a variety of additional more demanding tasks. During these latter activities, discrepancies in the KB are often found. Again, traditionally this is resolved by the domain expert and knowledge engineer (KE) making changes to the KB, and then re-running the tasks on which the discrepancies occurred to see if the changes resolve the problem(s). As KBs become larger this becomes a fairly daunting task; hence the interest in (semi-) automating this process. Several systems have now been implemented which address this issue; here I shall review systems which have taken discernibly different approaches. LEAP (Mitchell, Mahadevan and Stein-berg, 1985) was the first 'explanation-based' learning system and worked in the domain of VLSI design. Whereas 'similarity-based' learning systems need many examples to learn a concept, explanation-based learning systems need only a single example, as they generalize the solution by accessing a completely specified domain theory. This is a major disadvantage, of course, because *complete* domain theories are available for relatively few 'interesting' domains. DISCIPLE (Kodratoff and Tecuci, 1987) and BLIP (Morik, 1987) have a similar objective but can cope with *partially* specified domain theories. KRUST (Craw and Sleeman, 1988) uses previous task–solution pairs and partial meta-knowledge, or background knowledge, in the refinement process (see below). INFER* (Sleeman *et al.*, 1989) uses a range of focusing heuristics, and infers previously unencountered mal-rules from protocols of students solving algebra problems. MALGEN (Sleeman *et al.*, 1989) also addresses the issue of inferring previously unencountered mal-rules; it applies perturbations to correct domain rules.

The last two systems to be reviewed refine a database of stored cases; the so-called case-based reasoning approach. (For the advantages of case-based reasoning over more traditional forms of knowledge elicitation, see Kolodner, 1984).

PROTOS (Porter and Bareiss, 1986) is, in fact, a combination of explanation-based learning (EBL) and case-based reasoning subsystems. The case-based classification subsystem suggests a reference pattern, a case which matches the unknown, and the EBL subsystem then attempts to create an explanation for this justification using background domain knowledge. However, the task is made easier as a human-teacher specifies which characteristics are 'critical' and which are 'spurious'; and further, if PROTOS is unable to explain a feature, it asks the 'teacher' for additional domain knowledge to enable it to make the discrimination.

REFINER (Sharma and Sleeman, 1988) creates prototypes and non-prototypes for several disease categories, and if necessary highlights the inconsistencies which exist in the KB; further, in many situations, it suggests how these inconsistencies may be removed.

In the next subsections the KRUST and REFINER systems are discussed in more detail.

The KRUST System

Waterman (1970) described a system, called POKER, which could modify its behaviour. The domain knowledge of Poker was represented as a series of production rules, and the system used a simple conflict-resolution strategy; namely that the first rule which is satisfied fires. A typical rule-set is shown in Figure 12.3, where the Cs are the condition parts of the rules and the As the action parts. In the figure A_s represents the decision actually made by the rule-set (that is, this is the rule which under these conditions would 'fire'), and A_e corresponds to the action which the expert indicated would be appropriate.

$$C_1 \rightarrow A_1$$
$$C_2 \rightarrow A_e \quad \text{.... TARGET RULE}$$
$$C_3 \rightarrow A_s \quad \leftarrow \text{ERROR-CAUSING RULE}$$
$$C_4 \rightarrow A_e \quad \text{.... TARGET RULE}$$
$$C_5 \rightarrow A_s$$

FIGURE 12.3 Stylized version of the rule-base used in Waterman's POKER system and KRUST.

Waterman introduced the terminology of *error-causing* rule for the rule which fired mistakenly and *target rule* for the rule which *should* have fired. Waterman used a series of heuristics to attempt to change the rule-set so that the first target rule in the rule-set would fire (instead of the error-causing rule). The POKER system proposed at most one modified KB as a result of this process. As with POKER, KRUST requires the expert to say what the result should be. KRUST extends his work in several ways:

a) It is able to generalize and specialize symbolic as well as numerical values.
b) It can cope with rule-sets which have multiple firing cycles.
c) It generates a *series* of KBs each of which is unique and corresponds to a distinct target rule.

Before presenting this set to the expert, KRUST rejects KBs which do not give correct answers for previously worked tasks; additionally it uses domain-specific meta-knowledge to further screen the set for acceptable KBs. The fact that length and time are never negative entities is an example of domain-specific meta-knowledge for physics. More generally, it could be knowledge about the acceptable range for a particular variable (for example, blood pressure or IQ).

A further system, LIBRA, is planned which will additionally use *statistical* and *rule-justification* knowledge to propose likely faulty rules. These same additional knowledge sources will be used to eliminate unacceptable KBs.

The REFINER System

As mentioned earlier, REFINER is a system which helps the expert refine a KB consisting of a set of cases and their assigned diagnoses or, more generally, classifications. (Kolodner (1984) discusses advantages of case-based reasoning over more traditional approaches to knowledge elicitation.) REFINER is provided with a series of cases and their classifications; further, the system is told whether the expert believes the case to be a prototypical or non-prototypical example of the category. By using background knowledge stored in a 'semantic network', REFINER infers descriptions of prototypes and non-prototypes for each of the categories. (The description for the non-prototype of Class A is a generalization of the prototype for class A.)

Figure 12.4 gives a graphical view of a KB which contains four classes: A, B, C and D. In this case the KB is consistent. If the KB had been inconsistent then two of the categories would have overlapped. In this situation there would be at least *one* case which the KB would be unable to uniquely identify.

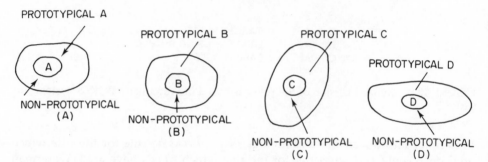

FIGURE 12.4 Schematic sketch of prototypical and non-prototypical descriptions for classes A, B, C and D.

Assumptions

Assumptions which underlie this work include:

a) Each (disease) category must have some features to make it distinct.
b) A non-prototype must have at least one feature which is a variant of a feature found in a prototype; that is, a non-prototype must *not* have a set of completely unique features.

Features of a Simplified Algorithm

1) Presents a prototypical example of each class. REFINER infers a set of category-distinguishing-features (CDF) for each class.
2) Presentation of non-prototypes generalizes the appropriate CDF. Generalization can be performed on both numerical ranges (for example, 80–84 and 84–86 → 80–86), and semantic entities (arm and leg becomes a limb — this uses the semantic network mentioned earlier).
3) When encountering a case of D, as well as updating D's CDF also update the CDFs for A, B and C to remove all overlapping features (all the features in D) as these can no longer be distinctive for classes A, B and C.
4) Detection, and suggestions for how to remove inconsistencies (this is discussed later).

A Simple Example

PROTOYPE: DISEASE-A(P # 24) =
  Age = 50–54 *AND* DBP = 85–89 *AND* ADDITIONAL-DISEASE = DIABETES
PROTOTYPE: DISEASE-B(P # 85) =
  Age = 50–54 *AND* DBP = 105–109 *AND* ADDITIONAL-DISEASE = OBESITY

These are to be read as:

'Case P24 is a prototypical example of category A where the patient's age is in the range 50–54, the diastolic BP is in the range 85–89 and the patient also has diabetes.'

'Case P85 is a prototypical example of category B where the patient's age is in the range 50–54, the diastolic BP is in the range 105–109 and the patient additionally suffers from obesity'.

From this information REFINER rules out age as being a distinctive feature of either category (as the same range of values is present in both cases) and infers the following category-distinguishing features (CDFs):

CDF (DISEASE-A) =
DBP = 85–89 *AND* ADDITIONAL-DISEASE = DIABETES
CDF (DISEASE-B) =
DBP = 105–109 *AND* ADDITIONAL-DISEASE = OBESITY

Detection and Removal of Inconsistencies

An inconsistency occurs in the KB when any one of the CDFs is null, or empty (at which point REFINER will not be able to uniquely categorize at least one case). The example worked above gives some clue as to how such null CDFs occur. Any feature in a case identified as D causes all those features to be removed from the CDFs for classes A and B and C. If REFINER eventually has a null descriptor for A, say, it reconsiders all the cases (of other categories) which forced it to *remove* a feature from A's CDF; these cases are all *candidates* for investigation. Specifically, REFINER suggests that the following types of modifications should be considered:

1) Specific case(s) be reclassified.
2) Edit case(s) (e.g. a range).
3) Add new descriptor(s) to all cases.
4) Shelve case(s).

Summary

REFINER does a great deal of background processing of examples, and then presents the expert with the actual cases which cause the inconsistency to occur. Once confronted with highly focused information humans are often good at suggesting ways of overcoming the discrepancy. Thus, REFINER seems to have many of the desirable features of an Aide, and nicely illustrates our theme of cooperative problem-solving.

SYSTEMS FOR SCIENTIFIC THEORY REFINEMENT AND RULE FORMULATION

Scientific discovery is an intellectually very demanding activity, and as such has intrigued the AI community. Langley *et al.* (1987) argue that scientific discoveries have occurred as a result of both theory-driven and data-driven searches, but concede that the process often involves both. That is, a high-level theory *suggests* what the relevant parameters influencing a process might be, and a data-driven search confirms what relationship, if any, *actually* exists between the parameters.

Meta-DENDRAL (Buchanan and Feigenbaum, 1978) was the first AI discovery program and used a theory-driven approach. The BACON series of programs (Langley *et al.*, 1987) have essentially explored the data-driven approach. We at Aberdeen have developed a framework (Gray, Sleeman and Stacey, 1988) which allows both approaches to be brought to bear, but have so far only implemented a system which can summarize data once the appropriate parameters have been identified.

In the next sub-sections the BACON system as well as the Aberdeen framework will be outlined in some further detail.*

BACON

As noted earlier, this important set of programs does data-driven inference of scientific laws. BACON attempts to discover quantitative laws describing the relationships between a set of prespecified parameters; it creates terms until a constant is derived (or a resource limit is exceeded).

Example

BACON is able to discover Kepler's law (which is $d^3/p^2 = k$, where p is the period of a planet's revolution, d is the distance of that planet from the sun, and k is a constant) from the following data:

PLANET	p	d
MERCURY	1	1
VENUS	8	4
EARTH	27	9

It uses the heuristics given in Figure 12.5. As shown below, BACON first generates the term d/p, then d^2/p, d^2/p^2, and finally d^3/p^2:

PLANET	p	d	d/p	$d^2 p$	d^2/p^2	$d^3 p^2$
MERCURY	1	1	1	1	1	1
VENUS	8	4	0.5	2	0.25	1
EARTH	27	9	0.33	3	0.11	1

Four Heuristics applied recursively.

1. IF Y has the value V in a number of cases, THEN hypothesise that Y always has that value.
2. IF X and Y are linearly related with slope S and intercept I in a number of cases, THEN hypothesise that this relation always holds.
3. IF X increases as Y decreases and X and Y are not linearly related, THEN define a new term T as the PRODUCT of X and Y.
4. IF X increases as Y increases and X and Y are not linearly related, THEN define a new term T as the RATIO of X and Y.

FIGURE 12.5   Heuristics used by BACON for trend and constancy detection.

---

*Readers may wish to note that AM carried out discovery in a mathematical domain; and EURISKO discovered domain heuristics (Lenat, 1982).

d/p is formed by using the heuristic 4 (RATIO); d^2/p is formed from d/p and d using heuristic 3 (PRODUCT); d^2/p^2 is formed from d^2/p and p using heuristic 4; and d^3/p^2 is formed from d^2/p^2 and d using heuristic 3.

The basic BACON mechanism has been considerably extended. Amongst the interesting extensions are facilities to detect recurring sequences and to infer polynomial terms by calculating repeated differences.

There are limitations of the BACON system. It cannot cope well with noisy data, the *order* of data sets is sometimes important, and it does not handle irrelevant variables. On the other hand, the systems (BACON and its family of related systems) are very useful for producing *summaries* of datasets.

Aberdeen's Framework for Scientific Theory Refinement

We accept the position argued by Langley *et al.* (1987) that scientific theory formation needs a combination of theory-driven and data-driven approaches for many situations.

Many theories (for example, Schrodinger's equation) are either only solvable in a limited number of simple situations or are not sufficiently specified to be tractable. In either case, the scientist needs to add some additional assumptions to make the theory tractable. If we are lucky this 'enhanced theory' will suggest that a small set of parameters can be used to predict further parameter(s). In which case it is usual for a scientist to perform a series of experiments, and for data-driven techniques to be used to determine the nature of the relationship, if any, between the parameters.

The investigators in this project used *their* higher-order knowledge of chemistry to hypothesize that the solubility of an organic liquid in water is dependent on some aspect of the molecule's size—most probably its surface area. Further, chemical knowledge was used to hypothesize that the solubility was likely to be

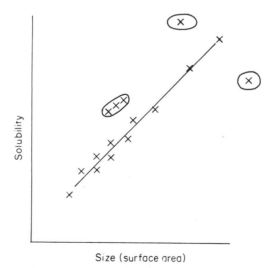

FIGURE 12.6   Plot of solubility versus size (surface area) for ketones.

greatly influenced by the principal chemical group and so the hypothesis was investigated for particular chemical groups.

From Figure 12.6 one can see that the relationship seems to be true for the majority of the points. However, one also observes clusters of points and the occasional outlier. The challenge for the scientist looking at the results is to decide between *special*, *spurious* and *interesting* cases. Trained scientists have knowledge about frequently recurring special cases; chemists, for example, know that small atoms (like hydrogen) often have anomalous behaviour. On the other hand, it is frequently very difficult to separate spurious from interesting cases; interesting cases being those for which a revised theory needs to be proposed.

Suppose one decides that a group of points are not spurious then one looks for common attributes which make them perform differently from the *majority* of the points. For instance, we found that one of the 'groups of points' contained molecules which had a particular nonlinear shape; in general, one searches one's domain-specific concept bank for attributes common to all members of such groups which are not shared by other molecules.

Again, this work highlights the desirability of having a program do the basic data analysis, and to bring anomalous situations to the expert's attention. Confronted with such stark evidence of the inadequacy of the proposed hypothesis, humans can frequently be extremely creative in suggesting solutions.

SHORTCOMINGS OF CURRENT MACHINE LEARNING APPROACHES

Systems which refine KBs and refine scientific theories are part of a wider sub-area of AI known as Machine Learning, and as such suffer from the limitations of this sub-field. An identified weakness in machine learning, and indeed in the whole of AI, is the current lack of powerful representational schemata. Additionally, the machine-learning sub-field has identified a further range of peculiar problems: needing to specify in advance the concept description language (CDL), the inherent bias of CDLs (Utgoff, 1986), and the need to introduce new predicates (Muggleton, 1988) into the CDL. Finally, Rendell (1986) has argued convincingly that machine-learning systems, like humans, need to use *purpose* to guide their learning.

In this section I report a study in which the Aberdeen group investigated how humans infer appropriate description languages. After all, no one tells a child which descriptors to use to describe a chair—one simply states that several objects are chairs and the child 'acquires' an appropriate description which enables the child to classify previously unencountered objects as chairs. Intriguingly, these same complex classification tasks seem to be at the heart of scientific discovery.

Put another way, Feigenbaum (1977) has rightly said that knowledge acquisition is the bottleneck which is preventing widespread use of expert-systems technology. Several authors have suggested that machine-learning techniques are the answer to the knowledge-acquisition problem. I, similarly, wish to assert that inferring the appropriate 'concept description language' is the current bottleneck of machine learning.

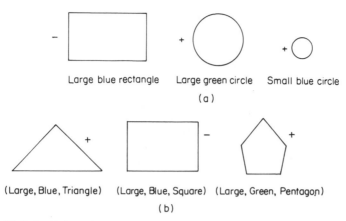

Large blue rectangle   Large green circle   Small blue circle

(a)

(Large, Blue, Triangle)   (Large, Blue, Square)   (Large, Green, Pentagon)

(b)

FIGURE 12.7   Rule inference and the effect of the concept description language.

Figure 12.7a shows that the correct concept (the underlying concept is 'circle') can be inferred given those examples and the concept description language:

{(large small)   (blue green)   (rectangle circle)}.

Figure 12.7b shows that if the CDL is extended to include 'triangle' and 'pentagon' (and if disjunctions and negations are not allowed), then the examples cannot be correctly classified. The CDL needs to be further enhanced to include:

{(even-sidedness odd-sidedness)}.

As mentioned earlier, machines also need the capability to extend their CDLs.

A Study of Humans Classifying Natural Concepts

For the reasons given above it was thought to be important to see how people classified natural concepts. (The term natural is used in contrast with the type of concepts used by Bruner, Goodnow and Austin (1956), where the subject was told the set of relevant descriptors in advance.) There were two other major differences between our study and the classical studies of Bruner. Firstly, we recorded talk-aloud protocols; and secondly, we gave the subjects a set of stimuli which forced them into a problem-solving mode. Figure 12.8 shows a typical set

Cow	+
Bull	−
Goat	+
Grocery store	+
Fish	−
Ham	−
Refrigerator	+

FIGURE 12.8   Set of 'natural' stimuli used in the experiment.

of stimuli used in the study (Korpi, 1988); the items above the dotted line would lead the subject to suppose the concept was, say, a female domestic animal. The fourth item in the list, 'grocery store', is not consistent with this evolving hypothesis and frequently forces subjects to radically re-evaluate their hypotheses.

Figure 12.9 gives the protocol for one of the subjects with this set of stimuli; the subject's comments just after he sees the fourth item (grocery store) are worth looking at in detail. In the second column of this figure I give the output from a program which aims to replicate the gross features of the subject's protocol (Sharma, 1988). For a detailed analysis of these subjects' protocols and for a discussion of the proposed underlying models, see Korpi (1988). Below I quote from Korpi's analysis:

> 'Successful strategies most often involved spontaneous activations of relevant information or search of the (subject's) Knowledge Base, and modification of hypotheses. This implies that subjects possess the necessary information to make unusual connections between concepts, and that their task is to find that information and put it together in appropriate ways.'

HUMAN trace

E: COW, (+)
cow = example
category animals
this is only example, → unsure
not enough information.
don't have anything to associate it with,
could be a number of things.
animal, living things, things
you find on farms, those come to mind.
unsure, because haven't seen anything else.

E: BULL (−)
bull not = example.
rules out things on farm,
because bull on farm, as well as cow.
also, bull = animals,
so animals not = category.

Animals not = category;
things on farm not = category.
What other things did I mention?
living things. It can't be living things!
Cows, now what else ... cows, cows.

bulls have horns; cows don't have horns.
Yet they're still kind of the same family.
things without horns,
unsure, just based on these two.

E: GOAT (+)
Goat = example. Goat.
goat = animal, but so is bull.

MODEL trace

Please give an example: COW
Is it a Positive example? (Y or N) y

... COW
... COW
... FARM
... ANIMAL
A number of concepts come to mind:
Could be LIVING, ANIMAL, FARM

Please give an example: BULL
Is it a Positive example? (Y or N) n

... BULL
... ANIMAL
It isn't ANIMAL
... FARM
It isn't FARM
Thinking of ...
... BULL
... HORNS
Hypothesis might be related to HORNS
I'm Unsure, though!

Please give an example: GOAT
Is it a Positive example? (Y or N) y

... GOAT
... HORNS
It isn't HORNS

Goats have horns,
so can't be animals without horns.
And goats are found on a farm.

bulls much bigger than cows. And goats,
but goats are a lot smaller than cows.
Hmm,
if restrict category to farm animals that are
— well, goats are not necessarily friendly,
but they're friendlier than bulls.
I'm going to say non-violent farm animals,
unsure
Non-violent farm animals sounds like pacifist
[Laughter] farm animals,
so unsure.

E: GROCERY-STORE (+)
Grocery-store nothing to do with these things
These things are animals.
Grocery-store isn't an animal.
And grocery-stores are not found on farms.
Cows ... and goats are living things.
Grocery-store is a place.

not animals, because of the bull.
not non-violent because of the grocery-store.

Uh, could be ...
cows and goats ... grocery-store ...
you eat cows, like to eat beef,
which could buy in grocery-store.
yet, wouldn't find goat meat
[laughing] in grocery-store
— at least, not in the States.
so you can eat those things ...
could be food,
except this [store] is different.
cows and goats could be food,
food items, except so could bulls
if goat = food, then bull = food.
that wouldn't explain grocery-store as item.
Cows, cows ... and grocery-store.
cows slaughtered for beef,
and could be in grocery-store.
But goats wouldn't be.
that doesn't sound right,
because grocery-store part of same category.

Cows ... you get milk from cows ...
You don't get milk from bulls.
You could get milk from goats,
but goat milk is pretty rare.
could say you get milk at grocery-store,
or from grocery-store,
not in way you get milk from cow.
yet couldn't do that at all with a bull.

Thinking of ...
... GOAT
... BULL
... BIG
It isn't BIG
Thinking of ...
... Bull
... VIOLENT

Hypothesis might be related to VIOLENT
I'm Unsure, though!

Please give an example: GROCERY-STORE
Is it a Positive example? (Y or N) y

... GROCERY-STORE
... VIOLENT
It isn't VIOLENT
Thinking of ...
... ANIMAL
It isn't ANIMAL
... LIVING
It isn't LIVING
Thinking of ...
... GROCERY-STORE
... PLACE
It isn't PLACE
Thinking of ...
... GROCERY-STORE
... BEEF
It isn't BEEF
... FOOD
It isn't FOOD
Thinking of ...
... GROCERY-STORE
... COW
... BULL
... GOAT
... GOAT
... BULL
... COW
... ANIMAL
... LIVING
... FARM
... HORNS
... BEEF
... FOOD
... GROCERY-STORE
... PLACE
... MILK
... MILK

Hypothesis is related to MILK
Very Sure!

continued

could be Things from which you get milk ...
although, that—

I'll say things from which you get milk,
somewhat sure.

E. FISH (−)
Fish not = example
don't get milk from fish.
looking back at current category,
having ruled out other categories,
if apply fish to current category,
I see that category still stands,
because can't get milk from a fish.

How many more examples so you give me?
E: won't tell. Just tell what you think.
pretty sure,
category is Things from which you get milk.

E: HAM (−)
Ham not = example.
I'm pretty sure category is things from
which you get milk,
because can't get milk from ham.
even, though could find ham in grocery store,
I'm pretty sure.

E: REFRIGERATOR (+)
Refrigerator = example?
You get milk from refrigerator.
You get milk from cow;
you get milk from grocery-store;
you get milk from goat.
I'm pretty sure that's category:
things from which you could get milk.

E: Good

Please give an example: FISH
Is it a Positive example? (Y or N) n

... FISH
... MILK

Hypothesis is related to milk
Pretty Sure!

Please give an example: HAM
Is it a Positive example? (Y or N) n

... HAM
... MILK

Hypothesis is related to MILK
Pretty Sure!

Please give an example: FRIDGE
Is it a Positive example? (Y or N) y

... FRIDGE
... MILK

Hypothesis is related to MILK
Pretty Sure!

Please give an example: NIL

BYE.

FIGURE 12.9   A subject's protocol and the corresponding simulation protocol.

Korpi argues that her experiment supports a focusing (or as she calls it, a flashlight) model. This model assumes that all the necessary information (say about *cow* and *grocery store*) are already stored in memory and merely have to be 'brought into focus'.[*]

---

[*] At my presentation at the 'Thinking' conference in Aberdeen in August 1988, several questioners raised the issue of whether, in fact, some information might have to be created, and not just found. This seems to me, in retrospect, to be a perfectly reasonable explanation. Unfortunately, I have so far been unable to think of an experiment to discriminate between these possible mechanisms; timing studies would appear to me to be too insensitive, but it is possible that clues might be contained in protocols.

The Simulation Model

Sharma (1988) describes a model which has replicated the main features of all the protocols collected by Korpi. (Note that I am *not* claiming that these are precise cognitive models; but nonetheless I believe this to be an interesting, a suggestive, simulation).

The model's knowledge is stored as a graph with links between the several nodes. There are both 'strong' and 'weak' links, and in general the strength of the link from A to B can be different from that from B to A. Figure 12.10 shows part of the network needed to cope with this set of stimuli. In this system, 0 represents an *inactive* node and 100 an *active* or *saturated* node. The simulation uses the following propagation rules:

1) Concepts *one strong* link away from a fully saturated node have 20 points added to their 'score' or activation.
2) Concepts *two strong* links away from a fully saturated node have 10 points added to their 'score'.
3) Concepts *one weak* line away have 10 added to their 'score'.
4) Values are additive (to a maximum of 100).
5) There is an in-built decay mechanism which operates at the end of each time period.

The numbers in square brackets give the values of the nodes after the node 'living' becomes an active node, and is saturated (giving it a score of 100) (cf. Anderson 1983).

Typical output from this simulation is given in the right-hand column of Figure 12.9; and as noted earlier, by merely changing the strengths of several links Sharma has been able to replicate the several protocols collected by Korpi.

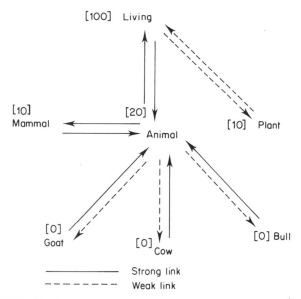

FIGURE 12.10 Part of the semantic network used by the simulator.

Conclusions

Korpi's study seems to be an important contribution to understanding how people classify natural concepts, be they toddler or scientific researcher.

However, the implications of the study for AI and machine learning seem to be somewhat daunting. Humans solve complex problems of this kind because they already have encoded *vast* amounts of information about concepts; both the 'normal' attributes, say, about a *cow* and obscure facts that cows can be pets, when they were first domesticated, etc. Even if *some* of the information is created *in vivo*, as suggested earlier in this chapter, it is certain that vast amounts of information *is* stored. If AI systems are to discover important new relationships, we need to provide the system with 'rich' knowledge structures and with the ability to infer new knowledge.

To date, by and large, AI systems have been provided with minimal knowledge bases and these have enabled the systems to tackle well-specified specific tasks. By its very nature, the task of a Discovery System *cannot* be that well-specified, and hence the need for an extensive knowledge base.

GENERAL CONCLUSIONS

The major theme of this chapter has been the use of AI systems to filter information which is presented to the user. In particular, it is expected that such a system would highlight difficulties which it was unable to resolve with its knowledge base, and get the human expert to consider and resolve such conflicts. I hope the review has been persuasive of the power and generality of this approach, and of the need for building systems in which the computer and the human solve problems cooperatively.

REFERENCES

Anderson, J. R. (1983). *The architecture of cognition*. Cambridge, MA: Harvard University Press.

Bruner, J.S., Goodnow, J. J., & Austin, G. A. (1956). *A study of thinking*. New York: John Wiley.

Buchanan, B. G, & Feigenbaum, E. A. (1978). DENDRAL and meta-DENDRAL: their application dimension. *Artificial Intelligence, 11*, 5–24.

Craw, S. M., & Sleeman, D. (1988). The refinement of dynamic knowledge bases by collecting evidence. Technical report, Computing Science Department, The University, Aberdeen.

Feigenbaum, E. A. (1977) The art of AI: themes and case studies of knowledge engineering. In *Proceedings of 5th IJCAI conference* (pp. 1014–1029).

Frase, L. T. (1980). Computer aids for text editing and design. Paper presented to annual American Educational Association meeting, Boston.

Gray, N. A. B., Sleeman, D., & Stacey, M. K. (1988). Machine discovery and the operationalisation of scientific theories. Technical Report, TR 8801, Computing Science Department, The University, Aberdeen.

Jackson, P. (1986). *Introduction to expert systems*. (pp. 86–89). Wokingham: Addison-Wesley.

Kodratoff, Y., & Tecuci, G. (1987). DISCIPLE-1: Interactive apprentice system in weak theory fields. In *Proceedings of IJCAI '87*, Vol. 1 (pp. 271–276).

Kolodner, J. L., (1984). Knowledge-based self-organising memory for events. In A. Elithorn & R. Banerji (eds.), *Artificial and human intelligence* (pp. 57–66). Amsterdam: Elsevier.

Korpi, M. (1988). *Making conceptual connections: An investigation of cognitive strategies and heuristics for inductive categorisation with natural concepts*. PhD thesis, Stanford University.

Langley, P., Simon, H. A., Bradshaw, G. L., & Zytkow, J. M. (1987). *Scientific discovery: Computational explorations of the creative processes*. Cambridge, MA: MIT press.

Lenat, D. B. (1982). The nature of heuristics. *Artificial Intelligence*, **19**, 189–249.

Michalski, R. S., Carbonell, J. G. & Mitchell, T. M. (eds.) (1983). *Machine Learning: An AI approach*. Tioga press.

Michalski, R. S., Carbonell, J. G. & Mitchell, T. M. (eds.) (1986). *Machine learning: An AI approach*, Vol. II. Los Altos: Morgan-Kaufmann.

Mitchell, T. M., Mahadevan, S., & Steinberg, L. I. (1985). LEAP: a learning apprentice for VLSI. In *Proceedings of IJCAI '85*, Vol. 1 (pp. 573–580).

Morik, K. (1987). Acquiring domain models. *International Journal of Man–Machine Studies*, **26**, 93–104.

Muggleton, S. (1988). A strategy for constructing new predicates in first order logic. In D. Sleeman (ed.), *Proceedings of EWSL '88* (pp. 201–210). London: Pitman.

Nilsson, N. J. (1971). *Problem-solving methods in artificial intelligence*. New York: McGraw-Hill.

Porter, B. W., & Bareiss, E. R. (1986). Protos: an experiment in knowledge acquisition for heuristic classification tasks. In *Proceedings of the international meeting on advances in machine learning*, Les Arcs, France (pp. 159–174).

Rendell, L. (1986). A general framework for induction and a study of selective induction. *Machine Learning*, **1**, 177–226.

Rouvray, D. H. (1986). Predicting chemistry for topology. *Scientific American*, **255**, 36–43.

Samuel, A. L. (1967). Some studies in machine learning using the game of checkers. II Recent progress. *IBM Journal of Research and Development*, **11**, 601–617.

Sharma, S. (1988). *Case-based knowledge acquisition and refinement*. PhD thesis, University of Aberdeen.

Sharma, S., & Sleeman, D. (1988). REFINER: a case-based differential diagnosis aide for knowledge acquisition and knowledge refinement. In D. Sleeman (ed.), *Proceedings of EWSL-88* (pp. 201–210). London: Pitman.

Sleeman, D. (1987). Some challenges for intelligent tutoring systems. In *Proceedings of IJCAI-87* (pp. 1166–1168). Palo Alto: Morgan-Kaufmann.

Sleeman, D., Hirsh, H., Ellery, I., & Kim, I. (1989). Expanding an incomplete domain theory: two case studies. *Machine Learning Journal*.

Sridharan, N. S. (1973). Search strategies for the task of organic chemical synthesis. In *Proceedings of IJCAI-73*, (pp. 95–104).

Utgoff, P. E. (1986). Shift of bias for inductive concept learning. In R. S., Michalski, J. G. Carbonell & T. M. Mitchell, (eds.), *Machine learning: An AI approach*, Vol. 2. Los Altos: Morgan-Kaufmann.

Waterman, D. A. (1970). Generalisation learning techniques for automating the learning of heuristics. *Artificial Intelligence*, **1**, 121–170.

13

Psychosemantic Foundations of Creativity

HANS KREITLER AND SHULAMITH KREITLER
Tel Aviv University

IMPACTS OF MEANING ON CREATIVE PROCESSES

Like all kinds of human performance, creativity has its motivational, emotional and cognitive aspects. In each of these domains a great many theoretical and empirical studies have been carried out, so that any attempt to review them here would either have to be shamefully superficial or would exceed the framework of this chapter. Therefore, from the very start we shall concentrate on our own attempts to understand a particular aspect of creativity; namely, the most elementary means required for overt or covert creative performance as well as methods for the improvement of these means.

Our work on creativity is based on our theory about the nature of meaning and symbolization and their function in cognitive performance (Kreitler, 1986; Kreitler and Kreitler, 1976, 1982, 1984, 1985a). We regard cognition as the meaning-processing as well as the meaning-processed system (that is, the system that acquires meaning, produces meaning, elaborates meaning and stores meaning), but its processing is co-determined by the meaning it processes. Thus, in contrast to the information-processing paradigm, we treat meaning not only as something that is processed but as an active agent that, by force of its own laws and implications, co-determines the course of the cognitive process. Try to imagine what would have happened with modern physics if Einstein, in his thought experiment of 1904, had assumed—perhaps precognitively influenced by Asimov—that the observer in the elevator travels with a speed greater than the speed of light, or how Hamlet's monologue would have developed had he started with the sentence 'To be or not to care, that is the question'. In other words, to our mind, it is utterly mistaken to disregard the impact of cognitive contents on cognitive processing.

Yet, if one assumes that the meaning of each cognitive content has a specific impact on the course and results of cognitive processing, one has to cope with a

Lines of Thinking, Volume 2 Edited by K.J. Gilhooly, M.T.G. Keane, R.H. Logie and G. Erdos
© 1990 John Wiley & Sons Ltd

vast, almost infinite multitude of meanings. Investigators in the information-processing tradition were probably not up to this task. Thus, they conformed to Bartlett's saying that good researchers are opportunistic in selecting as a theme that which can be researched with the available means while ignoring that which cannot yet be studied. In the absence of means for assessing contents, they ignored the impact of contents and instead focused almost exclusively on strategies. We found the means for dealing with contents by developing a theoretically based systematization of meaning which allowed for satisfactory characterization and quantification of meaning required for studying the role of cognitive contents in cognitive processes such as planning in children and adults (Kreitler and Kreitler, 1986, 1987a, 1987b), overcoming functional fixedness (Arnon and Kreitler, 1984), improving analogical thinking (see below), resolving the problem of horizontal decalage in Piaget's theory (Kreitler and Kreitler, 1988), and, last but not least, illuminating some hitherto overlooked aspects of creativity.

It is obvious that understanding our research in creativity presupposes some knowledge of our meaning system and the manner in which it may be applied in cognitive research.

A NEW THEORY OF MEANING AND ITS MEASUREMENT

We define meaning as a referent-centred pattern of cognitive content items which we call 'meaning values'. Referent and meaning values are in fact complementary terms, because cognitive contents turn into meaning values by being assigned to a referent, whereas anything to which meaning is assigned (for example, an input, an internal stimulation, an auditory or visual image and so on) becomes a referent owing to the meaning assigned to it. Thus, the word 'blue' or the notion *blue* may function once as referent for the meaning value 'it is a colour' and at another time as a meaning value assigned to a referent (for example, 'the Mediterranean').

The meaning values required for characterizing the referent by way of meaning assignment are derived from the universe of cognitive contents. We regard this universe not as something static that could be properly understood in terms of identities, oppositions and inclusions, in the sense of Katz' (1972) tree formations or any other kind of static content categories, but rather as a fully dynamized 22-dimensional space. Each of the 22 dimensions—we call them *meaning dimensions* (see Table 13.1)—can be conceptualized either as a strategy for activation and retrieval of cognitive contents that characterizes the referent in a particular manner, or as a field that, if activated, brings to the fore meaning values that fulfil a particular function in regard to the referent (for instance, being the cause of the referent, describing its sensory qualities, being its superordinate category, and so on). In principle, each referent can be characterized in terms of meaning values of each of the 22 meaning dimensions, though some of these characterizations would be rather far-fetched, unconventional or bizarre. Again, meaning dimensions are not content categories but principles of characterization, because the same cognitive contents such as *brown* can be used once for expressing a sensory quality (for example, 'The strawberry

Table 13.1 Major variables of the meaning system

1) MEANING DIMENSIONS

Dim. 1 Contextual allocation
Dim. 2 Range of inclusion (2a: subclasses of referent; 2b: parts of referent)
Dim. 3 Function, purpose and role
Dim. 4 Actions and potentialities for action (4a: by referent; 4b: to/with referent)
Dim. 5 Manner of occurrence or operation
Dim. 6 Antecedents and causes
Dim. 7 Consequences and results
Dim. 8 Domain of application (8a: referent as subject; 8b: referent as object)
Dim. 9 Material
Dim. 10 Structure
Dim. 11 State and possible changes in state
Dim. 12 Weight and mass
Dim. 13 Size and dimensionality
Dim. 14 Quantity and number
Dim. 15 Locational qualities
Dim. 16 Temporal qualities
Dim. 17 Possessions (17a) and belongingness (17b)
Dim. 18 Development
Dim. 19 Sensory qualities (19a: of referent; 19b: by referent)
Dim. 20 Feelings and emotions (20a: evoked by referent; 20b: felt by referent)
Dim. 21 Judgements and evaluations (21a: about referent; 21b: by referent)
Dim. 22 Cognitive qualities (22a: evoked by referent; 22b: of referent)

2) TYPES OF RELATION

TR 1 Attributive (1a: qualities to substance; 1b: actions to agent)
TR 2 Comparative (2a: similarity; 2b: difference; 2c: complementarity; 2d: relationality)
TR 3 Exemplifying-Illustrative (3a: exemplifying instance; 3b: exemplifying situation; 3c: exemplifying scene)
TR 4 Metaphoric-symbolic (4a: interpretation; 4b: conventional metaphor; 4c: original metaphor; 4d: symbol)

MODES OF MEANING

Lexical mode   (TR 1 + TR 2)
Personal mode (TR 3 + TR4)

3) FORMS OF RELATION

FR 1 Positive
FR 2 Negative
FR 3 Mixed positive and negative
FR 4 Conjunctive
FR 5 Disjunctive
FR 6 Combined positive and negative
FR 7 Obligatory

4) SHIFTS OF REFERENT

SR 1 Identical
SR 2 Opposite
SR 3 Partial
SR 4 Previous meaning value
SR 5 Modified
SR 6 Higher-level referent
SR 7 Associative
SR 8 Grammatical variation
SR 9 Linguistic label
SR 10 Unrelated

Close shifts   (SR 1 + SR 8 + SR 9)
Medium shifts (SR 3 + SR 4 + SR 5 + SR 6)
Far shifts   (SR 2 + SR 7 + SR 10)

is brown') and, at another time, as the reason why one does not want to eat it. Therefore, cognitive contents *per se* cannot be coded on a particular meaning dimension unless it functions as a meaning value assigned to a particular referent. Our experience has shown that in order to promote the full understanding of this point it is often useful to choose a referent, then check the list of meaning dimensions in Table 13.1 and assign a meaning value to the referent in line with several or all of the 22 dimensions.

However, meaning regarded as the relation between the referent and the meaning value (for example, knowing and/or saying something about something) cannot be fully understood in terms of meaning dimensions alone. There are four other aspects of the referent–meaning value relations that must be considered.

One of these aspects is the *types of relation*. The types of referent–meaning value relations characterize the immediacy, directness or complexity of the relation. The attributive relation (for example, 'The tree—is tall') is the simplest or most direct one. The comparative relation ('The tree—is higher than a house') is less direct because it requires the introduction of another term. Semantically more complex and distant are the exemplifying–illustrative and the metaphoric –symbolic relations which, owing to their overall importance for creativity, will be discussed later in this chapter.

The third set of meaning variables are *forms of relation*. The forms of relation—mainly assertion, negation, conjunction and disjunction—are psychologically more indicative of the relating process than of the formed relation and hence correlate with different cognitive proficiencies, such as logical or probabilistic thinking (Kreitler and Kreitler, 1990).

The fourth set of variables codes the intriguing phenomenon of *referent shift*. When assigning meaning to a term, the subject invariably deviates from the originally presented referent by assigning meaning values to a part of the referent, to one of its prior meaning values, to a superordinate class, or even to a completely new referent, and so on (see Table 13.1). For instance, to the referent 'Girls' one subject provided the following meaning values: 'females, giggling creatures, giggling is a charming mixture of repression and confession'. In normal subjects referent shift is not a kind of confabulation, because eventually the subjects return to the original referent. Rather it is the cognitive equivalent of Piaget's decentring and recentring that prevent a Ditchburm-like vanishing of the stimulus (Piaget, 1958).

Finally, the two *modes of meaning*—namely, the lexical interpersonally-shared meaning and the personal–subjective meaning—are not to be mistaken for denotation and connotation. Lexical meaning is or is intended to be interpersonally shared. It uses primarily the attributive type of relation and in a conventional way also the comparative type. In contrast, the personal–subjective mode of meaning relies primarily on the use of instantiation, dynamic scenes, interpretation, metaphors and symbols proper (see Table 13.1).

Thus, for evaluating meaning, each meaning value must be coded five-fold; namely, it must get at least one coding on each of the five sets of variables. The codings are then summed up across the different meaning values. The coding of meaning may be done in regard to any statement or communication of meaning, primarily verbal statements or any written text.

In order to determine the meaning potentials of a subject, a *meaning test* was developed. The subject is presented with a standard set of 11 words and is asked to communicate what each term means in general and to him or her personally to an imaginary person who understands language and other means of expression but presumably does not know the meaning of the presented term(s). The answers may be given verbally (orally or in written form), as well as through gestures or drawings (enacted, drawn or described). Summing up the coded responses of a subject to the meaning test yields the subject's meaning profile; namely, the frequencies with which the subject used each of the meaning variables in responding to the test (Kreitler and Kreitler, 1982, 1985b, 1990).

Normal adults with about eight years of education make active use of 11–13 meaning dimensions, with idiosyncratic differences in frequency, the attributive and exemplifying types of relation, at least two forms of relation (assertion and negation) and some shifts of referent. In addition, normal adults can be expected to have passive command—in the sense of inducement by direct questioning or obvious input demands—of all meaning dimensions, all forms of relation, and can be trained to grasp metaphors and to a certain extent even symbols proper (Kreitler, 1986; Kreitler, Kreitler and Wanounou, 1987/88). As may be expected, there are high and significant positive correlations between the results of the meaning test and the IQ (Kalmar, 1980). Yet in contrast to the IQ, the meaning test provides insight into cognitive performance and, even more importantly, it points the way to cognitive improvement and rehabilitation (Kreitler and Kreitler, 1989).

MEANING IMPACTS ON FUNCTIONAL FIXEDNESS, DECALAGE AND PLANNING

A case in point is functional fixedness. It was shown that adolescent girls confronted with the task of completing an electric circuit which could be done only by using a metal screwdriver as a connecting link did significantly better after training of 11 meaning dimensions, none of which was particularly task-specific (Arnon and Kreitler, 1984). Another example is the horizontal decalage; namely, the inability to solve a particular problem although the schema for solving the task has already been acquired and successfully applied for solving similar tasks. Piaget himself did not provide a satisfactory explanation for this phenomenon plaguing his theory. The results of four studies based on the meaning system led to a reasonable resolution of the problem (Kreitler and Kreitler, 1988). One of these studies showed that decalage in regard to conservation was much more pronounced in those children who had only a poor active command of the task-relevant meaning dimension than in those who had a good command of this dimension, as assessed by the meaning test. Likewise, we found that planning abilities in children as well as in adults, though strongly determined by cognitive motivational factors as outlined by our theory of cognitive orientation, are co-determined by meaning factors too. Thus, in adults the correlation between the motivational factors of cognitive orientation and successful and systematic planning was in the range 0.40–0.60 (for different planning tasks) but was raised to 0.70–0.99 when the relevant meaning variables were also taken into account (Kreitler and Kreitler, 1987a,b).

In sum, there is ample evidence for the crucial role of meaning in cognitive functioning. The more there is active use of meaning dimensions and other meaning variables, including referent shift, the better is performance in cognitive tasks. However, since cognitive tasks in general and creative acts in particular are highly specific, the active use of many meaning variables does not warrant successful performance if the two or three meaning variables required specifically for the task at hand are not used by the subject at all or only infrequently, as evidenced by the subject's meaning profile. A case in point is analogical thinking, which according to the lore in creativity is often mentioned in the reported or assumed process leading to scientific inventions, particularly in physics and mathematics (Arieti, 1976; Gentner and Gentner, 1983; Gordon, 1961; Ortony, 1979; Perkins, 1981). It seems fairly obvious that analogical thinking involves comparison. But it is no less obvious that comparison without the active use of the dimension relevant for the content domain of the task at hand would not suffice for a successful act of analogy to occur. Thus, it is likely that when Stevenson looked at his steaming teapot, mere comparison would not have given rise to the conception of the steam engine without prior meaning assignment to the observed phenomenon in terms of the meaning dimensions *causes* and *results*.

ANALOGICAL AND LOGICAL THINKING AND THEIR CREATIVE USE

For the clarification of this issue we performed a study designed, among other things, to investigate the role of the comparative type of relation and the specific meaning dimensions involved in the analogies. We hypothesized, first, that subjects who make frequent use of the comparative type of relation in the meaning test would perform on the whole better on a test of analogies than subjects using this type of relation less frequently; and second, that subjects who in the meaning test make frequent use of the meaning dimension required for completing a particular analogy would succeed better in resolving the analogies than subjects who use this dimension infrequently (for example, the analogy 'A river relates to a brook as the ocean to...' is based on applying the meaning dimension *size*).

The subjects were 96 undergraduates of the social sciences, half men and half women. They were administered, in two separate sessions in randomized order, the meaning test and a test of analogies that included 24 items: eight relating to the meaning dimension *size*, eight relating to *state* (for example, strength, status, liquidity), and eight relating to *temporal qualities*. The results showed that the frequency of the comparative type of relation in the subjects' meaning profile was correlated 0.65 with their overall performance on the analogies test ($p < 0.001$). Then we added a second predictor which was the frequency, in the subject's meaning profile, of the meaning dimension involved in the content of the items (namely, *size, state* or *temporal qualities*). The addition of this predictor, each for the relevant group of items, appreciably increased the multiple correlation between the predictors and the performance on analogies: it raised it to 0.85 in the case of *size* items, 0.90 in the case of *state* items, and 0.97 in the case of *temporal qualities* items.

As a sequel to this experiment we carried out another study which was designed to examine whether the above-reported correlation between the comparative type of relation and performance on the analogies test was actually based on a causal relation between this type of relation and analogical thinking. For this purpose we selected out of a larger pool of subjects (undergraduates in the social sciences) 60 subjects who had in the meaning profile frequencies of the comparative type of relation one standard deviation below the group's mean. They were administered the 24-item analogies test before they were divided randomly into two groups (in each, $n = 30$), one of which got a brief training designed to increase the use of the comparative type of relation (three 45-minute group sessions), whereas the other served as a control group. Two weeks after termination of the training all the subjects were administered a parallel form of the analogies test. The performance of the experimental subjects was significantly higher than that of the controls (see means and standard deviations in Table 13.2). An analysis of variance showed a significant main effect for the training/control factor (see Table 13.3).

Encouraged by the above results, we used the same experimental design for checking the cognitive potentials of the attributive type of relation which appeared as a factor likely to contribute to coherence and rigor in thinking (Kreitler, Kreitler and Wanounou, 1987/88). Thus, we hypothesized that subjects using frequently the attributive type of relation in their meaning profile would perform better on a test of syllogisms than those scoring low on this type of relation. For 86 undergraduates (43 controls) the correlation was 0.72. (Needless to mention, also other meaning variables were correlated with high

Table 13.2 Means and standard deviations (in parentheses) on the test of analogies before and after training

	Experimental subjects	Control subjects
Pre-training	10.6(4.5)	9.9(5.0)
Post-training	18.5(5.7)	10.3(4.8)

Each item solved correctly was scored as one point.

Table 13.3 Results of the analysis of variance with performance on the analogies test as the dependent variable

Source of variation	df	MS	F
Training/control	1	14.56	7.10[a]
Error	58	2.05	

[a] $p < 0.01$.

Table 13.4 Means and standard deviations (in parentheses) on the test of syllogisms before and after training

	Experimental subjects	Control subjects
Pre-training	9.5(3.4)	9.0(4.1)
Post-training	16.8(5.0)	9.9(4.8)

Each item solved correctly was scored as one point.

Table 13.5 Results of the analysis of variance with performance on the test of syllogisms as the dependent variable

Source of variation	df	MS	F
Training/control	1	13.44	4.00[a]
Error	84	3.36	

[a] $p < 0.05$.

scores on the syllogisms test.) A training study of the attributive type of relation, performed exactly as the above-described training study on the comparative type of relation, showed that the training of the attributive type of relation increased performance appreciably on the logical thinking test (see Tables 13.4 and 13.5).

Obviously, scientific and artistic creativity may frequently require additional cognitive abilities, but the fundamental contribution of analogical and logical thinking is evidenced by many examples in both domains. Freud used the analogy of the hydraulic model to explain the functioning of the id–ego–superego structure energized by the libido and the death drive. Another salient analogy in Freudian theory which initiated a new trend in social psychology compares the role of the leader in regard to the masses to that of the superego in regard to the id. Also, despite his so-frequent daring conclusions, he was rarely if ever caught committing a logical mistake. The beautifully constructed psychoanalytic theory, like Hull's impressive structure, is found wanting not on logic but on evidence.

In contrast to psychoanalysis that relied on analogies, there was no trace of analogical thinking but only pure logical thinking in Arnold Schoenberg's twelve-tone revolution that broke with about 500 years of pre-fixed seven-tone scales. Reportedly, Schoenberg regarded the harmonic, modulational and melodic possibilities of the traditional scales as exhausted and the possibilities offered by a twelve-tone chromatic as having been used to their limits in Wagner's *Tristan*, Mahler's symphonies and in his own *Transfigured Night*. Foreseeing that every new scale tradition would likewise be exhausted soon, he drew the rather obvious conclusion that triviality could only be avoided if the composer constructed for each composition its own specific and unique twelve-tone sequence that would serve as the frame of reference for this composition (Anton von Webern, personal communication; Kreitler and Kreitler, 1972).

A less serious or sympathetic commentator would be tempted to interpret some of the above reasoning in terms of analogical thinking—for example, that composers should be their own Pope Gregor—but the Schoenbergians insist on the purely logical reasoning that has guided Schoenberg to his revolution.

METAPHORIZATION, SYMBOLIZATION AND THEIR EXPERIMENTAL ENHANCEMENT

A different, though perhaps additional, aspect of creativity was explored by applying some other variables of our meaning system, particularly the variables of the exemplifying–illustrative and metaphoric–symbolic types of relation. The popular belief that only or mainly artists are metaphorizers and symbolizers is utterly erroneous. Scientists metaphorize too. Mathematics as the major language of the hard sciences can be and is actually used and understood lexically as well as metaphorically, as, for instance, when regarding a vector as an ordered set of numbers or in physics as a directed force of given strength. However, according to our more precise categorizations of the metaphoric–symbolic meaning variables, Newton's falling apple served him merely as an illustrative instance of gravity, regaining its purely lexical meaning the moment Newton picked it up and ate it.

Table 13.1 shows that in the meaning system there is a distinction between metaphor and symbol. We define metaphor as a referent–meaning value combination in which the meaning value is drawn from a sphere of content and/or degree of concretization not conventionally related to the referent (for example, blue monday, sleepy river). The symbol is an elaborate metaphor that includes an incongruity or a conflict and resolves it on the level of the image by being a complex good *Gestalt* (Kreitler, 1986; Kreitler and Kreitler, 1972). The Indian Mandallas combining harmoniously squares or triangles with a circle or triangles with circles are symbols. So is the image of a snake catching its tail that led Kekula to the discovery of the benzene rings; or the door destined only for the particular peasant who is not allowed to enter through it (Kafka, 'Before the Law'). Freud's censor or Maxwell's demon opening or closing the door for molecules seem to have been scientifically highly potent metaphors. Picasso's Guernica is both an illustrative instance of the Spanish Civil war and a metaphor of all the wars. Whether Plato's image of the cave is grasped as a metaphor or a symbol depends on one's belief or disbelief in the possibility of obtaining absolute knowledge. Most of Freud's so-called sexual symbols, as for instance the cigar as the penis symbol, are not at all symbolic but merely representations by way of similarities in sensory qualities, or, in the case of the box standing for the vagina, similarities of function or use.

Considering the so-obvious potentials of the exemplifying–illustrative and metaphoric–symbolic types of relation for creative thinking (see also Kreitler, Kreitler and Wanounou, 1987/88), we decided to check experimentally the contribution of these variables to the scores on common creativity tests. Thus, in one study a group of undergraduates in the social sciences and the humanities

($n = 74$, half men and half women) were administered, in two separate group sessions and in random order, the meaning test and a standardized version of the Kogan–Wallach creativity test that provides scores on fluency, flexibility, elaboration and originality. The results showed that the subjects' scores on the exemplifying–illustrative type of relation were correlated positively and significantly with their scores on fluency ($r = 0.59$, $p < 0.01$) while their scores on the metaphoric–symbolic type of relation were correlated positively and significantly with originality ($r = 0.65$, $p < 0.01$) and to a certain extent with elaboration ($r = 0.39$, $p < 0.01$). It should be emphasized at this point that not all significant correlations between the meaning variables and creativity scores are presented in this context, but only those that refer to the relevant types of relation.

Again, in order to learn about the direction of the causal impact a training study was conducted. The subjects were 80 adolescents 14–15 years old. They were selected out of a larger pool of subjects in line with their scores on the types of relation that were of interest: they had scores below the group's mean either on the exemplifying–illustrative type of relation ($n = 40$) or the metaphoric–symbolic type of relation ($n = 40$).

The subjects of these two groups were first administered one of the two parallel versions of the Kogan–Wallach test of creativity. The subjects of each group were then divided randomly into two subgroups, one of which served as experimental and the other as a control subgroup. The experimental subjects who were low on the exemplifying–illustrative type of relation got four 30-minute group training sessions designed to increase their use of this type of relation. The experimental subjects who were low on the metaphoric–symbolic type of relation got a comparable training designed to increase their use of this type of relation. The methods used in the training were pre-tested in previous studies (see, for example, Kreitler, 1986) and consisted essentially in an extended version of the induction methods of personal–subjective meaning applied by Kreitler, Kreitler and Wanounou (1987/88). The control groups got no training at all. Three weeks after termination of the training all subjects were administered the second parallel version of the Kogan–Wallach creativity test.

Table 13.6 Means and standard deviations (in parentheses) of four creativity scores before and after training

Creativity score	Pre/post	Subjects trained in exemplifying–illustrative types of relations		Subjects trained in metaphoric–symbolic types of relations	
		Experimental	Controls	Experimental	Controls
Fluency	Pre	3.46(1.03)	3.59(1.24)	3.80(0.95)	3.67(1.42)
	Post	7.21(2.52)	4.05(1.79)	8.54(2.87)	4.10(1.64)
Flexibility	Pre	2.79(0.87)	2.40(0.74)	2.63(1.04)	2.39(0.77)
	Post	4.50(1.24)	2.45(0.82)	9.80(3.00)	3.52(1.10)
Elaboration	Pre	1.59(0.36)	1.70(0.46)	1.65(0.97)	1.55(0.62)
	Post	2.75(0.97)	2.01(0.86)	5.13(2.20)	1.46(0.53)
Originality	Pre	0.85(0.23)	1.01(0.44)	0.94(0.56)	0.80(0.37)
	Post	0.62(0.35)	0.93(0.42)	6.74(2.02)	1.00(0.50)

Table 13.7   Results of analyses of variance with scores on creativity test as dependent variables

Group	Source of variation	df	MS	F
Training: Exemp–Illustr	Training/control	1	7.78	4.25[a]
Dependent variable: Fluency	Error	78	1.83	
Training: Metaph–Symb	Training/control	1	8.21	4.69[a]
Dependent variable: Fluency	Error	78	1.75	
Training: Metaph–Symb	Training/control	1	13.52	9.13[b]
Dependent variable: Flexibil	Error	78	1.48	
Training: Metaph–Symb	Training/control	1	4.26	5.07[a]
Dependent variable: Elab	Error	78	0.84	
Training: Metaph–Symb	Training/control	1	10.69	12.73[c]
Dependent variable: Original	Error		0.84	

Note: Only analyses with significant results are presented.
[a] $p < 0.05$; [b] $p < 0.01$; [c] $p < 0.001$.

The results showed that the trained groups had significantly higher scores on the creativity test than did the controls and than they themselves had obtained prior to the training. Again, the group that was trained on the exemplifying–illustrative type of relation got higher scores only on fluency, but the group that was trained on the metaphoric–symbolic type of relation got higher scores on all four scores of creativity (see Table 13.6 for the means and Table 13.7 for the results of the analyses of variance).

CONCLUSIONS

In summing up our findings it must be reiterated that we did not intend to provide a fully fledged and satisfactory solution to the riddle of scientific and artistic creativity—nor did we succeed in doing so. True to our intent to explore the cognitive foundations of creativity, we had to ignore personality factors, environmental influences, the state of the domain before the creative performance, the difficulty of the task that had to be resolved creatively, and a host of other more and less important variables. But we hope to have succeeded in showing that a well-developed meaning system in general and the frequent application of some meaning variables in particular exert a decisive impact on creative performance. Moreover, since it was shown that by training these meaning variables it is possible to obtain an increase in creativity scores, symbolization and symbol understanding (Kreitler, 1986), we may regard a well-developed meaning system in general and the above-discussed meaning variables in particular as the core of the cognitive foundations of creativity.

REFERENCES

Arieti, S. (1976). *Creativity: The magic synthesis.* New York: Basic Books.
Arnon, R., & Kreitler, S. (1984). Effects of meaning training on overcoming functional fixedness. *Current Psychological Research and Reviews*, **3**, 11–24.

Gentner, D., & Gentner, D. R. (1983). Flowing waters or teeming crowds: mental models of electricity. In D. Gentner & D.L. Stevens (eds.), *Mental models*, (pp. 99–129). Hillsdale, NJ: Erlbaum.

Gordon, W. J. (1961). *Synectics: The development of creative capacity*. New York: Harper.

Kalmar, Y. (1980). *Relations of meaning to social class and to some personality and cognitive variables*. Master's thesis, Department of Psychology, Tel Aviv University.

Katz, J. J. (1972). *Semantic theory*. New York: Harper and Row.

Kreitler, S. (1986). *The psychology of symbols* (revised and enlarged edition). Tel Aviv: Papirus. (Originally published in 1965 as *Symbolschoepfung und Symbolerfassung* by Reinhardt, Basel.)

Kreitler, H., & Kreitler, S. (1972). *Psychology of the arts*, Durham, Duke University Press.

Kreitler, H., & Kreitler, S. (1976). *Cognitive orientation and behavior*. New York: Springer.

Kreitler, H., & Kreitler, S. (1982). The theory of cognitive orientation: widening the scope of behavior prediction. In B. Maher & W. B. Maher (eds.), *Progress in experimental personality research*, Vol. 11 (pp. 101–169). New York: Academic Press.

Kreitler, S., & Kreitler, H. (1984). Meaning assignment in perception. In W. D. Froehlich, C. J. W. Smith, J. G. Draguns & U. Hentschel (eds.), *Psychological processes in cognition and personality*, (pp. 173–191). Washington, DC: Hemisphere.

Kreitler, S., & Kreitler, H. (1985a). The psychosemantic foundations of comprehension. *Theoretical Linguistics*, **12**, 185–195.

Kreitler, S., & Kreitler, H. (1985b). The psychosemantic determinants of anxiety: a cognitive approach. In H. van der Ploeg, R. Schwarzer & C. D. Spielberger (eds.), *Advances in Test Anxiety Research*, Vol. 4, (pp. 117–135). The Netherlands: Swets and Zeitlinger.

Kreitler, S., & Kreitler, H. (1986). Individuality in planning: meaning patterns of planning styles. *International Journal of Psychology*, **21**, 565–587.

Kreitler, S., & Kreitler, H. (1987a). Plans and planning: their motivational and cognitive antecedents. In S. L. Friedman, E. K. Scholnick & R. R. Cocking (eds.), *Blueprints for thinking: the role of planning in cognitive development*, (pp. 110–178). New York: Cambridge University Press.

Kreitler, S., & Kreitler, H. (1987b). The motivational and cognitive determinants of individual planning. *Genetic, Social and General Psychology Monographs*, **113**, 81–107.

Kreitler, S., & Kreitler, H. (1988). Horizontal decalage: a problem and its resolution. *Cognitive Development*, **4**, 89–119.

Kreitler, S., & Kreitler, H. (1989). *The cognitive rehabilitation of the retarded*. Unpublished manuscript. Tel Aviv University.

Kreitler, S., & Kreitler, H. (1990). *The cognitive foundations of personality traits*. New York: Plenum.

Kreitler, S., Kreitler, H., & Wanounou, V. (1987/88). Cognitive modification of test performance in schizophrenics and normals. *Imagination, Cognition and Personality*, **7**, 227–249.

Ortony, A. (1979). The role of similarity in similes and metaphors. In A. Ortony (ed.), *Metaphor and thought* (pp. 186–201). Cambridge: Cambridge University Press.

Perkins, D. N. (1981). *The minds best work*. Cambridge, MA: Harvard University Press.

Piaget, J. (1958). Assimilation and connaissance. In A. Jonckheere, B. Mandelbrot & J. Piaget (eds.), *Etudes d'epistemologie genetique*, Vol. 5 (pp. 49–108). Paris: Presses Universitaires de France.

14

The Embodyment Theory of Pre-reflexive Thought and Creativity

J. T. HAWORTH
University of Manchester

MAIN TENETS OF THE EMBODYMENT THEORY

In modern life, reflective thought and the search for ideas and 'testable truth' is taken as the prime route to knowledge and creativity. Questions concerning the primary origins of knowledge and meaning are rarely raised. Yet these are crucial to an understanding of thinking, creativity, and daily life.

The major contribution of Merleau-Ponty is that, unlike other phenomenologists, he focuses on the origins of perceptual knowledge and consciousness. In stressing the prime importance of the body and its operations, he argues that our fundamental knowledge of the world comes through our body's exploration of it. Primary meaning is reached through coexisting with the world in distinction to intellectual meaning reached through analysis. This primary meaning is brought about mainly by pre-reflection. The body does not find meaning pre-existent in the world but calls such meaning into existence by its own activity and by virtue of it being combined with time and space, in distinction to it being in and conceiving time and space. The body has its world or understands its world without having to use its symbolical objectifying function '... to perceive is to render oneself present to something through the body', and 'consciousness is in the first place not a matter of "I think", but of "I can".'

This 'Embodyment Theory' of Merleau-Ponty proposes that the visible unfolds and is concentrated by the body over time. It has a style across time. We do not see the world but see with the world. Vision commences in things. It is not to apprehend first by constructing an intellectual immanence but by coexisting over time.

Perception, it is argued, can no longer be considered a constitution of the true object but as our *inherence* in things. Perceptual, emotional and cognitive life are

Lines of Thinking, Volume 2   Edited by K.J. Gilhooly, M.T.G. Keane, R.H. Logie and G. Erdos
© 1990 John Wiley & Sons Ltd

viewed as subtended by an *intentional arc* which situates us in our past, our future, our human setting, and physical, ideological and moral situation. Perceptual synthesis is thus seen as a temporal synthesis. This involves structures from all the past sensory and affective life of a person (the *carnal formula*) sedimented in pre-reflexive thought, and *lines of intentionality* which trace out at least the *style* of what is to come; that is, a certain manner of dealing with situations which has issued from perception in distinction to being consciously imposed.

THE 'EMBODYMENT THEORY OF ART'

The previous characteristics of perception can be seen in artistic activity, perhaps more easily than in the creative act of living. Merleau-Ponty's analysis of art, scattered throughout his writings, constitutes an 'Embodment Theory of Art', which is used in evidence for his embodment theory of perception. The theory is in direct contrast to traditional theories of art emphasizing 'artistic intentions' and the search for 'ideas' and 'truths' as the main driving force in art, and viewing the substrate of the work as subsidiary to the artistic value of the work. The embodment theory views the art work as 'enriched being' in its own right, in distinction to it being an analogue for an external 'truth' or 'essence'. It proposes that this enriched being is not produced primarily by 'intentional acts', but by the reciprocal influence of consciousness, the body, techniques and materials. The work of art is also considered to be visible or meaningful in a stronger sense than everyday perception. It 'gives visible existence to what profane vision believes to be invisible'.

The embodment theory of art recognizes that in the production of a work of art the artist does not have to ask what important 'truth' or idea he wishes to portray. Rather, works of art can come about through the continuous interaction of the artist with the ideational and physical fabric of the world. As Picasso has said, 'Je ne cherche pas, je trouve'. What prompts artistic creation is not simply objects or situations, but 'carnal formulae' and personal 'style'.

Merleau-Ponty quotes Max Ernst, who said that 'the role of the painter is to grasp and project what is seen in him', and Paul Klee '... I think the painter must be penetrated by the world—perhaps I paint to break out.' He believes that in modern art the painter's vision 'is not a view on the outside, a merely 'physical–optical' relationship with the world—but a concentration or coming to itself of the visible'. What prompts artistic creativity, he considers, is not simply a response to objects or situations, but involves *carnal formulae*; and a painter does not put his immediate self into a painting but instead his *style* which he has had to master. This style is not something developed consciously to depict the world, but is an 'exigency that has issued from perception'. It is a personal system of equivalences that he makes for himself for the work which manifests the world as he sees it: 'It is the universal index of the "coherent deformation" by which he concentrates the still scattered meanings of his perception and makes it exist expressively.'

Merleau-Ponty does not say that ideas are not important in art, rather that they have their origins in embodment. In raising the question of what is implacable in a work of art, he answers:

> 'The fact that it contains, better than ideas, matrices of ideas, the fact that it provides us with symbols whose meaning we never stop developing. Precisely because it dwells and makes us dwell in a world we do not have the key to, the work of art teaches us to see and ultimately give us something to think about as no analytic work can; because when we analyse an object, we find only what we have [consciously] put into it.' (p. 76; my insertion in brackets)

Thus, when we view a work of art:

> '... (we) do not look at it as (we) do a thing; ... [rather] ... my gaze wanders in it as in the halos of being. It is more accurate to say that I see according to it, or with it, than I see it'.

Some further quotes from Merleau-Ponty's analysis of art may serve to illustrate this. In *Phenomenology of perception*, Merleau-Ponty states:

> 'Aesthetic expression confers on what it expresses an existence in itself, it installs it in nature as a thing perceived and accessible to all, or conversely plucks the signs themselves ... the colours and canvas of the painter — from their emperical existence and bears them off into another world. No one will deny that here the process of expression brings the meaning into being or makes it effective, and does not merely translate it.' (p. 183)

> 'The effort of modern painting [he considers] has been directed not so much towards choosing between line and colour, or even between the figuration of things and the creation of signs, as it has been towards multiplying the system of equivalences (a logos of lines, of lighting, of colours, of reliefs, of masses—a conceptless presentation of a Universal Being), towards severing their adherence to the envelope of things. This effort might force us to create new materials or new means of expression, but it could well be realised at times by re-examination and re-investment of those which existed already' (p. 182)

In painting he believes that 'depth' is a crucial consideration, citing Giacometti ('I believe Cezanne was seeking depth all his life') and Robert Delauney ('Depth is the new inspiration'). This depth is not that of Euclidean space, but rather *global locality*—'a locality from which height, width and depth are abstracted—a voluminosity' (pp. 180–181).

From his analysis of modern art Merleau-Ponty concludes:

> 'Now perhaps we have a better sense of what is meant by that little verb "to see". Vision is not a certain mode of thought or presence to the self; it is the means given me for being absent from myself, for being present at the fission of Being from the inside ...' (p. 166)

CONTEMPORARY PRINTMAKING

In contemporary fine art the process of creativity and the art work can illustrate the importance of Merleau-Ponty's emphasis on both *matrices of ideas* and the *reciprocal influence of consciousness, the body, technique and materials*. There is creative tension between, on the one hand, a process of working which lets an image or idea emerge through interaction with the medium, and on the other hand an approach where, as in conceptual art, the idea is considered of prime importance, but where the exploitation of a medium can result in the art work being stunningly beautiful and even metaphysical, irrespective of the value of the original idea *per se*. This can be seen most readily in contemporary printmaking, which uses a range of materials and retains the developmental stages of the work, making the creative act more open to inspection.

Kaelin (1962, p. 392) notes that the claim of Merleau-Ponty that expression is a bodily movement allows it to be said that an artist thinks with his materials, not with the ideas that he imposes on them. Typical of this is the work of Sam Frances, for example, who has used lithography to fulfil his inquisitive interest in things mystical, acknowledging 'a mysterious element which remains partially beyond his control and which causes the image to rise out of the stone' (Einstein, 1975, p. 227).

In contrast to Frances, the conceptual artist Sol le Witt has used etching to convey an idea, first working out a complex set of combinations of four types of line—vertical, horizontal, left and right diagonal—and then producing a series of etchings. Sol le Witt, who coined the term 'conceptual art' in 1964, believes that 'the initial idea is paramount'. Nevertheless, as one reviewer notes, '... his art has turned out stunningly beautiful' (Sol le Witt, 1978). It can also be perceived as coherently combining structure, certainty and uncertainty, ambiguity and depth—a structured voluminosity, at least for those whose gaze 'wanders in it as in the halos of being'.

While these two examples typify the continuing discourse in art on the relative importance of ideas/cognition versus more primordial methods of contact with the world, many printmakers work on a broad basis, synthesizing ideas with 'affective' responses to situations and materials. Gilmour (1978) notes that 'Truth to materials has been one of the most important concepts in establishing the autonomy of print ...' (p. 24). And Castleman (1976) stresses, 'It is the compatibility of technique and concept that has characterized quality in creative work—whatever the medium' (p. 11). Picasso and Dubuffet are two renowned examples of artist–printmakers whose work illustrates this.

Picasso in his printmaking shows a subtle use of materials and process which echo with Berger's (1981) comments on his paintings showing a recognition of the indeterminacy of objects, of things just coming into visibility. Dubuffet is an artist–printmaker, whose art appears to contain concrete references to reality, but whose concern in printing from a vast range of materials is with the creation of the imaginary, with liberating pre-reflexive thought, and to show that all objects may be sources of fascination and illumination (Dubuffet, 1973).

Other printmakers exploit the serial property of prints, and this area is also illustrative of the dynamic interplay between the properties and potentialities of art processes and ideational influences. Prints are made in stages and several copies can be made at each stage, some of which may be used as a basis for creative explorations in new directions. Some artists—Jasper Johns, for example—use the serial property of prints to chronicle a process of visibility. The critic Geelhaar (1980) notes that, through John's repeated transformations of a printed object:

'... motifs develop further complexities of content, the distinction before and after results in a record of time; the traces of transformations awaken memories of an earlier state. In this way, prints have become chronicles of their own process.' (p. 26)

Some conceptual printmakers also combine grids, maps, time-sequence photographs and diaries. Such work can give a new feeling for 'space and depth', a concern of many artists, as Merleau-Ponty has indicated. This approach echoes comments by Woods, Thompson and Williams (1972):

'The activity of art today is less concerned with the possibility of a finite solution than with the possibility of reaching discoveries in a diversity of media. The process is analogous to keeping a diary.' (pp. 121–123)

RESEARCH

Two internationally renowned artists whom the author has studied and interviewed, and whose methods of working highlight and develop aspects of the embodyment theory, are Michael Rothenstein and Alan Green. Michael Rothenstein is in the tradition of art concerned with the pictorial image. His work and approach could almost be said to constitute a paradigmatic case for the embodyment thesis. Alan Green is concerned with the image (art work) as object and with the serial property of printmaking. His work illustrates how 'the process' and 'the idea' can interact in a manner consistent with the embodyment thesis.

Michael Rothenstein

Rothenstein is concerned with the printed image and with the power of prints, like art in general, to open up new experiences of quality. In *Frontiers of printmaking* (1962) he points out that many artists have constantly attempted to widen the means of expression to include all possible *materials* and all practical *techniques*.

In citing Braque, Picasso and Dubuffet as important explorers of *materials* in printmaking, Rothenstein considers that this has not been wilful adventure on their part, but has served a philosophic intention affecting the whole basis of present aesthetic judgement. The printmaker has grown more flexible, more resourceful in answering the question: 'Which of these will give my image its most potent expression'. He also notes that the choice of materials is a fundamental one and may be partly the subject of the image.

Rothenstein has emphasized the importance to him of the 'wild shapes' that wood can have, creating an avalanche of movement within and by its shape. The irregular nature of these shapes meant that he did not need to work with the rectangle or square; it was 'a total escape from the idea that the plate or the block, or the lithostone forms the image':

'If I use this [wild shape] I am in free space ... that was fundamental to my thinking. Free space connecting everywhere—outside the curves themselves—and in the movement of the wood—as against the hemmed-in look of a print whose outer dimension is set by the plate.'

In using wild shapes, he stressed that he was conspiring with nature:

> 'I didn't really want those hard edge, faceless abstract shapes. I wanted images, however abstract, that had the resonance of 'thereness', of something real, of something one could respond to and feel, that was part of this extraordinary world we live in, not cut off as an aesthetic system of hard shapes.' (video)

Rothenstein has often used photographic images as found objects, combining them with relief printing from a variety of materials. Latterly he has combined his own photographs and woodcuts. His philosophy regarding use of photographic images with other marks, particularly those from relief printing, is of relevance.

In *Relief printing* (1970) he notes that the arrival of photographic aids placed entirely new areas of expression in the printmaker's hand. Photographs excite him: 'Photos have occasionally a strangeness, a gripping suggestiveness' (Gallery F15 Catalogue, 1980); 'In particular I found news photos exciting, I collected them avidly' (Drumcroon Catalogue, 1983). Some of the photoscreen prints he made combine photo images from very different periods. The print 'He's dead' combines images collected over a 30-year period, alienating one, Rothenstein believes, from a natural relationship with time. As such they distinctly resemble Merleau-Ponty's concepts of 'carnal formulae' subtended by an 'intentional arc'.

The important relationship between consciousness, the body, technique and materials, espoused in the embodyment theory, is reflected in Rothenstein's longstanding concern with *technique* and its relationship to creativity. This concern runs through his writing. For example, he considers that gestures which the eye can follow engender a state of empathy between onlooker and artist, and that a line or shape cut in resistant material can have a unique vital characteristic. In *Relief printing* Rothenstein makes the point that the act of cutting a line in wood or lino is demanding and needs a form of concentration that both frees energies and removes the unnecessary constraint of artistic responsibilities—of being swamped by the explosion of ideas, information and possibilities in art.

In discussing his discovery of caustic etch for obtaining controlled textures on lino, he notes that the 'traditional procedure of trying to get a graded tone—by use of a multiple tool to give fine line systems has been found to be slow and restrictive, laborious to the point of inhibiting the free run of creative sensation'. In colour proofing he advocates 'that this should be done in the spirit of excitement—often quickly and spontaneously to catch colours appropriate to the block on the wing'.

This creative interaction with the medium, this conspiracy with the object, does not apply just to the mark or to colour. It also applies to designs and design systems. Once the initial statement is made, printmaking can open up opportunities for considerable experimentation. As Rothenstein indicates, a series of first prints can be treated differently, the statement can be handled in different ways, it can be printed repeatedly in varying positions and orientations. Combined multiple images can be produced quickly without the unnecessary labour of outlining and filling in with paint, a process which may well deaden the grasp of the design system. Elements can be printed in different tones to give an impression of movement, and the initial statement can be combined with other images. Thus the print evolves along lines anticipated in the embodyment theory of Merleau-Ponty.

Rothenstein does not believe in technique for its own sake. When 'conspiring with nature', he stresses that virtuosity is not enough—there has to be an idea: 'Images taken from found objects must be incorporated in the natural flow of vision' (*Frontiers of printmaking*, p. 22). When interacting with the mediums he 'listens to the voices' which emanate from the process, and quotes Haytor (with whom he worked for a short period) on technique: 'Only when the use of such devices reveal an image previously unknown, inaccessible by other means, does it become vital.'

Style and One's Nature

Rothenstein's approach to printmaking has not remained static. He has noted that the artist does not need to live by establishing a style and practising that style all his life. However, as the Drumcroon Catalogue of his work notes: the earlier work and the mature work he sees as *intersecting arches*, each springing from a different area of possibility. There is an underlying style 'subtended', perhaps, by an 'intentional arc', to use Merleau-Ponty's terminology:

> 'When you see the work together you can see that it is all done by the same chap ... I would always centralise an image. Certain characteristics of space and pacing—I think they are just as much in these [late] woodcuts as those photographic prints. You can't really get away from the basic sort of *substructure of one's nature* [a point which emerged several times in interviews]. I get a satisfaction from drawing with a knife or gouge, a satisfaction unobtainable by other means .... I love the sculptural feel of working with tough material and I see it as something substantial'.

This outline of Michael Rothenstein's written views and work demonstrates the process of 'embodyment' as developed by Merleau-Ponty. Rothenstein 'conspires with objects' and exploits the unique characteristics of materials and tools through a process of mind and body, reacting with the 'voices' which emanate from the process. Images and ideas can emerge in the process and be incorporated in the 'flow of vision' to produce prints as 'enriched being' in distinction to the print functioning as an analogue for a preconceived idea. At the same time there are grounds for considering that images can be sedimented in 'pre-reflexive' thought as 'carnal formulae' and emerge later through an 'intentional arc' via the process of 'style'. The interviews I had with Michael Rothenstein demonstrate and elaborate on this (Haworth, 1985).

Images, the Carnal Formula and the Intentional Arc

Rothenstein has been an avid collector of images for many years and discussion indicated how images could excite him: 'At a certain point they excite you to a point where there's a kind of integration between what's out there, the image, and what's in here, the response.' The photo images for a sporting print he was making had been collected over a long period of time. In discussing how they came to be in the print, Rothenstein commented;

> 'You have a certain reaction to them which over a period becomes rather substantial. You want to get back to them. You want to do something with them. These are all news photos I've had for a long time. Some of them go back years. There is a kind of background feeling in the choice.'

This impact on perception of an image, whose 'weight' can be carried forward and build up over time, is termed in Merleau-Ponty's thesis 'carnal formula subtended by an intentional arc'. This is a prevalent characteristic of Rothenstein's creative process and images recur throughout his work. For example, he drew cockerels as a child and some of his most recent work still uses the cockerel image. As Rothenstein notes, he works very much 'out of obsession'.

The relevance of the term 'carnal formula' was also indicated in reference to the print 'Japanese kites'. In discussion of how things became 'encoded in one's imagination', Rothenstein noted:

> 'One day I remember seeing a girl wearing a shirt with big, strong, startling cubist colours against a rippling torso, like an element from cubist art. Although I did some drawings of friends holding up kites before I did the print, it was a memory, quite a remote memory of that particular combination—coloured lines against the torso—which came alive when I came to do the print.'

Rothenstein's comments on his latest wood carvings, which contain rather 'crude' imagery, also referred to the process of 'encoding':

> 'I don't call this drawing, I call it anti-drawing. It's setting down really rough metaphors for faces or actions or whatever—I don't know how it's happened. Other artists are doing it in America. Jim Dine has started woodcutting using the most direct means.'

> 'When I say that now I do anti-drawing, I don't want to return to this idea of drawing, of trying to make things look real ... I'm not trying to make it as real as it could look, but trying to make it encoded in terms of my own imagination, which is something quite different. But it's something that is hard to talk about.'

Meaning

In many of Rothenstein's prints the 'meanings' arise as the work is done. In the print of the girl with the burning candle, Rothenstein said that it had sexual connotations: the girl with the burning candle, the upturned umbrella, the cock as a pun on the physical features of the man. But he said:

> 'I did the image because of the forms that excited me, the colours that excited me, the movement that excited me. I simply went to work and did it. But when I looked at it afterwards I realized that this is a sexual scenario.'

In discussing one of his semi-abstract prints, Rothenstein said that with this category of his prints he was obsessed with the forms. The form in this print, he saw as a metaphor for the body, arms and legs, breast and nipples. But he added:

'The artist, he doesn't always know himself what he's trying to say. What is important is that he wants to say it—that's what's important. Perhaps it was by chance that I came across the clues that this print is about the body image.'

For Michael Rothenstein in his concern with the image, and perhaps also for other artists, the 'process' is influenced not only by the materials but also by philosophical concerns, predispositions and the substructure of one's nature. His process of artistic creation demonstrates *in detail* a reciprocal influence between consciousness in its broadest sense, the body and materials, producing prints as enriched being, in contrast to subordinating expression to the demands of truth.

Alan Green

Green is a painter and printmaker concerned with the image (art work) as object, with structure and multiple meanings, with the 'flesh of things' in Merleau-Ponty's terminology. He is also concerned with the serial property of printmaking. His work is pertinent to the embodment thesis in that it illustrates how 'the process' and 'the idea' can interact in a manner consistent with this thesis.

The art of Alan Green is strongly influenced by his attitudes and conceptions. He believes that painters have learnt a great deal from conceptual artists, while some have neglected this area to their peril. His paintings and prints, which have delicately structured surfaces located in a square, could be thought to be about 'certainty and uncertainty', ideas of concern to conceptual artists.

The way in which the 'concept' or 'idea' influences the work of Alan Green, however, is not in the sense of an artist 'chasing after an idea', of the artist trying to *portray* a particular concept, idea or truth. Rather, what he has derived from conceptual art is an *attitude* towards art and the creative process. This attitude sets the stage for his work. He is not interested in conveying illusion or encouraging virtuosity by sleight of hand, but in structure and the object qualities of works of art and the multiple meanings they can have. In tune with what he sees as the needs of society, he believes in conservation of resources, including ideas as well as physical resources. He believes in making the most of the working process itself. As Martin Lignon (1980) has noted, Green, unlike the minimalist artists, does not have to chase after an idea in his work: 'His demarche on the contrary consists in making the most of a situation which emerges from the working process itself ...' (p. viii).

'Parallel Worlds'

The interview with Green and examination of his paintings and prints illustrated that when the artist is working he does not need to be continually thinking of how to comment on society, or how to communicate. He does not have to subordinate his expression to the demands of 'truth'. Instead, the artist works in a 'parallel world' where the physical, ideational and emotional climate created by the conditions prevalent in society can exert an effect. Artistic meaning and 'comment' can emerge by the two parallel worlds of the art process and social considerations meeting in the artist by a process of embodyment. This has analogies with the claim made by Merleau-Ponty: 'that modes of thought correspond to technical methods, and that to use Goethe's phrase, "What is inside is also outside".'

In his painting Green is trying to go beyond pre-givens in art, in the sense of past ideas. He believes that while one has to have ideas, it is a question of how basic one can be. Thus in his painting he responds to what has happened the previous day to the surface of the work in line with his belief that an important lesson of conceptual art is not so much a concept, as trying to maintain an attitude of realism. At the same time one aspect of this 'attitude of realism' for Green is that paintings as objects can be used to stretch the mind and perception.

This intermeshing of attitudes with technical methods is also shown in Green's reasons for making many of his prints in series and small editions. He likes prints because:

> '... you can take an image and put it on a plate of copper, process and print it and then still have an image left on the plate. You can return to it and carry on with it. You can't do that so directly with drawing or painting. *With prints it's a natural thing that it should be like that.*'

This property of printmaking is utilized by Green to bring 'images into visibility', to use Merleau-Ponty's terminology. There is coexistence with techniques; the medium, and the outside world in its influence on attitudes.

Inherence

In discussing Green's paintings and printmaking it was apparent that Green *inheres* in the process, and that issues of *freedom, constraint* and *process* are interrelated. He considers there is an element of process and behaviour in his work. Behaviour influences his work in that if one is tired one works one way; if one is fresh another. If one runs out of a certain paint, one works another way. All this, he considered, fed into his work.

In undertaking a painting, Green lives and exists with it over time. The *constraints* imposed by the square give him an enormous amount of *freedom* to exploit colour and structure. While the square may appear the blandest of shapes, it is perhaps the simplest way of putting different colours in relation without interference from form. Green still has a myriad of decisions to make regarding canvas size, colour, method of application of paint, reaction of paint and nature of surface produced, etc. But for Green, in painting, the constraint of the square appears to help him 'inhere' in things. And, as in perception, on the embodyment thesis; this 'inherence' helps him to bring forth 'meanings'—'truths' in the art work.

In his printmaking Green also 'inheres' in the process over time. This process, by the nature of its technical methods, sets constraints. The number of plates and printing is limited, unless overthrown by money. The press and materials available can influence the print size, and the nature of line may relate to tools and materials. As in painting, these constraints can enforce discipline and enhance focus. And in this 'inherence' options can be opened up through interaction with surface texture, overprinting and the re-use of images, etc. The art work can come into visibility in the process.

Much of Green's printmaking is concerned with the production of series of prints where the individual members of a suite bear some relationship to each other. Printing plates may be used in whole or part several times to produce different images by variations of overprinting or rotating the position of plates, etc. For example, a print termed 'half to the right' was produced by grinding away the cross-hatched image on the right of the plate and overscreening the left-hand side and part of the black image with white.

A lot of time and effort may go into the structure of the prints. Lines may be painstakingly drawn. Sometimes if there was a mark Green did not like he would spend hours burnishing it out so as not to get what he didn't want, while still letting the plate evolve. Green notes that some things come about through the history of the plate. In one print a certain tone had appeared owing to the process of combination. He took it (accepted it) but he had not made the decision to do it, noting: 'That is what is meant by this conceptual thing ... You are setting up an *attitude* where events are decided by what's gone on in the process, by what's gone before. It's a self-fulfilling work in the end.'

This 'inhering' in the work, and living an idea through a particular attitude, may be one approach to 'brute' perception, to the 'nerve of things'. Coupled with the influence of the 'parallel world' of 'lived experience' it can produce prints as 'enriched being' of current significance. In a statement on Green's prints, agreed with the artist, Hart (1983) points out that the images in a suite show the interconnectness of things, 'the knock-on effect of all activity' which can act as a metaphor for human relationship and creativity.

In his work Green is treading a fine line between letting work happen, experimenting with both surface and ideas, and at the same time terminating experiments. His concluding thoughts were that he was concerned with providing restricted areas for chance to occur, and partly controlling this. However, it is equally apparent that he is very much concerned with the traditional artistic matters of enjoying colours, lines, tones and textures, with structure and strength, with subtlety and fragility, with not being too obvious, and with caring.

In connection with this, Martin Lignon (1980), discussing the work and philosophy of Green, makes the interesting point that conscious action can only take a certain amount of information if it wants to remain operational, to concentrate on the job in hand. To paraphrase Lignon: 'Theorising practice ... and becoming fully aware of the philosophical implications of pictorial action ... could weaken the rhythm and skills needed to produce ...' (p. xii). These comments have obvious parallels in the importance attached by Merleau-Ponty to pre-reflexive thought in perception and artistic creation. At the same time Green is concerned not to be carried away by technique. The interplay of 'ideas' with technique is necessary, even if these ideas are merely setting a background structure, which may aid in the production of what Melanie Hart has termed 'objects of contemplation', objects which are forged through Green living an idea.

CONCLUSIONS

Merleau-Ponty considers that the painter 'is a certain speech in the discourse of painting which awakens echoes from the past and the future to the exact degree that it does not look for them, and because he is linked to all other attempts to the exact degree that he buries himself resolutely with his world.' As the present study shows, both Rothenstein and Green bury themselves resolutely in their world. They inhere in their work over time, and the process produces art works which are 'enriched being', a characteristic which is shared by other artists.

While this model of artistic creativity emphasizes the importance of pre-reflexive thought, it does not deny the importance of reflection. In defending his embodyment thesis in *The Primacy of perception* (1964), Merleau-Ponty states 'It is the unreflected which is understood and conquered by the reflective. Left to itself perception forgets itself and is ignorant of its own accomplishments' (p. 203).

Reflection may take place after an art work has been produced. The artist may look at it to discover why it seems better or worse than a previous work, and even, as Rothenstein has noted, to discover what it means. This can inform the artist's 'intentional arc', and what Peguy has called his 'historical inscription' in which can be recognized the filiations or kinships in the work of past and present artists.

Reflection can, of course, also take place in the process of making an art work. As this review and study of artistic creativity shows, there is a reciprocal relationship between consciousness, materials and technique involving both pre-reflexive and reflexive thought. The work of Rothenstein and Green shows that knowing and operating in the world is as much an interactive process as one based on initial intentions. Artistic creativity involves 'keeping options open' as well as taking decisions, and 'being spontaneous' as well as disciplined, and doing and evaluating during the process and over a period of time.

Various features of the interactive aspect of creativity have been documented by such writers as De Bono (1970), Hudson (1966), Vernon (1970), Perkins (1981) and Barron and Harrington (1981). This chapter has highlighted the importance in artistic creativity of the dynamic reciprocal influence and simultaneous intertwining of attitudes, philosophy, predisposition and 'self' with the physical and ideational fabric of the world through the process of embodyment involving pre-reflexive and reflexive thought.

Interestingly there are parallels with the embodyment thesis in recent concepts and approaches in the study of person–situation interactions. For example, concepts of activity and action theory (Frese and Sabini, 1985), affordances (Gibson, 1979; Von Hofsten, 1985), and flow experiences (Csikszentmihalyi, 1975; Privette, 1983) resonate with Merleau-Ponty's concept of 'inherence' in things. Life trajectories and personal life histories are also seen to be important (Roberts, 1986). Approaches are being adopted which aim to render visible the 'unrecognized' influences of formal and informal institutions on behaviour (Jahoda, 1986). While in this area there is some recognition of the complex and simultaneous interweaving of the person and the environment, a detailed juxtaposition of the embodyment theory of perception and pre-reflexive thought with these concepts and approaches could be mutually informative.

REFERENCES

Barron, F., & Harrington, D. M. (1981). Creativity, intelligence and personality. *Annual Review of Psychology*, **32**, 439–476.

Berger, J. (1981). The island of appearances. *New Society*, 8 October, 68–69.

Castleman, R. (1976). *Prints of the twentieth century: A history*. London: Thames and Hudson.

Csikszentmihalyi, M. (1975). *Beyond boredom and anxiety*. San Francisco: Jossey-Bass.

de Bono, E. (1970). *Lateral Thinking*. Harmondsworth: Penguin.

Drumcroon Catalogue (1983). *Michael Rothenstein*. Wigan: Art Education Centre.

Dubuffet, J. (1973). *Dubuffet Restrospective*. New York: Guggenheim Museum.

Einstein, S. (1975). The prints of Sam Frances. In P. Selz (ed.), *Sam Frances*. New York: Abrams.

Frese, M., & Sabini, J. (eds.) (1985). *Goal-directed behaviour: The concept of action in psychology*. Hillside: Erlbaum.

Gallery F15 Catalogue (1980). *Michael Rothenstein*. Sweden: Jeloy.

Geelhaar, C. (1980). *Jasper Johns' working proofs*. New York: Petersberg Press.

Gibson, J. J. (1979). *The ecological approach to visual perception*. Boston: Houghton Mifflin.

Gilmour, P. (1978). *The mechanised image*. London: Arts Council of Great Britain.

Hart, M. (1983). *Alan Green: Prints*. British Council Catalogue.

Haworth, J. T. (1985). *Contemporary printmaking and the embodyment theory of Merleau-Ponty*. Unpublished M.Litt. thesis, University of Lancaster.

Hudson, L. (1966). *Contrary imaginations*. London: Methuen.

Jahoda, M. (1986). In defence of a non-reductionist social psychology. *Social Behaviour*, **1**, 25–29.

Kaelin, E.F. (1962). *An existentialist aesthetic*. London: University of Wisconsin Press.

Le Witt, S. (1978). *Sol Le Witt*. New York: Museum of Modern Art.

Lignon, M. (1980). Alan Green. In *Alan Green: Paintings 1969–1979*. Oxford: Museum of Modern Art.

Merleau-Ponty, M. (1962) *Phenomenology of perception*. London: Routledge and Kegan Paul.

Merleau-Ponty, M. (1964). *The primacy of perception* (J. M. Eddie, ed.). Evanston: North Western University Press.

Perkins, D.N. (1981). *The mind's best work*. London: Harvard University Press.

Privette, G. (1983). Peak experience, peak performance, and flow: a comparative analysis of positive human experiences. *Journal of Personality and Social Psychology*, **45**, 1361–1368.

Roberts, K. (1986). *ESRC young people in society/16–19 initiative: A sociological view of the issues*. London: Economic and Social Research Council.

Rothenstein, M. (1962). *Frontiers of printmaking*. London: Studio Vista.

Rothenstein, M. (1970). *Relief printing*. London: Studio Vista.

Vernon, P.E. (1970). *Creativity*. Harmondsworth: Penguin.

Woods, G., Thompson, P., & Williams, J. (1972). *Art without boundaries*. London: Thames and Hudson.

15

Creativity: A New Evolutionary Perspective on the Relationship Between 'Person', 'Process' and 'Press'

JANE GEAR
University of Hull

INTRODUCTION

The fact that research into creativity conventionally falls under a number of different subheadings—namely, 'person', 'process', 'product' and, less frequently, but inclusive of environmental factors, what Messick (1976) calls 'press'—seems to suggest that creativity itself might merit a more central place in human psychology than is currently the case. Although it may be viewed as only one element of thinking, creativity involves what are regarded by anthropologists, among others, as our most human capacities of mind: our abilities to hypothesize and symbolize (Davis, 1981). Significantly, in the context of this paper, it is also said to incorporate what Arieti refers to as 'paleologic thinking' (Arieti, 1976); that is, our most primitive, 'free', primary process thinking.

Of established theories of creativity, none actually centres on the role of stress, nor even on the autonomic nervous system (ANS), despite the fact that the concepts of 'crisis' and 'stress in early childhood', for example, have gained at least some legendary significance. Similarly, although it is not new to relate phylogenic and ontogenic processes to each other, and evolutionary hypotheses about creativity have been proposed before, existent theories tend to relate to certain kinds of creativity only. None, so far, has served either to reduce the fragmentation of the weight of relevant research which falls into so many sub-fields, or succeeded in defining similarities and/or differences between artistic and scientific creativity, although distinctions are frequently made.

The purpose of this chapter, therefore, is to introduce one application of a new approach to understanding the human mind which allows creativity to be

Lines of Thinking, Volume 2 Edited by K.J. Gilhooly, M.T.G. Keane, R.H. Logie and G. Erdos
© 1990 John Wiley & Sons Ltd

viewed within a broader context of human experience and behaviour (Gear, 1989). One effect of this is that it allows artistic style to be related to other aspects of individual style, as will be explained. The approach in question is called APM–A theory, because it is rooted in the interactive processes of attention, perception, memory and arousal. It would be simpler to say that the theory centres on the effects of different levels and kinds of arousal on attention (A), perception (P) and memory (M), were it not for the fact that events of A, P and M

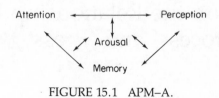

FIGURE 15.1   APM–A.

UNCONSCIOUS SCANNING AND FOCUS	CONSCIOUS SCANNING AND FOCUS	
Increasing tendency towards highly individual interpretations of and/or increase in physical activity		
Creativity – given 'purpose' (identified problem) and medium	IMAGINATION Anticipation, flexibility of thought and action; predominance of scanning over focus	Creativity – given 'purpose' and medium
Increase in arousal and increase in 'orientation needs' to include greater anticipation, more future planning (given 'purpose') and anxiety		
Unconscious and sub–threshold selection from alternatives	AWARENESS Use of expectancy and prediction	Consciousness of choice and selection from alternatives
Increase in arousal and in sub–threshold and conscious scanning activity		
As species learning	Highly specific REACTIVITY	As a result of individual learning (conditioning)
Increase in arousal and resources for coping with current internal and external demands		
	Environmental change LOW AROUSAL AND HIGH FOCUS	

The left axis reads: UNCONSCIOUS ATTENTION / PERCEPTION / MEMORY
The right axis reads: CONSCIOUS ATTENTION / PERCEPTION / MEMORY

FIGURE 15.2   A unidimensional view of changes in awareness and behaviour associated with increases in arousal. It is unidimensional because it does not, for instance, take into account the inverted-U shape created by correlates of efficiency and arousal, nor increases in arousal identified in Figures 15.3 and 15.4.

are also seen to affect arousal (−A); just as they are all seen to affect each other. Graphically, instead of any suggestion of a particular, linear and/or constant sequence of events such as attention → perception → thought → feeling → memory, it is being argued that—despite the conclusions of Zajonc (1980), for instance, on the separability of feeling and thinking—an interactive model of our reactions to environmental information (see Figure 15.1) provides a more useful explanatory tool.

Before moving on to making some crucial distinctions between kinds of arousal which, it is argued, are likely to underlie individual differences—not simply in degrees and style of creativity, but also in other aspects of experience and behaviour—Figure 15.2 describes some of the effects on thinking and behaviour of changes in levels of arousal. The figure describes shifts in levels of activity, as well as increases in awareness, which are part of our evolutionary history (Razran, 1971; Lancaster, 1975), as well as being aspects of individual experience and behaviour. The kinds of changes in question are most familiar as effects of the 'fight–flight' response or as drug-induced states (Huxley, 1977); but they also amount to increases in creative potential.

THE APM–A HYPOTHESIS

The APM–A hypothesis which provides the theoretical link between changes at species level and changes which take place in individuals depends on a number of well-known findings about arousal and performance. One of the most significant is a conclusion drawn by the Russian neurosurgeon Luria, as long ago as 1932. He concluded that some degree of motor disorganization is a fundamental organic reaction to affect. In turn, this finding is taken elsewhere to suggest a fundamental need for the externalization of neuronal excitation (Gear, 1989). Such a need viewed alongside the findings of Hebb on arousal and performance (1955), and those of Yerkes and Dodson on optimal levels of arousal (1908), provides the basis of an explanation of what Ardrey (1977) has suggested were the beginnings of both art *and* technology — the Acheulian axe.

The Acheulian axe represents the first known, and hitherto apparently inexplicable, unnecessary embellishment of a functional object: the transformation of a tool into an object of beauty. It coincided with the end of the harsh climatic conditions of the Pleistocene, the end of the last ice-age which was marked by a number of qualitative advances, including the production of beautiful decoration which bore no apparent relationship to functional demands. A possible explanation can be arrived at, however, if it is argued that the autonomic nervous system is as vital an element of species adaptation as it is to individual responsiveness to change: that it provides a steady 'tuning' of the organism to prevailing environmental conditions. If this is the case, base levels of sympathetic nervous system (SNS) activity are likely to have increased, in response to increased demands on physical and mental resources. But as SNS activity is both self-perpetuating and wears off only slowly, the coincidence of the Acheulian culture with the disappearance of former omnipresent threats can be seen to be highly significant. A relatively sudden easing of conditions and lessening of external demands is, after all, likely to have favoured those able to direct their new, excess (to survival needs) energies into other kinds of productive activity.

It would obviously have been counter-productive for individuals (and, ultimately, the species) for surplus energies to have been expressed randomly, or directed, perhaps in the form of gratuitous violence, towards fellow tribesmen or—at more indirect risk to self but for the gratification of equally primitive urges—towards the mates of fellow tribesmen. The harmless (by comparison) embellishers-of-axes, and others who found productive outlets for their energies, are therefore likely to have been amongst those who survived long enough to procreate and exert influence over others; while the hominid equivalent of the sociopath, or even the innocent sensation seeker (Zuckerman, 1979) expressing freed energies without the rudimentary benefits of emergency rescue services, let alone comprehensive accident insurance, are likely to have increased significantly in numbers only temporarily, until more recent times.

Clearly, there is more to creativity that this—the mere use of otherwise potentially self-destructive or socially disruptive energies. Further, current evidence of anti-social behaviour and sensation seeking is plentiful enough for us to realize that such behaviours were not selected against *per se*. Besides, creativity is surely about ideas as well as the expression of energy in socially acceptable ways. There are many repetitive activities which could have served this end. But before reconsidering changes in awareness and thinking identified in Figure 15.2, a question arises about how the hypothesis above differs from what might be seen as other displacement theories. Differentiation from Freudian theory, for example, is quite simple. Freudian theory would tell us neither why the ego should suddenly have become so much more active half a million years ago, nor, conversely, why the id should suddenly have become so much more turbulent at that point in time. Similarly, Lorenz's 'hydraulic' model fails to explain evolutionary changes in levels of motor activity, let alone changes in experience. Further, neither of these, nor other 'tension-release' or 'drive-reduction' theories, offers any insight into any qualitative prerequisites of perception or thinking necessary for creativity to occur.

In order to move to a position from which to address some of the other questions raised above, as well as to be able to focus on the relevance of 'environmental press' to artistically creative persons, it is necessary briefly to consider some aspects of psychological and physiological processes in a little more detail. The hypothesized shift in consciousness and concomitant evolution of new needs has already been attributed to species-wide changes in SNS activity. This also inevitably implies changes in balancing parasympathetic nervous system (PNS) activity, incidentally compounding potential for human variability alongside increased adaptability. Even more significantly, it is necessary to take into account the fact that adrenalin *and* noradrenalin—both hormones secreted during SNS activity—affect perceptual processes *and* behaviour in different ways.

A DYNAMIC MODEL OF STYLE

The best-known research into the effects of adrenalin and noradrenalin is by Ax (1953) and Funkenstein (1956). Ax correlated anger with a mixed adrenalin/

noradrenalin-like pattern, while Funkenstein made an association between *anger* and noradrenalin; but both associated *fear* with adrenalin. Others have associated adrenalin variously with apprehension and anxiety, mental pain and discomfort, and increased mental activity. Similarly, increased secretion of noradrenalin has been associated with reactions to unpleasant stimuli, increase in blood sugars (Van Toller, 1979), and increased activity in rats (Campbell and Singer, 1979). These findings and others allow us, with some confidence, to make a very simple correlation between the secretion of noradrenalin and observable changes in physical activity, and between the secretion of adrenalin and changes in mental activity. They also allow a conception of arousal and activation of the ANS which suggests increase in two different kinds of energy, which, in turn, promote different *kinds* of physical *and* mental activity, according both to intensity and kind of SNS activity and the patterning of balancing PNS response.

Given that the association of adrenalin with anxiety and fear also relates directly to a capacity to hypothesize, the generally acknowledged shift to 'higher-order needs', which happened approximately half a million years ago, is likely, in APM–A terms, to have included a shift to heightened needs for reassurance, best thought of in terms of 'orientation needs'; this is because of their perceived relationship to the orientation reflex, another term for limbic arousal, alternatively and appropriately labelled by Pavlov as the 'What-is-it?' response. Elsewhere (Gear, 1989) these needs are defined in detail. There is insufficient space to do so here, but their definition derives from a weight of evidence from a number of different fields which suggests, first, that as vulnerable beings we share fundamental needs for environmental feedback of both sensory and cognitive kinds. Secondly, our needs are chiefly, although to varying extents, for feedback from our physical and social environments. Thirdly, we also have varying levels of need for reassurance from our cultural and intellectual environments. Most importantly, however, individuals are seen to differ in *terms* of their needs: one of the differences being in degree of orientation towards their physical, social and/or cultural surroundings.

It is not in fact new to argue that individuals differ according to their needs (Murray, 1938), nor is it new to suggest that people differ in terms of SNS–PNS interaction (Eppinger and Hess, 1915). However, what is being suggested here is that people differ according to needs which arise *from* different patterning of autonomic nervous system activity; and needs are redefined beyond physical survival needs, chiefly as needs for different kinds and levels of reassurance.

The APM–A analysis also differs from others in identifying two different kinds of SNS activity, each of which increases availability of different kinds of energy which, in turn, being subject to variability and to balancing PNS activity, promote different kinds of experience and behaviour. This view, as the figures below illustrate, offers potential for accounting for a considerably greater range of human variability than hitherto, including variability in kinds and levels of creative potential. It actually offers the possibility of relating what is being called 'individual adaptive style' (including fundamental styles of perceiving, conceptualizing and behaving) to potential for, and styles of, creativity.

The significance of the identification of different kinds of SNS activity is shown in the figures below. They illustrate the fact that, given a relative bias towards

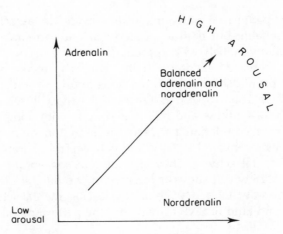

FIGURE 15.3 Three different kinds of increase in hormonal release associated with increase in arousal.

SNS activity, an individual may or may not display a *further* bias: towards increase in either mental energy (and activity)—as a phenomenon researched by Beatty (1982)—or physical activity.

This is a view which allows an APM–A identification of three key aspects of limbic arousal: (i) intensity of arousal, (ii) predominantly adrenalin-biased arousal, and (iii) predominantly noradrenalin-biased arousal; the interplay of which can be seen to provide for a vast range of variability. In fact support for the likelihood of differential responses of this kind is already available (Gale and Edwards, 1983).

Expressed diagrammatically, this concept offers the basis of the APM–A model in Figure 15.3. Intensity and bias of arousal may also be expressed in terms of their incidental effects (see Figure 15.4); that is, as promoting *different intensities and kinds of mental and physical activity* and, it is being argued, the most fundamental changes in, and characteristic styles of, experience and behaviour.

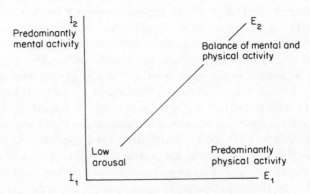

FIGURE 15.4 Intensities and biases of mental and physical activity associated with levels of arousal and internal and external styles.

VARIABILITY AMONG 'INTERNALIZERS' AND 'EXTERNALIZERS'

Most obviously, and in the most general terms, it is possible now to locate types referred to as 'internalizers' on the side of low physical activity (see Figure 15.5). (The phrase 'physical activity' is used in its broadest possible sense to include all behavioural gestures, from finger-tapping to more gross and obvious behaviours.) This location implies either relative PNS dominance in the lower half of the model at I_1 representing *first-order* internalizers, or strongly adrenalin-biased, rather than noradrenalin-biased, arousal in the upper half (I_2), representing *second-order* internalizers. Similarly, first- and second-order 'externalizers' can be located on the side on which high levels of physical activity either predominate over mental activity (at E_1) or are manifest *alongside* intense mental activity as a result of high levels of both adrenalin *and* noradrenalin (at E_2).

Instead of simply providing stereotypes to describe the polar-extreme types, the model being developed allows for the possibility of differences within and between the two major groups (Es and Is) which include *relative* degrees of *both* mental and physical activity of different kinds; relative degrees of scanning *and* focus (see Figure 15.2); and relative degrees of disorganization (or flexibility) *and* organization (or rigidity) of experience and behaviour. Importantly, alongside this potential for accommodating a much wider range of variability, the model allows for these kinds of activity to be manifested in socially acceptable *or* unacceptable ways. This is to suggest that the biological bases—as opposed to environmental influences—for criminality, for instance, may be the *same* as those for artistic achievement, so allowing the same physiological type to be expressed in either, or even both, forms, as well as other possibilities.

In the detailed explanation of the whole theory (Gear, 1989) it becomes possible at this stage to begin not only to develop the model in terms of a typology of individual style and to add definitions of 'personality', but also to include the new definition of needs; a definition of *kinds* of intelligence; and to

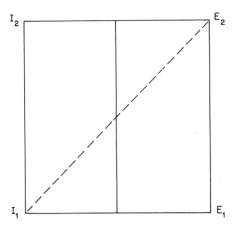

FIGURE 15.5 Externalizers (E_1 and E_2) and internalizers (I_1 and I_2) viewed in terms of intensity and bias of kinds of arousal and kinds of activity according to Figures 15.3 and 15.4.

locate the many different forms of behaviour which fall under the general heading of 'creativity'. The model also provides a means of relating these to so-called 'abnormal' behaviours. As a model of fundamental process, it also accommodates different possible manifestations of the variable intensities and biases of arousal which it represents, and takes into account dynamic relationships *within and between* the various extremes. The most significant of these are represented by the lower half of the left-hand side of the model, the corner marked I_1 (lowest arousal of any kind and archetypal internalizers), and the top right-hand corner marked E_2 representing highest levels of adrenalin and noradrenalin secretion, highest arousal, and archetypal externalizers. Incidentally, this diagonal *also* represents the simplest possible way of defining individual differences and accommodates the Eysenckian definitions of extrovert and introvert. The model also accommodates Eysenck's other dimensions of neuroticism and psychotism, as well as personality and perceptual disorders such as psychopathy and autism, but rather different explanations are offered in the book cited above.

Figure 15.6 sets out some of the differences seen to exist between first- and second-order externalizers (E_1s and E_2s and first- and second-order internalizers (I_1s and I_2s).

Although multiple continua are eventually used to cut into and across the model, in order to explore its dynamics, it has to be remembered that each area

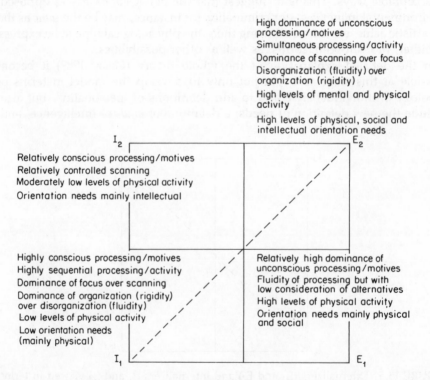

High dominance of unconscious processing/motives
Simultaneous processing/activity
Dominance of scanning over focus
Disorganization (fluidity) over organization (rigidity)
High levels of mental and physical activity
High levels of physical, social and intellectual orientation needs

I_2

Relatively conscious processing/motives
Relatively controlled scanning
Moderately low levels of physical activity
Orientation needs mainly intellectual

E_2

Highly conscious processing/motives
Highly sequential processing/activity
Dominance of focus over scanning
Dominance of organization (rigidity) over disorganization (fluidity)
Low levels of physical activity
Low orientation needs (mainly physical)

Relatively high dominance of unconscious processing/motives
Fluidity of processing but with low consideration of alternatives
High levels of physical activity
Orientation needs mainly physical and social

I_1

E_1

FIGURE 15.6 Some fundamental differences within and between the major internal and external adaptive styles.

represents an extremely wide range of variability in itself. On the other hand, despite offering a representation of psychological variability much nearer to probability than simple bipolar or trait models, this dynamic model is still based on a relatively *simple* interpretation of hypothesized differences in patterning of SNS–PNS activity. It is based on the relatively simple notion of gradual dominance of SNS over PNS activity, as arousal increases. But to attempt to give as complete a picture as possible of likely 'real' variability, it would be necessary to place many overlays of possible different patterns of 'balancing' PNS activity over our existing simple model. This is because variation in intensity and bias of aspects of SNS activity must surely be compounded by variations in patterns of SNS–PNS *interaction*. This implies that, in addition to the possibility of an evenly balanced relationship, providing a simple hyphenated pattern, as it were, of SNS–PNS activity (of low *or* high intensity), patterning may be *uneven* providing a bias in the form of a dot–dash, rather than a dash–dash pattern; so that SNS activity is seemingly either under- or over-compensated by PNS activity, again at different possible intensities.

'ADAPTIVE STYLE' AND CREATIVITY

The model as it stands, however, is already adequate to be able to begin to relate some general aspects of 'adaptive style' to different levels and kinds of creativity. Necessity being the 'mother of invention', it can be argued that all of us have some capacity for creative thought and action when 'pressed', but the literature on 'person' and 'process' in relation to creativity offers extremely strong support for identifying the most creative among us as second-order (E_2) externalizers as defined in detail elsewhere (Gear, 1989). This places archetypal 'creatives' in the area of the model consistent with findings which typify them as highly motivated, having strong 'libidos', being 'flexible', 'dominant' and 'open' (Stein, 1974; Freeman, 1971). This location of creativity on the model is also consistent with findings from a number of related fields, including research into cognitive styles and lateralization of brain function. This is what Cropley (1970) has to say about cognitive styles and creativity:

> 'Most cognitive styles ... have in common the property that they involve a dichotomy between, on the one hand, taking the world in in large lumps and, on the other, selectively attending only to chosen portions of the environment. The dichotomy can be restated as being a matter of paying attention to as wide a range of environmental properties as possible, or selecting a few attributes of the environment and concentrating on them and processing them. ... taking in as much information as possible involves cognitive strain, necessitates frequent modification of existing categories and makes intellectual functioning an arduous task ... it involves the advantages of being able to change one's existing mental structures very readily, of being able to relate widely different looking data and, in fact, of being in a state highly favourable to the appearance of creative thinking.'

Cropley goes on to say that a variable closely related to category width is that of risk-taking, which is another factor in research findings—as well as part of the folklore and legend—which identifies creative people as E_2 externalizers, in which way Zuckerman's sensation seekers are also identified. But creativity is manifested in many different ways, and it cannot be assumed, for example, that because externalizers are seen to make more 'connections' than internalizers, they are necessarily more 'imaginative'. Imagination is surely as susceptible to 'style' as any other aspect of feeling or thinking, and it is being argued that different kinds and levels of arousal (feeling) have fundamental effects on styles of thought. For instance, imagination may involve the manipulation of accurately remembered imagery and be typical of those being defined as second-order internalizers; just as it may be fired by more generalized feeling, or external stimulation of a more fragmentary nature, and be more typical of externalizers. Further, different kinds of creative production demand different levels of focus, as well as different levels of energy expenditure which, in turn, relate to differing demands, and preferences, for accuracy or freedom of expression (Gear, 1986).

Messick was able to identify nine cognitive styles in 1970 and nineteen by 1976. By adding to these the tens of strikingly similar dichotomies identified by researchers into cerebral lateralization, the number of dichotomous descriptions of psychological processes swells to at least fifty. All are consistent with the APM–A polar extremes of I_1—E_2 (see Figure 15.7) which are defined in detail elsewhere (Gear, 1989). This association of dichotomies with the simple continuum—which incidentally also locates right hemisphere characteristics at E_2—is consistent with the established association of the right hemisphere with artistic, and particularly musical, abilities (Young, 1983).

Springer and Deutsch (1981) conclude that the left hemisphere processes information 'in terms of details and features ... something like a digital computer', while the right 'perceives simultaneous relationships and more global properties and patterns ... more like an analogue computer'. There are obvious connections to be made between these conclusions and those of Liam Hudson (1967) on arts/science differences; and a very wide range of findings would allow us to conceptualize arts activities in general to be represented by the right side of the model, and technological and scientific activities of the left.

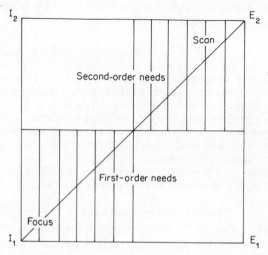

FIGURE 15.7   Key dimensions of individual style holding in common the polarity I_1—E_2.

But obviously there are very wide ranges of individual differences between people involved in the arts and the sciences and some people excel in both. By taking account of intensities *and* biases in patterning of hormonal responses, however, such differences can be accommodated.

Elsewhere (Gear, 1989) the concepts of 'vulnerability', 'high-order needs' and 'urgency of processing', with reference to high levels of limbic arousal, have been invoked in order to relate to each other the fields of personality, cognitive style and lateralization of brain function. The same concepts have also been used, in turn, to apply the 'dynamic model of style', which has been described in part, to so-called 'abnormal' styles of experience and behaviour. Indeed, the field of creativity itself frequently touches on those of neuroticism, psychoticism and psychopathy. In a sense, creativity—in its most obvious form—is by definition 'abnormal', being concerned with novel responses and the making of *unusual* associations. Magaro (1980) actually concludes that the processes of creativity and schizophrenia are the same although the outcomes are different. Storr (1976) draws attention to the fact that many of the world's great creators have exhibited obsessional symptoms; and Prentky (1980) devotes a book to creativity and psychopathy.

Further, Mannheim (1965) cites an identification of three types of criminals, of which one is 'predominantly creative'. He also draws links between criminality and 'creative genius' and refers to numerous examples from the arts and sciences of creative individuals found guilty of criminal offences. The line between creativity and 'madness'—or even creativity and social deviancy—is not just thin, but extremely wavy, even suggesting the existence of what might be called 'biological alternatives'. One possible living example is Jimmy Boyle, well-known convicted murderer, sculptor, writer (1977) and now also dedicated social worker. He actually describes a turning point in his life as being given the 'tools' to express his energies. It would seem that environmental 'press' holds evolutionary significance in the emergence of creative 'persons' and 'processes': that, in the development of creativity, physiological factors play a fundamental role if environmental factors allow necessary periods of 'incubation' *and* if appropriate 'tools' for the productive expression of ideas and energies happen to be available.

REFERENCES

Ardrey, R. (1977). *The hunting hypothesis*. Suffolk: William Collins.

Arieti, S. (1976). *Creativity: The magic synthesis*. New York: Basic Books.

Ax, A. F. (1953). The physiological differentiation between fear and anger in humans. *Psychosomatic Medicine*, **15**, 433–443.

Beatty, J. (1982). Task-evoked pupillary responses, processing load and the structure of processing resources. *Psychological Bulletin*, **91**, 276–292.

Boyle, J. (1977). *A sense of freedom*. London: Pan.

Boyle, J. (1977). *The hard man*. Edinburgh: Canongate.

Campbell, F., & Singer, G. (1979). *Brain and behaviour*. Australia: Pergamon Press.

Cropley, A. J. (1970). S–R psychology and cognitive psychology. In P. E. Vernon, (ed.), *Creativity*. Middlesex: Penguin.

Davis, D. D. (1981). *The unique animal*. London: Prytaneum Press.

Eppinger, J., & Hess, L. (1915). Die vagotonie. *Mental and Nervous Disease Monographs*, **20**.

Freeman, J. *et al.* (1971). *Creativity: A selective review of research* (2nd edn.). London: Society for Research into Higher Education.

Funkenstein, D. H. (1956). Norepinephrine-like and epinephrine-like substances in relation to human behaviour. *Journal of Nervous and Mental Diseases*, **124**, 58–66.

Gale, A., & Edwards, J. A. (1983). *Physiological correlates of human behaviour*. New York: Academic Press.

Gear, J. (1986). A new means of discrimination or a measure of 'good taste'? A critique of Eysenck's visual aesthetic sensitivity test (VAST) [and subsequent exchange with H. J. Eysenck]. In M. Ross (ed.), *Curriculum issues in art education*, Vol, 6: *Assessment in the arts*. Oxford: Pergamon Press.

Gear, J. (1989). *Perception and the evolution of style: A new model of mind*. London: Routledge.

Hebb, D. O. (1985). Drives and the conceptual nervous system. *Psychological Bulletin*, **62**, 243–254.

Hudson, L. (1967). *Contrary imaginations*. Middlesex: Penguin.

Lancaster, J. B. (1975). *Primate behaviour and the emergence of human culture*. New York: Holt, Rinehart and Winston.

Luria, A. R. (1976). *The nature of human conflicts*. New York: Liveright (first published in 1932).

Magaro, P. A. (1980). *Cognition and schizophrenia and paranoia: The interpretation of cognitive processes*. Hillsdale, NJ: Erlbaum.

Mannheim, H. (1965). *Comparative criminology*. London: Routledge.

Messic, S. *et al.* (1976). *Individuality and learning*. San Francisco: Jossey Bass.

Murray, H. (1938). *Explorations in personality: A clinical and experimental study of fifty men of college age*. New York: Oxford University Press.

Prentkey, R. A. (1980). *Creativity and psychopathology*. New York: Praegar Press.

Razran, G. (1971). *Mind in evolution: An East–West synthesis of learned behaviour and cognition*. Boston: Houghton Mifflin.

Springer, S. P., & Deutsch, D. (1981). *Left-brain, right brain*. San Francisco: W. H. Freeman.

Stein, M. I. (1974). *Stimulating Creativity*, Vol. 1. New York: Academic Press.

Storr, A. (1976). *The dynamics of creation*. Middlesex: Penguin.

Von Toller, C. (1979). *The nervous body*. Chichester: John Wiley.

Yerkes, R. M., & Dodson, J. D. (1908). The relation of strength of stimulus to rapidity of habit formations. *Journal of Comparative Neurology and Psychology*, **18**, 459–482.

Young, A. W. (1983). *Functions of the right hemisphere*. London: Academic Press.

Zajonc, R. R. (1980). Feeling and thinking—preferences need no inferences. *American Psychology*, **35**, 151–175.

Zuckerman, M. (1979) *Sensation seeking: Beyond the optimal level of arousal*. Hillsdale, NJ: Erlbaum.

Part IV

Individual Differences

Individual Differences in Thinking

ROBERT H. LOGIE
University of Aberdeen

In attempting to provide an overview of a section on individual differences, there is a danger of being confronted with papers on disparate topics, having no common theme other than that they form a less coherent group than other sections of the book. On closer reading, it became apparent that the papers in this section were much more coherent than they might seem initially. What these papers contribute is a converging insight into the possible variables which might determine thinking efficiency.

The chapter by Deary and Caryl discusses the relationship between intellectual speed and the time an individual takes to extract information from a stimulus. The 'inspection time' paradigm is an ingenious method for assessing perceptual speed in the absence of a manual response. The authors report the rather intriguing finding that inspection time correlates with measures of intelligence, and is related to the P200 cortical evoked response. These results taken together suggest that inspection time may be a much purer measure of the efficiency of information processing, in the absence of motor output as a confounding factor.

One speculative extension of the argument by Deary and Caryl is the notion that intellectual speed underlies much of the individual variation in thinking ability. This issue is addressed to some extent in the paper by Morris, Downes and Robbins. It is clear that neurological damage can result in cognitive deficits, although the severity and nature of such deficits varies widely with the severity and nature of the damage. The clinically oriented study of Parkinson's disease has a long history. However, the nature of the associated cognitive deficits is equivocal. In particular it has been difficult to dissociate any cognitive deficits from the severe problems of tremor and of initiating movement suffered by Parkinson's patients. This effectively rules out tasks that rely on response time measures or fine motor control, although there are a number of published studies which seem unaware of this limitation—see Della Sala *et al.* (1986) for a review.

Morris, Downes and Robbins use a version of the 'Tower of London' task, and they measure the 'planning time' required independently of the motor output required in solving problems of this type. It appears that there is indeed an impairment in initial thinking time suffered by such patients, but that they were otherwise cognitively unimpaired on this task. The picture that emerges is of a general slowing of information processing and reduced thinking efficiency. One potential for future development seems to be to try combining the Deary and Caryl 'inspection time' task with the study of Parkinson's patients.

Morris *et al.* interpret their findings in terms of a 'dysexecutive syndrome' within the context of working memory (Baddeley, 1986). The relationship is very unclear between Baddeley's working memory and the cognition required for reasoning and problem solving. Other aspects of working memory have benefited from neuropsychological studies, and as such the approach taken by Morris and colleagues holds considerable potential for elucidating the concept of a central executive and its role in thinking and problem solving.

The chapter by Gregory takes a more qualitative approach in the study of concept formation. Gregory collected verbal protocols in groups of elderly and younger people, and found few differences, with age, in the frequencies of the chosen strategies. However, there was evidence that older people were less likely to choose one particularly efficient strategy. Also, the elderly were impaired relative to controls when they were specifically requested to use this strategy, suggesting a loss of flexibility in strategy choice, and, as such, a loss of flexibility of thinking with age. It is interesting that Morris *et al.* also advocate the use of verbal protocols in problem solving, and Gregory clearly demonstrates the promise of this technique.

Finally, the chapter by Casey, Winner, Brabeck and Sullivan explores the efficiency of particular kinds of thinking. They examine the issue of individual propensities for visuo-spatial thinking, and find that individuals who choose careers in mathematics and the visual arts have good visual memories. Also, individuals having a career in mathematics and sciences are particularly adept at manipulating spatial images, and this ability seems to be distinct from memory for static visual images.

Casey *et al.* set their studies within the context of a saying derived from the first epistle of Alexander Pope (1688–1744): 'Tis education forms the common mind, Just as the twig is bent, the tree's inclined'. The thesis is that individuals who have a genetic predisposition for a particular skill will seek out experience which will build on that skill. As further evidence, the chapter demonstrates that female subjects who are right-handed, but who have close relatives who are left-handed, tend to have good visual and spatial memories. Thus individuals without such a genetic predisposition are less efficient in visual and spatial thinking.

Do the views in all four chapters converge? They certainly all address the issue of thinking efficiency, and reasons for its variation. Speed and flexibility of thinking do appear to deteriorate in a systematic fashion with age and with brain disease. In normal adults variations occur related to processing speed and this in turn may vary with the nature of the processing. We can also draw some parallels between chapters, as outlined above. However, there are a number of issues that could be explored to provide further insights into individual differences in thinking. For example, in Volume 1 of this set, the chapter by Byrne and Johnson-Laird refers to the notion of mental models in reasoning. To what extent are these parallels between manipulation of mental models of a problem, and manipulation of images for spatial reasoning as studied by Casey *et al.*? To what extent does Deary and Caryl's view of intellectual speed relate to efficiency in reasoning and problem solving? A major role for these chapters may then be to stimulate further explicit exploration of these issues.

REFERENCES

Baddeley, A. D. (1986). *Working memory*. London: Oxford University Press.
Della Sala, S., Di Lorenzo, G., Giordano, A., & Spinnler, H. (1986). Is there a specific visuo-spatial impairment in Parkinsonians? *Journal of Neurology, Neurosurgery and Psychiatry*, **49**, 1258–1265.

16

Inspection Time and Cognitive Ability

IAN. J. DEARY AND PETER G. CARYL
University of Edinburgh

INTRODUCTION

The search for a basic information processing measure that would explain a substantial proportion of the between-individual variance in psychometric intelligence test scores will provide future historians of psychology with a saga whose dates span the twentieth century. Hunt (1980) compared the effort with the search for the holy grail, and it is easy to see why: from glorious, if misinterpreted, failures (Wissler, 1901), through passed-over clues (McK. Cattell, 1886; Burt 1909/10; and see Deary, 1986) and partly justified hubris (Brand and Deary, 1982) the tale has enough scandal, folly, disappointment and, perhaps, achievement to match King Arthur's escapades. But, myth and romanticism aside, there are tangible results from the hypothesis, held by many psychologists since their subject began and by the layman (Sternberg *et al.*, 1981), that some form of mental speed is related, if not causal, to intelligence.

Most fanciers of this hypothesis have reached for their reaction time (RT) apparatus. Why they have done so in such numbers is not clear. It may have been nothing more complicated than the sheer convenience of having RT devices to hand, as opposed to having to invent new *mental* speed tests. Nevertheless, there is sufficient evidence to show that the correlation between intelligence test scores and RT indices will account for a small but significant proportion of variance (Beck, 1933; Jensen and Vernon, 1986). As early as 1890, McK. Cattell warned that RT involved too much variance attributable to motor processes and that a more mental index should be used.

It is ironic that, while he was still at Leipzig with Wundt, Cattell (1886) had devised a reaction-free mental speed task and had already proposed that 'perception time' might have an ontogenic relationship with later mental ability. In parallel with the significant but meagre IQ–RT correlations, there is a history

Lines of Thinking, Volume 2   Edited by K.J. Gilhooly, M.T.G. Keane, R.H. Logie and G. Erdos
© 1990 John Wiley & Sons Ltd

of much stronger correlations between IQ-type test scores and measures of perceptual intake speed, where the dependent variable is the stimulus presentation time needed by a subject in order to make a correct decision, not the time it takes to react to a standard stimulus (see Deary, 1986, for a review). However, these studies did not form a united body of research (most of the authors seemed unaware of their predecessors) and were not developed further to provide a theory of how the mental speed–intelligence relationship came about.

The inspection time measure did not appear on the scene as yet another arbitrary performance index to be unthinkingly correlated with IQ test scores; it emerged from a psychophysical theory developed by Vickers, Nettelbeck and Willson (1972) in order to give a statistical account of how individuals sample information from visual stimuli when making a decision in a two-choice discrimination task. They proposed that information from the stimulus is sampled in quanta, through the execution of a number of 'inspections'. Reliably correct discriminations are made when a subject has had sufficient time to perceive the stimulus. 'Inspection time' is the name given to the time (in ms) that is required by an individual, under given standard conditions, to make an accurate (usually, but arbitrarily, set at about the 85% correct point on the psychometric curve) decision concerning a simple stimulus. The theory states that, if a stimulus is simple enough, it may require only a single inspection to make an accurate discrimination.

Vickers, Nettelbeck and Willson (1972) hypothesized that IT was a measurable parameter of an individual's thinking processes, reflecting stable individual differences. To date, the most popular form of the IT test uses a stimulus consisting of two parallel vertical lines of markedly different lengths. The lines are presented via a tachistoscope or a LED display and are immediately backward masked. Subjects are required to indicate whether the longer of the lines was on the right or on the left. Responses are made at leisure and, usually, no RT is recorded, only the correctness of the judgement. Stimulus time is varied from the very easy to the impossible, including enough points in between to map the subject's psychometric curve. Subjects' ITs are estimated using various psychophysical techniques, including adaptive algorithms and methods of constant stimuli and, over more than a dozen studies, the IT test–retest reliability is greater than 0.7 (Nettelbeck, 1987).

Interest in, and controversy surrounding, IT grew when it was reported to have a substantial correlation with psychometric measures of intelligence (Nettelbeck and Lally, 1976; Brand and Deary, 1982; Mackintosh, 1981; Nettelbeck, 1983). Two near-complete reviews of the IQ–IT literature (Brand and Deary, 1982; Nettelbeck, 1987) concluded that there is a moderate correlation between these two variables, and that it is probably in the region of − 0.5 (that is, higher-IQ subjects have shorter ITs). The correlation between IT and cognitive ability holds for both verbal and non-verbal ('culture-fair') tests and in many different subject populations (normal and mentally handicapped adults, children, the elderly and undergraduates).

There have been various attempts to explain the correlation between cognitive ability and IT. Some have tested the possibility that the correlation occurs because high-IQ subjects adopt task-specific strategies (Mackenzie and Bingham, 1985; Mackenzie and Cumming, 1986), while others (for example, Mackintosh, 1986) have suggested that high-IQ subjects remain more attentive during, and become less bored by, the IT task. If a fast IT involves little more than adopting a particular visual strategy in (or maintaining concentration in) a repetitive and artificial task, then its value as an explanation of human thinking efficiency is limited. Here, IT is seen as a consequence of intelligence.

Others have argued that the IT–IQ correlation arises because IT is a basic feature or component of human information processing or that it might represent neural efficiency (Deary, 1988; Nettelbeck, 1987; Jensen, 1985). In this view IT may be seen as causal to measured intelligence: advantages in the early stages of information encoding, or in general neural information transfer, are said to lead to more accurate and quickly constructed internal representations and to higher levels of fluid and crystallized intelligence.

We shall now report the results of two sets of experiments carried out recently in Edinburgh. In the first section we deal with results from experiments on an auditory version of the IT task. It was felt that if the IT–IQ result could not be replicated using stimuli in another modality, then those who suspected that IT might be a task-specific skill would remain to be answered. In the second section we consider the results obtained when subjects' cerebral evoked potentials are recorded while they perform IT tasks. These experiments were undertaken in the belief that, if there are evoked potential parameters which correlate with IT performance, then we may be able to say something about its importance and place in human information processing.

AUDITORY INSPECTION TIME

While Nettelbeck (1987) was in a position to review more than two dozen studies examining the relationship between intelligence and visual IT, there are only six studies on the auditory IT–IQ correlation. In various permutations these have addressed one or more of the following questions:

a) Do auditory IT and psychometric intelligence test scores correlate significantly?
b) Is there a significant correlation between visual and auditory IT?
c) Is any auditory IT–IQ correlation which exists due to individual differences in pitch discrimination ability?

Deary (1980; reported in Brand and Deary, 1982) devised an auditory IT task intended to tap auditory processing speed in a manner analogous to the visual task. Instead of the lengths of lines, the pitches of two tones (of 880 and 770 Hz) were chosen as the discriminanda. Using the method of constant stimuli, these were presented to subjects as a pair at tone durations ranging from 100 ms to 2.7 ms. The pairs, with one tone played 500 ms after the other had finished, came in the order 'high–low' or 'low–high'. They were backward- and forward-masked with white noise. Subjects were required to state, in their own time, the temporal order of the tones. The task was exploratory and imperfect—white noise was not effective as a mask and the 500 ms inter-tone gap allowed subjects to rehearse the first tone—but auditory IT correlated at − 0.66 with Mill Hill IQ scores and at − 0.70 with scores on Raven's Progressive Matrices ($n = 13$). Excluding two mentally handicapped subjects, the correlation with Mill Hill IQ remained significant at − 0.61, but the correlation with Raven scores fell to a non-significant − 0.28.

The correlation between visual and auditory IT was 0.99, but it was entirely dependent upon the inclusion of the two mentally handicapped subjects. This study provided tentative evidence that IT might be a general, not solely visual, information processing or encoding speed. However, a series of objections to any such conclusion came in the study of Irwin (1984). Despite replicating the auditory IT–IQ correlation in a sample of 50 schoolchildren, Irwin noted the following:

1) Using a task very like that of Deary (1980), his subjects often obtained ITs at brief durations where there was overlap of frequency spectra for the stimulus tones, making the task, in effect, partly a pitch discrimination task.
2) There was a significant correlation between auditory IT and pitch discrimination ($r = − 0.54$).
3) There was a near-zero correlation between auditory and visual IT.

Clearly, Irwin's (1984) results argue against a general information-intake ability and against an auditory processing speed–IQ relationship.

There were problems with Irwin's study. Chiefly, he did not report having pretested, as Deary (1980) did, his subjects for pitch discrimination ability before including them in the auditory IT analysis. This is equivalent to not excluding subjects with poor visual acuity from a visual IT study. About one-third of normal adults and up to one-half of samples of 12-year-old children (Deary *et al.*, 1989) cannot reliably discriminate 880 from 770 Hz, however long the presentation time. If these subjects were not excluded from the auditory IT analyses there would be a spurious inflation of any existing pitch discrimination–auditory IT correlation.

Nettelbeck, Edwards and Vreugdenhil (1986) improved the auditory IT task by replacing the white noise mask with a mask consisting of rapidly alternating 15 ms bursts of both stimulus tones and white noise. The inter-tone gap remained and, perhaps owing to the non-exclusion of poor pitch discriminators, the authors obtained a very skewed (towards long ITs) distribution of auditory ITs. Nevertheless, in their sample ($n = 29$) auditory and visual IT correlated significantly with Raven's Advanced Progressive Matrices (at − 0.38 and − 0.41, respectively) and with each other (− 0.39).

Three recent experiments in our laboratory have addressed the above issues using a further improvement of the auditory IT task. To achieve mean IT values in a range that does not involve the overlap of the stimulus tones' frequency spectra, we have made two changes:

a) the inter-tone gap has been removed; and
b) we have introduced a more effective mask, consisting of alternating 10 ms bursts of the stimulus tones.

In contrast with previous studies, we obtain, when those subjects with poor pitch discrimination skills are excluded, relatively unskewed distributions for auditory IT and mean values of about 70 ms for 90% accuracy levels.

In a study on undergraduates we found that auditory IT correlated significantly with Alice Heim 5 ($n = 40$, $r = -0.31$) and Mill Hill Vocabulary scores ($n = 80$, $r = -0.27$) but not with Raven's Advanced Progressive Matrices scores ($n = 80$, $r = -0.05$) (Deary et al., 1989). In the same study auditory IT estimates were correlated with three different IT tasks, some more vulnerable to strategy use than others, resulting in coefficients of 0.20 (ns), 0.24 ($p < 0.05$) and 0.53 ($p < 0.001$). This result, together with that of Nettelbeck, Edwards and Vreugdenhil (1986), supports the hypothesis that auditory and visual IT share common variance, at least in adults.

Using the same auditory IT task with a new sample of 34 undergraduates, we have replicated the correlation between auditory IT and Alice Heim 6 Verbal scores (-0.45), but we found a non-significant correlation with Alice Heim 6 Non-verbal scores (-0.27) (Deary, Head and Egan, 1989). In this group there was a near-zero correlation between Seashore Pitch Perception scores and cognitive ability, and a non-significant correlation between auditory IT and pitch perception scores (-0.20). In a group of schoolchildren ($n = 53$) we found that the auditory IT correlated significantly with both Raven's Matrices (-0.26) and Mill Hill Vocabulary scores (-0.36). However, in the schoolchildren ($n = 119$) pitch discrimination ability did correlate significantly, but at levels around 0.17, with IQ-type test scores (Deary, Head and Egan, 1989). When partial correlations were calculated for auditory IT and IQ, controlling for pitch discrimination ability, they deviated very little from the original estimates.

There are still too few studies on auditory IT to draw firm conclusions, but the above evidence allows us to state the following interim hypotheses:

1) Auditory IT ability correlates significantly with psychometric intelligence test scores, particularly verbal test scores.
2) This correlation is not dependent upon pitch discrimination ability.
3) There is a moderate correlation between auditory and visual IT.

The correlations mentioned above are uncorrected for restriction of ability range in samples and for unreliability of the IT and IQ measures and are, therefore, underestimates of the true IT–IQ correlation. At this stage, then, it is still possible credibly to maintain that information encoding speed accounts for a moderate amount of IQ variance and that this encoding speed is not a property of just one sensory modality.

EVOKED POTENTIAL STUDIES OF INSPECTION TIME

Posner (1986) makes the case that, in what he terms 'mental chronometry', analyses of averaged evoked potentials (AEPs) can provide converging evidence which is a useful adjunct to the methods of experimental psychology. We now discuss experiments which establish the existence of individual differences in AEP measures which can be related to the individual's IT, and to psychometric intelligence.

Earlier analysis of AEP–intelligence relationships involved relatively gross measures (for example, Blinkhorn and Hendrickson's (1982) string-length measure) of response to simple, repetitive stimuli, where the task (e.g. simply listening) imposed minimal demands on the subjects. It is important to stress that our experiments are distinct from this earlier literature. Our subjects were faced with the equivalent of an IT-task, with presentation durations chosen to ensure 10% or 15% errors, and we are concerned with individual differences in latency, amplitude or speed of development of specific AEP peaks.

All experiments in this section involve basically simple visual discriminations, such as whether the longer of two lines (presented on a 7-segment LED display, with one line twice the length of the other) is on the left or the right. The task is made difficult by imposing, after a suitable interval, a backward mask.

It is conventional in analyses of evoked potentials to present the stimuli for a fixed duration. Because of individual differences in speed of discrimination, adoption of a constant stimulus duration before mask onset would produce a task which differed in difficulty for different subjects. To ensure that the features identified are not merely correlates of differences in task difficulty, we presented subjects in each experiment with discriminations of constant *psychological* difficulty, presenting stimuli for a duration equal to their (previously determined) inspection time.

Having chosen to match across subjects for psychological difficulty, we need to establish that the differences we report are not a trivial side effect of differences in physical duration. The first two experiments introduce the AEP measures of interest, and establish that they are unaffected by gross variation in physical duration of the stimuli used in the task.

Both experiments were small-sample studies (Zhang, Caryl and Deary, 1989b), in which subjects' IT (to a 90% correct criterion) had been tested immediately before the AEP session, using the stimuli to be presented in the AEP work. All testing took place in a darkened room, and stimuli were presented with a 7-segment LED display. Subjects were required to respond at leisure (and never before the mask was switched off) rather than to treat the experiment as a reaction time task. Speed of responding was unimportant, and was not recorded. Each trial began from two to three seconds after the previous response.

Silver–silver chloride electrodes were used. The active electrode at the vertex was referred to the left mastoid, with the right mastoid as earth. 1024 points following cue onset were sampled at 1 kHz.

In both experiments, response to stimuli at the subject's IT duration was contrasted with that to stimuli representing much easier or much harder discrimination tasks. In experiment 1, easy stimuli were presented for 1.75 times the subject's IT duration, before mask onset, difficult stimuli for only 0.25 times his IT. In experiment 2, easy stimuli were completely unmasked, while in the 'difficult' trials, the mask was presented synchronously with stimulus onset, so that the stimulus was completely obscured. In each experiment, subjects were presented with 75 trials at IT-duration, randomly intermixed with 70 easy and 70 difficult trials, and separate AEPs were generated for each of the three conditions, using the first 64 stimuli without visible artefacts. Measures used were P200 and P300 latencies and amplitudes, and a measure of the rise-time of the P200 wave (P200T) (Zhang, Caryl and Deary, 1989a).

The IT task requires a subject to encode rapidly the discriminative stimulus into STM, before onset of the mask; once encoding has taken place, the decision about which alternative was presented can be made at leisure. Chapman, McCary and Chapman (1978) identified a factorial component, peaking slightly later than the conventionally recognized P200 wave, whose size was correlated with degree of encoding of a discriminative stimulus into STM. This evidence, and pilot work from our laboratory, identified the P200 wave as one of particular interest. The P300 to stimuli of psychological significance is often considered to mark completion of decision-making, and provides an index of this which is unaffected by variation in time required for response selection (Pritchard, 1981). P300 amplitude should reflect confidence in the decision.

As expected, P300 amplitude did vary significantly between the three categories of trials in each experiment (repeated measures ANOVA, $F(2,14) = 5.49$ in experiment 1 and 4.34 in experiment 2, both $p < 0.05$). Page's test for trend confirmed that, in each experiment, P300 amplitude was greatest for the easy discrimination, intermediate for the IT-duration condition, and smallest for the condition where the discrimination was very difficult or impossible. In neither experiment was there significant variation in P300 latency across the three categories of trial ($F(2,14) = 0.19$ and 1.82, respectively). The contrast with experiments in which decision latency increases with difficulty (see, for example, McCarthy and Donchin, 1981; Duncan Johnson and Kopell, 1981) presumably reflects the fact that stimulus information remained available in these alternative paradigms, allowing further sampling where the discrimination was difficult, while in our experiments early masking eliminates this possibility.

Turning to the P200 measures, we found that the rise-time measure P200T was correlated with IT more highly and more consistently than other measures. Focusing initially on the IT-duration trials, which are of a constant difficulty for all subjects in both experiments, and combining data from the two experiments to avoid some of the problems of interpretation of results based on very small numbers, we found a correlation between P200T and IT of 0.57 ($n = 16$, $p < 0.05$).

This correlation is based on data in which higher-IT subjects receive longer stimulus presentations before mask onset. To find whether this variation in pre-mask stimulus duration might be important, we need to look for an effect of the seven-fold variation in stimulus duration across the three types of trial in experiment 1. A repeated-measures ANOVA test revealed no significant effect of presentation duration on any P200 measure ($F(2,14) = 0.61$, 0.71 and 1.96 for P200T, P200A and P200L, respectively), but confirmed the presence of significant differences between subjects for all three measures ($F(7,14) = 20.23$ for P200T and 14.47 for P200A, both $p < 0.01$, and 3.27, $p < 0.05$, for P200L). Thus individual differences, and not the variation in stimulus duration, appear to underlie the IT–P200T correlation.

Could we influence these P200 measures consistently by the more drastic manipulation of eliciting stimuli in experiment 2? Again, there were no significant differences between experimental conditions for any P200 measure ($F(2,14) = 0.14$, 0.67 and 2.12 for P200T, P200A and P200L), but highly significant differences between subjects ($F(7,14) = 6.84$, 20.45 and 34.34 for P200T, P200A and P200L, $p < 0.01$ or better in each case). Note that in both experiments, the AEP measure (P300A) which reflected ease of the discrimination did vary between conditions. We can safely conclude that the individual differences in P200T which we are interested in are not an artefact of differences in stimulus duration or the ease of the discrimination.

As might be expected, in view of the insensitivity of the P200T measure to major variation in presentation duration, we have also found that individual differences in this measure can be identified in responses to the variable-duration stimuli presented while the subject's IT is being measured using the PEST procedure, as well as with standard-length stimuli, and that here too the P200T measure is correlated with IT (Zhang, Caryl and Deary, 1989a).

If the correlation between IT and IQ is approximately 0.5 in the overall population, there must be a considerable task-specific component of the IT variance. We now argue as follows: Since IT and IQ correlate, and since we have demonstrated a correlation between P200T and IT, then:

1) Might the P200T index be a correlate of IQ?
2) Alternatively, might the P200T index be a non IQ-related (i.e. task-specific) component of IT variance?

We also wanted to know whether the difference in P200T we have described is present in potentials evoked only by the IT stimuli (requiring rapid encoding or discrimination), by any stimuli requiring discrimination (even if presented for several hundred milliseconds), or by any stimuli at all, no matter whether or not they require a response.

Experiment 3 involved a larger number of subjects, and addressed these questions (Zhang, Caryl and Deary, 1989b). The experimental procedure was more complex than in the previous experiments, and we shall summarize only the most relevant results.

Subjects had their IT measured in a pre-test session, and in the main session were presented with post-masked IT-duration stimuli, as before. Their response had to be delayed until a response signal was presented (on the same LED panel). In only half the trials was the subject required to attend to and discriminate the IT-duration stimuli; in the other half, the IT stimulus could be neglected, but to maintain attention to the LED panel, on these trials we required subjects to look for the response signal, and respond as rapidly as possible when it appeared, pressing a standard key for these RT responses. (Note that in this experiment rapid responding was also required on the trials in which IT-stimuli were *discriminated*, but that two response keys were used for this discriminative response). The pre-stimulus cue was used both to alert the subject for the trial, and to signal whether the trial to follow required an IT-discrimination, or an RT response to the response signal. The pre-stimulus cues used were the digits 2 and 6, also presented on the LED panel. Evoked responses to the cues, and to the IT stimuli (whether or not these were to be discriminated) were recorded. Evoked responses to the response cues were not recorded. The meaning of the different cue digits, order of presentation of trials, etc., were appropriately randomized.

We shall deal here with results for the vertex electrode only (Table 16.1). In

Table 16.1 Correlations of AEP measures, IT and IQ

AEP measure	Stimulus	Correlation with	
		IT ($n = 37$)	IQ ($n = 35$)
P200$_T$	IT(discriminated)	0.645[c]	0.111
	IT(ignored)	0.117	0.047
	Cue	0.290[d]	−0.339[a]
P200$_L$	IT(discriminated)	0.442[b]	−0.017
	IT(ignored)	0.070	0.160
	Cue	−0.003	0.119
P200$_A$	IT(discriminated)	0.332[a]	0.101
	IT(ignored)	0.253	−0.095
	Cue	−0.000	0.195
P300$_A$	IT(discriminated)	0.503[b]	0.173
	IT(ignored)	0.068	0.069
P300$_L$	IT(discriminated)	0.055	0.066
	IT(ignored)	0.061	−0.062

IT(discriminated) represents the responses to IT stimuli to which the subject was required to make a discriminative response. IT(ignored) represents the responses to IT stimuli which the subject could ignore, being required to make a RT response but no discrimination. Cue represents responses to the digit used both as a cue and to indicate whether a RT or discriminative response to the subsequent IT stimulus was required.
[a] $p = 0.05$; [b] $p = 0.01$; [c] $p = 0.001$; [d] $p = 0.05$ (one-tailed).

this experiment there were significant correlations between IT and the P200T of potentials elicited both by IT stimuli on trials requiring discrimination, and by the cues. In contrast, potentials evoked by the IT stimulus on trials in which it could be disregarded had a P200T which was not correlated with IT. This correlation is evidently dependent on the need to encode and subsequently discriminate the stimulus (as was true both for the cues, and for task-related IT stimuli), but does not depend on the speed of encoding required with the IT stimuli.

In contrast to the previous experiment, there were also correlations between the P200L and P200A measures and IT. These were only obtained for responses to the IT-stimuli which were to be discriminated; for these stimuli, P300A was also significantly correlated with IT.

Do these relationships reveal anything about psychometric intelligence? The P200T measure of responses evoked by the cue (but not the IT stimulus) was correlated with AH5 total score ($r = 0.34$, $p < 0.05$). The sign of this correlation is as expected in view of the IT–IQ relationship. The correlation was stronger with part I of the AH5 test (verbal–mathematical) rather than part II (pictorial–spatial). None of the other evoked potential measures which correlated with IT correlated with intelligence.

The pattern of relationships can be most conveniently summarized by a small principal components analysis of the correlations (Table 16.2), which reveals three factors, each extracting approximately 24% of the variance, the third of which (with loadings on IT, AH5, and the P200T to the cue) presumably reflects

Table 16.2 Principal components analysis of selected
AEP measures, IT and IQ (based on correlations for 35
subjects)

Measure	Sorted factor loadings		
	Factor 1	Factor 2	Factor 3
P200$_L$	0.923	−0.102	0.068
P200$_T$	0.872	0.300	0.013
IT	0.611	0.496	−0.469
P300$_A$	0.151	0.876	0.066
P200$_A$	0.034	0.874	0.031
AH5 (part 1)	0.117	0.197	0.846
P200$_T$ (to cue)	0.119	0.087	−0.687
AH5 (part II)	0.021	0.008	0.644
Variance	25%	24%	23%

Except where specified, all AEP measures are for responses
evoked by IT stimuli which were to be discriminated by the
subject.

general intelligence. The first and second factors, which have loadings on IT and
evoked potential measures but not on intelligence, must reflect task-specific
components of the variance.

In summary, our results suggest that differences in IT performance depend on
individual differences in stimulus processing, which can be detected as early as
200 ms after stimulus onset, in responses to unmasked as well as the conventional backward-masked stimuli used in IT tests, provided the stimulus must be
encoded. The differences are apparently not shown to stimuli which can be
neglected. Our AEP measures revealed an important task-specific component in
responses to IT stimuli, as well as a non-specific component related to general
intelligence.

REFERENCES

Beck, L. F. (1933). The role of speed in intelligence. *Psychological Bulletin*, **30**, 169–178.
Blinkhorn, S.F., & Hendrickson, D. E. (1982). Average evoked responses and psychomet-
ric intelligence. *Nature*, **295**, 596–597.
Brand, C. R., & Deary, I. J. (1982). Intelligence and 'inspection time'. In H.J. Eysenck
(ed.), *A model for intelligence*. New York: Springer.
Burt, C. R. (1909/10). Experimental tests of general intelligence. *British Journal of
Psychology*, **3**, 94–117.
Cattell, J. McK. (1886). The inertia of eye and brain. *Brain*, **8**, 295–381.
Cattell, J. McK. (1890). Mental tests and measurements. *Mind*, **15**, 373–381.
Chapman, R. M., McCary, J. W., & Chapman, J. A. (1978). Short-term memory: the
'storage' component of the human response predicts recall. *Science*, **202**, 1211–1214.
Deary, I. J. (1980). How general is the mental speed factor in 'general intelligence'? B.Sc.
Hons. thesis, University of Edinburgh.
Deary, I. J. (1986). Inspection time: discovery or rediscovery? *Personality and Individual
Differences*, **7**, 625–631.

Deary, I. J. (1988). Basic processes in human intelligence. In H. J. Jerison and I. Jerison (eds.), *Intelligence and evolutionary biology*. Berlin: Springer.

Deary, I. J., Caryl, P. G., Egan, V., & Wight, D. (1989). Visual and auditory inspection time: their interrelationship and correlations with IQ in high ability subjects. *Personality and Individual Differences*, **10**, 525–534.

Deary, I. J., Head, B., & Egan, V. (1989). Auditory inspection time, intelligence and pitch discrimination. *Intelligence*, **13**, 135–148.

Duncan Johnson, C. C., & Kopell, B. S. (1981). The Stroop effect: brain potentials localise the source of interference. *Science*, **214**, 938–941.

Hunt, E. (1980). Intelligence as an information processing concept. *British Journal of Psychology*, **71**, 449–474.

Irwin, R. J. (1984). Inspection time and its relation to intelligence. *Intelligence*, **8**, 47–65.

Jensen, A. R. (1985). The plasticity of 'intelligence' at different levels of analysis. In J. Bishop & D. Perkins, (eds.), *Thinking: Progress in research and teaching*. Franklin Institute Press.

Jensen, A. R., & Vernon, P. A. (1986). Jensen's reaction time studies: a reply to Longstreth, *Intelligence*, **10**, 153–179.

McCarthy, G., & Donchin, E. (1981). A metric for thought: a comparison of P300 latency and reaction time. *Science*, **211**, 77–80.

Mackenzie, B., & Bingham, E. (1985). IQ, inspection time and response strategies in a university population. *Australian Journal of Psychology*, **37**, 257–268.

Mackenzie, B., & Cumming, S. (1986). Inspection time and apparent motion. *Personality and Individual Differences*, **7**, 721–729.

Mackintosh, N. J. (1981). A new measure of intelligence? *Nature*, **289**, 529–530.

Nettelbeck, T. (1982). Inspection time: an index for intelligence? *Quarterly Journal of Experimental Psychology*, **34A**, 299–312.

Nettelbeck, T. (1987). Inspection time and intelligence. In P. A. Vernon (ed.), *Speed of information processing and intelligence*. Norwood, NJ: Ablex.

Nettelbeck, T., Edwards, C., & Vreugdenhil, A. (1986). Inspection time and IQ: evidence for a mental speed–ability association. *Personality and Individual Differences*, **7**, 633–641.

Nettelbeck, T., & Lally, M. (1976). Inspection time and measured intelligence. *British Journal of Psychology*, **67**, 17–22.

Posner, M. I. (1986). *Chronometric explorations of mind*. Oxford: Oxford University Press.

Pritchard, W. S. (1981). Psychophysiology of P300. *Psychological Bulletin*, **89**, 506–540.

Sternberg, R. J., Conway, B. E., Ketron, B. L., & Bernstein, M. (1981). People's conceptions of intelligence. *Journal of Personality and Social Psychology*, **41**, 37–55.

Vickers, D., Nettelbeck, T., & Willson, R. J. (1972). Perceptual indices of performance: the measurement of 'inspection time' and 'noise' in the visual system. *Perception*, **1**, 263–295.

Wissler, C. (1901). The correlation of mental and physical tests. *Psychological Review Monographs*, **3**.

Zhang, Y., Caryl, P. G., & Deary, I. J. (1989a). Evoked potential correlates of inspection time. *Personality and Individual Differences*, **10**, 379–384.

Zhang, Y., Caryl, P. G., & Deary, I. J. (1989b). Evoked potentials, inspection time and intelligence. *Personality and Individual Differences*, **10**, 1079–1094.

17

The Nature of the Dysexecutive Syndrome in Parkinson's Disease[*]

ROBIN G. MORRIS
Institute of Psychiatry, London

JOHN J. DOWNES
University of Cambridge

TREVOR W. ROBBINS
University of Cambridge

INTRODUCTION

Over the past few years neuropsychology has provided a significant input to cognitive psychology, allowing a greater specification of detail in some theories of information processing. Examples can be drawn from the study of memory, reading and perceptual disorders (Ellis and Young, 1988). The study of higher-level cognitive dysfunctions, for example planning, has also been used to specify the neuropsychological processes involved in thinking and problem solving (Duncan, 1986; Shallice, 1982).

Baddeley (1986) has coined the term 'dysexecutive syndrome' (DES) for the class of disorders involving higher-level cognitive dysfunction. For this, the underlying impairment is assumed to be in the supervisory control of information processing, which includes the sequencing of subcomponents of tasks and directing the flow of information processing between cognitive subsystems. The frontal lobes, and in particular the prefrontal cortex, has for many years been linked with such executive functioning. Although damage to the frontal lobes

[*]The research was supported by a major award from the Welcome Trust to T. W. Robbins, B. J. Everitt and S. B. Dunnett. The authors would like to thank Drs J. Evenden and B. Sahakian for their helpful comments.

may lead to a DES, disorders with the main focus of damage in areas others than the frontal lobes may also lead to a form of DES. In Parkinson's disease (PD) the impairment is in motor functioning, but there is also evidence that such patients have deficits in problem solving and tasks that are sensitive to frontal lobe dysfunction (Brown and Marsden, 1987; Gotham, Brown and Marsden, 1988; Lees and Smith, 1983; Sahakian et al., 1988). More specifically, there have been reports that PD patients are impaired on the Wisconsin Card Sorting test (WCST), which requires subjects to focus on and use attribute information (colour, number or shape) to sort cards. PD patients have been found to make more errors in completing this task and are able to sort stimuli into fewer categories (Bowen et al., 1975; Lees and Smith, 1983; Taylor, Saint-Cyr and Lang, 1986). On a simpler categorization task in which subjects had to determine the 'odd-man-out' in a series of three or four figures, Flowers and Robertson (1985) found that PD patients were less able to alter response sets to sort by a different rule or to maintain their attention on the relevant attributes of the task. Finally, there is evidence from the studies of Cools et al. (1984) that PD patients have difficulty in a variety of motor and cognitive tasks that involve 'switching' between procedures, such as alternatively generating animal names and professions on a verbal fluency task.

In PD these deficits have been variously characterized as a deficit in switching and maintaining mental set (Bowen et al., 1975; Lees and Smith, 1983), an impairment in the internal control for the regulation of behaviour (Brown and Marsden, 1987), or an inability to generate efficient strategies for problem solving when relying on internal cues to drive activity (Taylor, Saint-Cyr and Lang, 1986). The specific neuropathology responsible for this type of impairment is unclear, but there have been several theories relating to neurochemical abnormalities in subcortical structures. Studies by DeLong and his colleagues (De Long, Georgopoulos and Crutcher, 1983; De Long et al., 1984) have led to the suggestions of 'motor' and 'complex' loops linking the basal ganglia and frontal cortical areas. These neuroanatomical pathways have recently been suggested to share common modulatory functions in terms of the control of movement and cognition (Nauta, 1984; Marsden, 1984). If, as proposed by Marsden (1984), the initiation and execution of complex motor acts are dependent on the integrity of these systems, then a reduction in dopaminergic activity in the striatum might contribute to an impairment of the control and organization of cognitive functioning.

One way of conceptualizing executive functioning is through the model proposed by Norman and Shallice (1980) which is based on the notion that both cognition and action depend partly on the execution of highly automatic routine programmes or schemata. Only a small subset of these schemata can be activated at any one time, and in order to regulate this process there is a 'contention scheduling mechanism' that involves the mutual inhibition of competing schemata, after selection of the strongest. Overriding this mechanism is the 'supervisory attentional system' (SAS) which controls non-routine action by biasing the activation of particular schemata. To investigate executive functioning in relation to neuropsychological disorders, Shallice (1982) developed the Tower of London test, a simplified version of the Tower of Hanoi

(Egan and Greeno, 1974). For this, subjects are required to rearrange coloured beads between upright rods so as to achieve a given configuration. Shallice has used this task to investigate planning abilities in patients with frontal lobe damage; the results indicate that those with left anterior lesions make significantly more errors in completing the task. He attributes this deficit to an impairment of the SAS such that the patients are impaired in their ability to select non-routine schemata and engage in efficient planning.

In relation to Parkinson's disease it is not clear what aspects, if any, of the model are impaired, although Norman and Shallice (1980) have suggested tentatively that 'contention scheduling' may be linked with basal ganglia functioning. If so, then this part of the system may be impaired in PD, but damage may also take place at a different level, for example the SAS, given the possible implication of the frontal lobes in the neuropathology of the disorder. In order to investigate this possibility further the Tower of London task was used on a sample of Parkinson's disease patients. In Shallice's (1982) version of the task, performance was measured in terms of the number of moves needed to reach the solutions within one minute of starting. The version that we developed involved a two-dimensional representation of the problem on the VDU screen of a microcomputer fitted with a touch sensitive screen. The beads were represented by two-dimensional blocks that could be moved around the screen by the subject, as explained below.

The computerized version of the Tower of London test allows for an accurate measurement not only of errors, but also of a breakdown of the times required to complete the subcomponents of the task. This was thought to be particularly important because of the possibility of a trade-off between speed and accuracy in the test. With Parkinson's disease patients a problem is that movements are inevitably slower because of the motor impairment. Therefore, a control condition was used in which the subjects were 'led' through a series of moves equivalent to the correct solutions, thus providing movement times that could be used to derive corrected measures of thinking time. Using this method it was possible to obtain measures of accuracy and speed with separate estimates for the time taken to plan and execute a sequence of moves.

THE METHOD

Subjects

A group of 12 patients with idiopathic Parkinson's disease was included in the study. Their mean age was 64.6 years ($SD = 1.3$ years) and mean years of education was 9.5 years ($SD = 0.4$ years). Each patient was diagnosed by a physician and assessed for the severity of symptoms using the Hoehn and Yahr (1967) scale. According to this scale four patients were classified as being at severity level I, two at level II and six at level III. For five of the patients the symptoms were predominantly right-sided and for the remaining seven predominantly left-sided. All patients were on levodopa preparation and four were also on anticholinergic medication.

These patients were compared with a group of 18 control subjects, free from

Table 17.1 Summary of characteristics of Parkinson's disease patients and matched control group

	PD		Controls	
	Mean	SD	Mean	SD
NART-predicted IQ	111.1	1.9	113.3	2.0
WAIS				
Verbal IQ	110.0	3.7	113.9	3.0
Performance IQ	105.4	3.9	117.0	4.1
Age-scaled subscores:				
Comprehension	13.2	0.7	12.3	0.6
Vocabulary	11.8	0.5	11.3	0.5
Block design	10.8	0.8	12.8	0.8
Object assembly	9.4	0.5	11.7	0.8[a]
Corsi Block Span	5.0	0.3	4.6	0.2

[a] Significant at $p = 0.05$ level using two-tailed t-test.

neurological or psychiatric disorder. These subjects had a mean age of 63.7 years ($SD = 1.0$ years) and mean years of education 9.7 years ($SD = 0.5$ years).

The two groups of subjects were given a background neuropsychological assessment, including a short form of the Wechsler Adult Intelligence Scale (WAIS) (using the comprehension, vocabulary, block design and object assembly subtests), the National Adult Reading test (NART) (Nelson, 1982) and a computerized version of the Corsi Block Span test. A summary of the characteristics of the groups is given in Table 17.1, indicating that they were matched for verbal intelligence, measured using the WAIS subtests and the NART. The Performance IQ for the PD group was lower than for the controls, but the difference was not significant. However, there was a significant difference on the Object Assembly subtest ($t(28) = 2.2$, $p < 0.05$), a test of visuospatial organizational ability sensitive to motor speed.

Procedure

The subjects were tested using an Acorn BBC B$^+$ microcomputer fitted with a high-resolution VDU and a Microvitec touch-sensitive screen. They sat approximately 0.5 m in front of the VDU and were instructed to make their response by touching the screen. Initially a procedure was used to train the subjects to point correctly at the screen, requiring the subjects to touch a sequence of flashing crosses with the index finger of their dominant hand. When a cross appeared the subject's finger had to be held over the cross for six seconds before it was replaced by another cross in a different position.

The computerized Tower of London task was a two-dimensional representation of the original task developed by Shallice (1982). The beads in the Shallice task were represented by coloured rectangular blocks superimposed on rod-like structures. In the top half of the VDU screen was shown the 'goal' arrangement that the subject had to copy, and in the bottom half were the blocks that the subjects had to move. The blocks could be moved about by touching the block, and then touching the desired position. In order to signal that a block had been touched, the rim of the block flashed and a short tone was emitted. When the destination position was touched the block moved to the new position and the rim stopped flashing. If the subject initially touched a block and changed his or her mind, the block could be 'deactivated' by touching it once more. The rules for moving a block followed the practical limitations set by the Tower of London task, namely that a block could not be moved to occupy a position with space underneath it, nor could it be moved if there was another block above it. If the subject attempted to break these rules, the computer emitted a series of short tones to act as a warning. The computer measured the number of moves required to complete a problem and the latencies for each response. In the control conditions, the bottom arrangement differed from the top one by just one move at a time. As soon as the appropriate move was made the top arrangement would change, thus leading the subjects through a sequence of moves identical to that required to solve each problem but with no planning involved.

In order to avoid the effects of differential practice for the test and control problems, these were interspersed as follows. There were two sets of six test problems alternating with two sets of six control problems. In the first set there were two problems that could be solved in two, three and four moves. In the second set there were two problems that could be solved in four moves and four problems that were soluble in five moves. Thus, throughout the procedure there was a graded increase in difficulty. Before each set, two practice problems were given in order to familiarize the subject with the procedure.

Results

Number of Moves

The average number of moves for the test problems is shown in Figure 17.1. The mean scores for each group show that as the difficulty of the problems increased, the mean number of moves increased over and above the minimum number of moves required. It is clear from these results that across the levels of difficulty the difference between the two groups is slight.

This pattern was confirmed by statistical analysis using a two-way ANOVA test with 'group' (PD versus controls) as the between-subject factor and 'difficulty' (2, 3, 4 or 5 moves) as the within-subject factor. Neither the interaction between the two factors was significant nor the group main effect, but there was a significant main effect of difficulty ($F(3,84) = 175.7$, $p < 0.001$).

Response Latencies

Motor initiation and execution. An estimate of response time in the absence of planning was derived from the control problems, in which the subjects were 'led' through a sequence of moves. For all of the problems an average was taken for the time taken to touch the block that the subject intended to move (the

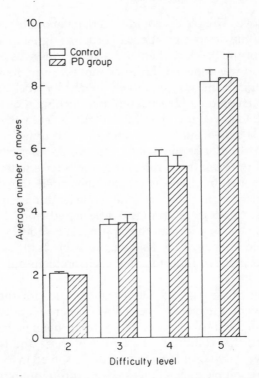

FIGURE 17.1   Average number of moves on the Tower of London test.

motor initiation time) and the subsequent delay until the destination position was touched (the motor execution time). As would be predicted from the motor impairment in PD, this group showed longer motor initiation and execution times (see Table 17.2). A two-way ANOVA test with 'group' as the between-subject factor and 'movement time' (initiation versus execution time) as the within-subject factor showed only a main effect of group ($F(1,28) = 16.1$, $p < 0.001$).

Thinking times. The measurement of motor initiation and execution times can be used as a means for extracting the thinking time from the performance latencies. Two measures of thinking time were used in the analysis:

a) *Planning time* — the latency for the first response during which time the subject would be planning a sequence of moves.
b) *Subsequent thinking time* — the time between the first move and the end of the test.

It was thought that following the first move subjects might still devote time to planning, particularly for the more difficult tasks where the subject might pause to assess their progress and consider what further moves to make.

Adjusted measures of planning and subsequent thinking time were calculated taking into account the control conditions. Where T_1 is the planning time and T_2 the subsequent thinking time, the corresponding adjusted times t_1 and t_2 were

Table 17.2 Motor initiation and execution times for Parkinson's disease and control group

	PD		Controls	
	Mean	SD	Mean	SD
Initiation time (s)	2.33	0.43	1.27	0.05
Execution time (s)	1.90	0.13	1.28	0.06

calculated as follows:

$$t_1 = T_1 - i$$
$$t_2 = T_2 - (n-1)i - ne,$$

where i is the motor initiation time, e is the motor execution time, and n is the number of moves taken.

The variables were also derived from three related data sets:

1) based only on attempts that were correct using the minimum number of moves;
2) based on all correct solutions irrespective of the number of moves; and
3) averaged across all attempts, including those that did not achieve solution in the maximum number of moves.

Each set was analysed, yielding the same results, so only the analyses for data set (1) are presented below.

The adjusted scores are shown in Figure 17.2, giving the thinking time as a function of difficulty level. It is notable that the 'planning time' prior to the first move appears to peak with the three-move problems. In contrast, there is an increase in the 'subsequent thinking time', reaching a maximum with the most difficult problems.

The two measures were analysed separately using two-way ANOVA tests with 'group' as a between-subject factor (PD versus controls) and 'difficulty level' as a within-subject factor (levels 2, 3, 4 and 5). Because the standard errors, and therefore the variance of the data, increased with the mean values, the latencies were log-transformed ($\log(x+1)$) to satisfy the assumptions of the ANOVA test. For the initial planning time this revealed a main effect of group ($F(1,28) = 6.3$, $p < 0.05$), a main effect of difficulty ($F(3,84) = 1.4$, $p < 0.05$) but no interaction between the factors ($F(3,84) < 1$). It can be seen from Figure 17.2(a) that the main effect of difficulty is mainly accounted for by increase in initial planning time from the two-move to the three-move problems for the PD group.

For the subsequent thinking time there was no main effect of group or interaction ($F < 1$), but the main effect of difficulty was significant ($F(3,84) = 36.1$, $p < 0.01$). Figure 17.2(b) indicates that this effect is mainly due to the difference in thinking times between difficulty levels three and four. Thus the initial planning latencies were significantly longer for the PD group, and thinking times varied significantly with difficulty level.

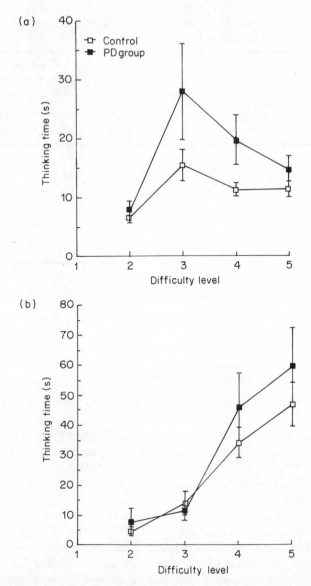

FIGURE 17.2   Average thinking times (a) prior to and (b) subsequent to the first move as a function of difficulty (minimum number of moves to solution).

DISCUSSION

The average number of moves to complete the Tower of London task was the same in the two groups of subjects. As the minimum number of moves to solve a particular problem increased, there was a relative increase in the actual number of moves taken, but this was the same across the groups. In contrast the PD group took longer to plan their moves, when allowance was made for the speed at which individual moves could be made.

A notable feature of the results is that the thinking time prior to the first move appears to peak when the difficulty level reaches three moves to solve a problem. Conversely the thinking time subsequent to the first move increases substantially above the three-move level of difficulty. One explanation of this result is that, for the three-move problems, the subjects have sufficient processing capacity to formulate the total sequence of moves to achieve the end-state. With these problems more time is put into the initial planning and less thinking time is required in between moves. With the more complex problems the processing capacity of the subjects is strained, forcing them into a different strategy of formulating subgoals (Egan and Greeno, 1974; Greeno, 1978). The sequence of moves for achieving the first subgoal can be decided upon more rapidly, hence the decrease in the initial thinking time; but more time is required subsequently to formulate and achieve the subsequent subgoals. This explanation fits with the observation by Egan and Greeno (1974) that, in the more complicated Tower of Hanoi task, people formulate subgoals and work on them one at a time.

The fact that there was no difference in number of moves to complete the tasks between the groups indicates that the general programming ability of Parkinson's disease patients is intact. If the SAS is responsible for general programming (Norman and Shallice, 1980), then this appears to be fairly strong evidence that this system is not grossly impaired in Parkinson's disease. The increase in initial thinking time in the PD group indicates that the processing involved in formulating plans takes place less rapidly. Several questions arise from this finding. What are the possible reasons for slowed planning processes and how can they be distinguished? What are the implications of the results for understanding the dysexecutive syndrome, and the functions of the frontal lobes and basal ganglia?

The slowed thinking time in patients with PD could be accounted for in many ways. The first class of explanation focuses on speed/accuracy trade-offs. It is possible that the SAS in patients with PD is indeed less efficient than normal, but the deficiency is overcome by longer processing time. Thus, PD patients could be considering more incorrect move orders than normal and hence spend more time rejecting them before arriving at the correct solution.

A second account is similar to that previously proposed by Morris et al. (1988) and commensurate with the other cognitive deficits observed in PD, the slowed thinking time is suggested to represent delays in switching between different representations—for example of the goal (and subgoals), and of the schemata governing the sequences of moves under consideration. This impaired articulation of different representations could be seen as resulting from a deficit in the SAS. Specifically, when several false or poor solutions are considered the PD patient is prone to perseverate in this vein of thinking because the SAS no longer provides an effective input for resolving the impasse, and thus other potentially correct sequences are not allowed to become activated.

A third account suggests that the increased thinking time does not necessarily represent extra time spent considering the problems, but includes mental activity not devoted to their solution. The PD patient may then be prone to distractions away from solving the problems. As Shallice (1982) has argued, a deficient SAS would be less capable of resolving conflicts between the schemata governing problem-orientated thinking and non-problem-orientated thought. Thus, for example, one version of this hypothesis suggests that the PD patients may have the solution to the problem ready for output, but are distracted from committing it to action. Although this remains a possibility, to the author's knowledge there is no direct evidence that Parkinson's disease patients are more prone to distraction.

Each of the accounts has to make special assumptions to explain why a deficient SAS leads to slowed thinking without a concomitant increase in errors. In the patients with left-anterior cortical lesions described by Shallice (1982), increases in errors also occurred together with slow thinking times. Thus slow thinking times are sometimes associated with increased number of errors and sometimes not. This conclusion suggests that it may be profitable to consider the mechanisms controlling thinking time to be somewhat different from those controlling move selection. In the case of the anterior cortical lesions, where both types of change occur, it is quite possible that the elevated errors may have led to slow responding, perhaps by reducing motivation. However, this possibility is ruled out for the PD patients of the present study, because of their relatively accurate performance.

In psychological terms, the slowed thinking could reflect an effect of apathy or motivational impairment. In Shallice's model, energizing influences of motivation are mediated by 'vertical threads' providing activation to the contention scheduling process. In neural terms, it has been pointed out that the dopaminergic innervation of the basal ganglia is a likely substrate for such activational influences (Robbins and Sahakian, 1983). Although associated classically with the bradykinesia of PD, dopamine depletion could also affect cognitive processes by disrupting the function of the caudate nucleus, and, conceivably, the ventral striatum, including the nucleus accumbens. Both of these terminal regions are depleted of dopamine in PD, though to a lesser extent than the putamen, which has been linked most closely with the motor disorder. The apparent lack of relationship with the effects of levodopa on the thinking deficit may argue against dopamine depletion being a relevant factor. However, it has been pointed out recently that levodopa dosage is typically titrated more optimally to combat the bradykinesia of PD, rather than the cognitive deficit (Gotham, Brown and Marsden, 1988). There is also an innervation by dopaminergic pathways of the frontal cortex itself, which is also affected in PD (Agid et al., 1987). The functions of this pathway are not well understood, but it is clearly not wise to equate dopaminergic activity solely with basal ganglia function. Other neurotransmitter deficits in the innervation of the frontal cortex, including noradrenergic, serotoninergic (Scatton et al., 1983) and cholinergic (Edwardson et al., 1985) forms could also potentially contribute to the cognitive deficit in PD (see also Agid et al., 1987).

Finally, it is notable that the PD patients in this study were receiving levodopa preparations, raising the question as how much the impaired thinking times were an effect of medication? In fact, there were no correlations between any parameter of thinking time with the dose of levodopa medication (for the initial thinking time, Pearson's $R = 0.06$; for the subsequent thinking time, Pearson's $R = -0.06$). The two least equivocal ways of showing a lack of effect of levodopa would be either (1) to show deficits regardless of whether the PD patients were on or off medication, or (2) to demonstrate deficits in patients early in the course of PD who were not yet receiving medication. In a preliminary study we have shown no deficits in a small ($n = 6$) group of unmedicated patients with PD, but interpretation of this result is confounded by the fact that these subjects were only in the first stages of the disease and the impairment in thinking time might be related to disease severity.

Many questions remain for further research. In particular, a major challenge is to define ways of separating supervisory (perhaps cortical?) and energetic (subcortical?) contributions to the thinking deficit in PD. This could perhaps be done using more subtle measures of thinking, or by manipulating the load on processing by the use of subsidiary tasks which tap particular specific functions, along the lines of the working-memory model (Baddeley, 1986). Another approach would be to collect protocols of the move-by-move thoughts of the subjects, as has been done previously in studies of thought processes in chess players (de Groot, 1965; Holding, 1985). Such protocols, for example, would allow us to determine if patients with PD consider more moves, and longer 'trees' (possibly continuations), than do control subjects.

It has been suggested by some (Hornykiewicz, 1984) that thinking is no more than internalized action. This perhaps surprising insight seems particularly plausible in the case of patients with PD. However, the present study suggests that PD may lead us to consider the different ways in which this comparison can be made, and in which thinking processes can lose their customary efficiency.

REFERENCES

Agid, Y., Ruberg, M., Dubois, B., & Pillon, B. (1987). Anatomical and biochemical concepts of subcortical dementia. In S. M. Stahl, S. D. Iversen & S. E. Goodman. *Cognitive neurochemistry*, (pp. 248–271). London: Oxford University Press.

Baddeley, A. D. (1986). *Working memory*. Oxford: Clarendon Press.

Bowen, F. P., Kamienny, R. S., Burns, M. M., & Yahr, M. D. (1975). Parkinsonism: effect of levodopa on concept formation. *Neurology*, **25**, 701–704.

Brown, R. G., & Marsden, C. D. (1987). Neuropsychology and cognitive function in Parkinson's disease: an overview. In C. D. Marsden & S. Fahn (eds.), *Movement disorders*, Vol. II. New York: Butterworth.

Cools, A. R., Van Den Bercken, J. H. L., Horskink, M. W. I., Van Spaendonck, K. P. M., & Berger, H. J. C. (1984). Cognitive and motor shifting aptitude disorder in Parkinson's disease. *Journal of Neurology, Neurosurgery and Psychiatry*, **47**, 443–453.

de Groot, A.D. (1965). *Thought and choice in chess*. The Hague: Mouton.

De Long, M. R., Georgopoulos, A. P., & Crutcher, M. D. (1983). Cortioc-basal ganglia relations and coding of motor performance. *Journal of Neurology, Neurosurgery and Psychiatry*, **36**, 192–194.

De Long, M. R., Georgopoulous, A. P., Crutcher, M. D., Mitchell, S. J., & Richardson, R. T. (1984). Functional organisation of the basal ganglia: contributions of single cell recording studies. In *Functions of the basal ganglia*—Ciba Foundation Symposium **107** (pp. 64–82). London: Pitman.

Duncan, J. (1986). Disorganisation of behaviour after frontal damage. *Cognitive Neuropsychology*, **3**, 271–290.

Edwardson, J. A., Bloxham, C. A., Candy, J. M., Oakley, A. E., Perry, R. H., & Perry, E. K. (1985). Alzheimer's disease and Parkinson's disease: pathological and biochemical changes associated with dementia. In: S. D. Iversen, (ed.), *Psychopharmacology: Recent advances and future prospects*. London: Oxford University Press.

Egan, D. E., & Greeno, J. G. (1974). Theory of rule induction: knowledge acquired in concept learning, serial pattern learning and problem solving. In L.W. Gregg (ed.), *Knowledge and cognition*, (pp. 43–103). Potomac, MD: Erlbaum.

Ellis, A. W., & Young, A. W. (1988). *Human cognitive psychology*. Hillsdale, NJ: Erlbaum.

Flowers, K. A., & Robertson, C. (1985). The effects of Parkinson's disease on the ability to maintain a mental set. *Journal of Neurology, Neurosurgery and Psychiatry*, **48**, 517–529.

Gotham, A. M., Brown, R. G., & Marsden, C. D. (1988). 'Frontal' cognitive function in patients with Parkinson's disease 'on' and 'off' levodopa. *Brain*, **111**, 299–321.

Greeno, J. G. (1978). Nature of problem solving abilities. In W. K. Estes (ed.), *Handbook of learning and cognitive processes*, Vol. 5, (pp. 239–270). Hillsdale, NJ: Erlbaum.

Hoehn, M. M., & Yahr, M. D. (1967). Parkinsonism: onset, progression and mortality. *Neurology* (Minneapolis) **17**, 427–442.

Holding, D. (1985). *The psychology of chess skill*. Hillsdale, NJ: Erlbaum.

Hornykiewicz, O. (1984). Discussion. In *Functions of the basal ganglia*—CIBA Foundation Symposium **107** (p. 241). London: Pitman.

Lees, A. J., & Smith, E. (1983). Cognitive deficits in the early stages of Parkinson's disease. *Brain*, **106**, 257–270.

Marsden, C. D. (1984). Which motor disorder in Parkinson's disease indicates the true motor function of the basal ganglia? In *Functions of the basal ganglia*—Ciba Foundation Symposium **107** (pp. 225–237). London: Pitman.

Morris, R. G., Downes, J. J., Sahakian, B. J., Evenden, J. L., Heald, A., & Robbins, T. W. (1988). Planning and spatial working memory in Parkinson's disease. *Journal of Neurology, Neurosurgery and Psychiatry*, **51**, 757–766.

Nauta, D. (1984). Discussion. In *Functions of the basal ganglia*—Ciba Foundation Symposium **107** (pp. 237–241). London: Pitman.

Nelson, H. E. (1982). *National adult reading test manual*. Windsor: NFER–Nelson.

Norman, D. A., & Shallice, T. (1980). *Attention to action: Willed and automatic control of behaviour*. San Diego: University of California Centre for Human Information Processing, (report 8006).

Robbins, T. W., & Sahakian, B. J. (1983). Behaviour effects of psychomotor stimulant drugs: clinical and neuropsychological implications. In I. Creese (ed.), *Stimulants: Neurochemical, behavioral and clinical perspectives*, (pp. 301–338). New York: Raven Press.

Sahakian, B. J., Morris, R. G., Evenden, J. L., Heald, A., Levy, R., Philpot, M., & Robbins, T. W. (1988). A comparative study of visuospatial memory and learning functioning in Alzheimer-type dementia and Parkinson's disease. *Brain*, **111**, 695–718.

Scatton, B., Javoy-Agid, F., Rouquier, L., Dubois, B., & Agid, Y. (1983). Reduction in cortical dopamine, noradrenaline, serotonin and their metabolites in Parkinson's disease. *Brain Research*, **275**, 321–328.

Shallice, T. (1982). Specific impairments in planning. In D.E. Broadbent & L. Weiskrantz (eds.), *The neuropsychology of cognitive function*, (pp. 199–209). London: The Royal Society.

Taylor, A. E., Saint-Cyr, J. A., & Lang, A. E. (1986). Frontal lobe dysfunction in Parkinson's disease: the cortical focus of neostriatal outflow. *Brain*, **109**, 845–883.

18

Concept Attainment Solution Strategies and Age

DIANE GREGORY
Humberside College of Higher Education

INTRODUCTION

The formation of concepts is crucial to adequate intellectual functioning. The value of the organization they provide has clearly been demonstrated for all our basic cognitive processes—perception, memory, learning and attention. It lies at the heart of our use of language, and without it thinking and problem-solving would be virtually impossible. In the light of the many reports of age-related deficits in performance on many cognitive tasks, it is clearly important for us to achieve some understanding of how concepts are formed and of how this process changes with age.

Many studies of concept attainment have reported a decline in success rate with advancing age. (Reviews of this area have been provided by, for example, Rabbitt (1977), Giambra and Arenberg (1980) and Denny (1982).) Most involve a memory component and so confound age-related changes in concept attainment with the well-documented decrement in memory for recent events found among older subjects. Two types of concept-attainment methodology are relatively free from this memory confound. The first involves the popular 'sequential method' of presenting, one at a time, the instances from which the subject is required to form a concept. To avoid memory load, after each instance is presented subjects are required to write down the instance, its outcome, and the list of hypotheses they hold as to what the concept could be (see, for example, Arenberg, 1968; Beavan and Wetherick, 1986). This method links with Levine's (1975) theory of concept attainment. He postulates that subjects should have two pools of hypotheses available to them, one consisting of those tested and rejected, and another consisting of those yet to be eliminated. As a sequentially presented concept problem unfolds, subjects are expected to eliminate from their written list of still-viable hypotheses, until only one—the answer—remains.

An alternative is the less cumbersome 'simultaneous method', where all the instances required to form the concept are presented to the subject at one go, along with their outcomes. The subject has all the necessary information made available to him with no need to remember anything. All that is required is the answer (i.e. a single hypothesis).

If, as has been supposed (by, for example, Levine, 1975), subjects attain concepts by generating all the viable hypotheses and then systematically eliminating from among them the ones which presented instances show to be invalid, then subjects should perform equally well on both the sequential and simultaneous methods of presentation. The author, with Norman Wetherick, found evidence that these two methods of presentation were not operationally equivalent (Beavan and Wetherick, 1986). Comparison of scores obtained from the same subjects on logically identical versions of the same task presented both sequentially and simultaneously yielded a difference in scores which was designated the 'sequential decrement effect'. In essence, this is represented by a fall-off in performance, as measured by the number of correct solutions, on sequentially presented problems in comparison with the same task presented simultaneously.

This appears to be a stable effect, found at all ages and with both abstract and concrete types of material. Although initially only evidenced by older subjects (in their sixties and seventies) on one-from-three single-attribute concept-attainment problems, it was also induced in younger subjects (in their twenties and forties) by using harder two-from-four conjunctive concepts. It was also present in older subjects when the simpler task was presented in abstract form, as opposed to the original concrete task, although the use of this type of material had a generally adverse effect on their performance under both presentation conditions. Although the sequential method reliably showed age-related deficits, no convincing age effects were found when the simultaneous method of presentation was used. A pilot sample of subjects in their eighties indicated that performance on this version of the concept-attainment task will eventually break down with age, but that this is likely to follow a considerable number of years after deficits have appeared on the sequential task.

Clearly we need to find out how subjects tackle concept attainment when left to their own devices, as with the simultaneous method. The recent resurgence of interest in the concurrent verbal reports of subjects, following the work of Ericsson and Simon (1984), has meant that we can now tap into the concept-attainment processes during simultaneous presentation. We simply ask subjects to think aloud as they form the concepts. If they are using the same strategy as they do with the sequential method, then we should expect them to report that they are generating a list of viable hypotheses after consideration of the first instance, then considering each subsequent instance in turn, eliminating hypotheses as they go.

THE METHOD

To keep continuity between the results of this study and that of Beavan and Wetherick (1986), the same task and subjects drawn from the same pool were used. Two sets of 'poisoned food' problems were constructed, following Arenberg's (1968) suggestion for a concrete task. One set comprised single-attribute problems and the other set comprised two-from-four conjunctive concept-attainment problems. The attributes in these problems were represented by courses in a meal; the three levels of each were choices of foods within each course, and a positive instance was designated as 'died', negative as 'lived'. The instructions to subjects explained that someone had put lethal poison into one of the foods being served in a restaurant. By examining the meals people ate and whether they lived or died as a result, the subjects' task was to discover the poisoned food. Where they were dealing with the more complex two-from-four conjunctive problems, the story was further complicated by the poisoner having been disturbed half way through tampering with the food, with the result that half the poison was in one item and the rest in another. Neither food would be lethal on its own, but death would result from eating both foods. The easier, single-attribute set was presented first, followed by the harder two-from-four conjunctive set. The construction of items in these sets of problems is shown in Figure 18.1, and actual examples in Figure 18.2.

Fifteen subjects aged between 20 and 50 (six males and nine females) and 15 subjects aged between 60 and 80 (six males and nine females) were tested individually. All were members of the volunteer subject panel of the Department of Psychology, University of Aberdeen.

The subjects were simply told to 'think aloud' as they solved each problem, their verbalizations being recorded on audio tape. Care needs to be taken to ensure that reports obtained in this way do indeed produce a useful record of subjects' cognitive processes. Byrne (1983) provides us with some good advice concerning the best techniques to use when eliciting verbal reports. We should

(a) 1. +, +
     2. +, +, +
     3. +, −
     4. +, −, −
     5. +, +, +, +
     6. +, −, +, −
     7. +, −, −, −
     8. +, −, −, +, −
     9. +, −, +, −, −

(b) 1. +, +
     2. +, +, +
     3. +, +, −, −
     4. +, −, −
     5. +, −, −, −
     6. +, +, +, +
     7. +, −, −, −
     8. +, +, +, −, −
     9. +, +, −, −, −
    10. +, −, −, +, −, −
    11. +, −, −, −, +, −

FIGURE 18.1 Construction of (a) single-attribute and (b) two-from-four conjunctive concept-attainment problems.

(a) Meal 1: Lamb, Beans, Coffee   died
     Meal 2: Pork, Beans, Tea   lived
     Meal 3: Lamb, Carrots, Coffee   died
     Meal 4: Lamb, Peas, Tea   lived

(b) Meal 1: Beef, Beans, Tart, Coffee   died
     Meal 2: Lamb, Beans, Tart, Coffee   died
     Meal 3: Pork, Beans, Sponge, Coffee   lived
     Meal 4: Pork, Peas, Tart, Coffee   lived

FIGURE 18.2 Specimen problems: (a) single-attribute and (b) two-from-four conjunctive concept attainment.

use psychologically naive subjects. The subjects here were non-psychologists and, as far as is known, had not received any training in introspective reporting. A simple 'think-aloud' instruction was used to avoid encouraging subjects to try to explain their behaviour, yet still elicit the information required. The task appears to be easily verbalized since Beavan and Wetherick (1986) noted that some subjects spontaneously verbalized during its performance. This would also be expected from the use of verbal material, rather than, for example, a manipulative or psychomotor task. Byrne cautions us against the use of retrospective reporting, where bias can be introduced as a result of information having to be retrieved from long-term memory. The use of concurrent protocols here avoids this source of contamination.

Analysis

Once the taped verbal protocols were transcribed to produce 'hard copy', care still needed to be taken in their analysis. Byrne tells us to look at patterns in this data, not just content. Since analysis in this study is at the level of global strategies, the whole protocol for each problem was taken as the unit for encoding, thus directing the encoder's attention to its pattern, rather than its detailed specific content. However, before analysis of this verbal data could begin, some checks had to be made to make sure that the transcribed protocols obtained were indeed pertinent to the cognitive processes under scrutiny.

Firstly, did the verbalization disrupt performance? Since the same subjects were used here as in Beavan and Wetherick's (1986) study, it was possible to compare 'silent' and 'think-aloud' performance on a logically identical, but different, set of single-attribute problems to test for any fall-off in the number of concept-attainment problems correctly solved. No significant difference was found between the two sets of scores (see Table 18.1). This suggests that there was no disruption of performance due to the request to verbalize. Although the 'silent' condition always came first, there was no evidence of a learning effect, backing up Johnson's (1962, 1964) finding that subjects do not recognize problem types when they meet them a second time.

Secondly, Ericsson and Simon (1984) offer some useful criteria for assessing whether our verbal reports are epiphenomena and, therefore, not true representations of cognitive processes. The data obtained should correspond to

Table 18.1 Mean number of single-attribute problems correctly solved under 'silent' and 'think-aloud' conditions

Age groups	'Silent' scores	'Think-aloud' scores
20 and 40 years	8.8	9.0
60 and 70 years	8.3	8.5

the stimuli used. A glance at the examples of protocols included in the text of the 'Results' section will confirm that this was the case; also, that the verbalizations were relevant to the task and represent a plausible approach to the solution of the problem. The verbalizations further showed the necessary consistency across similar situations.

Turning our attention to the encoding itself, this study is both theory-driven and data-driven. It is theory-driven in so far as the simple hypothesis put forward for testing is that subjects solving concept-attainment problems under simultaneous presentation conditions will not exclusively use the strategy required of them by the sequential method of presentation (instance-by-instance elimination from a list of possible answers). However, an encoding procedure aimed at simply testing for the presence or absence of this single strategy will not do justice to the richness of the verbal report data obtained, nor represent the best use of the not inconsiderable amount of time invested in garnering that data. Since there is no theoretical basis available to indicate clearly what other strategies might be found, a data-driven encoding scheme was developed from analysis of a subset of the data (the first ten subjects to be tested). These protocols were then put back into the sample and encoded afresh.

All this was done by the experimenter and needed to be checked for reliability by an independent encoder. This person was kept naive as to the experimental design and hypothesis in order to avoid biasing his judgements. Enough information was provided to enable him to perform the task effectively without having to resolve ambiguities by resort to inferences based on prior expectations brought to the task with him. To this end, he was provided with anonymous copies of the transcribed protocols, copies of the problems and instructions, and descriptions of the strategies to be encoded.

The encoding instructions for the strategies were as follows:

Examine the protocol for clear evidence that the subject solved the problem by:
CD: Taking a food/pair of foods common to all meals where the outcome was death.
$CD + e$: First selecting the foods/pairs of foods common to the meals which resulted in death, then sequentially considering the remaining meals in order to eliminate all but one of these.
e: Taking the foods/pairs of foods from the initial meal resulting in death and sequentially considering the subsequent meals so as to eliminate all but one of these.

O: Selecting the food/pair of foods which were present in the initial meal resulting in death, but not in any subsequent meals where death was not the outcome.

OF: Deciding on one member of the poisoned food pair, then independently selecting the other.

OF + e: Deciding on one member of the poisoned food pair, then sequentially considering the meals for evidence of its fatality in combination with another food.

Results

Analysis of covariance taking into account the effects of sex, education and WAIS scores for Arithmetic, Vocabulary, Block Design and Picture Arrangement tests (data available from Beavan and Wetherick, 1986) revealed that there were no age effects on numbers of concepts correctly attained on either set of problems. None of the covariates included was found to have a significant effect on either of these scores.

Turning to the results of the protocol analysis, I shall begin by considering those problems which were correctly solved and for which both the experimenter and independent encoder produced a coding, the experimenter's codings being taken for use here. The independent encoder emerged as consistently more willing to infer a strategy from any given protocol than was the experimenter, and this resulted in 20.1% of protocols being excluded from the frequency data for each problem. Analysis of these cases showed that their encodings followed the same pattern as those where the experimenter also gave a code. Overall agreement between the experimenter and the independent encoder as to the actual codes given was a healthy 88.2%.

It became immediately apparent that the elimination type of approach, as suggested by Levine's model, was not the only one that subjects used. The strategy which most closely corresponds to this approach is the 'e' (elimination) strategy. Rather than appearing universally, this strategy turned out to be only one of a number of strategies used. Further, the types of strategy subjects employed seemed to be strongly linked to the structure of the particular problem being tackled in terms of the combination of positive, or 'died', and negative, or 'lived', instances it contained (see Table 18.2).

Table 18.2 Overall percentages of encodings by problem construction for single-attribute problems

Problem construction	CD	CD + e	e	O
All positive	100	—	—	—
Mixed (multiple positive)	20.6	39.7	39.7	—
Mixed (single positive)	—	—	55.1	44.9

Single-Attribute Problems

Looking first at the easier, single-attribute set of problems, it was found that the 'e' strategy was, in fact, not used at all where a problem consisted of all positive

Table 18.3 Encodings for problems 1, 2 and 5: all-positive-instance, single-attribute problems

	20 and 40 year-olds	60 and 70 year-olds	Totals
CD strategy	31	30	61
Total number of problems	43	45	88

instances. For problems 1, 2 and 5 (see Figure 18.1) the only strategy encoded was 'CD' (common denominator), where subjects simply looked for the food which all the meals shared in common (see Table 18.3). This strategy was both popular and effective, and showed no age-related trend in its usage. Inter-coder agreement was 98.7% for this group of problems. Examples of the comments encoded as 'CD' are:

'They all died. All the meals must have something in common. As far as I can see the only thing they have in common is the tea. So ... the poisoned food is the tea.'

This subject is quite explicitly looking for the single item present in all the instances, although there is no account of why.

'They died in them all and the only one that's common to them all is tea, so its tea.'

The line of reasoning is, again, one of searching for a food present in all the fatal meals.

For problems 6, 8 and 9, where two or more positive instances were combined with negative ones, three strategies came into play. Both 'CD' and 'e' were represented, plus a composite of these two strategies, 'CD + e'. No one strategy was dominant, nor were there any age-related differences in their usage (see Table 18.4). Inter-coder agreement was 97.3% for this group of problems.

Examples of comments encoded as 'CD' are:

'Common denominator there seems to be coffee.'

No mention is made of any other food common between the two positive instances which are only implied as the source of the answer.

Table 18.4 Encodings for problems 6, 8 and 9: mixed-instance, multiple-positive single-attribute problems

	20 and 40 year-olds	60 and 70 year-olds	Totals
CD strategy	4	9	13
CD + e strategy	13	12	25
e strategy	14	11	25
Errors	0	3	3
Total number of problems	43	45	88

'So the first meal is lamb, carrots and tea. I take it it's the same with Meal 4 beef, carrots and tea, they died. So I take it it was tea.'

This subject also seems to completely overlook the second common food between the two positive instances.

Examples of comments encoded as 'CD + e' are:

'Obviously something that's common to those two. It could be beef or it could be beans. But that man had beans and lived, so it's obviously beef.'

The initial sentence here refers to the two positive instances presented. The 'CD' strategy is used first and followed up with the 'e' strategy in order to eliminate one of the two remaining candidates.

'What is common to 1 and 3? It must be beef because beans in Meal 5 and that person lived, so it's something—it must be beef.'

Again, the 'CD' strategy is explicit at the start, followed by elimination.

Examples of comments encoded as 'e' are:

'Lamb, beans and coffee is infected. Pork, beans, tea they lived. So beans is okay. Lamb, carrots, coffee somebody died. It must be lamb or coffee. Lamb, peas, tea and they lived. It must be coffee that's infected.'

This subject does a thorough job of elimination by considering each meal in turn.

'Died with lamb, carrots and tea. So lamb is out when he lived, and he lived with carrots. Tea he died, tea died, tea died.'

In this case, the answer appears to be being checked again against the two positive instances.

In problems 3, 4 and 7 there was only a single positive instance at the start which was followed by one or more negative instances. This seemed to represent the kind of situation where the 'e' strategy would be most useful. However, the 'O' (odd-one-out) strategy claimed an almost equal share of the protocols encoded by the experimenter (see Table 18.5), but there were encoding problems with this category. The independent encoder failed to use the 'O' category at all, using the 'e' and 'CD + e' categories instead. This was the only

Table 18.5 Encodings for problems 3, 4 and 7: mixed-instance, single-positive-attribute problems

	20 and 40 year-olds	60 and 70 year-olds	Totals
O strategy	10	12	22
e strategy	16	11	27
Errors	0	1	1
Total number of problems	42	45	87

systematic bias found in the use of the category labels and reduced inter-coder agreement to only 53.1%.

In the experimenter's view, the 'O' strategy places emphasis on the positive instance as a source of information, whereas the 'e' strategy places this emphasis on the disconfirmatory information contained in the negative instances. This is, however, a subtle difference which the following examples may, or may not, clarify for the reader. It also highlights one of the difficulties of the use of this kind of data.

Examples of comments encoded as 'O' are:

> 'Pork, peas, tea died. The others all lived, so it has to be something different in the first one. None of the others had pork.'

Here the subject seems to be disregarding similarities between the positive and negative instances and looking for the odd food out from the first, positive instance. This must be the answer since, by implication, only people who died ate it.

> 'Two meals, the only difference being that the one took milk and one took tea. The person with milk died and the person with tea didn't, so the milk is containing the poison.'

This subject makes more explicit the odd-food-out approach.

Examples of comments encoded as 'e' are:

> 'Beef, beans, coffee. First person died. So, second person had the beans, so it couldn't have been the beans, and the next person had the beef and lived. So it wasn't the beef, so it must have been the coffee.'

Here the elimination of two out of the three foods from the positive instance is quite explicit.

> 'Somebody died having eaten lamb, beans and coffee. Meal 2 beans are clear, and Meal 4 the lamb is clear, so it must be coffee.'

Again we see that the answer is arrived at by elimination of the alternatives.

Two-From-Four Problems

A similar picture of varied strategies linked to problem construction emerged for the harder set of problems (see Table 18.6).

Table 18.6 Overall percentages of encodings by problem construction for two-from-four conjunctive problems

Problem construction	CD	CD + e	e	OF	OF + e
All positive	98.1	—	1.9	—	—
Mixed (multiple positive)	31.5	51.5	8.5	8.5	—
Mixed (single positive)	—	—	57.0	18.0	25.0

Table 18.7 Encodings for problems 1, 2 and 6: all-positive-instance, two-from-four conjunctive problems

	20 and 40 year-olds	60 and 70 year-olds	Totals
CD strategy	33	20	53
e strategy	1	0	1
Errors	0	7	7
Total number of problems	45	45	90

Again, where all the instances were positive (that is, in problems 1, 2, and 6) the 'CD' strategy was almost unanimously used and its reported use was not related to age. The two encoders agreed on 98.2% of occasions for these problems (see Table 18.7).

An example of the comments encoded as 'CD' is:

'All died. All took lamb and beans. So I would say lamb and beans.'

The subject is searching for the pair of foods shared by all the positive instances and disregarding anything else.

Where two or more positive instances were combined with negative ones (i.e. 3, 8, 9, 10 and 11) four strategies emerged with the 'e' approach accounting for only 8.5% of coded protocols. An equally small percentage of protocols were encoded 'OF', leaving the 'CD + e' and 'CD' strategies to account for the bulk of protocols for these problems. The most popular strategy, 'CD + e', was found to be more frequently used by the group of subjects in the 20–50 age range (Mann–Whitney, $p < 0.01$, two-tailed). None of the other strategies showed any significant relationship with age, although the use of the 'e' strategy was limited to only a few subjects in the younger group. Agreement between encoders here was 84.1% (see Table 18.8).

An example of a comment encoded as 'CD' is:

'I'll have the beans and the jelly for those two. Both died and both had that. It makes sense.'

Table 18.8 Encodings for problems 3, 8, 9, 10 and 11: mixed-instance, multiple-positive two-from-four conjunctive problems

	20 and 40 year-olds	60 and 70 year-olds	Totals
CD strategy	12	10	22
CD + e strategy	29	7	36
e strategy	6	0	6
OF strategy	1	5	6
Errors	10	24	34
Total number of problems	75	69	144

Here the subject apparently does not notice a third common food between the two positive instances.

Examples of comments encoded as 'CD + e' are:

'1 and 5 died this time. Both ate the beans and the jelly and the coffee. But number 6 ate the jelly and the coffee, so it has to be just one of those. Number 2 ate the beans and the coffee. So it has to be the beans and the jelly.'

This younger subject has no trouble keeping track of the pairs to be decided between here.

'Meal 1 person died with beef, beans, tart and coffee, and Meal 2 person died with lamb, beans, tart and coffee. So it must be either two out of three beans, tart and coffee. Beans and coffee person lived. Peas and coffee person lived. Peas and coffee person lived. So coffee must be clear. Sorry, Meal 4 it was the tart and coffee person lived. Coffee is clear. Therefore it's the beans and tart.'

In this older subject the sequence of 'CD' and then 'e' strategies is clearly seen. The 'e' part seems to cause strain.

An example of a comment encoded as 'e' is:

'The combination can't be jelly and milk 'cos someone ate that and lived. It can't be jelly and peas 'cos someone ate it and lived. It can't be beef and peas, just by going through and taking any combination from the meal the person lived from. Peas and milk.'

This time a much more long-winded process of pairwise elimination.

An example of a comment encoded as 'OF' is:

'Common factor is there as well as the beef. There, right. What else has he got to have before he dies that's in all this? Milk, is that right? Now think. If he has beef and milk and dies, and that one has beef and milk and dies, but this one has milk. Beef and died. He has beef and milk and lived, so that's not right. Well it can't be the milk, it might well be the beef. Now what's the next one, peas. What am I looking for? I'm looking for a common something else that's on the top two lines. Sponge. Beef and sponge would do it. Now what happens here, he's had beef and sponge, oh and he died. He had sponge, oh yes. Now, where have I got? Beef and sponge, What an effort.'

Although this subject seems aware of the search for a pair, items are considered independently of each other for at least part of the time. One food out of the pair is settled first, and a rather unsystematic search for its partner then follows.

As with the easier set of problems, where there was only one positive instance available (i.e. problems 4, 5 and 7) the 'e' strategy came more into its own and claimed 57% of coded protocols. However, it was still only one of three strategies found, with 'OF' and the composite 'OF + e' strategies each representing a sizeable minority (see Table 18.9).

Use of the 'e' strategy fell significantly with age (Mann–Whitney, $p < 0.05$, two-tailed). Neither of the other strategies showed any age-related change. Inter-coder agreement for these problems was 97.7%.

Table 18.9   Encodings for problems 4, 5 and 7: mixed-instance, single-positive two-from-four conjunctive problems

	20 and 40 year-olds	60 and 70 year-olds	Totals
e strategy	14	2	16
OF strategy	1	4	5
OF + e strategy	5	2	7
Errors	7	19	26
Total number of problems	45	45	90

An example of a comment encoded as 'e' is:

'One died, three lived. Looking through any meal that someone survived from to see if there are two items that's in the one meal people have died from. It can't be pork and peas. It can't be pork and jelly. It can't be pork and coffee. Rule out pork. It can't be jelly and coffee. It must be peas and jelly.'

The rationale behind this strategy is made explicit at the start by this subject who then systematically eliminates pairs of foods from the first instance until only one remains. This subject was from the younger group.

An example of a comment encoded as 'OF' is:

'Person died having eaten beef, peas, jelly and milk. So two of those are poisoned. Person lived having eaten beef, jelly and milk so peas is one of the poisoned ones. A person lived having eaten beef, peas, jelly and coffee, so that clears beef and jelly, so it must be peas and milk.'

Although this subject isolates one food, this is not followed up with a systematic elimination of this in pairs with others from the positive instance.

An example of a comment encoded 'OF + e' is:

'Person died having pork, peas, tart and tea. Must be two of those. Number 2 peas, tart and tea are included and the person lived, so pork must be one of the poisoned foods. Pork and peas person lived, with pork and tart the person lived, so it must be pork and tea.'

The two stages of this strategy are made quite clear here.

Of the total of 71 errors recorded, only 14 received an encoding. The category encodings for these were evenly distributed across all the strategies used and did not appear to indicate any change of approach to solution from situations where correct answers were produced. Possibly the task was not sufficiently difficult for performance to break down completely.

DISCUSSION

The simplest version of the experimental hypothesis under test here was that subjects would not exclusively use the instance-by-instance elimination, or 'e' strategy as they would be forced to under sequential presentation conditions.

This proved to be the case. What is more, for some types of problem construction this strategy was not used at all. It is difficult not to conclude that such sequential studies are, at best, simply detailed examinations of the use of one concept-attainment strategy. They test its robustness on the type of problem construction where such a solution method may reasonably be expected to be used by a certain percentage of subjects, and also the extent to which subjects can generalize its application to problem constructions where they would not normally use it. As we have discovered, this is not the only strategy available to subjects, and some subjects may not use it at all when left to their own devices.

Although some subjects' verbal reports indicated that they were using an exact replica of the sequential solution method when encoded as exhibiting the 'e' strategy, many others were not using a strictly equivalent approach although they received the same encoding. What tended to happen was that a food or pair of foods (i.e. one hypothesis) was selected and tested out before being retained or discarded. So, rather than progressing through the instances in an orderly manner, the subjects tended to progress through the hypotheses in a systematic fashion. This often entailed jumping about from instance to instance as hypotheses were considered in turn. Of course, this is not possible under sequential presentation conditions and even further weakens the case for the generality of results from such studies on the assumption that their implicit strategy is universal.

The findings of this study indicate that the strategy used to solve a simultaneously presented concept-attainment problem depends on the particular construction of that problem in terms of the positive and negative instances it contains. The more complex the problem, the greater the range of strategies encountered. There was a basic core of strategies which were applied to both easier and harder sets of problems where the construction was the same. Many of the strategies appear to have an economic, rather than logical, foundation. Some were almost universal, others were not. Where more than one positive instance was available, subjects tended to capitalize on the easily extracted information from these before turning to look at negative instances.

It is noteworthy that the only age effects found in this study were for the use of the dominant 'e' strategy on single-positive-instance problems, and the 'CD + e' strategy on multiple-positive, mixed-instance problems, both of the harder type. This suggests that the use of the 'e' strategy, either alone or in combination with another, falls off with age. This may reflect the difficulty older subjects are reported to have in dealing with negative instances (Wetherick, 1966). In the light of this, it is not surprising that constraining elderly subjects to use it in sequentially presented problems leads to performance decrements at a lower level of problem difficulty than is found in younger subjects. The greater flexibility afforded them under simultaneous presentation conditions enables this difficulty to be largely overcome, and suggests an explanation of the 'sequential decrement effect.'

Clearly the 'elimination' strategy suggested by Levine's model is insufficient to account for performance on the simultaneously presented version of the task. Subjects' strategies are much more flexible, economic of effort and, at times, not even logical. We need a more broadly based model to account for them. Evans

(1984) has provided one which has been developed to cope with evidence from a variety of thinking and problem-solving tasks. Evans proposes that thinking is a two-stage process. Firstly, 'heuristic' processes separate out those features of a problem deemed to be relevant and worthy of further attention. We would not expect to find evidence of these in verbal protocol data since they are not considered to be accessible to a subject's focal attention, so would not be available for verbal report (Ericsson and Simon, 1984). They represent quick screening processes designed to narrow down the field of possibilities, and we see only the evidence of their results. The closely defined nature of the kind of laboratory task used here means that the subjects are aware that they are working with a limited set of possibilities, so the scope for these 'heuristic' processes is rather narrow.

Evans' second stage involves effortful 'analytic' processes acting on the information resulting from the first stage, and is in focal attention so accessible for verbal report. These 'analytic' processes need not be logical or rational, so we might have predicted the disjunction found between Levine's logical strategy and the less formal, rule-of-thumb strategies shown by many subjects here.

The constraints of the traditional method severely limit the scope for both stages of Evans' model. The instance-by-instance method of presentation gives no opportunity for 'heuristic' processes at all, and the subject is reduced to only one 'analytic' strategy, the 'elimination' one. That subjects when left to their own devices during simultaneous presentation rely heavily on positive instances and turn to negative ones almost as a last resort suggests that the 'elimination' strategy forced on them by the sequential method is the weakest and least practised in their repertoire, since it may involve constantly switching between types of instances. It also appears to be the one whose use is most readily abandoned by older subjects. It is not, therefore, surprising that the 'sequential decrement effect' occurs, and that it appears on relatively easy problems with older subjects.

REFERENCES

Arenberg, D. (1968). Concept problem solving in young and old adults. *Journal of Gerontology*, **23**, 279–282.

Beavan, D., & Wetherick, N. (1986). An investigation of concept problem-solving in relation to age using sequential and simultaneous presentation. Paper delivered at the BPS Conference, London, 1985 (*Abst. Bull. BPS*, **39**, A34).

Byrne, R. (1983). Protocol analysis in problem solving. In J. St. B. T. Evans (ed.), *Thinking and reasoning*. London: Routledge and Kegan Paul.

Denny, N. W. (1982). Aging and cognitive change. In B. B. Woolman & G. Stricker (eds.), *Handbook of developmental psychology*. Englewood Cliffs, NJ: Prentice-Hall.

Ericsson, K. A., & Simon, H. A. (1984). *Protocol analysis: verbal reports as data*. Cambridge, MA: MIT Press.

Evans, J. St. B. T. (1984). Heuristic and analytic processes in reasoning. *British Journal of Psychology*, **75**, 451–468.

Giambra, L. M., & Arenberg, D. (1980). Problem solving, concept learning and aging. In L. W. Poon (ed.), *Aging in the 1980s: Psychological issues*. Washington, DC: American Psychological Association.

Gregory, D. J. (1986). *Age-related changes in inductive reasoning processes*. Unpublished Ph.D. thesis, University of Aberdeen.

Johnson, E.S. (1962). The simulation of human problem solving from an empirically derived model. *Dissertation Abstracts International*, **24**, 3435P (order number 63-3497).

Johnson, E.S. (1964). An information processing model of one kind of problem solving. *Psychological Monographs*, **78** (whole number 581).

Levine, M. (1975). *A cognitive theory of learning*. Hillsdale, NJ: Erlbaum.

Rabbitt, P. (1977). Changes in problem-solving ability in older age. In J. E. Birren & K. W. Schaie (eds.), *Handbook of the psychology of aging*. New York: Van Nostrand Reinhold.

Wetherick, N. E. (1966). The inferential basis of concept attainment. *British Journal of Psychology*, **57**, 61–69.

19

Visual–Spatial Abilities in Art, Maths and Science Majors: Effects of Sex, Family Handedness and Spatial Experience*

M. Beth Casey
Boston College

Ellen Winner
Boston College and Harvard Project Zero

Mary Brabeck
Boston College

Kate Sullivan
Boston College

INTRODUCTION

It has often been argued that certain professions depend on visual–spatial abilities. Such fields include the visual arts, mathematics, the physical sciences, architecture and engineering. This position has been taken by individuals actively engaged in these fields as well as by psychologists (cf. Benbow, 1988; D'Amico and Kimura, 1987; Gardner, 1983; Krutetskii, 1976; Maccoby and Jacklin, 1974).

Our research focuses on three of the 'visual–spatial' fields: the visual arts, mathematics, and science. An individual's choice of these professions may be influenced by the ability to attend to visual–spatial patterns, to encode and

*This research was partially funded by a Boston College Faculty Research Grant to M. B. Casey and M. Brabeck, and by Boston College Psychology Department funds granted to E. Winner. We thank Howard Gardner and Ron Nuttall for helpful comments on an earlier draft of this chapter.

Lines of Thinking, Volume 2   Edited by K.J. Gilhooly, M.T.G. Keane, R.H. Logie and G. Erdos retrieve them at will, and to manipulate these mental images in two- and three-dimensional space. Artists report using these skills when holding an image in mind while painting, when planning how a three-dimensional scene can be transposed onto a two-dimensional canvas, and when contemplating changes in composition (Winner and Pariser, 1985).

Mathematicians use such skills when they visualize mathematical relations and solutions to problems (Krutetskii, 1976). Indeed, one area of mathematics, topology, is the study of how space is organized. The mathematician Stanislaw Ulam recalls his childhood fascination with the intricate patterns on an Oriental rug, and suggests that such visual patterns embody mathematical relations to which those with mathematical ability are attracted (Gardner, 1983).

Physical scientists use such skills when they visualize and reason about models of the physical world. For instance, Einstein reported that he thought in images (Ghiselin, 1952), and the chemist Fredrich August von Kekulè reported that he discovered the ring-like structure of the benzene molecule when he recognized its similarity to a snake curling and seizing its own tail (Perkins, 1981). In short, on the basis of introspective reports of individual creators and analyses of these fields by psychologists, the hypothesis that visual–spatial abilities are particularly important in these fields deserves serious consideration.

In this chapter, we explore two related sets of questions. First, we ask whether individuals who select these fields do in fact demonstrate superior visual–spatial abilities relative to individuals who select more verbal fields. If so, does the pattern of skills found differ depending on the field which the individual has chosen? We have selected two kinds of skills to investigate, one primarily visual (visual memory, which involves the ability to retrieve faithful images) and one primarily spatial (spatial visualization, which involves the ability to transform shapes and spatial relations in one's mind). Henceforth we refer to both as types of 'spatial' skill, and to the fields under investigation as 'spatial' fields. Visual memory and spatial visualization are considered to be two major components of visual–spatial ability (Thurstone, 1938). We shall present evidence that individuals who select spatial fields do indeed excel in one or both of these spatial skills. Such superiority may be due to learning (these individuals have extensive experience in spatial fields) or to an initial proclivity. We do not attempt to resolve this issue of nature versus nurture.

The second question to be addressed concerns the issue of sex differences in spatial ability. The profession of maths, science, and to a lesser extent art have fewer women than men. Why this is so is controversial. Certainly, societal pressures play a major role (Eccles, 1986). In addition, women may have less well-developed spatial skills than men, and thus may be placed at a disadvantage in fields which depend on such skills (Benbow, 1988; Burnett, Lane and Dratt, 1979; McGee, 1979; Sherman, 1978). In fact, the largest and most consistently reported cognitive sex difference is found on one measure of spatial visualization, mental rotation (Linn and Petersen, 1985).

Whether sex differences in spatial skills are causally related to sex differences in maths and science performance has not been conclusively established (Linn and Petersen, 1986). However, Burnett, Lane and Dratt (1979) found that, when spatial ability was statistically controlled, sex differences on the mathematics

Scholastic Aptitude Test (SAT–M) were no longer significant. We have replicated this effect using the Vandenberg Mental Rotation test (Casey and Brabeck, in press).

To address the question of sex differences in spatial skills, it is useful to identify the characteristics of the women who perform as well as men on the Vandenberg and other spatial tasks. We develop and present some evidence for a 'bent twig' explanation of the superior performance of those women who excel (Harris, 1978; Sherman, 1978). This theory is based on the old saying: 'As the twig is bent, so grows the tree.' We suggest that women with a biological predisposition for spatial skill may seek out spatial experience which in turn may stimulate their initial biological proclivity.

To address the two sets of questions summarized above, we have divided this chapter into two parts. In the first we establish that individuals who select spatial fields do demonstrate superior visual memory and spatial visualization. The studies addressing this question have been a primary focus of Ellen Winner's research programme. In the second part we take up the question of why so few women enter these fields. We approach this question by identifying the characteristics of the women who excel spatially within these fields. The second series of studies has been conducted by Beth Casey and Mary Brabeck.

VISUAL–SPATIAL SKILLS IN ART, MATHS AND SCIENCE STUDENTS

Visual Memory

We have demonstrated in two studies that artists have superior visual memory skills. We have shown this with instructed as well as non-instructed (incidental) memory tasks, using both children identified as talented in art and college studio art students. We have no data yet on maths and science students, but we are currently comparing art, maths and science majors on an instructed visual memory task (Winner *et al.*, 1988).

Study 1: Incidental Visual Memory in Artists

We first demonstrated superior incidental memory for visual patterns in both adult studio art majors (at a liberal arts college) and children identified by their art teachers as talented in art (Rosenblatt and Winner, 1988). Incidental memory tasks assess the ability to retain information passively, without intent to remember. The studio art majors' performance was compared with that of students majoring in other fields; the talented children's performance was compared with that of children selected as showing 'average' artistic ability.

Subjects were presented with pairs of pictures and were asked to select the one they preferred. This instruction was designed to ensure that subjects looked at the stimuli, but that they did so without knowledge that their memory was to be tested. Both members of the pair were either representational or non-representational. After viewing the pictures and taking a short break, subjects were shown the pairs again, with one member of each pair slightly altered. Subjects were asked to identify the altered member, and to indicate what had

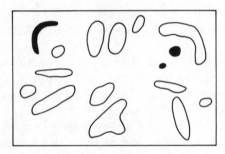

FIGURE 19.1 ETS Shape Memory test: sample item. From Ekstrom *et al.* (1976). Kit of factor-referenced cognitive tests. Educational Testing Service. Reproduced by permission.

been changed. The altered aspects included changes in composition (same components but rearranged), colour (for example, from dark to light green), form (for example, a rounded shape was elongated), line quality (for example, smooth to rough), and content (for example, caterpillar changed to a leaf). Both the adult and the child artists proved better able than the control group to identify the altered pictures and to recall what had been altered. No sex differences were found. This study has been more fully reported in Rosenblatt and Winner (1988).

Study 2: Instructed Visual Memory in Artists

In a second study, we investigated whether this same superiority would be demonstrated on an instructed visual memory task in which subjects deliberately try to retain patterns in memory (Sullivan and Winner, 1989). We compared the performance of studio art majors in a four-year college of art with psychology undergraduates in a four-year liberal arts college. The test administered was the Shape Memory test from the ETS Service Kit of Factor-Referenced Cognitive Tests (Ekstrom *et al.*, 1976). As shown in Figure 19.1, this task is composed of a complex pattern of non-representational, irregular shapes. Subjects are given four minutes to study this picture. They are then shown small segments of the picture, some of which have been altered. The task is to decide whether the frame shown is identical to that segment of the original picture.

As predicted, the art students outperformed the psychology students on this task ($F(1,60) = 4.07$, $p = 0.048$). Out of a possible 20 points, the mean art score was 16.21 ($SD = 6.92$, $N = 27$); the mean psychology score was 12.62 ($SD = 5.64$, $N = 29$). No sex differences were found. Possible reasons for this are discussed later in the chapter.

The visual–memory superiority of the art students may well be IQ-independent: the mean Scholastic Aptitude Test (SAT) scores for both mathematical and verbal ability were lower at the art college (maths $M = 475$, verbal $M = 485$) than at the liberal arts college (maths $M = 578$, verbal $M = 527$).

Conclusions

Our findings are consistent with, and extend, those reported by other researchers. Children with either artistic or mathematical talent recall visual patterns better than do children lacking such talent, and this ability appears to be independent of IQ level (Hermelin and O'Connor, 1986). The IQ independence of certain feats of visual memory has been further demonstrated in severely retarded individuals with artistic talent (O'Connor and Hermelin, undated).

Taken together, we can conclude that artists (whether normal children or adults with artistic talent, or otherwise retarded individuals with a preserved island of artistic skill) show a superior ability to recall complex visual patterns. This superiority is demonstrated not only on incidental memory tasks, but also on instructed tasks. This issue has been less frequently studied for mathematically and scientifically talented individuals. However, we are now investigating this issue; and in the one pertinent study discussed above (Hermelin and O'Connor, 1986), mathematically talented children also showed superior visual memory on an instructed task.

Spatial Visualization

While visual memory has been investigated more frequently in artistically than in mathematically and scientifically talented individuals, spatial visualization has been investigated in all three groups. Although art students clearly demonstrate strong visual memory abilities, their superiority in spatial visualization is less clear. As we will show, this contrasts sharply with mathematics and science students. We report below two investigations of the spatial visualization abilities of art, maths and science students.

Study 3: Art Versus Maths Majors

We compared studio art majors and maths majors with a control group of students in non-spatial fields (Winner *et al.* 1988). Students came from a four-year liberal arts college and a four-year college of art. Control group students were selected at random from other majors: any student majoring in a subject which required six or more maths or natural science courses was omitted from the control sample.

Subjects were given the Surface Development Test from the ETS kit (Ekstrom *et al.*, 1976). As shown in Figure 19.2, this measures the ability to imagine folding up the sides of a paper cutout of a flattened three-dimensional object and then to match the sides of the cutout with those of the drawing of a three-dimensional object.

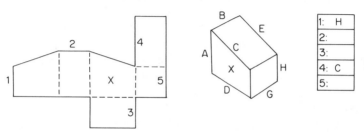

FIGURE 19.2 ETS Surface Development test: sample item. From Ekstrom *et al.* (1976). Kit of factor-referenced cognitive tests. Educational Testing Service. Reproduced by permission.

A main effect of 'major' was found ($F(2,106) = 3.52$, $p = 0.033$). *Post hoc* comparisons revealed that maths majors ($M = 20.20$, $SD = 5.99$, $N = 20$) outperformed the control group ($M = 15.26$, $SD = 6.97$, $N = 65$). In contrast, although art majors' scores did not differ significantly from those of maths majors, the art majors ($M = 18.11$, $SD = 6.80$, $N = 27$) proved only marginally better than the control group. No sex differences were found.

Study 4: Maths and Science Majors Versus Majors in Non-spatial Fields

The spatial visualization performance of maths and natural science majors was compared with that of a control group across three samples from two four-year liberal arts colleges (Casey and Brabeck, in press). The maths group was composed of students majoring in either pure mathematics or computer sciences; the science group was composed of students majoring in physics, chemistry and biology. Any student majoring in art or in fields requiring six or more maths or natural science courses was omitted from the control group.

The Vandenberg Mental Rotation test was administered (Vandenberg and Kuse, 1978). This test calls on the mental ability to rotate complex objects in three-dimensional space. Both maths majors ($M = 22.40$, $SD = 8.81$, $N = 68$) and science majors ($M = 21.60$, $SD = 8.55$, $N = 48$) outperformed the control group ($M = 18.11$, $SD = 8.94$, $N = 246$), ($F(2,345) = 6.94$, $p < 0.001$). This finding was replicated across the three samples. There was no interaction of 'major' with 'sample' or 'sex', but there was a main effect of sample (the third sample with lower overall SAT scores performed more poorly), and a main effect of sex. As has been previously found (Sanders, Soares and D'Aquila, 1982), females scored lower than males.

Conclusions

These results are consistent with previous findings showing that mathematically but not artistically talented individuals possess superior spatial visualization abilities. With respect to artists, two studies demonstrate no superior spatial visualization skills: Hermelin and O'Connor (1986) found that artistic children did not excel on spatial reasoning problems; and D'Amico and Kimura (1987) found that college art majors performed below average on tests of spatial visualization. However, in one study, art students at the School of the Art Institute in Chicago performed significantly above college norms on a mental rotation test (Getzels and Csikszentmihalyi, 1976). These artists may have been unusual, given the very selective standards of admission at the art school. Or the discrepancy in findings may come from a failure to separate artists who specialize in two-dimensional media (drawing, painting, printmaking) from those who work primarily in three-dimensional ones (sculpture, pottery). Our ongoing research addresses this issue.

With respect to maths and science students, other researchers have reported findings consistent with our own. Mathematically talented children excel at spatial reasoning tasks (Hermelin and O'Connor (1986)). Mathematically talented students show superior performance on spatial tests (Benbow *et al.*, 1983).

Indirect evidence for exceptional spatial visualization abilities of mathematics students come from Krutetskii's (1976) studies of problem solving by mathematically talented youths. Krutetskii identified three kinds of mathematically talented children: analytic (ones who find it difficult to solve problems visually and who thus use a verbal–analytic strategy), geometric (ones who solve problems visually), and harmonic (ones who can solve problems both ways). He found only a minority to be analytic.

With respect to science students, the results in the literature are consistent with our own findings and mirror those of mathematically talented individuals. Individuals who choose to study the physical sciences show superior skills in spatial visualization (D'Amico and Kimura, 1987).

What, then, can we conclude about the visual memory and spatial visualization abilities of students who select spatial fields? Students who go into the visual arts or mathematics appear to excel in visual memory. (We are currently investigating the visual memory ability of physical science majors.) The picture is more mixed when we consider spatial visualization. Students who select either mathematics or the sciences excel in spatial visualization. In contrast, artists do not consistently demonstrate such superiority. It should be noted that whether there is a causal relation between choice of discipline and pattern of abilities cannot be determined by these studies. We turn now to the issue of sex differences in spatial ability.

SEX DIFFERENCES IN SPATIAL ABILITIES: IDENTIFYING THE WOMEN WHO EXCEL

We now focus on women in maths and science. Our information on women in the visual arts is much less developed. However, in the discussion we shall return to the visual arts and offer some preliminary hypotheses and findings.

Rationale for Choice of Spatial Tasks

We have sought to identify the characteristics of those women who excel on spatial tests. For this purpose, it is necessary first of all to use spatial tests on which sex differences are obtained. Spatial tasks which reveal sex differences may be ones which depend heavily on the use of a 'spatial–configurational' rather than a 'verbal–feature' strategy. It is widely held that women as a group are more likely than men to depend on a verbal–feature strategy when solving spatial tasks (McGlone, 1980; Newcombe, 1982). With a verbal strategy, the stimulus is analysed feature-by-feature and coded into words. For instance, when solving the Surface Development task (Figure 19.2), one might reason verbally: 'If 4 is above 5 on the cutout, it must be perpendicular to it on the folded up form.' With a purely spatial strategy, the stimulus is coded directly as a visual image. For instance, on the Surface task, one simply forms an image of the folded up paper and then inspects the various sides. No additional verbal self-instructions are necessary.

The tests we selected were the Vandenberg Test of Mental Rotation (a test of spatial visualization) and the Rey–Osterrieth Complex Figure Test (Osterrieth,

Item type A: Items with mirror-image distractors

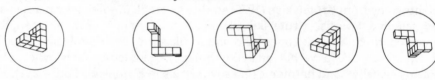

Correct answers: The first and fourth

Item type B: Items with feature distractors

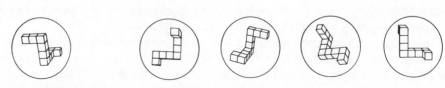

Correct answers: The second and fourth

FIGURE 19.3   The Vandenberg test: sample items. Reproduced by permission.

1944; Rey, 1941) (a test of visual memory used for neuropsychological assessment). Significant sex differences have been reported for both of these tasks (Bennett-Levy, 1984; Casey and Brabeck, 1989; Linn and Petersen, 1985), and neither can easily be solved with a verbal strategy. On the Vandenberg, subjects are instructed to use a mental rotation (spatial) strategy; moreover, a purely verbal strategy would be difficult on the mirror-image items which comprise half the test (see Item A in Figure 19.3). The Rey is an incidental memory test in which subjects are first asked to copy a complex, non-representational figure and then, without forewarning, to draw it in its entirety from memory (see Figure 19.4). This type of incidental visual recall task is less likely to prompt verbal coding than an instructed one, since subjects presumably do not rehearse, and thus must try to reconstruct the visual image to remember it. This task is difficult to solve without constructing and retaining an image of the total configuration. In contrast to the Rey and the Vandenberg, subjects may be able to use

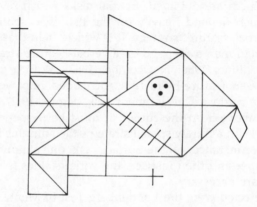

FIGURE 19.4   The Rey–Osterrieth Complex Figure.

verbal–analytic strategies on the memory tests in studies 1 and 2 and on the Surface test in study 3. This could account for the fact that no sex differences were found on these tasks.

Hypotheses and Predictions: The 'Bent Twig' Theory

We selected three variables as possible characteristics distinguishing women with superior spatial ability: family handedness, college major, and spatial experience. Here we were guided by a bent twig theory (cf. Halpern, 1986; Harris, 1978; Sherman, 1978). According to this theory, individuals are often drawn to activities in which their innate predisposition allows them to excel. Thus, biological potential can drive interest and choice of activities. In turn, participation in these activities helps to develop their initial abilities. Those lacking either such biological potential or the prerequisite experiences would fail to attain a superior level of ability. Only those with both would excel.

Family handedness. In an attempt to identify women's biological potential for spatial ability, we investigated the variable of family handedness, based on Annett's (1985) genetic model of handedness. Annett (1985) argues that the tendency for right-handedness is produced by the right-shift (rs) gene. This gene also affects brain organization and patterns of abilities. When the rs$^+$ allele is present on one or both chromosomes (rs^{+-} or rs^{++}), speech is lateralized to the left, with an accompanying preference for the right hand. Left-handed and ambidextrous individuals, as well as a small number of right-handers, do not inherit the right-shift factor (they are rs^{--}). For individuals with this rs^{--} genotype (approximately 19% of the population), handedness and cerebral organization are determined by random factors. Owing to this variability in their brain organization, no predictions can be made about the spatial abilities of non-right-handers (Annett, 1985).

However, differences in spatial ability can be predicted between those right-handed individuals carrying the heterozygous (rs^{+-}) and the homozygous (rs^{++}) right-shift factor (Annett, 1985). Annett proposes that the most common genotype is rs^{+-} (about 49% of the population). She also considers this genotype to be optimal in terms of a balance of spatial and verbal abilities. The incidence of this genotype is higher in right-handers with left-handed or ambidextrous relatives than in right-handers with only right-handed relatives. Individuals with this genotype carry the recessive rs$^-$ gene, but are right-handed owing to the dominant right-shift gene.

A smaller number of right-handers have the rs^{++} genotype (about 32% of the population). The incidence of this genotype is higher in right-handers with only right-handed relatives. Among women, this genotype results in a strong bias towards the left hemisphere when processing information, as well as a dependence on verbal strategies in solving spatial problems. This bias puts these individuals at a disadvantage on spatial tasks. Annett proposes that this left-hemisphere/language bias is greater for rs^{++} women than for rs^{++} men, because of more rapid maturation of both the left hemisphere and language ability in females. This sex difference is critical to our hypotheses, since it follows that the women, but not the men, with this genotype should be at a disadvantage on spatial tasks. These rs^{++} women should depend on verbal rather than spatial strategies when solving spatial tasks.

Based on Annett's (1985) predictions, we used family handedness as a marker for the right-shift factor (Casey and Brabeck, in press). We hypothesized that women with strong skills on the Vandenberg and Rey would be likely to come from a population of right-handers with non-right-handers in their immediate family (mixed family right-handers). Women who perform poorly would tend to be right-handers with only right-handed immediate relatives (consistent family right-handers). This latter group would be likely to have the rs^{++} genotype. In contrast, the former group, mixed family right-handed women should have the genetic potential (the rs^{+-} genotype) to excel on these tasks because they are less 'at risk' spatially.

Spatial activities and choice of college major.   We hypothesized that not only genetic but also environmental factors affect spatial ability in women. According to a 'bent twig' model, biological factors interact with environmental ones: women with the genetic potential to excel spatially are drawn to spatial activities which develop their spatial proclivities (Burnett, Lane and Dratt, 1982; Hyde, Geiringer and Yen, 1975). These experiences then provide women with the background and confidence to select typically male-identified fields such as maths and science. Once in these fields, their spatial ability should improve more than does that of women in the social sciences and humanities (Burnett and Lane, 1971). Thus, information about both choice of maths/science major and participation in spatial activities may be useful in identifying the women who excel spatially.

The choice of a maths/science major and the reporting of spatial experience are not by themselves enough to identify the women with superior spatial skill. First, there are many routes to success in maths and science. For instance, some maths/science majors may have poor spatial skills but successfully use their analytic abilities instead (cf. Hermelin and O'Connor, 1986; Krutetskii, 1976). Second, one may become involved in spatial activities for many reasons, even without an initial predisposition in that direction. We suggest that it is primarily the rs^{+-} women who capitalize on spatial experiences to develop their spatial ability. Thus, according to our bent twig hypothesis, the rs^{+-} genotype should interact with college major and/or spatial experience to influence spatial ability. While only longitudinal or training studies can confirm this prediction, such an interaction would provide strong, initial, supportive evidence for this hypothesis.

Study 5: Identifying the Women who Excel on the Vandenberg

The Vandenberg was administered to a total of 433 subjects including maths/science as well as non-maths/science majors (Casey and Brabeck, 1989). Maths and science fields were defined as college majors requiring at least six maths or natural science courses. Handedness information was obtained by using the Edinburgh Handedness Inventory (Oldfield, 1971). Right-handed subjects (scoring 0.41 or above on the Edinburgh) who reported having neither left-handed nor ambidextrous immediate relatives were classified as consistent family right-handers. Right-handers from families with one or more left-handed or ambidextrous immediate relatives were classified as mixed family right-handers. Left-handed or ambidextrous subjects (scoring 0.40 or below) were classified as non-right-handers. Standard scoring was used for the Vandenberg, with scores adjusted for guessing.

To examine the effect of practice, the test was administered two times, the second administration following directly after the first. There was a very strong effect of practice ($F(1,347) = 274.90$, $p < 0.001$) but no sex difference in amount of improvement was found. Thus, the gap between male and female performance was not narrowed through practice. Using average test performance across both administrations as the dependent variable, we showed that males ($M = 26.33$, $SD = 8.52$) had a large advantage over females ($M = 20.40$, $SD = 8.75$), ($F(1,397) = 27.64$, $p < 0.001$). Maths/science majors ($M = 23.87$, $SD = 9.07$) also strongly outperformed the non-maths/science majors ($M = 20.57$, $SD = 8.81$), ($F(1,397) = 10.15$, $p = 0.002$). There was no main effect of 'family handedness', but there was a three-way interaction of 'family handedness', 'major' and 'sex' ($F(2,421) = 5.15$, $p = 0.006$)—(see Table 19.1).

The simple effect analysis for males showed no main effects or interactions. In contrast, for the females, an interaction between 'family handedness' and

Table 19.1   Analysis of the average score on the Vandenberg test for the two administrations by family handedness, major and sex

	Mixed family right-handers		Consistent family right-handers		Individual non- right-handers	
	N	M^a	N	M	N	M
Female non-maths/science majors	70	19.01 (7.34)	64	19.67 (9.32)	39	16.26 (5.91)
Female maths/science majors	39	26.69^b (7.39)	61	20.70 (9.80)	41	21.42 (8.83)
Male non-maths/science majors	19	28.61 (6.63)	27	24.20 (10.23)	22	24.34 (9.15)
Male maths/science majors	15	25.63 (9.47)	26	28.46 (7.12)	10	27.65 (6.01)

[a] Figures in brackets are standard deviations.
[b] This subgroup of maths/science women outperformed the other two subgroups of maths/science women ($p < 0.05$, one-tailed).

'major' was found ($F(2,397) = 5.46$, $p = 0.011$). This interaction was in turn decomposed into simple effects for the two types of female majors. For the non-maths/science women, no difference in performance on the Vandenberg was found across the family handedness groups. However, for the maths/science women, a main effect of family handedness was found ($F(2,397) = 6.69$, $p = 0.004$).

Main results and conclusions. As predicted, simple contrast analyses demonstrated that the women who excelled on the Vandenberg were mixed family right-handers in maths/science fields (see Table 19.1). These women outperformed both consistent family right-handers in maths/science and non-right-handed women in maths/science. (The latter two groups did not differ). This effect was consistent across three samples (see Table 19.2).

The group of women who excelled ($M = 26.69$, $SD = 7.39$) was then compared (using a simple contrast effect) to the men across all subgroups ($M = 26.33$, $SD = 8.52$). This difference was not significant.

Furthermore, when verbal and maths SAT scores and parents' educational level were partialled out of the analysis of women's performance on the Vandenberg, the interaction between 'family handedness' and 'major' remained significant. The superior performance of our identified subgroup (female mixed family right-handers in maths/science) can be attributed neither to high math-

Table 19.2   Analysis of the average score on the Vandenberg test for the two administrations by sample for females

	Mixed family right-handers		Consistent family right-handers		Individual non-right-handers	
	N	M^a	N	M	N	M
Female non-maths/science majors						
Sample 1	34	19.21 (7.99)	27	21.43 (9.56)	12	16.50 (4.50)
Sample 2	23	19.61 (6.62)	19	20.05 (8.91)	10	17.60 (5.94)
Sample 3	14	17.57 (7.18)	18	16.64 (9.11)	17	15.29 (6.86)
Female maths/science majors						
Sample 1	12	27.15 (5.69)	16	19.91 (10.42)	8	25.00 (6.96)
Sample 2	14	28.25 (8.60)	20	23.55 (9.69)	16	20.22 (9.04)
Sample 3	12	24.38 (7.53)	25	18.92 (9.35)	17	20.85 (9.44)

[a] Figures in brackets are standard deviations.

ematical/verbal abilities, nor to SES. Our goal was thus achieved: we were able to identify the subgroup of women who perform as well as the men on the Vandenberg, and who outperform the other subgroups of women.

In order to provide an additional test of the right-shift theory, we obtained distant as well as immediate family handedness information. We reasoned that right-handed individuals with only right-handers among their distant as well as immediate relatives are those *most* likely to be rs^{++}. Consequently, parents of the consistent family right-handed women in the last sample were contacted to determine the handedness of grandparents, aunts and uncles. Among maths/science majors, the women predicted to score the lowest on the Vandenberg were those with exclusively right-handed first- and second-degree relatives.

The prediction was confirmed, since this group of maths/science majors ($M = 14.54$, $SD = 7.64$, $N = 14$) scored ten points lower than either those with distant non-right-handed relatives ($M = 24.50$, $SD = 8.53$, $N = 11$) or immediate non-right-handed relatives ($M = 24.38$, $SD = 7.53$, $N = 12$) out of a possible 40 points on the test. A t-test showed this difference to be significant ($t(35) = 3.76$, $p < 0.001$).

Although there is some disagreement about the degree to which family handedness reflects genetic or environmental factors, a genetic explanation for subgroup differences among women is supported by the extended family handedness data. The effect of handedness of grandparents, aunts and uncles is more likely genetic than environmental.

The lack of a family handedness effect for males. It might be asked why there was no significant family handedness effect for males. There are several possible explanations. According to an environmental explanation, males may be exposed to critical levels of spatial experience beyond that typically available to women. This in itself may be sufficient to overcome genetic differences in predisposition associated with family handedness. If so, this would have strong educational implications for women's spatial performance.

Alternatively, according to a biological explanation, family handedness may bear a different relation to brain organization in men than in women. There is evidence in the literature for a complex interaction between sex and family handedness for measures of cerebral laterality (McKeever, 1981), with males showing different laterality patterns for family handedness groups than females. As indicated earlier, Annett (1985) argues that rs^{++} males are less disadvantaged spatially than rs^{++} females because they are less lateralized. However, in contrast to Annett, the prevailing view is that men are more, rather than less, strongly lateralized (Bryden, 1982). This is a controversial issue, and the present results do not resolve it. However, they do provide support for Annett's hypothesis that, for women, the rs^{+-} genotype is associated with superior spatial skills. It remains for future research to determine the effect of genotype on brain organization.

Study 6: The Effect of Spatial Experience

As a result of the initial findings in study 5 with the first set of subjects (sample 1), a spatial activities measure was added to the protocol for the remaining subjects. The purpose was to test further the implications of the bent twig theory. Hence, a more direct measure of spatial experience was substituted in place of college major (Casey and Brabeck, in press). Subjects were divided into high and low spatial-experience groups. It was predicted that the mixed family right-handers with high spatial experience would outperform all other groups.

A shortened form of the Spatial Activities Questionnaire (SAQ) (Newcombe, Bandura and Taylor, 1983) was used to measure spatial experience. Independent judges selected those masculine-typed items which provided experience in visualizing either three-dimensional objects or two-dimensional representations of such objects. The items selected were carpentry, construction of go-karts, construction of model airplanes, sketching of house plans, design of electrical circuitry, and glass blowing. Subjects rated themselves on their degree of experience with these activities on a scale from 1 to 6. Subjects who rated themselves 4 or above on at least one of these activities were identified as having high spatial experience. (A more stringent criterion yielded the same results.)

Results and conclusions. A series of planned comparisons was performed on the first administration of the Vandenberg. We compared the high spatial experience/mixed family right-handers with the other groups of right-handed women (significance levels adjusted for number of comparisons)—see Table 19.3. The predictions were confirmed: the mixed family right-handers with high spatial experience outperformed each of the other three groups.

Moreover, for the mixed but not the consistent family right-handed women, choice of major was related to spatial experience. Chi-square tests were performed for the two right-handed groups to compare the frequency of maths/science versus non-maths/science majors for the women of high and low spatial experience. For the mixed family right-handers, fewer low-spatial-experience women selected maths/science as their major than in the high-spatial-experience group (22% versus 62%) ($\chi^2(1) = 9.29$, $p = 0.002$)—see Table 19.4. In contrast, no significant difference was found for the consistent family right-handers.

In conclusion these findings suggest that, for women with the rs^{+-} genotype,

Table 19.3 Analysis of women's performance on the Vandenberg test by family handedness and spatial experience level

	Mixed family right-handers		Consistent family right-handers	
	N	M^a	N	M
Low spatial experience	32	17.44 (7.07)	46	17.46 (8.68)
High spatial experience	30	22.30^b (8.59)	36	16.86 (9.50)

^{a} The figures in brackets are standard deviations.
^{b} The identified subgroup of women outperformed all other subgroups of women using planned comparisons ($p < 0.05$, one-tailed).

Table 19.4 The number of high and low spatial experience women within each major, for the family handedness groups

	Low-spatial experience group	High-spatial experience group
Mixed family right-handers		
Non-maths/science majors	25	11
Maths/science majors	7	19
Consistent family right-handers		
Non-maths/science majors	23	14
Maths/science majors	23	22

spatial experience makes a critical difference. Such experience may (1) have an impact on their spatial abilities, and (2) influence their choice of major. These experiences may be less important to women with the rs^{++} genotype. For this group, choice of major may be based on competencies unrelated to spatial potential or experience.

Given the importance of family handedness, major, and spatial experience in identifying the women who excel on the Vandenberg, a bent twig theory is supported. A subset of women with the genetic predisposition for mental rotation ability may be attracted to masculine-typed spatial experience and to college majors where such potential would be further developed.

Study 7: Identifying the Women who Excel on the Rey–Osterrieth Visual Memory Test

Finally, we sought to replicate our identified subgroup findings using a measure of incidental visual memory rather than a spatial visualization test. The women in the third sample were given the Rey–Osterrieth task. (The data on the Rey–Osterrieth were from Weinstein (1987) who used the Waber and Holmes (1986) scoring scheme.) Planned comparisons were performed, with significance levels adjusted for number of comparisons.

Based on a bent twig model, the consistent family right-handers who majored in maths/science were expected to score lower than the mixed family right-handed majors in maths/science. Predictions for the maths/science non-right-handers were less straightforward. Annett claims that non-right-handers lack the right-shift factor and hence have more variable brain organization, making their spatial ability less predictable. She did report a higher than average frequency of non-right-handers in a population of mathematicians (Annett and Kilshaw, 1982; see also Benbow, 1986). This is consistent with an analysis by Geschwind and Galaburda (1987), whose theory of brain organization and handedness is related to that of Annett (1985). They propose that non-right-handers tend to have either very high or very low spatial ability, and that those with high ability are likely to select spatial fields. Thus, those non-right-handers who major in maths or science might be expected to outperform non-right-handers in non-maths/science fields, and might perform as well as our identified subgroup. It should be noted that our non-right-handed population was homogeneous. No difference was found between the left and ambidextrous subjects for either the Vandenberg or the Rey. Moreover, only those non-right-handers with a family history of non-right-handedness were included in this last sample, in order to eliminate possible pathological non-right-handers (Satz, 1972).

Results and conclusions. Given the lack of clear predictions for non-right-handers in maths/science, we first carried out a planned comparison between maths/science mixed family right-handers and non-right-handers in these fields. The non-right-handed maths/science women did as well on the Rey as the mixed family right-handed maths/science women. Therefore, these groups were combined and compared with the maths/science consistent family group and with the three groups of non-maths/science majors. All of these comparisons were significant, with the combined group demonstrating superior recall.

These results for the Rey were consistent with the Vandenberg results for the identified subgroup. Overall, performance on the two tasks correlated 0.44, using the Pearson R test. However, the findings for the non-right-handed maths/science majors were inconsistent across the two tasks: they did poorly on the Vandenberg and yet they did well on the Rey. Why these subjects should perform worse on a spatial manipulation test than on a visual memory test deserves further investigation.

The inconsistency in performance found in the maths/science non-right-handers supports Annett's claim that this group has less predictable brain organization (cf. also Harshman, Hampson and Berenbaum, 1983). Non-right-handers continue to be a puzzle to researchers. However, the poor performance of the non-right-handed non-maths/science women on both tests, as well as the high performance of the non-right-handed maths/science women on at least the Rey, supports Geschwind and Galaburda's (1987) view that non-right-handers often perform at the two extremes on spatial tasks.

Table 19.5 Analysis of recall accuracy on the Rey–Osterrieth visual memory task by family handedness and major

	Mixed family right-handers		Consistent family right-handers		Individual non-right-handers	
	N	M^a	N	M	N	M
Female non-maths/science majors	14	43.07 (8.77)	10	40.89 (10.48)	14	38.79 (9.54)
Female maths/science majors	11	52.46[b] (7.10)	23	44.09 (10.33)	17	50.28[b] (8.24)

[a] The figures in brackets are standard deviations.
[b] These two subgroups of maths/science women combined outperformed the other subgroups of women using planned comparisons ($p < 0.025$, one-tailed).

GENERAL SUMMARY AND DISCUSSION

We asked two questions at the outset of this chapter. The first was whether individuals in spatial fields which are traditionally considered to invoke spatial reasoning skills actually have superior spatial abilities. We have provided positive evidence in answer to this question. However, the pattern of abilities depends on the spatial field in question. Visual artists excel in visual memory but their spatial visualization abilities are not unequivocally superior to those in non-spatial fields. In contrast, those in maths and science clearly excel in spatial visualization. See Winner *et al.* (1988) for a more systematic study of spatial abilities in these three fields in comparison with other specializations.

The second question was whether spatial ability relates to choice of maths or science as a major for women. Again, we provided positive evidence. First, the male advantage on the mathematics Scholastic Aptitude Test was eliminated when mental rotation ability was partialled out, suggesting that mental rotation ability may contribute to the sex difference on maths aptitude tests. (Note that the reverse was not true, since sex differences in mental rotation ability remained when mathematics SATs were partialled out.) Second, the women who excelled on both a mental rotation and a visual memory task were in maths/ science fields. Yet not all of the women in these fields were superior spatially. Handedness was a critical factor as well.

On the mental rotation task, the only maths/science subgroup to perform well was the one consisting of mixed family right-handers. On the visual memory task, among the maths/science majors, both the non-right-handers and mixed family right-handers excelled. The consistent family right-handers fared poorly on both types of tasks.

We based our interpretation of these data on Annett's (1985) genetic theory of handedness. It follows from her theory that consistent family right-handed women (the rs^{++} genotype) would be less likely to excel on spatial tasks than mixed family right-handed women (the rs^{+-} genotype).

Although these handedness findings do support a partial genetic component, the critical roles of college major and spatial experience suggest that environmental factors also influence spatial ability in women. The right-shift factor alone is not sufficient to explain sex differences in spatial ability. To begin with, the rs^{+-} is the most common genotype (Annett, 1985), and if this were the only factor contributing to spatial skill, then the majority of women would excel spatially.

We propose instead a 'bent twig' theory. Relevant spatial experience in childhood builds upon an initial genetic predisposition in spatial ability and influences choice of major in college. Longitudinal or training studies would clearly help to test this interpretation.

Finally, as promised, we return to the visual arts and offer a speculation about the nature of the spatial abilities of female artists. In a current study, we have begun to investigate the effect of family handedness patterns on women in art schools. An intriguing phenomenon has emerged. Out of the 21 right-handed women in our sample of art students, only five (24%) were consistent family right-handers. In contrast, for both maths/science and non-maths/science majors, there was a much higher percentage (57% and 55%, respectively). If this pattern remains stable over a larger sample, we would offer the following hypothesis. Success in the visual arts may depend much more exclusively on visual–spatial abilities than does success in maths and science. It has been shown that it is possible to perform well in maths and science using analytic–verbal skills as well as spatial ones (Krutetskii, 1976). Hence, those women with the rs^{++} genotype who also have strong verbal–analytic abilities may enter the fields of maths and science, but may be less likely to enter the field of visual art.

REFERENCES

Annett, M. (1985). *Left, right, hand, and brain: The right shift theory*. Hillsdale, NJ: Erlbaum.

Annett, M., & Kilshaw, D. (1982). Mathematical ability and lateral asymmetry. *Cortex*, **18**, 547–568.

Benbow, C. (1986). Physiological correlates of extreme intellectual precocity. *Neuropsychologia*, **24**, 719–725.

Benbow, C. (1988). Neuropsychological perspectives on mathematical talent. In L. Obler & D. Fein (eds.), *The exceptional brain: Neuropsychology of talent and special abilities*. New York: Guilford.

Benbow, C., Zonderman, A., & Stanley, J. (1983). Assortative marriage and the familiality of cognitive abilities in families of extremely gifted students. *Intelligence*, **7**, 153–161.

Bennett-Levy, J. (1984). Determinants of performance on the Rey–Osterrieth Complex Figure test: an analysis and a new technique for single-case assessment. *British Journal of Clinical Psychology*, **23**, 109–119.

Bryden, M. (1982). *Laterality: Functional asymmetry in the intact brain*. New York: Academic Press.

Burnett, S., & Lane, D. (1971). Effects of academic instruction on spatial visualization. *Intelligence*, **4**, 233–242.

Burnett, S., Lane, D., & Dratt, L. (1979). Spatial visualization and sex differences in quantitative ability. *Intelligence*, **3**, 345–354.

Burnett, S., Lane, D., & Dratt, L. (1982). Spatial ability and handedness. *Intelligence*, **6**, 57–69.

Casey, M., & Brabeck, M. (in press). Women who excel on a spatial task: proposed genetic and environmental factors. *Brain and Cognition*.

Casey, M., & Brabeck, M. (1989). Exceptions to the male advantage on a spatial task: family handedness and college major as factors identifying women who excel. *Neuropsychologia*, **27**, 689–696.

D'Amico, C., & Kimura, D. (1987). *Evidence for subgroups of adextrals based on speech lateralization and cognitive patterns*. Research Bulletin 664, Department of Psychology, University of Western Ontario.

Eccles, J. (1986). Gender roles and women's achievement. *Educational Researcher*, June/July, 15–19.

Ekstrom, R., French, J., Harman, H., & Dermen, D. (1976). *Kit of factor-referenced cognitive tests*. Princeton, NJ: Educational Testing Service.

Gardner, H. (1983). *Frames of mind: The theory of multiple intelligences*. New York: Basic Books.

Geschwind, N., & Galaburda, A. (1987). *Cerebral lateralization: Biological mechanisms, associations, and pathology*. Cambridge: MA: MIT Press.

Getzels, J., & Csikszentmihalyi, M. (1976). *The creative vision: A longitudinal study of problem finding in art*. New York: John Wiley.

Ghiselin, B. (ed.) (1952). *The creative process*. New York: Mentor.

Halpern, D. (1986). *Sex differences in cognitive abilities*. Hillsdale, NJ: Erlbaum.

Harris, L. (1978). Sex differences in spatial ability: possible environmental, genetic, and neurological factors. In M. Kinsbourne (ed.), *Asymmetry function of the brain*. Cambridge: Cambridge University Press.

Harshman, R., Hamson, E., & Berenbaum, S. (1983). Individual differences in cognitive abilities and brain organization. I: Sex and handedness differences in ability. *Canadian Journal of Psychology*, **37**, 144–192.

Hermelin, B., & O'Connor, N. (1986). Spatial representations in mathematically and in artistically gifted children. *British Journal of Educational Psychology*, **56**, 150–157.

Hyde, J., Geiringer, E., & Yen, W. (1975). On the empirical relation between spatial ability and sex differences in other aspects of cognitive performance. *Multivariate Behavioral Research*, **10**, 289–309.

Krutetskii, V. (1976). *The psychology of mathematical abilities in school children* (translated by J. Teller). Chicago: University of Chicago Press.

Linn, M., & Petersen, A. (1985). Emergence and characterization of sex differences in spatial ability: a meta-analysis. *Child Development*, **56**, 1479–1498.

Linn, M., & Petersen, A. (1986). A meta-analysis of gender differences in spatial ability: implications for mathematics and science achievement. In J. Hyde & M. Linn (eds.), *The psychology of gender*. Baltimore: Johns Hopkins University Press.

Maccoby, E., & Jacklin, C. (1974). *The psychology of sex differences*. Stanford: Stanford University Press.

McGee, M. (1979). Human spatial abilities: psychometric studies and environmental, genetic, hormonal, and neurological influences. *Psychological Bulletin*, **86**, 889–918.

McGlone, J. (1980). Sex differences in human brain asymmetry: critical survey. *Behavioral and Brain Sciences*, **3**, 215–227.

McKeever, W. (1981). Sex and cerebral organization: is it really so simple? In A. Ansara, N. Geschwind, A. Galaburda, M. Albert & N. Gartrell (eds.), *Sex differences in dyslexia*. Towson, MD: Orton Dyslexia Society.

Newcombe, N. (1982). Sex-related differences in spatial ability: problems and gaps in current approaches. In M. Potegal (ed.), *Spatial abilities: Development and physiological bases*. New York: Academic Press.

Newcombe, N., Bandura, M., & Taylor, D. (1983). Sex differences in spatial ability and spatial activities. *Sex Roles*, **9**, 377–386.

O'Connor, N., & Hermelin, B. (undated). *Visual and graphic abilities of the idiot-savant artist*. MRC Developmental Psychology Project, unpublished manuscript.

Oldfield, R. (1971). The assessment and analysis of handedness: the Edinburgh inventory. *Neuropsychologia*, **9**, 97–113.

Osterrieth, P. (1944). Le test du copie d'une figure complexe. *Archives de Psychologie*, **30**, 206–356.

Perkins, D. (1981). *The mind's best work*. Cambridge, MA: Harvard University Press.

Rey, A. (1941). L'examen psychologique dans les cas d'encephalopathie traumatique. *Archives of Psychology*, **25**, 286–340.

Rosenblatt, E., & Winner, E. (1988). Is superior visual memory a component of superior drawing ability? In L. Obler & D. Fein (eds.), *The exceptional brain: Neuropsychology of talent and special abilities*. New York: Guilford.

Sanders, B., Soares, M., & D'Aquila, J. (1982). The sex difference on one test of spatial visualization: a non-trivial difference. *Child Development*, **53**, 1106–1110.

Satz, P. (1972). Pathological left-handedness: an explanatory model. *Cortex*, **8**, 121–135.

Sherman, J. (1978). *Sex-related cognitive differences*. Springfield, IL: Charles Thomas.

Sullivan, K., & Winner, E. (1989). Recognising visual stimuli: does it help to be an artist? Paper presented at the American Psychological Association meeting, New Orleans, LA. August.

Thurstone, L. (1938). Primary mental abilities. *Psychometric Monographs*, **1**.

Vandenberg, S., & Kuse, A.R. (1978). Mental rotation: a group test of three-dimensional spatial visualization. *Perceptual Motor Skills*, **47**, 599–604.

Waber, D., & Holmes, J. (1986). Assessing children's copy production of the Rey–
    Osterrieth complex figure. *Journal of Clinical and Experimental Neuropsychology*, **3**,
    264–280.
Weinstein, C. (1987). *Delineation of female performance on the Rey–Osterrieth figure*. Unpub-
    lished dissertation.
Winner, E., Casey, M., DaSilva, D., & Hayes, R. (1988). Contrasting patterns of abilities
    and deficits in art and maths/science students. Paper presented at Conference, Art and
    the Brain, University of Chicago. May.
Winner, E., & Pariser, D. (1985). Giftedness in the visual arts. *Items*, December, 65–69.

Part V

Teaching Thinking

Teaching Thinking Skills

G. ERDOS
University of Newcastle upon Tyne

In addition to the quest for knowledge, most scientific research is motivated by applied considerations. Psychology is no exception. We want to understand behaviour, but also we would like to be able to put this understanding to good use. In the area of cognitive psychology and research on thinking, one of the most important considerations is how to make people better thinkers. There are a number of reasons for this. For example, changes in the work environment in the 'developed world' resulted in the ever-decreasing need for unskilled labour and in the steadily increasing need for decision-makers, designers, programmers and so on. Paradoxically, though, a number of measures for scholastic attainment show a decline; and the general level of academic competence is giving rise to serious concern both in Britain and in the United States.

If people show deficiencies in their thinking, could we teach them how to think? That thinking can be taught is a trivial statement, Bertrand Russell's remark notwithstanding. (He said: 'Some people would rather die than think. In fact they do.') People develop their thinking skills and the knowledge base to go with it. To facilitate this is the primary role of education. When psychologists and applied educational researchers discuss the teaching of thinking skills, they mean something slightly different. They usually refer to general strategies which would work across a number of domains.

There are a number of systematic programmes which have attempted to teach thinking skills. These vary greatly in their theoretical underpinnings, the materials used and their target population. A number of solid reviews are available surveying this field (see, for example, Baron and Sternberg, 1987; Chipman, Segal and Glaser, 1985; Segal, Chipman and Glaser, 1985; Nickerson, Perkins and Smyth, 1985). It is fair to say, though, that systematic evaluation of the available programmes is scarce.

In this section of the book there are four chapters addressing the issue of teaching thinking skills. One of their recurring themes is the role of *metacognition*. This, in common with many other psychological concepts, has a long tradition but a relatively short history. It entered the psychological literature around 1970 and it has been gaining popularity ever since, despite the difficulty concerning its definition and its delimitation from other concepts such as consciousness. Generally speaking, metacognition refers to knowledge about cognition itself, cognizing about cognition—thus, *meta*cognition. A closely linked concept to metacognition is that of the cognitive executive.

There are a number of prevailing reasons why metacognition is a central concept when one attempts to teach thinking skills. The cognitive processes involved within the overall framework of thinking include problem solving, decision making, evaluation and critical thinking, to name just a few. They are goal-orientated, motivated and often require commitment and effort over a considerable period of time. To some extent these processes are accessible to monitoring by the individual thinker and open to modification through experience. If one can diagnose cognitive deficiencies and identify the mechanisms likely to inhibit successful problem solving—such as impulsiveness, set and functional fixedness—then it should be possible to correct them through training and feedback. This requires the individual thinker to become aware of his or her own thinking processes and in addition to have knowledge about the nature of the thinking process itself. Several studies in which subjects were encouraged simply to reflect on their problem solving (that is, to engage in metacognitive activity) revealed this to have had a beneficial effect on performance (cf. Dörner, 1984).

One of the main exponents of metacognition, Brown (1987), considers that effective problem solving is based on evoking different forms of executive decision making. There is evidence that improving executive decision making will bring about an improvement in cognitive performance. Sternberg (1979) suggested that individual differences in executive functions may contribute to corresponding differences in intellectual performance. In his triarchic model of intelligence, he views metacomponents as being used to plan, monitor and evaluate activities, and he states that 'they are responsible for the higher-order information processing that is needed in order to regulate human mental functioning'. Sternberg, then, sees the metacomponents as instructors to the performance components, which then attempt to accomplish what the meta-components dictate needs to be carried out.

McGuinness' chapter is a theoretical analysis of the different attempts to teach thinking skills. She subdivides the current attempts into three groups, characterized by different antecedent traditions: the cognitive tradition which has a main emphasis on the information processing approach, critical thinking and knowledge restructuring with roots in constructivism. She points out that all three groups attempt to modify metacognition by the processes of *cognitive apprenticeship* and *cognitive modelling*. This involves the use of another person as a mediator in teaching thinking. As she puts it: 'The emphasis shifted from the metacognitions of the sole learner to the metacognitions of dyads, triads, and more; from reflection upon one's own thinking to dialogues about thought processes in the context of social interactions.'

The three empirical programmes reported here (Clark and Palm; Dominowski; Seagull and Erdos) have in common that they had a more limited objective than some of the more extensive programmes reported in the literature, in that they addressed specific target populations. This enabled them, however, to select specific aspects of certain thinking-skills training programmes and to put these to empirical test. While the results of each of them have to be treated with some caution, owing to methodological considerations, the overall picture which emerges is a positive one. If the objectives are clearly specified, individuals' thinking skills can be made more efficient with training.

Clark and Palm used an approach based mainly on Feuerstein's Instrumental Enrichment (Feuerstein *et al.*, 1980) to diagnose and correct cognitive deficiencies of industrial managers. They stress the point that 'training in metacognition is possibly one of the most useful areas in management training' and that exercises used in a programme for teaching thinking skills should be directly relevant to the work of the participants.

Dominowski undertook a two-pronged approach to study the improvement of undergraduates' problem solving ability. He investigated the effects of giving reasons for certain moves while solving problems and the impact of knowledge about cognition in general, gained through a course in cognitive psychology. Monitoring one's cognitive processes and relating this verbally to an observer has also been referred to as verbalizing or generating problem solving protocols. It is essentially a metacognitive activity and its impact on problem solving activity can be evaluated. Dominowski's evaluation of verbalizing links in closely with McGuinness' discussion of talking about thinking.

Seagull and Erdos describe a six-week intensive applied problem solving course intended as a science remediation programme within a college preparatory course for adult developmental students. Using an approach modified from Whimbey and Lochhead (1982), they also put a heavy emphasis on verbalizing and cognitive monitoring.

While the proliferation and diversity of the programmes for teaching thinking skills may baffle the uninitiated, it is nevertheless a testimony to the serious intention of psychology to convert theory into application. All the four papers presented here indicate that this area in the field of thinking is a vibrant one and that there is a promise of further progress.

REFERENCES

Baron, J. B., & Sternberg, R. J. (eds.) (1987). *Teaching thinking skills: Theory and practice.* Hillsdale, NJ: Erlbaum.

Brown, A. (1987). Metacognition, executive control, self-regulation, and other more mysterious mechanisms. In F. E. Weinert & R. H. Kluwe (eds.), *Metacognition, motivation and understanding* (pp. 65–116). Hillsdale, NJ: Erlbaum.

Chipman, S. F., Segal, J. W., & Glaser, R. (eds.) (1985). *Thinking and learning skills: Research and open questions.* Hillsdale, NJ: Erlbaum.

Dörner, D. (1984). Self-reflection and problem-solving. In F. Klix (ed.), *Human and artificial intelligence* (pp. 101–107). Amsterdam: North Holland.

Feuerstein, R., Rand, Y., Hoffman, M. B., & Miller, R. (1980). *Instrumental enrichment: An intervention for cognitive modifiability.* Baltimore, MD: University Park Press.

Nickerson, R. S., Perkins, D. N., & Smyth, E. E. (1985). *The teaching of thinking.* Hillsdale, NJ: Erlbaum.

Segal, J. W., Chipman, S. F., & Glaser, R. (eds.) (1985). *Thinking and learning skills: Relating instruction to research*. Hillsdale, NJ: Erlbaum.
Sternberg, R. J. (1979). The nature of mental abilities. *American Psychologist*, **34**, 214–230.
Whimbey, A., & Lochhead, J. (1982). *Problem solving and comprehension*. Philadelphia, PA: The Franklin Institute Press.

20

Talking About Thinking: The Role of Metacognition in Teaching Thinking

Carol McGuinness
The Queen's University, Belfast

INTRODUCTION AND OVERVIEW

Recently, a great deal of interest has been expressed in the task of promoting and enhancing thinking skills across the whole school system, at primary, secondary and tertiary levels. It stems from the realization that there is more to learning than rote memory and the routine application of familiar procedures and more to knowledge acquisition that the transmission of facts. It we want learners to engage in higher-order thinking, we cannot suppose that they will induce it from a content-based curriculum. We must make clear what we mean by higher-order thinking and then set out to teach it explicitly. Some excellent reviews and edited papers on these attempts to teach thinking, and on their research base, are now available (Baron and Sternberg, 1987; Bransford *et al.*, 1986; Chipman, Segal and Glaser, 1985; Glaser, 1984; Segal, Chipman and Glaser, 1985; Nickerson, Perkins and Smyth, 1985). Also available are a selection of curriculum materials to help instructors design and implement thinking courses in educational settings (Bransford and Stein, 1984; Hayes, 1981; Feuerstein *et al.*, 1980; Lipman, Sharp and Oscanyan, 1980; Whimbey and Lochhead, 1981). Much of this effort has come from the United States, although, in Great Britain, a set of curriculum materials, the Somerset Thinking Skills Course, has recently been published (Blagg, Ballinger and Gardner, 1988). Also, by far the largest scale effort to enhance thinking has been conducted in the Venezuelan school system at all levels (Dominguez, 1985; Hernstein *et al.*, 1986). Many writers view this emphasis on the process of thinking—compared with the product of thinking—as the curriculum reform movement of the 1980s. It is not the purpose of this chapter to evaluate the relative strengths and weaknesses of these different courses; that has been adequately done in many of the above publications. Rather, the goal of the chapter is to examine the instructional methods used in this new curriculum and, in particular, to explore the role of metacognition and metacognitive tools. Most thinking skills courses rely on enhancing metacognitive skills to a greater or lesser extent. But, over the years, the role of metacognition has been made more explicit and the variety of metacognitive tools has increased. Moreover, there is increasing recognition of the essential social nature of much metacognitive activity which, in turn, has led to theorizing about the role of social interaction and modelling as a mediator in cognitive change. For these reasons I would like (1) to trace the explicit and implicit role of metacognition in current attempts to teach thinking; (2) to describe examples of how metacognitive tools are used as instructional aids; and (3) to articulate a model of instruction and cognitive change which is captured in the notion of *cognitive apprenticeship*.

Promoting metacognitive activity is now accepted as the main tool for modifying both general and domain-specific thinking. Yet the concept of metacognition itself is not easy to define, even by those who coined the term (Brown, 1987; Flavell, 1987). It refers loosely to knowledge about, and control over, one's own cognitive system. Conclusions from metacognitive studies indicate that mature thinkers differ from novice thinkers because they have greater knowledge about when and how to use their cognitive resources. The methods used to study metacognition are self-assessment questionnaires, pre- or post-experimental questioning about the strategies used to complete cognitive tasks, and concurrent thinking-aloud protocols from which components of self-regulation can be observed. All the methods rely heavily on the person's verbalisations—or talk—as the main source of data about metacognitions, as indeed do training studies designed to enhance metacognitive skills (see, for example, Belmont, Butterfield and Ferretti, 1982; Flower and Hayes, 1980; Schoenfeld, 1982). Not only has metacognition become the prime target for enhancing thinking, but the methods of metacognitive research—talking about thinking—have become tools for instruction as well. I am calling this general trend the 'Talking about Thinking Movement' and it might appear to the naive observer that talking about thinking was sufficient for changing it! However, when current attempts to teach thinking are reviewed it will become clear that there is more to talking about thinking than casual conversation.

Talking about thinking takes many different forms. In order to explain these I shall examine three traditions in cognitive instruction which are influenced by different philosophical and epistemological viewpoints, have different ideas about the type of cognitive change they are trying to achieve, and are often critical of one another. Despite their differences, their practices to implement cognitive change are remarkably similar. The first of these traditions I shall call 'cognitive strategies' and it is most clearly influenced by ideas and concepts from cognitive psychology. The second tradition can be labelled 'critical thinking' and finds its origins in philosophers' discussions on informal logic and applied philosophy. Lastly, 'knowledge restructuring' owes much to the epistemological viewpoint of constructivism and has been concerned largely with domain-specific thinking, particularly in maths and science. Knowledge restructuring is also the concern of those cognitive scientists who study the development of expertise.

METACOGNITION AND COGNITIVE STRATEGIES

The theoretical roots of the attempts to teach thinking within this tradition are very influenced by the information-processing model of cognition in its many guises. Some of these attempts predate the current rise in cognitive psychology's interest in instruction, some are a direct result of it, while others have roots in slightly different traditions. Whatever the differences, they share the belief that if learners are encouraged to externalize thought process, if they are exposed to better patterns of thinking through direct verbal explanation, discussion, or modelling by expert thinkers, they will eventually internalize the new thought patterns and become better thinkers. Sternberg's (1986) *Intelligence applied* is a good example of a thinking course in the information-processing tradition. It is based on his componential model of human cognition, the triarchic model. According to this model thinking consists of information-processing components which serve different functions. Performance components are used to execute a task, knowledge acquisition components are used for learning new information, and metacomponents are engaged in planning, monitoring and evaluating performance on a task. Metacomponents essentially tell other components what to do. The course consists of training in all three types of components but, in comparison with other courses, *Intelligence applied* is very explicit about the role of metacognition. The method of instruction advised is verbal description of what is metacognitive knowledge, together with examples which demonstrate the benefits of planning, monitoring etc., and practical exercises. In general, this course encourages students to be more reflective about their own thought processes. A similar stance is adopted by Hayes (1981) in *The complete problem solver*, and by Bransford and Stein (1984) in *The IDEAL problem solver*. In contrast, Whimbey and Lochhead (1981) advocate a more systematic way of making thought processes explicit, through pair problem-solving. Their course on analytical reasoning and problem-solving puts great emphasis on precision in reasoning; they aim to eliminate errors caused by failure to observe and use all the facts, by jumping to premature conclusions and by not checking sufficiently for accuracy. To help students overcome these inadequacies they adopt the instructional procedure called pair problem-solving. Students think aloud as they solve well-defined problems in the presence of a listener-critic (usually a fellow student) who monitors the adequacy of the thinking. Students act both as problem-solvers and as listener-critics. Hence, they are provided both with an opportunity to make their own thought processes explicit as well as to listen to and monitor other students' thinking. The goal is to enhance thinking through metacognitive awareness. Although Whimbey and Lochhead also use descriptions of experts solving the same problems, they primarily use the students' peer-group as an instructional aid.

The explicit use of the 'other' as a mediator in the enhancement of cognitive strategies is central to Feuerstein's Instrumental Enrichment programme (Feuerstein *et al.*, 1980). Instrumental Enrichment is a specific application of Feuerstein's *et al.*'s more general approach to cognitive development. (The Somerset Thinking Skills' Course is a modification of Instrumental Enrichment). Feuerstein's approach centres on the concept of mediated learning experiences.

Cognitive mediation means that some agent (normally an adult) intentionally influences the interaction between the learner and the environment in a way that facilitates the learner's ability to organize and interpret it. Cognitive deficit is the result of 'mediation deprivation' which can be compensated for through systematic mediation intervention at a later stage. Instrumental Enrichment is designed to do just this. It consists of the intensive study of a series of progressively demanding exercises that provide the context for mediation. The teacher plays a critical role in a mediated learning session, exploring problem definitions, encouraging students to evaluate their strategies, helping them develop a language for discussing their thought processes, as well as engaging in bridging exercises to encourage transfer. The teacher's role is to intentionally facilitate the student to 'think about thinking' by talking about thinking.

The use of an expert adult as an explicit mediator of learning has been well developed in Palincsar and Brown's (1984) work on fostering reading comprehension strategies. Reciprocal teaching, as it is called, takes place in a cooperative learning group and consists of guided practice in applying the specific strategies of questioning, clarifying, summarizing, and predicting, to the task of text comprehension. A teacher and a group of students take turns at leading a discussion on a piece of text which they are jointly trying to understand. The teacher initially leads the group, actively models the desired comprehension strategies, and makes them overt, explicit and concrete. Then, each student takes a turn at modelling the strategies and leading the ensuing discussion. Gradually, the responsibility for the comprehension activities is transferred to the group and the teacher's role fades into the background. In reciprocal teaching the teacher acts as a mediator in two ways, as a model of expert performance as well as a scaffold or social support for the under-developed attempts of the novice. Brown (1986) reports that reciprocal teaching produces better results than either direct instruction in the desired strategies or even teacher modelling alone. Clearly, the use of an expert as a mediator for learning should not be haphazard if it is to produce maximum effect.

In summary, many methods for increasing metacognitive awareness are currently being used to promote thinking within the cognitive strategies tradition. Increasingly, there is a reliance on social interaction with fellow students or expert adults, both as facilitators for making thought processes explicit and as mediators in cognitive development.

METACOGNITION AND CRITICAL THINKING

Although attempts to enhance cognitive strategies and critical thinking have much in common, they originate from different theoretical traditions and have different emphases. In many respects the critical thinking movement is the more radical in its approach. It claims to be at 'the heart and core of educational reform' (Paul, 1985). Critical thinking, according to Ennis (1987), is 'reasonable reflective thinking that is focused on deciding what to believe and do' (p. 10). Since Ennis' (1962) discussion paper on the nature of critical thinking, there has been a lot of debate on the relationship between critical thinking and higher-order thinking skills (Presseisen, 1986). The main difference centres on the truth value of what to think (critical thinking) compared with the successful execution of strategies and procedures (cognitive strategies). Paul (1984) has distinguished between two conceptions of critical thinking. In a weak sense, he argues that critical thinking can be understood as a set of 'discrete micro-logical' skills which are extrinsic to the person and can be tacked on to other forms of learning, like a shopping list of new skills. Much of the teaching of cognitive strategies can be regarded as focusing on critical thinking in the weak sense (Paul, 1987). In contrast, critical thinking in the strong sense constitutes a frame of mind which is intrinsic to the character of the person and is fundamental to education in a free society. It has to do with the development of 'emancipatory reason' and is essential to the free, rational, and autonomous mind. So, the goals of critical thinking instruction are explicitly stated in terms of societal consequences as much as in terms of individual learning. What is to be believed does not depend on the authority of the source, but rather on the coherence of the arguments presented, their internal consistency, and the correspondence between arguments and available data. Hence, the critical thinker must be able to analyse arguments, identify assumptions, judge credibility, spot logical errors in inferences, and so on. How are such critical thinking skills to be developed?

The best example of a well-developed critical thinking skills course is Lipman's (1980, 1985) *Philosophy for children* and it takes a very novel approach to promoting metacognitive awareness. *Philosophy for children* is clearly not designed to teach philosophy to children but rather to enable learners to think philosophically. A mature critical thinker will have been raised with a spirit of reasonableness and in a community of inquiry. Lipman (1987) uses the Socratic framework and points to dialogue as the medium through which this spirit of reasonableness can be fostered. He has written works of fiction for children and adolescents in which characters figure out for themselves laws of reasoning, produce counterexamples, look for evidence for points of view, and, in general, argue in a philosophical way. The works themselves are about children talking and thinking about thinking. They are intended to provide a model, and indeed a language, for discussing thinking which can be exploited by the teacher in the classroom. Lipman has strong views on how philosophical discussion should be guided and proposes that teachers should be taught in the manner in which they are expected to teach! Lipman exploits dialogue in two ways, by modelling philosophical dialogue in the written works and by structuring classroom activity in ways which promote dialogue (for a critique, see Bransford *et al.*, 1985). It is Lipman's intention not just to model successful strategies for thinking, but also to create an educational atmosphere where a critical attitude and critical discourse is not only tolerated but actively pursued.

From the metacognitive point of view, the innovation in Lipman's work is the introduction of works of fiction as cognitive supports for both learner and teacher, and the use of a Socratic framework for conducting dialogue. In the Socratic framework the teacher helps the learner bring to light what he or she already knows and both partners explore and discover knowledge together. There are strong parallels between Socratic dialogue, reciprocal teaching and concepts of mediated learning.

METACOGNITION AND KNOWLEDGE RESTRUCTURING

A third tradition in current concerns about teaching thinking is deeply embedded in constructivist epistemology which has had its main influence on teaching thinking within specific subject domains. Advocated mainly by educational theorists, particularly science educators, the empirical work (if not the philosophical viewpoint) now finds common ground with cognitive psychologists and cognitive scientists who study the development of expertise (Carey, 1986). Constructivist epistemology is often contrasted with logical positivism and empiricism (Novak, 1987b) which holds that 'true' knowledge corresponds to how the world really works—the goal of knowing is to discover this true knowledge. In contrast, constructivism contends that knowledge is the invention of human minds and to gain knowledge is to manoeuvre through a series of conceptual structures. A constructivist viewpoint in education considers the learner as an active purveyor of meaning, and sees instruction as negotiation between two sets of conceptual structures—the teacher's and the learner's (Cobb, 1988; Pope, 1985). Thinking is essentially about sense-making. The goal of enhancing thinking within this tradition is about knowledge restructuring, not about teaching skills and strategies.

Using the Piagetian framework as a point of departure, there is widespread agreement that learners 'actively construct an individual world view based upon personal observation and experience and that they respond to formal instruction in terms of this pre-existing intuitive perspective' (Linn, 1986, p. 6). The implications of this statement for the teaching of science are far-reaching because learners actively assimilate new information with their own naive, and often erroneous, intuitive ideas. As Carey (1986) commented, there is now a 'highly productive cottage industry' documenting students' misconceptions, naive models, or alternative frameworks in maths, physics, chemistry, biology and economics (see Novak, 1987a, which is three volumes of proceedings from a recent conference on misconceptions, and a bibliography by Pfundt and Duit, 1988). The general finding is that students have naive conceptions of natural, and artefactual, phenomena which are highly resistant to change even after extensive formal instruction. Learners are not aware that their conceptions are at odds with the formal conceptions within the discipline, and, even more disastrously, neither are teachers. Teaching fails because the two participants in the learning process are failing to communicate (Cobb, 1988). The initial research interest focused on the content of specific scientific concepts, but there is increasing recognition that understanding can fail because of alternative meta-conceptions about the nature of science itself as well as about the nature of the learning process (Saljo, 1987).

Within the constructivist framework, teachers need to find ways to externalize these misconceptions and to facilitate cognitive change. Once again the burden falls on tools to increase metacognitive awareness. But naive conceptions are peculiarly resistant to diagnosis through self-reflection alone, and a number of more indirect methods have been developed to probe them into awareness (West and Pines, 1985). For example, Gilbert, Watts and Osborne (1985) use an interview-about-instances technique where students have to justify why some pictures are instances of a concept and others are not. Also, there are a number of concept-mapping and diagramming techniques developed by Novak and his colleagues (Novak, 1985) where students are trained to make their conceptions more explicit by organizing their concepts into network diagrams. While these techniques were initially developed for research purposes they are now used in the classroom to diagnose students' conceptions, to facilitate self-reflection, and to monitor change.

Diagnosing alternative conceptions is one thing, inducing conceptual change is another. As with changing cognitive strategies, many writers initially felt that reflection on misconceptions might be sufficient to change them. But more direct interventions are now being advocated, which give a special role to the teacher. Drawing on the analogy of conceptual change in the history of science, Posner *et al.* (1982) propose that students must feel dissatisfied with their current conceptions before they are likely to change them. Dissatisfactions can be induced by presenting students with anomalies so that they experience cognitive conflict. Cognitive conflict is proposed as the mechanism for change. In dialogues with students, they suggest that teachers should adopt an adversarial role, in the sense of being a Socratic tutor. Moreover, they should provide a model of scientific thinking which demonstrates a demand for consistency among beliefs, between theory and evidence, and so on. Champagne, Gunstone and Klopfer (1985) have shown how a number of different types of interactive teacher–student dialogues might work in the context of teaching mechanics. And indeed, it seems that expert teachers do adopt this style of teaching. Collins and Stevens (1982) report that inquiry teachers, as they call them, enable students to debug their current conceptions and move on to higher levels of knowledge and understanding, through the strategic use of interrogation and confrontation. Socrates rules again—it seems.

MODELS FOR INSTRUCTION AND COGNITIVE CHANGE

Whatever we may know about the components of good general thinking skills or about the nature of expertise, it is clear from the preceding discussion that the leap to instruction is still not easy. The instructional procedures which I have loosely called 'talking about thinking'—pair problem-solving, teacher modelling, scaffolding, reciprocal teaching, Socratic dialogue, concept-mapping, inquiry teaching—are not the most coherent list from which to infer a model of instruction. Yet, there is a recurrent theme. All efforts rely on talk in the context of social interaction as a means for promoting thinking. But it is a very special kind of talk which depends as much on the metacognitions of the teacher as of the learner. In a similar analysis of the cultivation of thinking, Resnick (1987, p. 432) says:

'When investigators of different theoretical orientations and disciplinary backgrounds converge in this way on a common prescription, it is worth considering what roles social interaction may be playing.'

The concept of mediation appears central to the role which social interaction plays in cognitive change. Mediation implies that the roots of cognitive change and development lie outside the immediate interaction between the learner and the environment. Mediation is well articulated in Feuerstein's Instrumental Enrichment programme, it is at the heart of reciprocal teaching and is echoed in the notions of Socratic dialogue and inquiry teaching. Vygotsky (1978) is rightly acknowledged by many writers as the father of this mediating view of cognitive development. Vygotsky proposed that learning involved internalizing activities originally witnessed and practised in cooperative group settings. He believed that higher mental functions first appear on the interpsychological or social plane and only later on the intrapsychological or individual plane. But, Wertsch (1979), a neo-Vygotskian, points out that researchers in the West have paid little attention to this transition from the interpsychological to the intrapsychological. Yet, it is the crux of the matter as far as current attempts to teach thinking are concerned.

So, what role does social interaction play in facilitating this transition? Resnick (1987) identifies some possibilities. First, she suggests that social interaction provides a model for effective thinking. Second, she says that the social setting provides a scaffold whereby learners initially depend on the expert but gradually take over limited aspects of the performance themselves before becoming completely independent learners and thinkers. Lastly, she hints that to promote thinking skills in social settings may have a profound effect on the learner because it encourages a disposition for critical thought such that talking about thinking becomes an acceptable form of social discourse. The way in which experts model and scaffold a teacher-learner interaction has been characterized by Collins, Seely-Brown and Newman (1987) as *cognitive apprenticeship*. In contrast with conventional schooling, where instruction is primarily didactic, the methods of cognitive apprenticeship are observation, coaching, and successive approximation in the context of ongoing tasks. The concepts involved are modelling, scaffolding and fading—while the learner moves from other-regulation to self-regulation. In their critique of current pedagogical practice, Collins *et al.* (1987) argue that 'skills and knowledge taught in schools have become abstracted from their uses in the world' (p. 1) and that 'standard pedagogical practices render aspects of expertise invisible to students' (p. 2). They point out that cognitive apprenticeship methods may prove powerful precisely because they require experts to externalize the mental processes they are using to comprehend, to categorize and to problem-solve in the context of meaningful and ongoing tasks. Students are given access, not only to conceptual and factual knowledge, but also to the strategic, and often tacit, knowledge of the expert performer. 'It is this dual focus on expert processes and situated learning that we expect to help solve the educational problems of brittle skills and inert knowledge' (p. 4). Collins *et al.* contrast cognitive apprenticeship with formal schooling which, they remind us, emerged only in the last century as a widespread method for education. They point out that apprenticeship is still the main method used to educate many professional groups, for example, in medicine, law, and the arts. Also, the everyday skills of language use and social interaction are acquired through informal apprenticeship methods. They advocate the 'retooling' of apprenticeship methods for the teaching and learning of cognitive skills.

But there is another sense in which a model can act as a facilitator of cognitive change which is not fully exploited in the cognitive apprenticeship characterization. Gilhooly (1987) has recently proposed the idea of mental modelling as a unifying concept for a wide range of cognitive activities (problem-solving, concept formation, logical reasoning, and even day-dreaming) and it bears further examination as a vehicle for instruction, particularly with regard to subject matter teaching. As we have seen, students develop naive models or conceptions. As they become expert, their naive concepts change and become more sophisticated but may still only approximate the full scientific conception. Glaser (1984, 1987) proposes that these transitory or temporary conceptions can act as "pedagogical theories" and can themselves be the target of instruction. Whatever the merits of Glaser's proposal, there is little doubt that tracing transitory stages in the development of domain-specific concepts so that they become pedagogical theories is a daunting task and may be accomplished in the long run. But a more immediate way forward had been outlined by Perkins (1986, 1987) in his analysis of *Knowledge as design*. Consistent with constructivist epistemology, Perkins argues for a radical rethink by educators about the nature of knowledge and how it is acquired. Knowledge is design, not information. If learners are made more aware of the role of models in the development of knowledge, then they will become more sensitive to the design-like and model-making nature of their own thinking. In *Knowledge as design*, Perkins sets out to show how any subject matter can be taught by organizing instruction around four basic design questions.

In summary, models can serve as mediators of cognitive change in several ways. A model can be an expert person to be mimicked (cognitive apprenticeship); or it can be a mental model which is itself the target for instruction (models as pedagogical theories); or it can be an overarching epistemological principle which provides a context for exploring the nature of knowledge and the nature of learning itself (knowledge as design). In any of the above meanings, the task of identifying the teacher–learner dialogues which use models to promote and build both general and domain-specific thinking has hardly begun.

CONCLUSIONS

This chapter began with an exploration of the metacognitive tools currently used to enhance and promote thinking skills. It ends with a characterization of instruction which can best be termed as cognitive apprenticeship and modelling. The emphasis shifted from the metacognitions of the sole learner to the metacognitions of dyads, triads, and more; from reflection upon one's own thinking to dialogues about thought processes in the context of social interactions. Although a host of questions remain to be answered about the validity and generalizability of the method of cognitive apprenticeship and the theory of cognitive development which it entails, the terrain is already being mapped out. Collins, Seely-Brown and Newman (1987) point to three cognitive apprenticeship 'success' models—Palincsar and Brown's (1984) reciprocal teaching for reading comprehension, Scardamalia, Bereiter and Steinbach's (1984) pro-cedural facilitation in writing compositions, and Schoenfeld's (1985) method of teaching mathematical problem-solving. And there are other examples which explore the influence of peer tutoring and peer collaboration (Forman and Cazden, 1985). A research agenda has been set in terms of the microscopic analysis (videotape/audiotape) of teacher–learner dialogues and peer interac-tions which enhance thinking processes. Also, Wertsch and others (Wertsch, 1985) are developing Vygotsky's developmental theory and applying it to educational settings in such a way that we may yet have a theory of cognitive development which can accommodate a theory of instruction.

REFERENCES

Baron, J. B., & Sternberg, R. J. (eds.), (1987). *Teaching thinking skills: Theory and practice.* New York: Freeman.

Belmont, J. M., Butterfield, E. C., & Ferretti, R. J. (1982). To secure transfer of training instruct self-management skills. In D. K. Detterman & R. J. Sternberg (eds.), *How and how much can intelligence be increased* (pp. 147–154). Norwood, NJ: Ablex.

Blagg, N., Ballinger, M., & Gardner, R. (1988). *Somerset thinking skills course: Handbook.* Oxford: Basil Blackwell.

Bransford, J. D., Arbitman-Smith, R., Stein, B., & Vye, N. J. (1985). Improving thinking and learning skills: an analysis of three approaches. In J. W. Segal, S. F. Chipman & R. Glaser (eds.), *Thinking and learning skills: Relating instruction to research,* Vol. 1 (pp. 133–206). Hillsdale, NJ: Erlbaum.

Bransford, J., Sherwood, R., Vye, N., & Rieser, J. (1986). Teaching thinking and problem-solving: research foundations. *American Psychologist,* **41,** 1078–1086.

Bransford, J. D., & Stein, B. S. (1984). *The IDEAL problem solver.* New York: Freeman.

Brown, A. (1987). Metacognition, executive control, self-regulation and other more mysterious mechanisms. In F. E. Weinert & R. H. Kluwe (eds.), *Metacognition, motivation, and understanding* (pp. 65–116). Hillsdale, NJ: Erlbaum.

Carey, S. (1986). Cognitive science and science education. *American Psychologist,* **41,** 1123–1130.

Champagne, A. B., Gunstone, R. E., & Klopfer, L. E. (1985). Instructional consequences of students' knowledge about physical phenomena. In L. H. T. West & A. L. Pines (eds.), *Cognitive structure and conceptual change* (pp. 61–90). Orlando: Academic Press.

Chipman, S. F., Segal, J. W., & Glaser, R. (eds.) (1985). *Thinking and learning skills: Research and open questions,* Vol. 2. Hillsdale, NJ: Erlbaum.

Cobb, P. (1988). The tension between theories of learning and instruction in mathematics education. *Educational Psychologist,* **23,** 87–103.

Collins, A., Seely-Brown, J., & Newman, S. E. (1987). *Cognitive apprenticeship: Teaching the craft of reading, writing, and mathematics* (ONR technical report 6459). Cambridge, MA: BBN Laboratories.

Collins, A., & Stevens, A. L. (1982). Goals and strategies of inquiry teachers. In R. Glaser (ed.), *Advances in instructional psychology,* Vol. 2. Hillsdale, NJ: Erlbaum.

Dominguez, J. (1985). The development of human intelligence: the Venezuelan case. In J. W. Segal, S. F. Chipman & R. Glaser (eds.), *Thinking and learning skills: Relating instruction to research,* Vol. 1, (pp. 529–536). Hillsdale, NJ: Erlbaum.

Ennis, R. H. (1962). A concept of critical thinking. *Harvard Educational Review,* **32,** 81–111.

Ennis, R. H. (1987). A taxonomy of critical thinking dispositions and abilities. In J. B. Baron & R. J. Sternberg (eds.), *Teaching thinking skills: Theory and practice* (pp. 9–26). New York: Freeman.

Feuerstein, R., Rand, Y., Hoffman, M. B. & Miller, R. (1980). *Instrumental enrichment: An intervention for cognitive modifiability.* Baltimore, MD: University Park Press.

Flavell, J. H. (1987). Speculations about the nature and development of metacognition. In F. E. Weinert & R. H. Kluwe (eds.), *Metacognition, motivation, and understanding* (pp. 21–29). Hillsdale, NJ: Erlbaum.

Flower, L. S. & Hayes, J. R. (1980). The dynamics of composing: making plans and juggling constraints. In L. Gregg & E. Steinberg (eds.), *Cognitive processes in writing: An interdisciplinary approach* (pp. 31–50). Hillsdale, NJ: Erlbaum.

Forman, E. A. & Cazden, C. B. (1985). Exploring Vygotskian perspectives in education: the cognitive value of peer interaction. In J. V. Wertsch (ed.), *Culture, communication, and cognition: Vygotskian perspectives* (pp. 323–347). Cambridge: Cambridge University Press.

Gilbert, J. K., Watts, D. M., & Osborne, R. J. (1985). Eliciting views using an interview-about-instances technique. In L. H. T. West & A. L. Pines (eds.), *Cognitive structure and conceptual change* (pp. 11–27). Orlando: Academic Press.

Gilhooly, K. J. (1987). Mental modelling: a framework for thinking. In D. N. Perkins, J. Lochhead & J. C. Bishop, (eds.), *Thinking: The second international conference* (pp. 19–32). Hillsdale, NJ: Erlbaum.

Glaser, R. (1984). Education and thinking: the role of thinking. *American Psychologist*, **39**, 93–104.

Glaser, R. (1987). Learning theory and theories of knowledge. In E. De Corte, H. Lodewijks, R. Parmentier & P. Span (eds.), *Learning and instruction*, Vol. 1 (pp. 397–414). Pergamon/Lueven University Press.

Hayes, J. R. (1981). *The complete problem solver*. Philadelphia, PA: The Franklin Institute Press.

Hernstein, R. J., Nickerson, R. S., De Sanchez, M., & Swets, J. A. (1986). Teaching thinking skills. *American Psychologist*, **41**, 1279–1289.

Linn, M. C. (1986). Establishing a research base for science education: challenges, trends and recommendations. *Teaching Thinking and Problem Solving*, **8**, no. 5.

Lipman, M., Sharp, A. M. & Oscanyan, F. S. (1980). *Philosophy in the classroom*. Philadelphia: Temple University Press.

Lipman, M. (1985). Thinking skills fostered by Philosophy for Children. In J. W. Segal, S. F. Chipman & R. Glaser (eds.), *Thinking and learning skills: Relating instruction to research*, Vol. 1 (pp. 83–108). Hillsdale, NJ: Erlbaum.

Lipman, M. (1987). Some thoughts on the foundations of reflective education. In J. B. Baron & R. J. Sternberg (eds), *Teaching thinking skills: Theory and practice* (pp. 151–161). New York: Freeman.

Nickerson, R. S., Perkins, D. N., & Smyth, E. S. (1985). *The teaching of thinking*. Hillsdale, NJ: Erlbaum.

Novak, J. D. (1985). Metalearning and metaknowledge strategies to help students learn how to learn. In L. H. T. West & A. L. Pines (eds.), *Cognitive structure and conceptual change* (pp. 189–209). Orlando: Academic Press.

Novak, J. D. (ed.) (1987a). *Proceedings of the second international seminar: Misconceptions and educational strategies in science and mathematics*, Vols I, II & III, Ithaca, NY: Cornell University.

Novak, J. D. (1987b). Human constructivism: towards a unity of psychological and epistemological meaning making. In J.D. Novak (ed.), *Proceedings of the second international seminar: Misconceptions and educational strategies in science and mathematics*, Vol. I (pp. 349–360). Ithaca, NY: Cornell University.

Palincsar, A. S., & Brown, A. L. (1984). Reciprocal teaching of comprehension-fostering and monitoring strategies. *Cognition and Instruction*, **1**, 117–175.

Paul, R. (1984). Critical thinking: fundamental to education in a free society. *Educational Leadership*, **42**, 4–14.

Paul, R. (1985). The heart and core of education reform. *Teaching Thinking and Problem Solving*, **7**, no. 7.

Paul, R. W. (1987). Dialogical thinking: critical thought essential to the acquisition of rational knowledge and passions. In J. B. Baron & R. J. Sternberg (eds.), *Teaching thinking skills: Theory and practice* (pp. 127–148). New York: Freeman.

Perkins, D. N. (1986). Knowledge as design. Hillsdale, NJ: Erlbaum.

Perkins, D. N. (1987). Knowledge as design: teaching thinking through content. In J. B. Baron & R. J. Sternberg (eds.), *Teaching thinking skills: Theory and practice* (pp. 62–85). New York: Freeman.

Pfundt, H., & Duit, R. (1988). *Bibliography: Students' alternative frameworks and science education* (2nd edn). Kiel: Institute for Science Education.

Pope, M. (1985). *Constructivist goggles: Implications for process in teaching and learning.* Invited paper presented to the British Educational Research Association, Sheffield.

Posner, G. J., Strike, K. A., Hewson, P. W. & Gertzog, W. A. (1982). Accommodation of a scientific conception: toward a theory of conceptual change. *Science Education,* **66**, 211–227.

Presseisen, B. Z. (1986). Critical thinking and thinking skills: state of the art definitions and practice in public schools. *Teaching Thinking and Problem Solving,* **8**, no. 4.

Resnick, L. B. (1987). Instruction and the cultivation of thinking. In E. De Corte, H. Lodewijks, R. Parmentier & P. Span (eds.), *Learning and instruction,* Vol. 1 (pp. 415–441). Pergamon/Lueven University Press.

Saljo, R. (1987). The educational construction of learning. In J. T. Richardson, M. W. Eysenck & D. W. Piper (eds.), *Student learning: Research in education and cognitive psychology* (pp. 101–108). Milton Keynes: Society for Research into Higher Education /Open University Press.

Scardamalia, M., Bereiter, C., & Steinbach, R. (1984). Teachability of reflective processes in written composition. *Cognitive Science,* **8**, 173–190.

Schoenfeld, A. H. (1982). Measures of problem-solving performance and of problem solving instruction. *Journal for Research in Mathematics Education,* **13**, 31–49.

Schoenfeld, A. H. (1985). *Mathematical problem solving.* New York: Academic Press.

Segal, J. W., Chipman, S. F. & Glaser, R. (eds.) (1985). *Thinking and learning skills: Relating instruction to research,* Vol. 1. Hillsdale, NJ: Erlbaum.

Sternberg, R. J. (1986). *Intelligence applied.* San Diego: Harcourt, Brace & Jovanovich.

Sternberg, R. J. (1987). Teaching intelligence: the application of cognitive psychology to the improvement of intellectual skills. In J. B. Baron & R. J. Sternberg (eds.), *Teaching thinking skills: Theory and practice* (pp. 182–218). New York: Freeman.

Vygotsky, L. S. (1978). In M. Cole, V. John-Steiner, S. Scribner & E. Souberman (eds. and trans.), *Mind in society: The development of higher psychological processes.* Cambridge, MA: Harvard University Press.

Wertsch, J. V. (1979). From social interaction to higher psychological processes: a clarification and application of Vygotsky's theory. *Human Development,* **22**, 1–22.

Wertsch, J. V. (ed.) (1985). *Culture, communication and cognition: Vygotskian perspectives.* Cambridge: Cambridge University Press.

West, L. H. T., & Pines, A. L. (eds.) (1985). *Cognitive structure and conceptual change.* Orlando: Academic Press.

Whimbey, A., & Lochhead, J. (1981). *Problem solving and comprehension: A short course in analytical reasoning.* Philadelphia, PA; The Franklin Institute Press.

21

Problem Solving and Metacognition

ROGER L. DOMINOWSKI
University of Illinois, Chicago

INTRODUCTION

Problem solving is a difficult enterprise, one that often leads to failure. By definition, problems are challenging, troublesome situations for which appropriate behaviour is *not* obvious; the very notion of problem solving is that one must discover, with less than compelling cues, how to achieve the desired goal in the particular situation. One who studies problem solving thus observes a considerable number of failures to solve. This experience quite naturally leads to questions concerning why people fail to solve problems, or what might be done to help people to be more successful in solving problems.

Earlier attempts to facilitate problem solving were not encouraging; that is, there were multiple reports of failures to find positive transfer where it might be expected (see, for example, Duncan, 1961). These efforts were 'flawed' by expecting too much from a single problem-solving or training experience. Any task has both concrete, specific features and more general features shared with other tasks. It is more likely that a person, having completed a task, would encode the specific, rather than the general features. If so, transfer from one (specific) task to another (specific) task is unlikely if the tasks have many different features even though sharing some common (general) features. It would take repeated encounters with tasks having different specific features but the same common features for general positive transfer to occur. This is, of course, what the studies of learning to learn had shown (see, for example, Duncan, 1958; Harlow, 1949). More recent research by my students and myself has shown that a greater amount of varied, successful practice yields positive transfer with problems for which earlier studies suggested no such transfer was possible (Jacobs and Dominowski, 1981; Lung and Dominowski, 1985).

These notions apply in a straightforward manner to recent research concerned with analogical problem solving (application of the solution of one problem to

Lines of Thinking, Volume 2 Edited by K.J. Gilhooly, M.T.G. Keane, R.H. Logie and G. Erdos
© 1990 John Wiley & Sons Ltd

another problem). Even though successive problems have identical *abstract* structures, no inter-problem transfer is found unless experimenters take rather extreme steps to stress the connections (Gick, 1985; Gick and Holyoak, 1980, 1983; Keane, 1985; Reed, Ernst and Banerji, 1974). In brief, people tend to encode the concrete specifics of a problem rather than its more abstract generalities. Consistent with earlier work on learning-to-learn, learning-to-solve, and concept formation, experience with multiple, varied exemplars is needed before more abstract and general features or relations will govern behaviour. The implication is that solving by analogy (that is, the application of the solution for particular problem X to particular problem Y) is unlikely to be the basis of problem-solving skill.

Historically, two distinct attitudes toward general intellectual skills may be identified. Those who study problem solving have tended to be pessimistic, expecting little or no inter-problem transfer. In contrast, the psychometric tradition has emphasized very general 'abilities', the most general of which would be 'g'. In recent times, several variations of more moderate positions have evolved, and these form the basis of research and debate.

Metacognition is the prime candidate for the basis of transferable more-or-less general intellectual skills. The distinction is now commonly made between declarative knowledge about cognition and metacognitive or executive processing. The terms vary, but the distinction seems constant and appears to reflect the contrast between declarative and procedural knowledge. In what follows, I will use the terms 'metacognitive knowledge' and 'executive processing' to refer to these two categories.

The initial emphasis was on metacognitive knowledge, based on the idea that what one knows about cognition might determine how one performs on cognitive tasks (see, for example, Kreutzer, Leonard and Flavell, 1975). Recently, greater emphasis has been given to the role of executive processes (Borkowski, 1985; Brown, 1978; Lohman, 1986). The idea is that performance depends on the effectiveness of executive or control processes such as planning, monitoring, evaluating, and modifying (performance). There is empirical support for the proposal that effective thinking is related to metacognitive knowledge and executive processing, but there are also empirical weaknesses and conceptual difficulties (Bransford *et al.*, 1986; Cavanaugh and Borkowski, 1980; Cavanaugh and Perlmutter, 1982; Hayes, 1985; Lohman, 1986). Metacognition is not afforded a major role in all formulations; an alternative view is that intellectual skills are heavily domain-specific, with metacognition of little importance (see, for example, Glaser, 1984).

Granting the uncertainties, it nonetheless seems reasonable to pursue questions regarding the relation between metacognition and problem solving. The proposed relations are quite plausible, and they have at least some empirical support. Investigating various metacognition–problem solving relations allows assessment of the merit or power of the approach and should lead to more refined formulations. Emphasis on the importance of domain-specific knowledge need not rule out an important role for metacognition. Even if it should prove correct that real expertise hinges on domain-specific knowledge, acquired over many years and used rather automatically, metacognition could be an important source of improvements in problem solving that, while falling short of full-blown expertise, are still real and worthwhile. There is a clear difference between, say, improving one's skill in solving quantitative problems and becoming a professional mathematician, and such improvements may very well be the result of better metacognitive processing.

The research reported here consists of two studies, each concerned with a different aspect of metacognition and its relation to problem solving; one concerns executive processing and the other concerns metacognitive knowledge. In both cases, the attempt is made to alter metacognition and assess the effects on cognitive performance.

EFFECTS OF GIVING REASONS

In the literature on problem solving, there are several reports of positive effects on problem solving that stem from 'verbalizing'. The task was the Tower of Hanoi, or disc-transfer problem. There are three pegs, A, B and C, with n discs stacked in order of size (smallest on top) on peg A. The problem is to produce the identical stack on peg C by moving discs one at a time, moving a disc only from one peg to another, and never covering a disc with one larger than itself. The minimum number of necessary moves, and especially the actual number of excess moves taken by subjects, increases dramatically as the number of discs to be transferred increases from two to six. People who were required to 'verbalize' while working on the problems have consistently been found to make fewer excess moves than control subjects (Ahlum-Heath and DiVesta, 1986; Gagne and Smith, 1962; Stinessen, 1985), both while verbalizing and on later transfer tasks where verbalization was not required. Curiously, the activity has consistently been labelled 'verbalizing', but it has in fact always been 'giving reasons for moves'! Subjects' stated reasons tend to be prosaic, and their content does not suggest why reason-giving should benefit performance. A very plausible explanation is that the requirement to give reasons for actions taken promotes monitoring, planfulness, evaluation and attention to problem features, and the sharpening of such executive processes yields the more efficient performance.

This account received support in a recent study from our department. Again using the Tower of Hanoi problem, Kristovich (1988) found that giving reasons reduced excess moves on practice problems (2–5 discs) and a subsequent transfer task (6 discs), whether reasons were given while working on each practice problem or only after a practice task had been completed. In contrast, on-line thinking aloud or post-task general retrospection had no effect on performance, compared with a no-verbalization control group. These findings implicate deeper, executive processing as central to the facilitation, and suggest that the timing of the activity is less critical.

Requiring reasons is a straightforward technique, it seems to suggest promoting executive processing, and it has been found to work! One wonders if it would be effective with problems different from the Tower of Hanoi. One problem that college students (among others) find very difficult, especially in its basic, abstract form, is Wason's four-card task. To quickly illustrate the task: Subjects are told that each of four cards has a letter on one side and a number on the other; they are shown one side of each card and see, respectively, A, B, 3 and 4. They are given a rule (for example, 'If a card has a vowel, then it must have an even number') and they are asked to indicate which cards they need to turn over in order to determine if the rule is true or false. In general terms, the rule is of the form 'If p, then q', the four cards display p, not-p, not-q and q, and the correct answer is 'p and not-q (A and 3 in the example).

Performance on the abstract (letter–number rule) version of the task is typically miserable, with fewer than 10% correct responses, and the majority of attempts to modify (improve) performance have focused on changing the content of the problem to something more concrete, familiar or meaningful (see, for example, Griggs, 1983; Wason, 1983; Wason and Johnson-Laird, 1972). In the course of working on such content manipulations, I was led to wonder if performance on this difficult problem might be affected by reason-giving. That is, compared with simply making choices (of cards to test), would performance be changed—would it be improved—if subjects were required to give reasons for their choices? In the literature, there were suggestions that this might be the case; Berry (1983) as well as Hoch and Tschirgi (1985) had found improvement after reason-giving, but in both studies this activity was part of a more complex treatment (for example, providing solutions or explanations, opportunities to review and change answers). Hence, I decided to examine the influence of reason giving *per se*, using a number of versions, differing in content, of the four-card task.

The Method

Eight versions of the four-card task, expected to show some differences in difficulty, were used; each will be described briefly. In the descriptions, the types of information on the two sides of the cards are arbitrarily labelled (a) and (b); for example, in problem 1 each card had (a) a purchase amount on one side and (b) a space for signature on the other.

1) *Checking charge slips*. Each slip has (a) a purchase amount and (b) space for signature. The rule is: 'If the purchase is over $50, then the slip must be signed by the manager'. The cards show: $75[*], a signature, a blank signature space[*], $25 ([*] = correct 'cards' to check).

2) *Postal regulations*. Each 'envelope' has (a) a stamp and (b) is sealed or not. The rule is: 'if sealed, the envelope must have a 20-cent stamp'. The cards show: 20-cent stamp, 10-cent stamp[*], sealed envelope[*], unsealed envelope.

3) *Checking regulations*. Each card shows (a) whether or not action A was taken and (b) whether or not precondition P was met. The rule is: 'If one is to take action A, then one must first satisfy precondition p'. The cards show: has taken action A[*], has not taken action A, has met precondition P, has not met precondition P[*].

4) *Checking travel passes*. Each 'pass' has (a) A or B and (b) blue strip or no blue strip. The rule is: 'If a pass has a blue strip, then it must have the letter A'. The cards show: no blue strip, blue strip[*], A, B[*].

5) *Checking diet.* Each 'meal' has (a) a kind of meat and (b) a kind of vegetable. The rule is: 'If you eat beef, then you must eat a green vegetable'. The cards show: chicken, corn*, peas, beef*.

6) *Checking labels.* Each label has (a) a letter (b) a number. The rule is: 'If a label has a vowel, then it must have an odd number'. The cards show: F, 8*, 7, E*.

7) *Letter–number, basic.* Each card has (a) a letter and (b) a number. The rule is: 'If vowel, then even number'. The cards show: A*, B, 1*, 2.

8) *Letter–number, justified.* Same as letter–number basic, with different specifics, and preceded by a paragraph explaining why an arbitrary rule is being used.

Each problem was contained on a single sheet of paper, with boxes representing 'cards'; subjects were required to indicate for each card whether they did or did not need to 'turn it over'. In the 'reasons' condition, there was an additional instruction to write briefly the reason for each decision made, in a space provided next to each card.

A total of 112 female, introductory-psychology students participated, 64 in the 'reasons' condition and 48 in the control ('no-reasons') condition. Each student worked through a booklet containing five problems; different booklets were constructed and distributed such that each problem was attempted by 25–52 subjects in the 'reasons' condition, by 23–48 subjects in the control condition. Data were collected in small-group sessions; participants worked at their own pace, and time to complete the booklet was recorded.

Results and Discussion

As might be expected, subjects in the 'reasons' condition took longer (mean = 34.6 minutes) to complete their booklets then did those in the control condition (mean = 24.4 minutes) ($t(110) = 12.09$, $p < 0.001$). The main results concern differences in solution rates; overall, the (unweighted) average percentage solutions were higher for the 'reasons' group (24.9%) than for the control group (12.8%) ($z = 3.63$, $p < 0.01$). The difference between conditions tended to be more noticeable for the easier problems (see Figure 21.1).

Additional analyses were made of subjects' tendencies to select (check) the various alternatives. Correct responding requires selecting the p and not-q instances while avoiding the selection of the q and not-p cases. Overall, selection tendencies were slightly more appropriate in the 'reasons' condition, but the differences were small (for example, 84% versus 80% selecting p) and nonsignificant. Other than the fact that there were more correct (p and not-q) selection patterns in the 'reasons' condition, there were no noticeable differences in selection patterns, either overall or on individual problems. In both groups, the most common incorrect pattern was selecting the p and q cases (about 30% in each condition). Other erroneous patterns occurred less often and with comparable frequencies in the two conditions.

Reason-giving improved performance, although the effect was relatively modest. The hardest and most abstract problems seem to present obstacles to

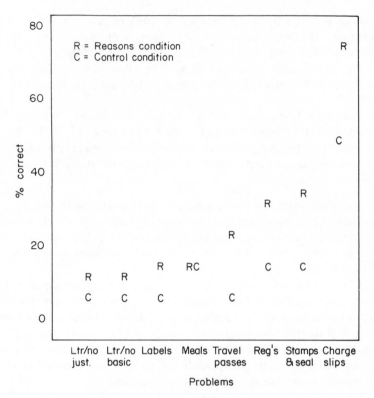

FIGURE 21.1   Solution rates for the 'reasons' and control conditions.

comprehending the scenario or the rule that are not removed by the sorts of processing that reason-giving might promote. Giving reasons was generally beneficial, however, and it seems most likely that the effect was due to greater care and attention to detail when making selections. It is not the case that those in the control condition 'had no reasons' for their choices—recall that overall selection patterns were similar across conditions. Rather, it would seem that reasons were more thoroughly and accurately developed in the 'reasons' condition. The present data do not allow more precise description of how this might have occurred (generating what might be on the other side, rechecking the rule, etc.); but they do suggest that processes such as monitoring and planning play a role in performance on this reasoning task. Whether reason-giving has properties different from other techniques that might evoke control processing is not known; simply asking subjects to 'THINK' (Duncan, 1963) or requiring them to reflect on their solution methods (Dorner, 1978) has been found advantageous. The findings imply that executive or control processes vary among normal young adults, with consequences for their cognitive performance (considering younger or less-developed subjects might well increase the impact). It would seem worthwhile to explore the effects of reason-giving and other, presumably similar, techniques across a carefully chosen range of problems, to establish the pattern and magnitude of influence. More detailed information about how the effects are generated will also be needed.

EFFECTS OF INSTRUCTION ABOUT COGNITION

Courses in critical thinking have been created, and instructional programs to foster higher-order thinking skills have been pursued. There are reports of success, but there also seem to be misgivings and questions about how effective such efforts have been (see, for example, Bransford, et al., 1986; Halpern, 1987; Lohman, 1986; Perkins, 1985). Such programmes focus on 'how to' think, providing instruction about strategies and the like. Less attention seems to have been given to the possible effects of completing the 'ordinary' college-level course on cognition. It is understandable that expectations of facilitation from such instruction might be uncertain: it is difficult to generate connections by which some course material might affect performance, there have been some weak results following quite direct attempts to teach higher-order strategies, and there have been questions concerning the relation between metacognitive knowledge and cognitive performance. Furthermore, Cheng et al. (1986) found that completing a one-semester course in logic did *not* lead to improvement on the four-card task. Granting these considerations, it is still the case that students in a course on cognition are exposed to information about strategies (a weak form of strategy instruction compared with the typical treatment), factors influencing task performance, discussions of better versus worse problem solvers, and the like. It is not unreasonable to suppose that some of this knowledge would prove useful to the student on at least some problem-solving tasks. I therefore decided to explore this question by giving a sample of problems of different types to students completing a course on cognition, as well as to students taking a non-cognitive psychology course.

The Method

Three undergraduate classes were involved: two were sections of the undergraduate course on cognition, whereas the third was a course on child development. The three classes were taught during the same ten-week quarter. (I am indebted to Bernadette Berardi-Coletta, Sharon Kristovich and Ray Wright for allowing me to recruit volunteers from their classes.) The two sections of the cognition course used the same textbook (instructor and the details of lecture content varied); neither the textbook nor the lectures for the course in development presented material directly relevant to the tasks used in this study. The two courses occupy similar places in the curriculum, having the same prerequisites and belonging to a set of lecture courses which are frequently taken by psychology majors. Early in the term, students were told by their instructors that a cognitive research project was being done that needed advanced students as participants, that they could earn a small number of 'bonus points' by participating, and that data would be collected throughout the quarter. Those who were interested signed a list of potential participants; from this list a small sample was randomly chosen, and these students were told that they had been selected to participate in sessions to be held 'immediately' and were given a set of times from which to choose. The others, as well as any selected students who could not attend an early session, were told that they would participate later in the quarter. Toward the end of the quarter, another set of sessions was made available to the students (including any who wished to participate but had not signed up at the beginning of the quarter). Thus the 'time 1' data were collected during the second and thirds weeks of the quarter (before coverage of problem solving and reasoning in the cognition classes), and the 'time 2' data were obtained during the ninth and tenth weeks (after the relevant coverage). The numbers of students participating, early and late, from each class were as follows: Cognition-A, 9 and 15; Cognition-B, 9 and 16; Development, 7 and 17.

Data were collected in small-group sessions. All students received the same tasks in the same order, as follows (maximum time allowed is shown in parentheses):

1) A sheet containing 30 five-letter anagrams (3 minutes).
2) A sheet of 25 syllogisms with abstract content (e.g. 'All A are B', 'Some B are C'), with students asked to select the appropriate A–C conclusion (or 'Can't say') (12 minutes).
3) The 'Hospital problem', a version of a deductive reasoning whodunit task (see Schwartz, 1971) requiring the relations among people, room numbers, and diseases to be worked out (4 minutes).
4) A two-task booklet containing two versions of Wason's four-card task, 'Checking meals' and 'Checking labels' (8 minutes).
5) A four-task booklet containing, on separate sheets, the 'Horse trade' problem, requiring one to determine the net gain or loss from a series of transactions; the 'Train' problem, requiring one to determine the number of opposite-travelling trains one would encounter during a train trip, in addition to answering three simpler questions; the 'Prisoner' problem, requiring one to find a path between two cells of a 4×4 matrix of cells under a set of constraints; and the 'Six dot' problem, requiring one to draw three straight lines connecting six dots without retracing or lifting the pencil from the paper (10 minutes). The 'Horse trade', 'Train' and 'Prisoner' problems are described more fully by Maier and Casselman (1970); the 'Six dot' problem was used by Lung and Dominowski (1985).

For both multiple-task booklets (4 and 5), students were allowed to move back-and-forth among the pages and were given periodic instructions to 'turn to the next problem' to ensure that they looked at all tasks in the booklet. Students also completed a brief academic history form and a self-report questionnaire about their problem-solving attitudes and habits. At the end of a session, participants were asked to avoid discussing any of the tasks with fellow students, as their final contribution to the research project.

Results and Discussion

Data from the questionnaire indicated that there were no significant group differences in number of psychology courses taken, grade-point-average in those courses, whether or not a course in logic had been taken, number of mathematics courses taken, age, gender, or year in college. The groups appeared comparable in terms of these demographic variables.

The primary analyses concerned differences in performance between the cognition course and the control (developmental) course. The data were subjected to multivariate analyses of variance with univariate analyses for the individual measures (unless otherwise indicated, reported F values have 1 and 69 df). References to the two sections of the cognition course will be made only when there were differences between them.

There were no course or time effects on the number of solutions for the anagram problems, valid syllogisms, the 'Hospital' (whodunit) problem, or the 'Horse trade' problem. Section B of the cognition course scored higher on valid syllogisms than did section A, ($F = 3.96$, $p < 0.06$). On the 'horse trade' problem, section A showed a sharp increase from Time 1 to Time 2 (11% versus 53% correct) while section B showed a decrease (56% versus 25%) ($F = 6.44$, $p < 0.01$); the control course showed no change (43% versus 41%). On the whole, no clear patterns of results appear for these measures.

Table 21.1 contains summary data for measures showing noticeable effects. Performance on invalid syllogisms is better for the cognition course, ($F = 5.66$, $p < 0.02$). The two sections of the cognition course show different patterns: section A had a large increase from time 1 to time 2 (21% versus 42%), whereas section B showed a decrease (38% versus 21%) ($F = 7.32$, $p < 0.01$). Correct responding to invalid syllogisms requires answering 'Can't say' (no conclusion can be drawn), and students in the cognition course gave this answer (rightly or wrongly) more often than those in the control course ($F = 7.30$, $p < 0.01$). Again, section A showed an increase over time (4.3 versus 10.7) but section B showed a decrease (6.7 versus 4.9) ($F = 8.88$, $p < 0.01$). It should be noted that, even with the differences between sections, performance in the cognition course is consistently above that in the control course.

Table 21.1 Mean performance by course and time of measurement

Task and measure	Course	Time 1	Time 2
% correct invalid syllogisms	Cognition	30.0	32.0
	Control	10.0	21.0
Number of 'Can't say', all syllogisms	Cognition	5.5	7.7
	Control	2.0	4.5
% solutions, checking meals	Cognition	33.0	61.0
	Control	14.0	23.0
% solutions, checking labels	Cognition	22.0	61.0
	Control	0.0	6.0
% solutions, 6-dot problem	Cognition	17.0	23.0
	Control	0.0	0.0
% extending lines, 6-dot problem	Cognition	33.0	45.0
	Control	14.0	0.0
% 'good effort' Prisoner problem[a]	Cognition	39.0	61.0
	Control	43.0	47.0

[a] No effects with this measure reached conventional levels of significance.

On the two versions of the four-card reasoning problem, students in the cognition course performed far better than those in the control course; for the 'meals' version, $F = 4.95$, $p < 0.03$, and for the 'labels' version, $F = 12.62$, $p < 0.001$. Although the conditions crossed with time interaction terms were not statistically significant, it can be seen that the performance gap between courses is much larger at time 2. Recall that, in the first study, these two versions were quite difficult (10–12% solutions); the control course data are in a comparable range, whereas the cognition students' performance at time 2 (61% correct) lies in an entirely different range. Consistent with the Cheng et al. (1986) finding, students who reported that they had taken a college course in logic performed no better on these problems (or on the syllogisms) than those without a logic course in their backgrounds.

On the six-dot problem, the cognition course performed better, both in terms of solutions, and with respect to extending (correct or incorrect) lines beyond the area of the dots. Owing to the lack of variance for the control course, ordinary tests are dubious. It can be seen that the difference in performance appears at time 1 and increases to a substantial gap by time 2. The two cognitive sections differed regarding extending lines (but not regarding solutions): section A showed a dramatic increase in the likelihood of extensions over time (0% versus 53%), whereas section B showed a decline (67% versus 38%). The difference is largely at time 1; at time 2 the two sections performed comparably and far better than the control course.

There were no solutions to the 'Train' problem (determining the number of opposite-travelling trains to be seen on a trip); the vast majority of students correctly answered the three, simpler, preliminary questions (when would a train leaving A at time x arrive at B; where would a train leaving A be at time y; would a train leaving A at time x 'meet' a train leaving B at time y). Other than showing that comprehending the problem instructions as assessed by these three questions is far from sufficient to solve the problem, this task yielded no interesting data. There was but one solution to the 'Prisoner' problem; however, there were differences among failures, and these were examined. Some students made reasonable (although unsuccessful) attempts to solve the problem—trying to construct a path from the start to the target cell while 'visiting' all the cells; others drew nothing or drew lines suggesting that they did not comprehend the task. The percentages of reasonable attempts ('good efforts') were calculated for the various groups. Although there were no significant effects with this measure, there was a suggestion that, by time 2, cognition students were making somewhat better efforts (see Table 21.1).

The findings give multiple indications of positive effects from a course on cognition. Several comments about the data are needed. First, the time 2 data are more reliable than those for time 1 (where quite small samples were used). Where differences between cognition sections occurred, they stemmed largely from the data for the section B, time 1 sample. That is, if one examines just time 2 data, the two sections are comparable (only a difference on invalid syllogisms appears). Section A quite consistently shows improvement from time 1 to time 2, whereas section B shows this pattern with some but not other measures. Where the 'reverse' pattern appears, it seems due more often to 'too high' a time

1 data point rather than 'too low' a time 2 data point. Second, although the instructors for both sections of the cognition course indicated that they did not, in class sessions, present relevant material prior to time 1 measurements, there was such material in the textbook (whether any students examined this material at that time is unknown). In sum, it does not seem reasonable to give equal weight to time 1 data or undue attention to changes from time 1 to time 2. In terms of academic demographic measures, the groups were similar—put differently, there is no hint that any section or course had a higher or lower density of better students. It seems reasonable to consider a difference in performance between courses, even if it sometimes shows up in time 1 data, to be suggestive of an instructional effect, so long as the difference appears at time 2.

Performance differences between the two courses varied across problems, and the tasks had varying relations to the instructional content of the cognition course. Anagram solving received coverage, including examples in the textbook, yet there was no hint of course differences on the anagram problems; it is not clear what students might learn that would help solving anagrams.

Syllogistic reasoning received textbook and lecture coverage in the cognition course, with examples, including some like those used in this study. There was no clear course effect for valid syllogisms, whereas cognition students performed better on invalid syllogisms and responded 'Can't say' more often. This pattern is sensible as an instructional outcome. Scores on the valid syllogisms are ambiguous, as it was possible to arrive at the correct conclusion for most of the valid problems on the basis of the shallow processing associated with atmosphere effects. The strongest error tendency in syllogistic reasoning is accepting invalid conclusions, so improvement in reasoning might be expected to appear more readily on invalid syllogisms. Learning to doubt, to be cautious, to resist the plausible-seeming conclusion would be a reasonable and positive outcome, one that would make a person better off in dealing with syllogisms (and arguments in general) without approaching expertise. The cognition students seem to learn to resist specific conclusions more often and are correct more often for invalid syllogisms. The data are *not* the result of the cognition students saying 'Can't say' more often in a non-discriminating fashion and obtaining more 'correct answers' on invalid syllogisms 'by chance'—in all groups, when students answered 'Can't say' they were correct about 70% of the time.

The four-card task was discussed in both textbook and lectures in the cognition course, although the specific versions used in this study were not presented. As mentioned earlier, the performance of the cognition students on these problems, especially at time 2, was impressive in the context of the typical, extreme difficulty of these problems and the obstacles often encountered when direct, very close-in-time attempts to aid performance on this task have been made. A substantial number of cognition students would seem to have learned to encode the rules and to understand the nature of the task, which would take them out of the realm of the majority of people when confronted with the problem. There would seem to be no need to invoke considerations of familiarity, concreteness, or the like (concepts which have been used to account for the limited success sometimes found by changing problem content). Whether the students had learned something that might affect their general thinking (for example, how they test hypotheses) is not known, but the observed effect is encouraging.

The cognition textbook described the 'popular' nine-dot problem and its solution, but the cognition students were not shown (in class or text) the six-dot problem used in this study. It would appear that some of them successfully transferred the knowledge that extending lines and trying multiple variations can be useful for 'unusual' dot-connecting problems. Their performance is not unlike that of strategy-instructed subjects (see Lung and Dominowski, 1985), although their instruction was indirect and separated in time from problem presentation.

One aspect of the procedures used in this study may have led to an underestimation of the effects of instruction. The exploratory nature of the study dictated using a variety of tasks — this idea, combined with the limited time for which participants were available, resulted in giving rather little time for a number of the tasks. Based on my observations, time constraints might have led to particularly low performance levels on the anagram problems, on syllogisms to a limited extent, and especially on the booklet containing the 'Horse trade', 'Train', 'Six-dot' and 'Prisoner' problems. The relevance of this consideration to an instructional effect is that, if students in the cognition course had acquired *general* knowledge that would help them cope with problems, that knowledge would be expected to help them 'work their way through' a problem rather than generate a quick solution. Consequently, the time limitations may not have allowed metacognitive knowledge to show its effects, in some cases.

Finally, one might ask just how 'meta' the knowledge was that seemed to help cognition students' performance. The pattern of results might suggest that, where cognition students performed better, it tended to be the case that the cognition course had included some reference to the task involved. The conjecture may be correct; that is, these data might reflect 'strategy training effects'. If so, the training would, minimally, appear to be less direct than the typical procedure, both in instructional orientation (there was here no deliberate attempt to teach task strategies) and in temporal separation between instruction and test. In addition, the students in the cognition course, where they showed some superiority, did so by transferring their knowledge to task variations they had not previously encountered, an accomplishment that deserves some appreciation.

CONCLUSIONS

The present results support the view that knowledge about cognition and generally applicable processes such as planning, monitoring, evaluating, re-checking and the like may play important roles in problem solving. In learning *about* cognition, a person can acquire a considerable amount of potentially useful information. Consider, for example, the following:

'Working-memory limitations can produce bottlenecks in problem solving. The most frequent error in syllogistic reasoning is accepting invalid conclusions for premises that logically yield no conclusion. Some problems are difficult precisely because their wording leads to inappropriate interpretations of the problem, provided that people adopt the most obvious interpretation.'

Acquiring, not the above or comparable sentences, but the knowledge that makes the sentences fully meaningful could make a person better able to cope with a variety of situations. In addition, as mentioned earlier, one could also learn about specific strategies, and about when to apply them, so that problem solving capability is enhanced.

For such knowledge to have any impact on problem solving, people must retrieve the information and apply it to their own problem solving efforts. Failures to do so would be expected. Given that much of the acquired information is relatively abstract, and given that the retrieval cues in the problem situation might be weak, one might expect that failures to apply potentially relevant knowledge would be inevitable. It is these plausible considerations that make the performance of the cognition students so intriguing and so encouraging. No attempt had been made to teach them 'how to solve problems', yet they retrieved and successfully made use of course material on a number of problems.

Two characteristics of instruction about cognition may be worth noting: the information is presented and acquired in a relatively abstract or weak context, and any specific item is only a part of a larger body of knowledge. Failures to obtain inter-problem transfer are commonly attributed to the relevant information being bound to the acquisition context and thus not applied in a new context. In many if not all of these situations, the relevant knowledge is an isolated bit of information, acquired in a very strong context. Perhaps it should be expected that such knowledge will not be transferred. Instruction about cognition, although having indirect connections to actual problem solving, might nonetheless lead to acquiring more transferable knowledge because of a weaker or abstract context and a richer, more integrated conceptual structure.

Using knowledge about cognition in a problem situation would seem to require metacognitive processing; that is, something equivalent to considering the question 'What do I know that might be useful here?' Questions of lesser scope might also be addressed ('What exactly am I being asked to do?' 'Are my assumptions correct?'). This kind of thinking exemplifies executive processing which, because it focuses on the act of problem solving rather than specific problem content, is a prime candidate for the basis of general skills.

There is no shortage of suggestions regarding what might be taught to foster the development of problem-solving ability (see Fredriksen, 1984). Some writers (for example, Glaser, 1984) stress the importance of knowledge of a domain (rather than general problem-solving skills), and some (Chase and Chi, 1980; Neves and Anderson, 1981) argue that expertise involves automatic pattern recognition which cues appropriate action, with extensive periods of practice, perhaps years, required for development. What role exists for metacognition? I offer the following suggestion.

There is some minimum amount of relevant knowledge that is necessary for any instance of problem solving to occur. If one lacks the knowledge, say, to understand what the problem is, then failure is assured, and neither metacognition nor any other proposed skill will be relevant. In some cases, the minimum declarative knowledge base may be quite large, specialized, and the outcome of extended study. Nonetheless, people seem to face many problem situations for which the minimum requisite knowledge is generally available (although perhaps not accessed). Even where specialized study may be required, it would seem to be true that, relative to any problem set, there will be people who have acquired sufficient declarative knowledge, but who may or may not solve a problem. Suppose it is true that expertise involves automatic, pattern-recognition-based responding. Even so, there is a huge space between lacking minimum requisite knowledge and being an expert, and a great deal of problem solving would seem to occur in this space. It is here that metacognition should play a role. Acquiring knowledge about cognition and sharpening one's executive processing will not guarantee success on any given problem. What might be expected is that a person would be successful more often, or more efficiently, over a variety of problem situations. The outcome would be, not expertise, but productive thinking (Wertheimer, 1982). Specifying the components of such thinking, investigating the conditions of their acquisition, and evaluating the strength of their influence on problem solving are worthy goals for research.

REFERENCES

Ahlum-Heath, M. E., & DiVesta, F. J. (1986). The effect of conscious controlled verbalization of a cognitive strategy on transfer in problem solving. *Memory and Cognition*, **14**, 281–285.

Berry, D. E., (1983). Metacognitive experience and transfer of logical reasoning. *Quarterly Journal of Experimental Psychology*, **35a**, 39–49.

Borkowski, J. G. (1985). Signs of intelligence: strategy generalization and metacognition. In S. Yussen (ed.), *The growth of reflection in children*. New York: Academic Press.

Bransford, J., Sherwood, R., Vye, N., & Rieser, J. (1986). Teaching thinking and problem solving: research foundations. *American Psychologist*, **41**, 1078–1089.

Brown, A. L. (1978). Knowing when, where and how to remember: a problem of metacognition. In R. Glaser (ed.), *Advances in instructional psychology*. Hillsdale, NJ: Erlbaum.

Cavanaugh, J. C., & Borkowski, J. G. (1980). Searching for metamemory–memory connections: a developmental study. *Developmental Psychology*, **16**, 441–453.

Cavanaugh, J. C., & Perlmutter, M. (1982). Metamemory: a critical examination. *Child Development*, **53**, 11–28.

Chase, W. G., & Chi, M. T. H. (1980). Cognitive skill: implications for spatial skill in large-scale environments. In J. Harvey (ed.), *Cognition, social behavior, and the environment*. Potomac, MD: Erlbaum.

Cheng, P. W., Holyoak, K. J., Nisbett, R. E., & Oliver, L. M. (1986). Pragmatic versus syntactic approaches to training deductive reasoning. *Cognitive Psychology*, **18**, 293–328.

Dorner, D. (1978). Self-reflection and problem solving. In F. Klix (ed.), *Human and artificial intelligence*. Berlin: Deutscher Verlag der Wissenschaften.

Duncan, C. P. (1958). Transfer after training with single versus multiple tasks. *Journal of Experimental Psychology*, **55**, 63–72.

Duncan, C. P. (1961). Attempts to influence performance on an insight problem. *Psychological Reports*, **9**, 35–42.

Duncan, C. P. (1963). Effects of instructions and information on problem solving. *Journal of Experimental Psychology*, **65**, 321–327.

Fredriksen, N. (1984). Implications of cognitive theory for instruction in problem solving. *Review of Educational Research*, **54**, 363–407.

Gagne, R. M. & Smith, E. C. (1962). A study of the effects of verbalizations on problem solving. *Journal of Experimental Psychology*, **63**, 12–18.

Gick, M. L. (1985). The effect of a diagram retrieval cue on spontaneous analogical transfer. *Canadian Journal of Psychology*, **39**, 460–466.

Gick, M. L., & Holyoak, K. J. (1980). Analogical problem solving. *Cognitive Psychology*, **12**, 306–355.

Gick, M. L. & Holyoak, K. J. (1983). Schema induction and analogical transfer. *Cognitive Psychology*, **15**, 1–38.

Glaser, R. (1984). Education and thinking. *American Psychologist*, **39**, 93–104.

Griggs, R. A. (1983). The role of problem content in the selection task and in the THOG problem. In J. St. B. T. Evans (ed.), *Thinking and reasoning: psychological approaches*. London: Routledge and Kegan Paul.

Halpern, D. F. (1987). Analogies as a critical thinking skill. In D. E. Berger, K. Pezdek & W. P. Banks (eds.), *Applications of cognitive psychology: Problem solving, education and computing*. Hillsdale, NJ: Erlbaum.

Harlow, H. F. (1949). The formation of learning sets. *Psychological Review*, **56**, 51–65.

Hayes, J. R. (1985). Three problems in teaching general skills. In J. Segal, S. Chipman & R. Glaser (eds.), *Thinking and learning*, Vol. 2, *Current research and open questions*. Hillsdale, NJ: Erlbaum.

Hoch, S. J., & Tschirgi, J. E. (1985). Logical knowledge and cue redundancy in deductive reasoning. *Memory and Cognition*, **13**, 453–462.

Jacobs, M. K., & Dominowski, R. L. (1981). Learning to solve insight problems. *Bulletin of the Psychonomic Society*, **17**, 171–174.

Keane, M. On drawing analogies when solving problems: a theory and test of solution generation in an analogical problem-solving task. *British Journal of Psychology*, **76**, 449–458.

Kreutzer, M. A., Leonard, S. C., & Flavell, J. H. (1975). An interview study of children's knowledge about memory. *Monographs of the Society for Research in Child Development*, **40**, serial no. 159.

Kristovich, S. A. R. (1988). *The effect of verbal report time and reason-generation on solution transfer*. Paper given at the 60th Annual Meeting of the Midwestern Psychological Association, Chicago, Illinois, April 1988.

Lohman, D. F. (1986). Predicting mathemathanic effects in the teaching of higher-order thinking skills. *Educational Psychologist*, **21**, 191–208.

Lung, C. T., & Dominowski, R. L. (1985). Effects of strategy instructions and practice on nine-dot problem solving. *Journal of Experimental Psychology: Learning, memory and cognition*, **11**, 804–811.

Maier, N. R. F., & Casselman, G. C. (1970). Locating the difficulty in insight problems: Individual and sex differences. *Psychological Reports*, **26**, 103–117.

Neves, D. M., & Anderson, J. R. (1981). Knowledge compilation: Mechanisms for the automatization of cognitive skills. In J. R. Anderson (ed.), *Cognitive skills and their acquisition*. Hillsdale, NJ: Erlbaum.

Perkins, D.N. (1985). General cognitive skills: why not? in S. Chipman, J. W. Segal & R. Glaser (eds.), *Thinking and learning skills*, Vol. 2, *Current research and open questions*. Hillsdale, NJ: Erlbaum.

Reed, S. K., Ernst, G. W., & Banerji, R. (1974). The role of analogy in transfer between similar problem states. *Cognitive Psychology*, **6**, 436–450.

Schwartz, S. H. (1971). Modes of representation and problem solving: well-evolved is half-solved. *Journal of Experimental Psychology*, **91**, 347–350.

Stinessen, L. The influence of verbalization on problem solving. *Scandinavian Journal of Psychology*, **26**, 342–347.

Wason, P. C. (1983). Realism and rationality in the selection task. In J. St. B. T. Evans (ed.), *Thinking and reasoning: Psychological approaches*, London: Routledge and Kegan Paul.

Wason, P. C., & Johnson-Laird, P. N. (1972). *Psychology of reasoning: Structure and content*. Cambridge, MA: Harvard University Press.

Wertheimer, M. (1982). *Productive thinking*. Chicago: University of Chicago Press.

22

Training in Metacognition: An Application to Industry

ALAN J. CLARK AND HENNIE PALM
Vista University, Pretoria

INTRODUCTION

Teaching thinking skills is becoming a new priority in cognitive psychology as we move away from a static conception of intelligence. In the past, intelligence was usually regarded as a finite skill which people possessed to a certain degree. It was especially the psychometric approach as characterized by theorists such as Spearman (1904), Eysenck (1979), Jensen (1969) and others, which perpetuated the view that the efficiency of an individual's thinking is a product of a genetically endowed intelligence.

More recent conceptions of thinking and intelligence approach these abilities as flexible characteristics which may be influenced by environmental intervention. For example, Feuerstein (1979) defines intelligence as 'the capacity of an individual to use previously acquired experiences to adjust to new situations' (p. 76). He implies that these experiences may be gained at any stage in the life-cycle, and in this way the individual's intelligence remains modifiable throughout life.

At this stage, there seems to be enough evidence that thinking can in fact be taught, as demonstrated by programmes such as those of Feuerstein (1980) and Sternberg (1986). The whole field is still surrounded by much controversy, but there is certainly as much reason to try to teach thinking as there is not to do so. The majority of thinking skills training programmes have focused on developing the abilities of children and college students. Although researchers such as Wagner and Sternberg (1986) have begun to pay attention to teaching thinking skills in developed adults, work in this area remains exploratory. This paper discusses one attempt to teach thinking skills in the world of work, and because of the lack of research in this area, relies quite heavily on the application of principles developed in work with children and college students.

Lines of Thinking, Volume 2 Edited by K.J. Gilhooly, M.T.G. Keane, R.H. Logie and G. Erdos
© 1990 John Wiley & Sons Ltd

THE PROBLEM

Developing the potential of their employees is an area of high concern for private companies. In an effort to retain what is referred to as the 'competitive edge', companies throughout the world realize that they must focus on developing the resources available to them. One of these resources is of course their staff, and in a world where sophisticated technology is becoming more available to everyone, maximizing the potential of what Sunter (1987) has referred to as 'invisible assets' is becoming an increasingly important area for retaining the competitive edge.

Rapidly advancing technology is making it more and more important for industrial nations to have an effective workforce, but at the same time, there seems to be a general consensus that the educational system in the Western world is not preparing its youth to meet the challenge of this technology. Paul (1987) suggests that the educational system in the United States, for example, teaches children how to solve monological problems whereas the 'most important issues ... are multilogical' (p. 131).

Late in 1987, we were approached by a large industrial corporation with a request to develop a thinking skills training programme for 1500 managers at the middle and senior levels. The management training division of this company felt that the efficiency of their managers could be significantly improved if they were more adept at problem-solving. They concurred with the belief that educational systems do not really teach people how to think effectively. Unfortunately, while they felt that their managers could be more creative, make better decisions, solve problems more effectively, and so on, they could not really provide a specific indication of the thinking skills deficits which needed attention. The authors decided to conduct a thorough evaluation of a sample group of the managers, and to develop a programme around the results of this evaluation.

One aspect which was clear from the outset of the project was that the research would be almost completely exploratory. The training programme would be designed as a pilot project, and many of the usual methodological issues would be ignored at this stage.

Evaluation and Findings

An evaluation was conducted on a sample of eight managers from the client company, and was chiefly qualitative in nature. The reason for this was partly because no standardized tests of thinking or cognitive skills exist, and because the psychometric tests of general problem-solving ability which are available tend to be contrived and artificial. It is usually very easy for subjects to decide what the 'correct' answer is, and they are then tempted to respond in a model fashion. For example, many of these tests contain questions such as: 'Do you consider all the alternatives before deciding on a solution?'

The majority of managers know the ideal model of problem-solving, and they would simply respond in terms of this model. Unfortunately, an ideal response set does not necessarily reflect effective problem-solving in real-life situations. It was felt that, in this case, ratings of the thinking skills deficits which were evident in the subject's attempts to solve actual work-related problems, would provide the best measure of areas of weakness.

Subjects were presented with problems which commonly occurred in their company, and had to solve these problems individually, in pairs and in groups. All attempts at problem-solving were audio-taped.

Feuerstein (1980) has provided an extensive list of cognitive deficits, and this list was used as a rating scale. Feuerstein has categorized these deficits in terms of four primary areas, namely the input, elaborational and output phases, and affective–motivational factors. The input phase covers eight factors, the elaborational phase thirteen, and the output phase seven. There are no specific factors listed for affective–motivational deficiencies.

The authors, who are both familiar with the work of Feuerstein, rated the frequency with which each deficit occurred in the different problem situations. Once this had been done, deficits which occurred as a theme across situations were selected as the focus of attention for programme development. In the end, seven primary deficits were selected as requiring attention.

Researchers working with adults will find that not all the factors apply equally well to their subjects. For example, in the input phase, impaired spatial orientation is listed as a possible deficiency, but it is unlikely that this will be found in corporate managers.

The seven deficits which were identified were:

1) *Impulsivity:* characterized by a disorganized approach to the problem, no careful exploration of alternatives, looking for instant solutions, and jumping to conclusions.

2) *Lack of precision and accuracy in data gathering:* characterized by ignoring some of the available data, making decisions on the basis of generalities, and accepting abstract, vague evidence.

3) *Inaccurate problem definition:* not recognizing that a problem exists; regarding symptoms as the actual problem, and first-order definitions of the problem.

4) *Lack of need for logical evidence:* accepting someone else's (incorrect) view of the problem, accepting a solution without evidence, refusing to change position when alternative evidence is presented.

5) *Egocentric communication modalities:* interpreted as 'my-side bias': refusing to listen to other points of view, allowing personal feelings undue influence when solving problems.

6) *Impaired accuracy in communicating responses:* communicating in generalities, issuing vague instructions, and setting vague goals.

7) *Trial-and-error responses:* failing to plan or consider a response, and testing the reception of a solution without first thinking through possible consequences.

When it came to developing the programme, a number of practical issues had to be considered. The most important of these was the time available for training. The industrial sector has a negative perception of long-term training programmes, because although training may have a positive effect, the time spent away from the job situation has a negative impact on productivity. While research on thinking skills training indicates that short-term programmes have very little potential impact (see, for example, Sternberg, 1987) the company in question was adamant that the programme should be of only limited duration.

After considering the time-pressure, it was decided that training in metacognition should form the main emphasis of the programme. The principal aim of training in metacognition is to allow subjects to be able to reflect on their thinking and problem-solving processes. This should allow them to engage in 'self-diagnosis', and they could then independently develop their thinking skills.

Why Teach Thinking

Teaching thinking is not a traditional area of concern in industry, so it is perhaps necessary to provide some motivation for doing so.

Nickerson (1987, pp. 30–31) suggests the following possible reasons for teaching thinking:

a) to allow people to be better equipped to compete effectively for jobs and recognition;

b) to make people better citizens;

c) to improve psychological well-being.

These reasons are still quite general and the authors would like to add a number of others. In the first place, free-market economies are increasingly moving towards decentralized decision-making, which will have the result that a multitude of effective decisions become necessary. It is no longer sufficient for a select few to be effective thinkers. The demands made on the average worker are becoming more complex and the distinction between those who make the decisions and those who do not is becoming increasingly blurred.

Secondly, specialized education very rapidly becomes obsolete. Technology is advancing at such a pace that the information which a graduate has is soon outdated. What industry needs more than ever is a workforce composed of autonomous learners, people who are capable of mastering new technology as it develops. The teaching of thinking could increase the number of people in a company who are autonomous learners.

Thirdly, the economic prosperity of an industrial state will increasingly depend on its capacity to develop and initially exploit new opportunities and products. In the past, the world was composed of a few advanced nations such as the United States and certain European countries, and a large number of poorly advanced states. This dichotomy between advanced and non-advanced nations is now far less evident. More nations are competing on the world trade markets, and countries such as Japan, Taiwan and South Korea are investing heavily in educating their populations. The emphasis is on developing 'entrepreneurs'—people who have finely developed critical thinking abilities, who can detect and exploit opportunities, and in this way ensure the economic survival of their nation.

In the authors' opinion, these reasons are sufficient motivation for teaching thinking in industry.

Training in Metacognition

Training in metacognition is not an entirely new field, but as with most areas of thinking skills training, very little work has been done with developed adults. The present study is therefore exploratory in nature, and conclusions reached are tentative at best.

The term metacognition refers to 'knowledge about knowledge', and in the present context may be defined as *awareness and control of one's thinking processes and problem-solving strategies*. This definition is a loose interpretation of Flavell's (1971) view of metamemory, but it is felt that it applies equally well to metacognition as a whole. Nickerson, Perkins and Smith (1985, p. 103) provide the following examples of metacognitive skills: 'planning, predicting, checking, reality testing, and monitoring and control of one's own deliberate attempts to perform intellectually demanding tasks'. The similarities between these examples and the definition provided are clear. These same authors note that not much work has been done in the area of training in metacognition, but that the little empirical work which has been done is encouraging. They point out:

> 'Metacognitive skills have a face validity that is very compelling: who can argue against the desirability of carefully managing one's time and resources, or of monitoring the effectiveness of an approach to a demanding task.' (p. 109)

There seem to be a number of advantages to training people in metacognitive analysis. The first is that experts generally seem to engage in more metacognition than do novices (Nickerson, Perkins and Smith 1985). Experts are more aware of their strengths and weaknesses, and spend more time monitoring their progress when solving problems.

A second advantage is that metacognitive skills more easily transfer across real-life situations which are not a specific focus of the training programme, and they also improve the transfer of other skills. This aspect is particularly important, because transfer is always difficult to achieve in training.

A final advantage is that the chances of success of training programmes in general seem to be improved if subjects are taught to analyse their own behaviour. Winfrey and Goldfried (1986) point out that one of the differences between successful and unsuccessful training programmes is that, in the successful programmes, subjects are taught how to monitor their own progress, and analyse and correct problem areas as they occur.

Summary

The aim of this study was to develop a thinking skills training programme, which would initially be applied to eight managers at a large industrial corporation. A qualitative evaluation of the sample group was conducted prior to programme development, and seven specific cognitive deficits were found to recur across various problem-solving situations. The description of these deficits was taken from the work of Feuerstein (1980). A decision was taken to make training in metacognition the main emphasis of the programme, for reasons which will be expounded upon in a later section.

THE METHOD

The Hypothesis

There will be a significant decrease in the frequency of thinking skills deficits shown by the subjects from before to after the metacognition training programme.

Research Design

A single-group pre-test/post-test design was used. This design has many methodological flaws, the most important being that it is not really possible to separate attention and treatment effects. However, this design was considered acceptable for the present study, as it was a pilot project initiating research in a new area. The client company was understandably reluctant to commit further staff members as controls, before any indication of the chances of success of the programme was available.

Subjects

The subjects were eight managers from the Head Office of a large industrial corporation, which employs in the region of 65 000 people. The subjects were selected from different departments. There were six men and two women, which is a fair representation of the proportion of men and women in managerial positions in the company as a whole.

One male subject dropped out of the programme after the first training module, which then left a total of seven subjects. At the rating stage, one tape was found to be inaudible, which left a total of six subjects to analyse.

Measures

Subjects were presented with a work-related problem both before and after the training programme, and asked to verbalize and audio-tape their attempts to solve the problem. They were instructed to speak aloud as they were solving the problem, and to try to verbalize all thoughts which they had. They were asked to tape a maximum of 30 minutes for each problem.

We then rated the frequency of occurrence of each of the seven primary deficits outlined earlier. However, one of the authors was blind to which problem represented the before and after measure, and this was regarded as a sufficient check for any possible bias. The two raters listened to a sample tape before beginning with the rating, in order to reach agreement on the verbal manifestation of each deficit. In addition, inter-rater reliability was checked by means of a direct comparison of frequency (observations), as described by Miller (1975).

This technique of using subject's verbal reports as a means of identifying thinking skills deficits is frequently used in studies of thinking (see, for example, Isenberg, 1987; Whimbey and Lochhead, 1982). Although verbal reports have traditionally been regarded as a rather weak form of measurement, Ericsson and Simon (1984) argue convincingly that they can be used effectively as measures of cognitive processes. These authors state:

'Two forms of verbal reports can claim to being the closest reflection of the cognitive processes. Foremost are concurrent verbal reports—We claim that cognitive processes are not modified by these verbal reports, and that task-directed cognitive processes determine what information is heeded and verbalized.' (p. 16)

Statistical Analysis

The Wilcoxon non-parametric test statistic was used throughout, and the level of significance for rejection of the null hypothesis was set at $p < 0.05$.

THE PROGRAMME

Previous research in thinking skills training has provided certain criteria to which such programmes should adhere, if they are to be successful. Sternberg (1983), for example, has outlined eight such criteria, and has expanded on some of these in later publications (e.g. 1987). However, in the present study, no attempt was made to develop a comprehensive training programme. The aim was more to explore the application of certain principles to managerial staff, and to generate hypotheses for future research.

The goals for this programme were very limited, as can be seen from the smaller number of thinking deficits which were addressed. The intention was that positive findings from the pilot programme would be used as a basis for more comprehensive programme development.

The decision to make training in metacognition the main emphasis of the programme was motivated by two factors. The first of these was the time-limitations placed on the training. Goals would need to be limited, but the maximum impact would need to be achieved in as short a time as possible. It was felt that training the subjects in metacognition would be the only way to meet both these requirements.

What one aims at when training in metacognition is essentially to provide the individual with a means of diagnosing his own thinking processes—to monitor his progress and correct ineffective thinking as it occurs. In theory, if a person can become proficient in this self-diagnosis, he should in a sense be able to teach himself thinking skills, or at least to improve the efficiency of his existing skills. This would then, of course, greatly reduce the time needed for training.

The second factor is that, by the time an employee reaches the managerial level in a modern corporation, the chances are good that he would have been through at least one course on effective problem-solving. The issue is not that managers do not know how to solve problems, but rather that they are not very good at detecting where they go wrong in the process. Improving their metacognitive abilities could help them to analyse this process, and to make it more effective.

The programme consisted of four 4-hour modules, spread over a period of two weeks. Homework exercises were set after each module, where the subjects had to apply the principles learned to their work situation.

In the first module, the concept of metacognition was introduced. The deficits which occurred with some frequency during the evaluation exercises were explained, and the way in which metacognition could help to control these deficits was discussed. Practical exercises were also used to demonstrate the existence of the different deficits. These exercises usually took the form of the subjects solving problems in a group setting, with the researchers commenting on the appearance of specific deficits as they occurred.

The homework exercise for this module was for subjects to try to detect the existence of any of the deficits in their colleagues' problem-solving.

The second module began with a discussion of the homework assignment. It is worth noting that the subjects were quite adept at detecting thinking deficits in other people, even though their exposure to this activity was very limited at this stage.

Subjects were then briefly trained in pair problem-solving, as described by Whimbey and Lochhead (1982), and had to work on problems in pairs. It was the role of the listener to make the problem-solver aware of thinking deficits as they occurred in his attempts to solve the problem. At the same time, the researchers moved between pairs of subjects to clear up any confusion, and to provide additional feedback.

The homework exercise was for subjects to personally analyse their attempts at problem-solving in the work situation, in terms of the deficits.

The third and fourth modules consisted of simulated committee meetings, in which half of the group acted as a committee solving a company-related problem, while the rest of the group rated them and provided feedback on the deficits which occurred.

In the third module, comprehensive feedback was provided by the observing group as well as by the researchers, once the 'committee' had arrived at a solution. In the fourth module, feedback was provided as soon as a deficit was noted by either the observing subjects or by the researchers. This could be at any stage of the problem-solving process, but the nature of the deficit was not explained. Instead, the committee had to stop their activity, decide which error had occurred, correct it, and move on.

The homework assignment between the third and fourth modules was for subjects to note thinking deficits that had occurred in committee meetings which they attended in the intervening period.

The process underlying the structure of the modules had two aims. The first was to move from a reliance on the researchers for feedback, to self-reliance. In other words, it was our intention that at the end of the programme the subjects should be proficient in analysing thinking deficits, both in themselves and in others. This would be useful in self-development as well as in the development of subordinates, which is one of the primary roles of a manager.

The second was to move from the relatively non-threatening situation of detecting thinking deficits in other people, to themselves, and then to their performance amongst peers in a group situation. The idea that one may be deficient in thinking skills is probably threatening to most people, and this threat is increased in a work situation, where one's performance is continually being evaluated. Because of this, it is important that subjects are exposed to criticism in a gradual manner, and in a situation where it is clear that deficiencies are not unique to any one individual.

RESULTS AND DISCUSSION

Inter-rater reliability was calculated at 88%, which is considered acceptable for further analysis of the data. In addition, all ratings were in the same direction, with five of the subjects showing a decrease in the frequency of thinking skills deficits from pre- to post-test, while the sixth subject showed no change.

As far as the Wilcoxon test of significance was concerned, t was found to be significant at the 5% level.

The metacognition training programme was found to have a significantly positive effect on the subject's thinking. In fact, most subjects showed a rather dramatic decrease in the frequency of thinking skills deficits from pre- to post-test. The results are interpreted as very encouraging, especially as the programme was of such short duration.

For the future, it would seem that it is worthwhile indeed to pursue training in metacognition with managers. The course was well-received and the participants's subjective evaluation was that the course was valuable to them.

This study has, of course, a number of limitations. The difficulty of separating attention and treatment effects has already been mentioned. Using a control group will be important in future research. The sample size was also very small, although if it had been possible to rate all eight original participants it would have been more acceptable. The method of rating was somewhat subjective, but evaluating subject's verbal reports remains the best method until such time as a standardized test of cognitive ability becomes available. At this stage, it is uncertain whether the effects of the programme will be durable. It was of very short duration, and this will need to be followed up at a later stage. It is also not clear to what extent transfer occurred, and this will also need to be evaluated.

In summary, we feel confident that a positive direction has been found for future research in thinking skills training, as well as management development. Training in metacognition is possibly one of the most useful areas in management training, especially when the limited training time available is taken into account. Subjects are provided with a means of diagnosing their own thinking skills deficit, and it is felt that this has more face validity than a much longer training programme which emphasizes basic thinking skills. One reason for this is, of course, that managers will often quite understandably feel that they are already reasonably effective in thinking and problem-solving.

A number of practical issues relevant to future research need to be highlighted. The first is that any thinking-skills training programme which is developed for managers should preferably be of short duration. A second is that exercises used in the programme should be directly relevant to the work situation of the subjects. While 'game-type' exercises have a strong fun element, they make the programme less personalized, and make transfer more difficult to achieve. Researchers such as Sternberg (1986) have referred to the importance of context, but unfortunately seem to have ignored this in the development of their own programmes. Finally, spaced-learning should be the chosen method of presentation. It decreases the possibility of information overload, and avoids the recency effect to some extent. When a programme must necessarily be of short duration, spaced-learning improves the chances of transfer and durability of treatment effects.

REFERENCES

Ericsson, K. A., & Simon, H. A. (1984). *Protocol analysis: Verbal reports as data*. Cambridge, MA: MIT Press.

Eysenck, H. J. (1979). *The structure and measurement of intelligence*. Berlin: Springer-Verlag.

Feuerstein, R. (1979). *The dynamic assessment of retarded performers: The LPAD, theory, instruments and techniques*. Baltimore: University Park Press.

Feuerstein, R. (1980). *Instrumental enrichment: An intervention program for cognitive modifiability*. Baltimore: University Park Press.

Flavell, J. H. (1971). First discussant's comments: What is memory development the development of? *Human Development*, 14, 272–278.

Isenberg, D. J. (1987). Inside the mind of the senior manager. In. D. N. Perkins, J. Lochhead & J. Bishop. (eds.), *Thinking: The second international conference*. Hillsdale, NJ: Erlbaum.

Jensen, A. R. (1969). How much can we boost IQ and scholastic achievement? *Harvard Educational Review*, 39, 1–123.

Miller, L. K. (1975). *Everyday behavior analysis*. Moterey: Brooks/Cole.

Nickerson, R. S. (1987). Why teach thinking? In: J. B. Baron & R. J. Sternberg (eds.), *Teaching thinking skills: Theory and practice*. New York: Freeman.

Nickerson, R. S., Perkins, D. N. & Smith, E. E. (1985). *The teaching of thinking*. Hillsdale, NJ: Erlbaum.

Paul, R. W. (1987). Dialogical thinking: critical thought essential to the acquisition of rational knowledge and passions. In: J. B. Baron & R. J. Sternberg (eds.), *Teaching thinking skills: Theory and practice*. New York: Freeman.

Spearman, C. (1904). General intelligence objectively determined and measured. *American Journal of Psychology*, 15, 201–293.

Sternberg, R. J. (1983). Criteria for intellectual skills training. *Educational Research*, 12, 6–26.

Sternberg, R. J. (1986). *Intelligence applied*. San Diego: Harcourt Brace Jovanovich.

Sternberg, R. J. (1987). Questions and answers about the nature and teaching of thinking skills. In: J. B. Baron & R. J. Sternberg (eds.), *Teaching thinking skills: Theory and practice*. New York: Freeman.

Sunter, C. (1987). *The world and South Africa in the 1990s*. Cape Town: Human & Rousseau.

Wagner, R. K., & Sternberg, R. J. (1986). Tacit knowledge and intelligence in the everyday world. In: R. J. Sternberg & R. K. Wagner (eds.), *Practical intelligence: Nature and origins of competence in the everyday world*. Cambridge: Cambridge University Press.

Whimbey, A., & Lochhead, J. (1982). *Problem solving and comprehension* (3rd edn.). Hillsdale, NJ: Erlbaum.

Winfrey, L. L., & Goldfried, M. R. (1986). Information processing and the human change process. In: E. R. Ingram (ed.), *Information processing approaches to clinical psychology*. Orlando: Academic Press.

23

Teaching Problem-Solving Skills to Adult Developmental Students

BEATRICE SEAGULL
NCAS, Rutgers University

GEORGE ERDOS
University of Newcastle upon Tyne

INTRODUCTION

In this chapter we report on the problem-solving course which has been in existence in its current form since 1982 at the Academic Foundations Department of the Faculty of Arts and Sciences, Newark, Rutgers University. The course on problem solving is part of an intensive summer programme which serves as pre-college preparation to adult developmental students. The label 'adult developmental student' is somewhat imprecise; but, generally speaking, it refers to students who have been admitted to colleges or universities, but who for a number of reasons show a lack in such basic academic skills as writing, reading and arithmetic.

There is a proliferation of courses teaching problem-solving and thinking skills. These range from the highly systematic and theory-linked ones to the pragmatic and ecclectic ones. The participants in these courses also vary between children with learning disabilities and adults with superior mental abilities. As Halpern (1987) points out, all the courses attempting to improve problem-solving skills share two basic assumptions:

> '(1) that there are clearly identifiable and definable thinking skills that students can be taught to recognize and apply appropriately, and (2) that if these skills are recognized and applied, the students will be more effective thinkers' (p. 76)

There are a number of workers in this field who believe that thinking and problem-solving skills have to be, by necessity, domain-specific, and attempts

Lines of Thinking, Volume 2   Edited by K.J. Gilhooly, M.T.G. Keane, R.H. Logie and G. Erdos
© 1990 John Wiley & Sons Ltd

to teach domain-independent problem-solving skills will meet with failure (Greeno, 1980; Glaser, 1984; Resnick, 1983). The argument is far from being settled, but reliable empirical evidence will have to be produced by both camps.

An area of interest to us concerned differences between expert and novice problem-solvers. Numerous studies (Bloom and Broder, 1950; Brown, 1978; Costa, 1984; Larkin *et al.*, 1980; Schoenfeld, 1979; Whimbey and Lochhead, 1979) support the observation that 'poor problem-solvers work too hastily, skip steps, lack the motivation to persist in analysing the problem, reason carelessly, and fail to check their solutions' (Maxwell, 1981). Some studies further suggest that differences in problem-solving performance are largely a function of metacognition, which is also referred to as 'executive processes' (Brown, 1978), 'cognitive monitoring' (Flavell, 1979), and 'comprehension monitoring' (Weinstein and Rogers, 1985). The topic of metacognition is closely linked with the difference between expert and novice problem-solvers. The experts know that they have a specific body of knowledge and a repertoire of techniques to solve problems within a specific domain. Their evaluation of the time and effort required to solve a given problem is more accurate than that of the novice. Since the concept of metacognition generally refers to individuals' 'knowledge about their own cognitive processes as well as their abilities to control these processes by organizing, monitoring, and modifying them as a function of learning outcomes' (Weinstein and Rogers, 1985), the teaching of problem-solving must involve a modification of this cognitive executive.

Based on this work, we decided that one of the possible forms of remediation would be a course explicitly targeted at thinking and problem-solving skills and an attempt to modify the metacognition of the students.

The Students

The Academic Foundations Department (AFD) students' profile is comparable to that of the 'New Student' (Cross, 1974), who ranks low on traditional tests of students' achievement and performs poorly in school. Lacking in self-esteem, self-confidence and perseverance, and faced with the pressure of quickly bridging broad educational gaps, the student may be intellectually immobilized by the inability realistically to evaluate performance (Coleman, 1966) and by the fear of failure (Holt, 1964).

It was a political decision to facilitate the admission of this type of student to colleges and universities and considerable financial resources were made available to offer support services to them to help with the academic difficulties all the way up to graduation. It was left to individual universities and colleges to work out the best strategy in terms of academic and personal counselling to achieve the politically and academically desirable objective of enabling these students to progress through higher education and to obtain a degree.

During their undergraduate training, students have to take 13 credits in science, including eight credits in laboratory science courses and three in algebra, irrespective of their major. The AFD addresses the needs of these students by providing counselling and tutoring services, developmental courses in mathematics, science, and language skills, and support classes for entry-level mathematics and science options.

Initially, however, AFD students participate in a six-week summer programme which focuses on the development of study skills in mathematics and English and the development of more general problem-solving skills. As part of this summer programme, we have been teaching a course on problem-solving to incoming freshmen from educationally deprived high schools since 1982. Our students are admitted to Rutgers University through the Educational Opportunity Program, part of a state-wide initiative to enhance the success of minority students in higher education. The students are from urban schools and have lower than average SAT scores. Every summer approximately 120 students are enrolled in the Summer Readiness Program for six weeks.

The problem-solving course was our response to the experience of preparing developmental students for college chemistry, physics, biology and geology courses. Most students, we found, had not the sophisticated means of thinking about scientific problems which the laboratory work and examinations required. The students' behaviours and comments revealed that they lacked the know-how to wade through terminology and extract meaningful information from it. Overwhelmed by the complexity of the problems, they were frequently unable to determine a starting point and would turn instead to trial and error. Confusion, anxiety, frustration and inappropriate answers followed. Furthermore, the students, upon entering the university, have a choice between four different laboratory science courses and very often they do not know which one they will choose up to registration. This makes subject-based remediation very difficult.

Motivated by J. R. Hayes' challenge (1981), which stated that if we know anything about problem-solving, then we should be able to teach it, we decided that the best preparation for our students was a course in problem-solving, concentrating on the learning-by-doing aspect of this undertaking.

What is Available

Our first step in developing a course to enable AFD students to become better problem-solvers was to investigate methods used at other institutions to solve similar problems. Xavier University in St Louis, for example, provided pre-college preparation for science majors through 'Project SOAR', a Piagetian-based programme having as one of its components 'cognitive therapy'. There were also 'Project ADAPT' at the University of Nebraska, Lincoln, 'Patterns of problem solving' at the University of California, Los Angeles, and the 'Cognitive Skills Project' at the University of Massachusetts. At California State University introductory science courses were supplemented by programme DORIS (Development Of Reasoning In Science: a course in abstract thinking) (cf. Nummedal, 1987). At Manhattan Community College the 'Cognitive studies project' was implemented in 1980 (Hutchinson, 1985).

We also examined a number of text-based programmes offering explicit instruction in general problem-solving, all of which eventually provided materials for our course: *'The ideal problem solver'* (Bransford and Stein, 1984),

'*CoRT thinking*' (deBono, 1973), '*The complete problem solver*' (Hayes, 1981), '*Concepts in problem solving*' (Rubinstein, 1975), '*Problem solving and comprehension*' (Whimbey and Lochhead, 1982), '*How to solve problems*' (Wickelgren, 1974), and last but not least '*How to solve it*' (Polya, 1957). As one can see there is a wide choice of courses and materials professing to teach problem-solving. The movement reached even the august portals of Yale (Sternberg and Davidson, 1987).

Our programme is one of the, by now, many attempts to teach general problem-solving strategies. It went through a number of modifications since its inception in 1969, and it has been in its current form since 1982. There is now also an increasing body of literature surveying this field (Nickerson, Perkins and Smith, 1985; Segal, Chipman and Glaser, 1985).

THE METHOD

'Problem-solving' was taught five hours a week, subdivided into two, two and one hour periods. Individual classes contained about 15 students. The students were grouped according to ability based on their performance on the New Jersey College Basic Skills Placement Test (NJCBSPT) and the Whimbey Analytical Skills Inventory (WASI). Parallel forms of these two tests were our pre-tests and post-tests to evaluate the impact of our course. The period between pre-test and post-test was six weeks—the duration of the course.

It is the declared goal of the New Jersey Basic Skills Council that every student entering any of the state's 30 public colleges or 11 participating independent institutions should be tested with the NJCBSPT. The test has been administered since 1978 and every year approximately 50 000 students are tested. The aim of the testing is to determine the levels of proficiency in collegiate basic skills of the entering freshmen and to assist colleges in placing already admitted students into remedial or first-level college English and mathematics courses. There is now a large-scale normative database available for this test and the results are published every year (see, for example, New Jersey Basic Skills Council, 1987a, b, c).

Even though the WASI is not a fully validated psychometric instrument, we chose it for the convenience of easy accessibility and low cost. Both the pre-test and post-test are included in Whimbey and Lochhead (1982). Analysis conducted by the New Jersey Task Force on Thinking (Morante and Ulesky, 1984) showed significant positive correlations between scores in the WASI and scores in each segment of the NJCBSPT. Since the WASI showed satisfactory correlation with the NJCBSPT and we were interested mainly in intragroup comparisons, we felt its use justifiable. We distinguished between three ability levels, 'high', 'medium' and 'low'. The main function of this grouping was to enable the instructors to find the most suitable speed for progress for the majority of students within each group.

The teachers, who were trained specifically to teach the course and have taught it since 1982, understood the ramifications of this type of teaching. They were assisted in the classroom by teaching assistants, also trained for this purpose. The majority of the teaching assistants were undergraduates who themselves went through the programme one or two years previously. In addition to the five hours spent in the classroom, there were a number of free periods when the students could request peer-tutoring of the teaching assistants. *Problem solving and comprehension*, by Whimbey & Lochhead (1982), was the main text. As the course progressed, additional materials were brought in to supplement the instruction.

Whimbey and Lochhead's method of paired problem-solving (Lochhead, 1985) appeared to us as one of the suitable techniques to modify the cognitive habits of our students and thus change their metacognition. In this method, two students work as a team. One reads and thinks aloud, while the other listens and monitors. As Lochhead (1985, p. 111) puts it: 'The partner who listens plays a critical role in the learning process. He or she must not sit back inattentively but, instead, must concentrate on two functions: (1) continually checking for accuracy: and (2) demanding constant vocalization.' However, with the exception of the highest level groups, two out of ten, as measured by the tests mentioned above, we have encountered difficulties with the above method. Across a number of different problems our students were unable to verbalize their thinking processes. When this happened, we took to the modelling approach and either the instructor or the teaching assistant solved the problem in front of the class, verbalizing his or her thinking processes. We also employed small-group problem-solving, with group sizes of three or four, facilitated by the instructor or teaching assistant. This method seemed to be most effective.

At the beginning of the course each student was given a course syllabus which outlined the objectives of the course, listed the topics to be covered and the thinking strategies which we wanted to practice. Furthermore, the students were given their own copy of the book *Problem solving and comprehension* after the WASI post-test had been carefully removed. In the class there was an emphasis on practical activity, discussion, awareness of strategies, and small-group problem-solving. In addition to the classroom exercises, the students had homework assignments which they had to hand in. These were mainly exercises from the course text. Since performance in the problem-solving course was part of the assessment of the students for placement for regular college courses, motivation and involvement with the course was high.

The following problem solving strategies were emphasized and demonstrated to the students:

Reading carefully
Determining what the problem is asking
Planning
Determining what has to be done
Reducing impulsivity
Breaking the problem into small parts
Determining which parts are to be dealt first
Following directions
Using drawings, models, diagrams
Creating mental images
Identifying variables

Listing attributes
Looking for patterns and relationships
Ranking information according to logical sequence
Defining terms
Determining relevant information
Eliminating irrelevant information
Using inferential reasoning
Working backwards
Role playing
Considering alternative solutions
Evaluating solutions

After the strategy was explained to the students, they were subdivided into pairs or small groups and they were asked to solve one or a number of suitable example problems.

Results

In addition to the subjective course evaluation, we measured the performance of the students in a pre-test post-test design using the New Jersey College Basic Skills Placement Test (NJCBSPT), and the Whimbey Analytical Skills Inventory (WASI). The NJCBSPT evaluates reading comprehension (RC), knowledge of sentence structure (SS), mathematical computation (ML), algebra (AL), and, through a 20-minute essay, writing skills (WS). Since the last one of these is the relatively most subjective measure, and showed the lowest correlation to the WASI in the Morante and Ulesky study ($r = 0.56$, $N = 513$, as opposed to 0.70 to 0.76 for the other four scales) we decided to exclude this scale from our analysis. Table 23.1 contains the pre-test and post-test scores. Using a one-way analysis of variance for dependent measures, all results proved to be significant at the 0.01 level.

In the course evaluation, students indicated that they had become more

Table 23.1   Mean raw scores and gains on the Whimbey Analytical Skills Inventory (WASI) and the New Jersey College Basic Skills Placement Test (NJCBSPT) segments ($N = 384$)

NJCBSPT segment	Number of questions	Pre-test	Post-test	Increase (%)
RC	47	25.01	28.24	12.9
MC	35	18.17	21.76	19.8
AL	35	13.24	15.89	20.0
SS	40	21.99	24.20	10.0
WASI	38	17.40	22.80	31.0

RC = Reading comprehension (47 questions, 50 minutes)
MC = mathematical computation (35 questions, 40 minutes)
AL = elementary algebra (35 questions, 40 minutes)
SS = sentence sense (40 questions, 35 minutes)
WASI = Whimbey Analytical Skills Inventory (38 questions, 40 minutes).

confident and more knowledgeable problem-solvers. In addition to listing specific strategies they had learned (e.g. diagrams, identifying variables), students also reported gains in more general abilities: reading analytically, drawing inferences, and learning from their own mistakes. Students stated that they were better able to persevere and overcome frustration, to accept and offer criticism, and to work with others.

DISCUSSION

Even though the statistical results are significant, it is difficult to argue from them that the actual problem-solving skills of the students have improved. It could be argued that what was gained was familiarity with the material and test-sophistication, even though the course was not geared to the tests. Since test-taking skills are one aspect of success at university, even if our results are not generalizable further than this, it is still a positive achievement.

The subjective course evaluation has to be treated with caution even though it was done anonymously. The students seem to have enjoyed the course which was certainly different from traditional subject-based courses. Owing to this fact, the students might have attributed a larger positive influence to the course, for improving their problem-solving skills, than would really be warranted. Since learned helplessness has been indicated as one of the obstacles to progress, an increase in self-confidence as a problem-solver must be considered as a positive outcome.

We would consider this as 'formative evaluation' in Nickerson, Perkins and Smith's term (1985). They distinguish between 'formative' and 'summative' evaluation. The former is carried out while the programme is being developed to provide results that can guide further development. The latter is usually done after the completion of the programme to assess the impact of the programme in terms of the developer's aims: 'Formative evaluation tends to be relatively informal, often largely qualitative, and usually focuses on specific aspects or components of a program rather than on the program as a whole' (Nickerson, Perkins and Smith, 1985, p. 314).

There are a number of obstacles to evaluation, and one of these we consider to be the major methodological shortcoming of this study. This concerns the separation of the actual teaching method and the materials used from the teaching personnel. Did our course succeed because of the course content or because of the enthusiasm and the motivating ability of a highly committed and well-trained teaching staff? Since there are a number of different programmes available to teach problem-solving skills, and success has been claimed for most of them, it is important to distinguish how far they are independent of their designers and transportable to different institutions.

Since the course on problem-solving was part of a larger programme, it will be difficult to ascertain whether it was the major contributing factor to long-term student progress measured by such variables as increased grade-point-average and decreased attrition. (Because part of the requirements for admission to the Educational Opportunity Programme is that the students participate in the six-weeks summer course, no comparable 'developmental' students were available to form a control group.) Under these circumstances it would be easy to dismiss courses teaching thinking and problem-solving skills as irrelevant. While we believe that problem-solving strategies do not replace knowledge, and that, to be an effective problem-solver in any given domain, an individual has to have sufficient knowledge of that domain, general problem-solving heuristics can supplement and foster domain-specific problem-solving skills.

Nickerson (1981) distinguishes four types of educational objectives: abilities, methods, knowledge, and attitudes. Nickerson, Perkins and Smith (1985) believe that the teaching of thinking should involve all four types: abilities that underlie thinking, methods that aid thinking, knowledge about thinking, and attitudes that are conducive to thinking. We believe that the problem-solving course we have been teaching to adult developmental students focused on two of these four types, namely methods that aid thinking and attitudes that are conducive to thinking.

The analogy we prefer to use to explain this belief is that of play. The function of play is to enable the child to learn about his or her environment, both social and physical, in a non-threatening manner. The puzzles and exercises used to teach problem-solving skills enable the students to find out about their thinking processes without the pressures of a minimum performance level in a domain-specific environment.

REFERENCES

Bloom, B. S., & Broder, L. J. (1950). *Problem-solving processes of college students: An exploratory investigation*. Chicago: University of Chicago Press.

Bransford, J. D., & Stein, B. S. (1984). *The ideal problem solver: A guide for improving thinking, learning and creativity*. New York: Freeman.

Brown, A. L. (1978). Knowing when, where, and how to remember: a problem of metacognition. In R. Glaser (ed.), *Advances in instructional psychology*, Vol. 1. Hillsdale, NJ: Erlbaum.

Coleman, J. (1966). *Equality of educational opportunity*. Washington, DC: US Government Printing Office.

Costa, A. L. (1984). Mediating the metacognitive. *Educational Leadership*, **42**, 57–62.

Cross, P. K. (1974). *Accent on learning*. San Francisco: Jossey-Bass.

deBono, E. (1973), *CoRT thinking*. Oxford: Pergamon Press.

Flavell, J. H. (1979). Metacognition and cognitive monitoring. *American Psychologist*, **34**, 906–911.

Glaser, R. (1984). Education and thinking: the role of knowledge. *American Psychologist*, **39**, 93–104.

Greeno, J. G. (1980). Trends in the theory of knowledge for problem solving. In D. Tuma & T. Reif (eds.), *Problem solving and education*. Hillsdale, NJ: Erlbaum.

Halpern, D. (1987). Analogies as a critical thinking skill. In D. E. Berger, K. Pezdek & W. P. Banks (eds.), *Applications of cognitive psychology: Problem solving, education and computing*. Hillsdale, NJ: Erlbaum.

Hayes, J. R. (1981). *The complete problem solver*. Philadelphia: Franklin Institute Press.

Holt, J. (1964). *How children fail*. New York: Dell Publishing Company.

Hutchinson, R. T. (1985). Teaching problem solving to developmental adults. In. J. W. Segal, S. F. Chipman, & R. Glaser (eds.), *Thinking and learning skills: Relating instruction to research*. Hillsdale, NJ: Erlbaum.

Larkin, J. J., McDermott, J., Simon, D. P., & Simon, H. (1980). Expert and novice performance in solving physics problems. *Science*, **208**, 1335–1342.

Lochhead, J. (1985). Teaching analytical reasoning skills through pair problem solving. In J. W. Segal, S. F. Chipman & R. Glaser (eds.), *Thinking and learning skills: Relating instruction to research*. Hillsdale, NJ: Erlbaum.

Maxwell, M. (1981). *Improving student learning skills*. San Francisco: Jossey-Bass.

Morante, E., & Ulesky, A. (1984). Assessment of reasoning abilities. *Educational Leadership*, **42**, 36–38.

New Jersey Basic Skills Council (1987a). *Results of the New Jersey College basic skills placement testing: Fall 1986*. Trenton, NJ: Department of Higher Education of the State of New Jersey.

New Jersey Basic Skills Council (1987b). *Interpreting scores on the New Jersey College basic skills placement test*. Trenton, NJ: Department of Higher Education of the State of New Jersey.

New Jersey Basic Skills Council (1987c). *Interpreting mathematics scores on the New Jersey College basic skills placement test*. Trenton, NJ: Department of Higher Education of the State of New Jersey.

Nickerson, R. S. (1981). Thoughts about teaching thinking. *Educational Leadership*, **39**, 21–24.

Nickerson, R. S., Perkins, D. N. & Smith, E. E. (1985). *The teaching of thinking*. Hillsdale, NJ: Erlbaum.

Nummedahl, S. G. (1987). Developing reasoning skills in college students. In D. E. Berger, K. Pezdek & W. P. Banks (eds.), *Applications of cognitive psychology: Problem solving, education and computing*. Hillsdale, NJ: Erlbaum.

Resnick, L. (1983). Mathematics and science learning: a new conception. *Science*, **220**, 477–478.

Rubinstein, M. F. (1975). *Patterns of problem solving*. Englewood Cliffs, NJ: Prentice-Hall.

Schoenfeld, A. H. (1979). Can heuristics be taught? In J. Lochhead & J. Clement (eds.), *Cognitive process instruction*. Philadelphia: Franklin Institute Press.

Segal, J. W., Chipman, S. F., & Glaser, R. (eds.). *Thinking and learning skills: Relating instruction to research*. Hillsdale, NJ: Erlbaum.

Sternberg, R. J. & Davidson, J. E. (1987). Teaching thinking to college students: some lessons learned from experience. *Teaching Thinking and Problem Solving*, **9**, 1–2 and 9–10.

Weinstein, C. E., & Rogers, B. T. (1985). Comprehension monitoring: the neglected strategy. *Journal of Developmental Education*, **9**, 6–29.

Whimbey, A., & Lochhead, J. (1982). *Problem solving and comprehension: A short course in analytical reasoning* (3rd edn.). Philadelphia: Franklin Institute Press.

Wickelgren, W. (1974). *How to solve problems: Elements of a theory of problems and problem solving*. San Francisco: Freeman.

Author Index

Subject Index

Contents of Volume 1

Part III: Analogy

Part IV: Decision Making